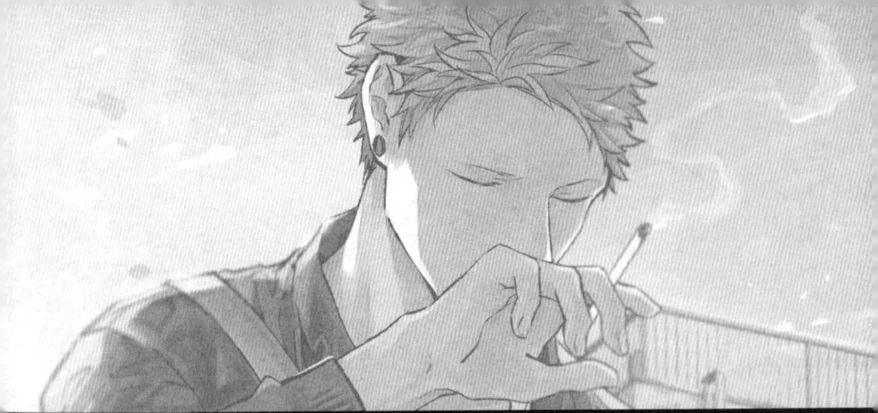

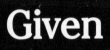

Given

Story and Art by **Natsuki Kizu** volume **5**

CONTENTS

SUBLIME

SuBLime Manga Edition

given

VOLUME 5

NATSUKI KIZU

RITSUKA UENOYAMA
(GUITAR)

Guitarist with skills far
beyond those of an average
high school student. Caring
and compassionate.
In a new relationship
with Mafuyu.

MAFUYU SATO
(GUITAR & VOCALS)

High school classmate of
Uenoyama's. Has an impressive
singing voice. Attached to
Uenoyama ever since he fixed
Mafuyu's broken guitar.

The band, now going by the name Given, enters a competition to take part in an upcoming a music festival. Haruki continues to nurse his secret crush on Akihiko, who's still entangled with his roommate and ex-boyfriend, professional violinist Ugetsu Murata. Driven into a corner by that dead-end relationship, Akihiko shows up at Haruki's place out of desperation. Haruki can't just stand by while Akihiro is suffering, but his heart breaks when even his offer to help is rejected. However, he still lets Akihiro move in with him, since the volatile drummer is effectively homeless after leaving the house he had shared with Ugetsu.

UGETSU MURATA

Violin prodigy. Akihiko's
ex-boyfriend. Even though he
and Akihiko broke up, they still
have an intense—and sometimes
sexual—relationship.

AKIHIKO KAJI

(DRUMMER)

University student.
His focus as a music major
is the violin, but he's also good
at playing guitar and bass.
Has known Ugetsu since
their high school days.

HARUKI NAKAYAMA

(BASSIST)

Graduate student at the same
university as Akihiko. The leader
of the band, as well as its manager
and peacemaker. Had his heart
broken by Akihiko, but still lets
him stay in his apartment.

When Ritsuka Uenoyama hears Mafuyu Sato sing for the first time, he's blown away by the other boy's raw talent and immediately asks Mafuyu to join his band. Uenoyama's bandmates Akihiko Kaji and Haruki Nakayama agree, and the three of them set a goal of coming up with a new song to perform at an upcoming concert. It falls to Mafuyu to write the lyrics, a task the quiet student finds impossible. Mafuyu lost his first love to suicide, which he partially blames himself for, a trauma that has left him reluctant to put his feelings into words.

However, during the concert, Mafuyu's pent-up emotions burst out of him and pour into the song. His spontaneous, powerful performance turns the show into an overwhelming success. Shocked into awareness, Uenoyama realizes he has feelings for Mafuyu and kisses him backstage. Before long, the two of them become a couple.

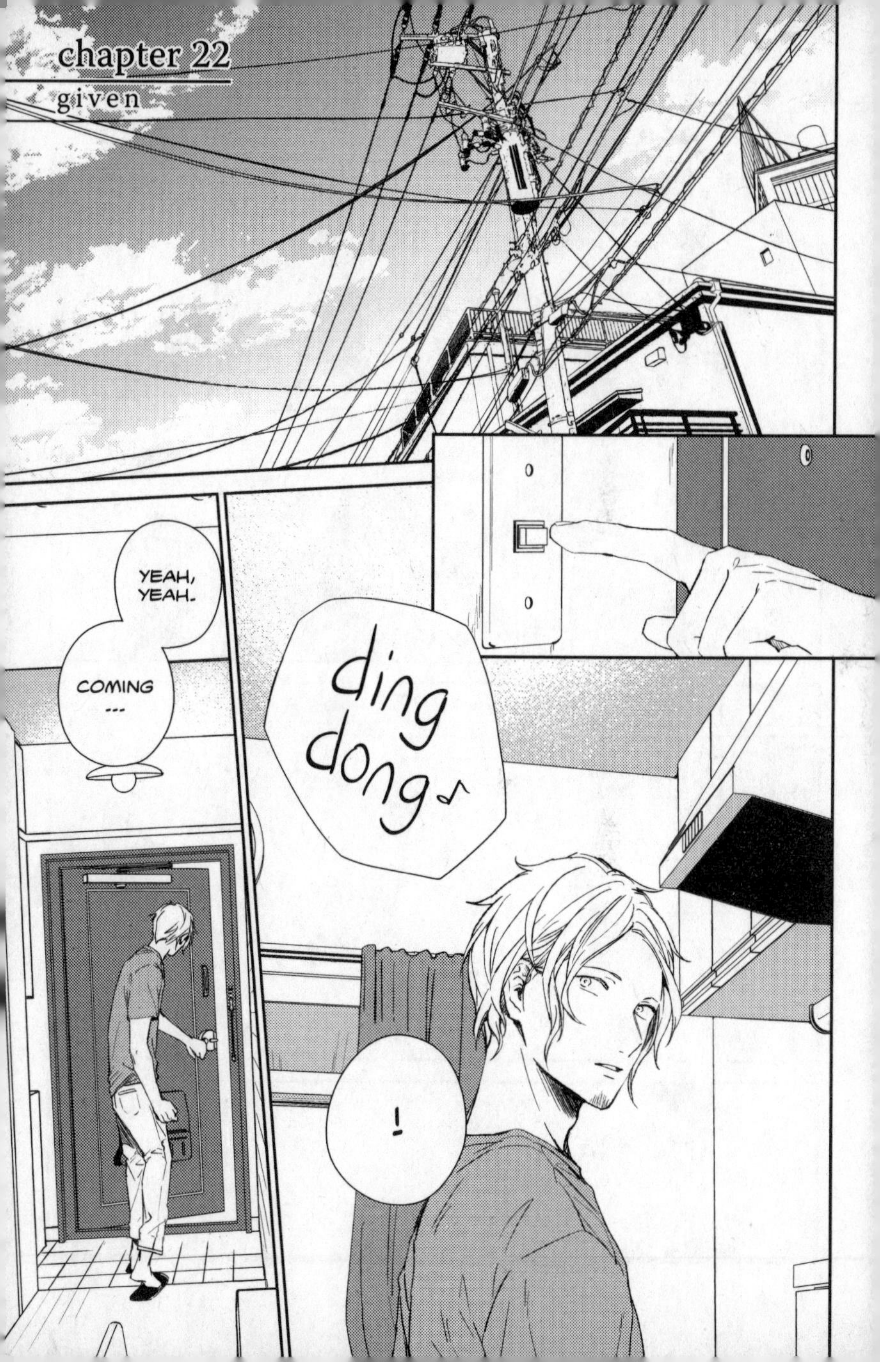
chapter 22
given
ding dong
!
YEAH, YEAH.
COMING ...

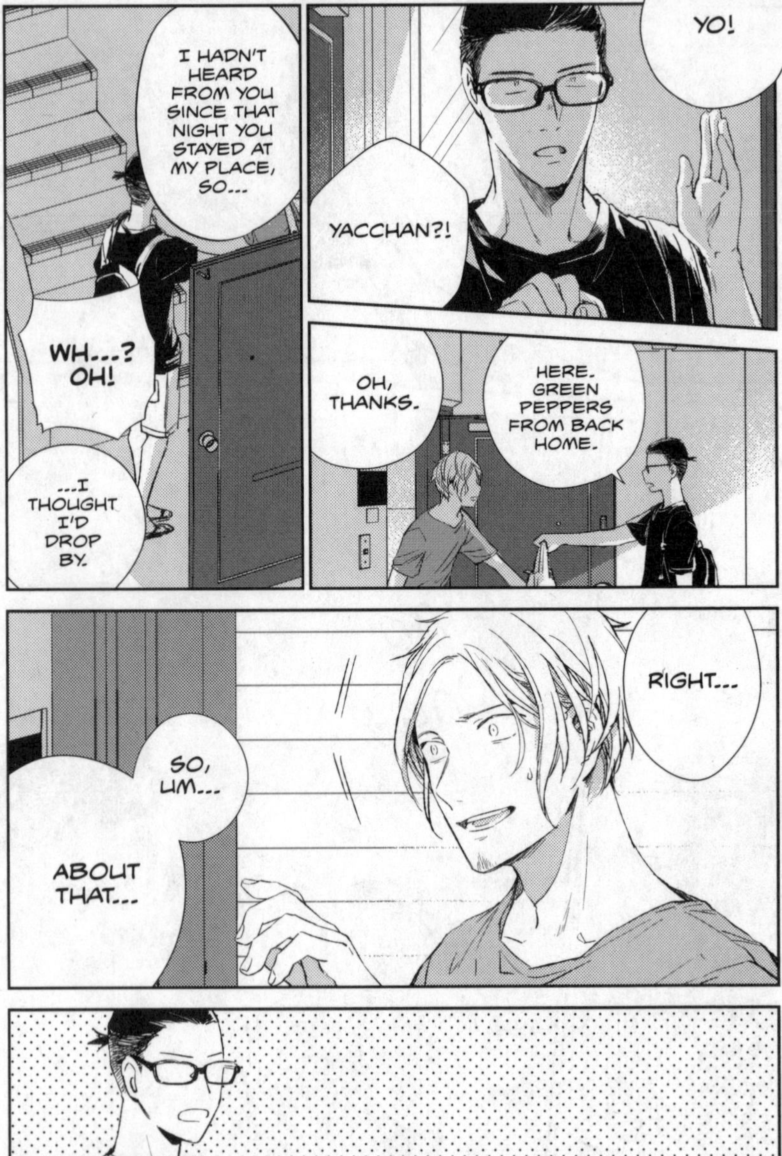
YO!
YACCHAN?!
HERE. GREEN PEPPERS FROM BACK HOME.
OH, THANKS.
I HADN'T HEARD FROM YOU SINCE THAT NIGHT YOU STAYED AT MY PLACE, SO...
WH...? OH!
...I THOUGHT I'D DROP BY.
RIGHT...
SO, UM...
ABOUT THAT...

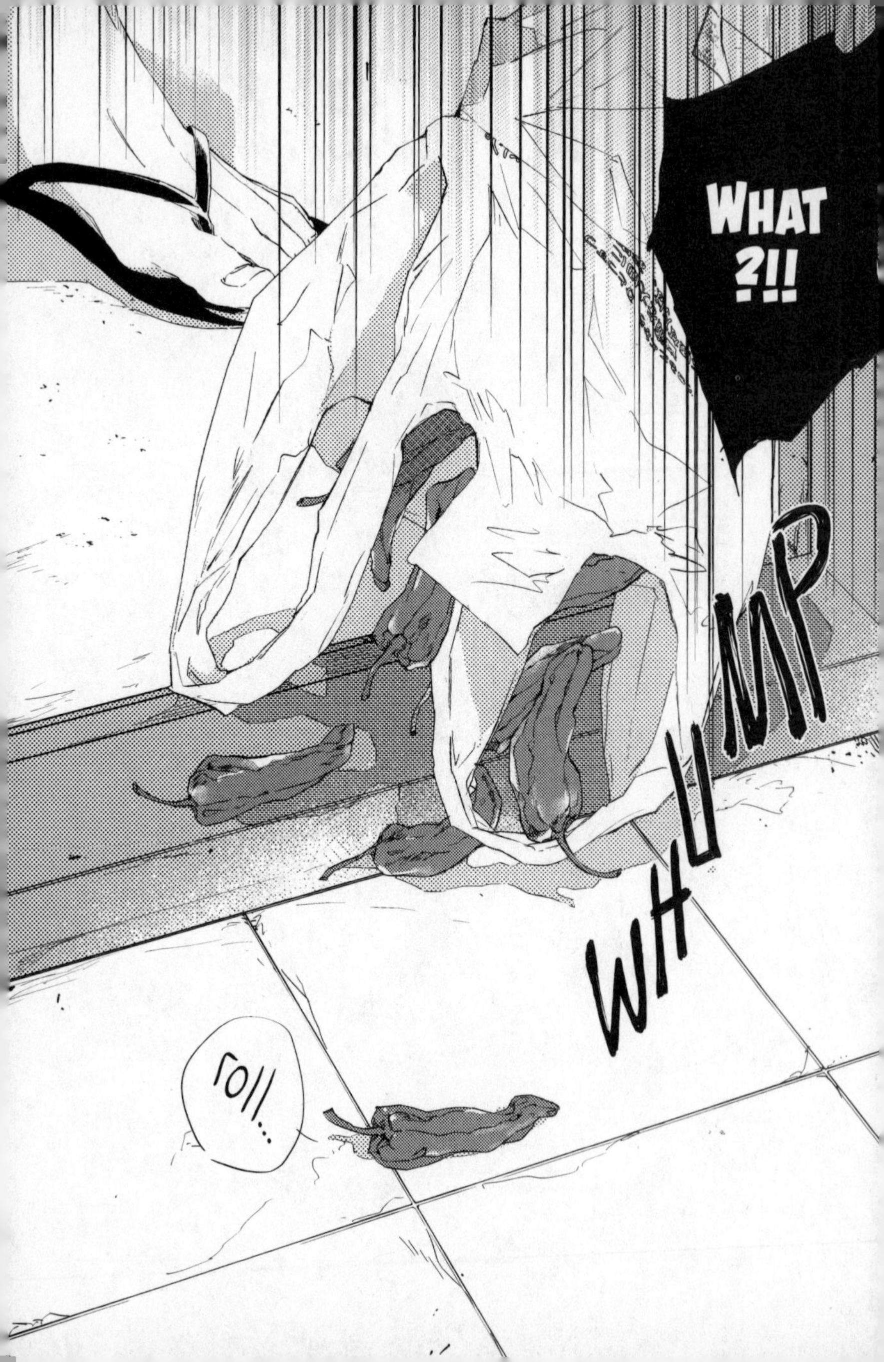
WHAT ?!!
WHUMP
roll...

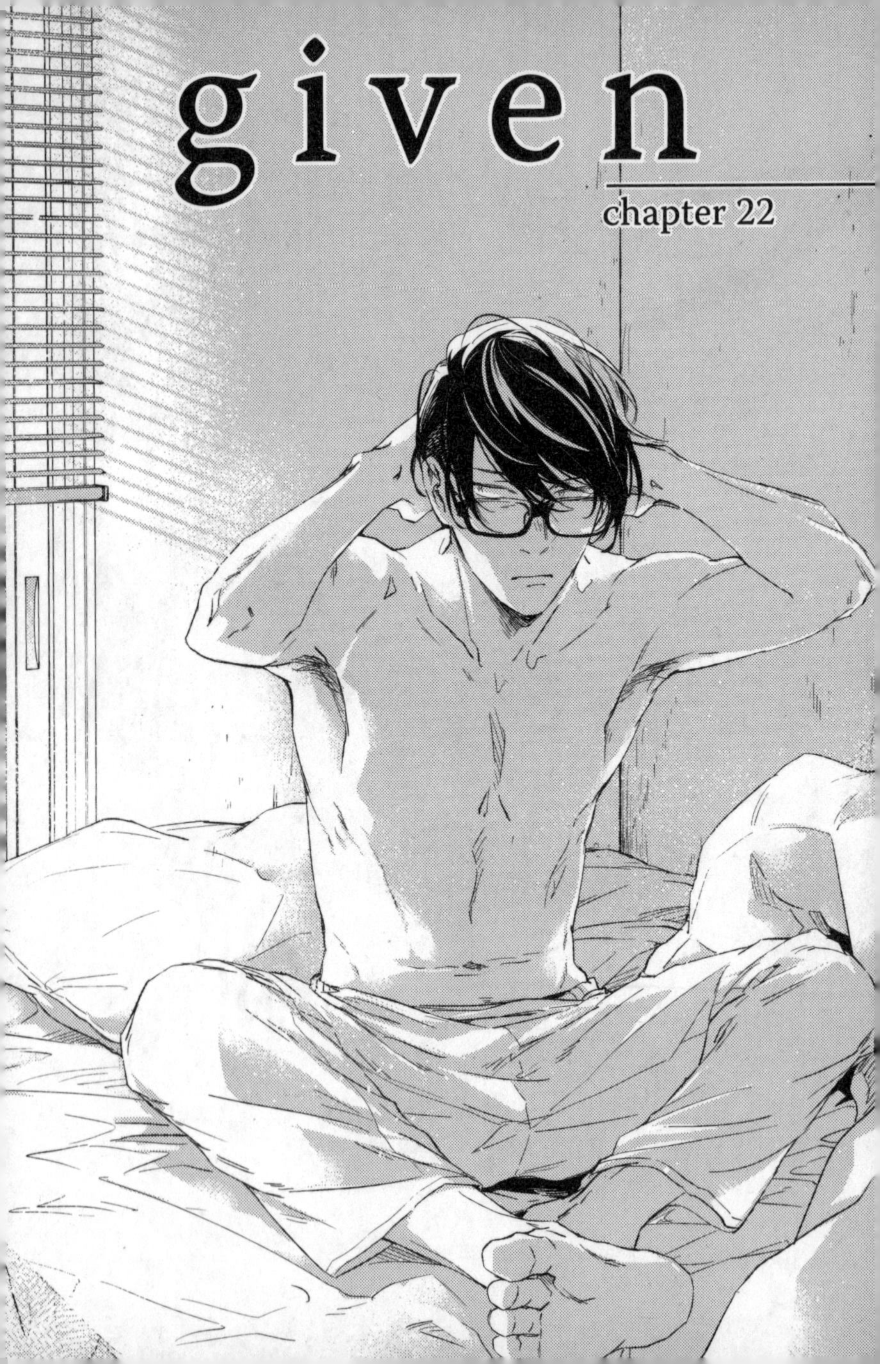
given
chapter 22

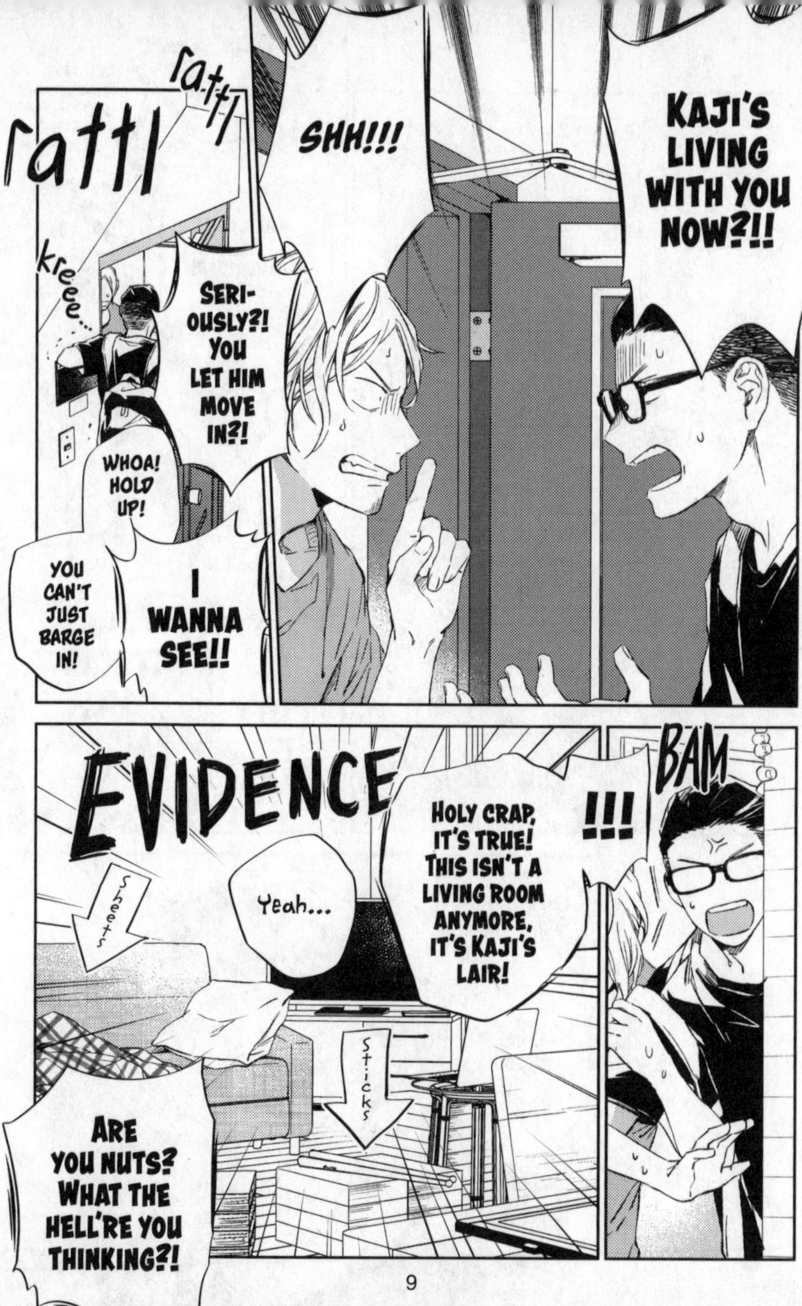
KAJI'S LIVING WITH YOU NOW?!!
SHH!!!
rattl
rattl
kreee...
SERI-OUSLY?! YOU LET HIM MOVE IN?!
WHOA! HOLD UP!
I WANNA SEE!!
YOU CAN'T JUST BARGE IN!
BAM
!!!
HOLY CRAP, IT'S TRUE! THIS ISN'T A LIVING ROOM ANYMORE, IT'S KAJI'S LAIR!
EVIDENCE
Yeah...
Sheets
Sticks
ARE YOU NUTS? WHAT THE HELL'RE YOU THINKING?!

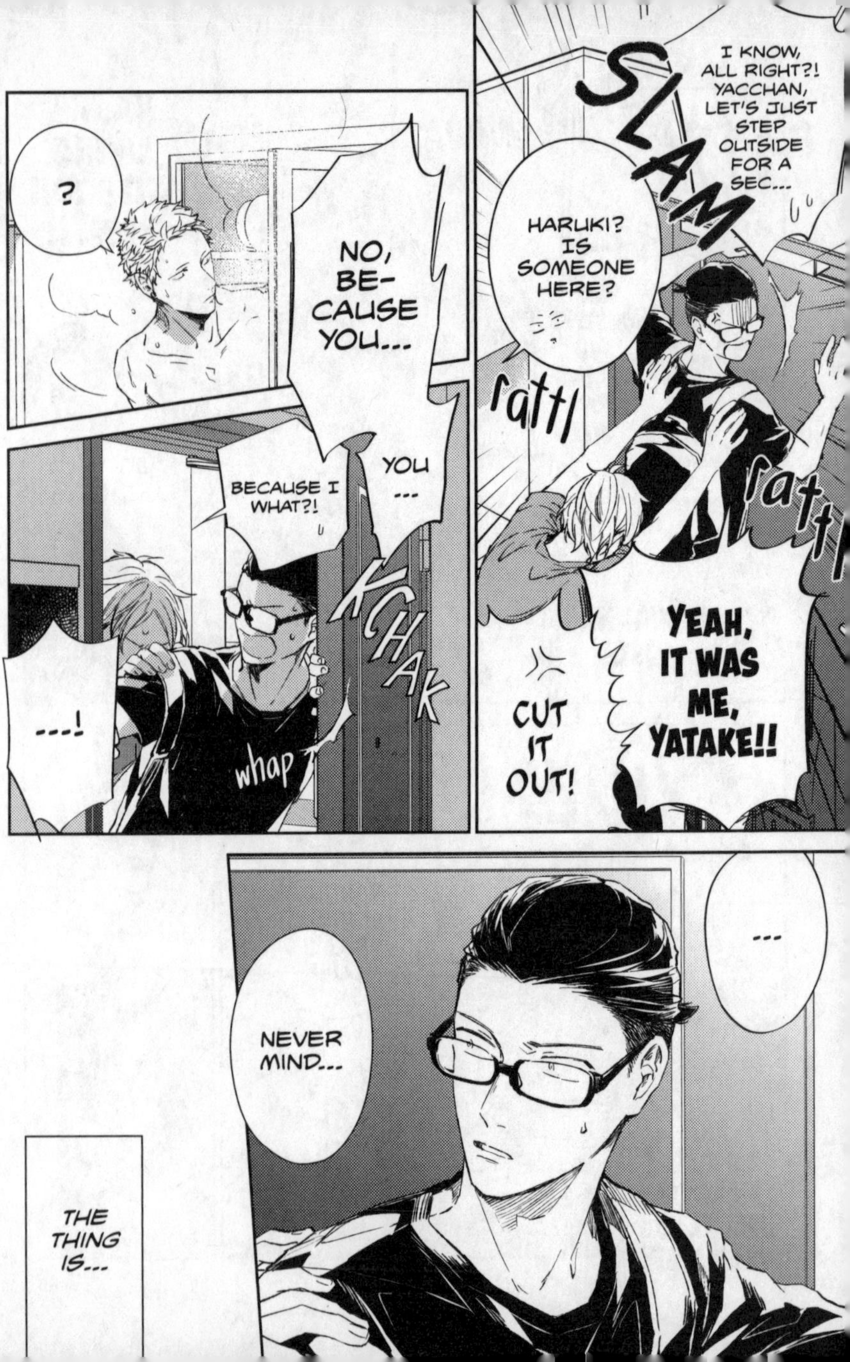
I KNOW, ALL RIGHT?! YACCHAN, LET'S JUST STEP OUTSIDE FOR A SEC...
SLAM
HARUKI? IS SOMEONE HERE?
rattl
rattl
YEAH, IT WAS ME, YATAKE!!
CUT IT OUT!
NO, BE-CAUSE YOU...
?
YOU ...
BECAUSE I WHAT?!
KCHAK
whap
...!
...
NEVER MIND...
THE THING IS...

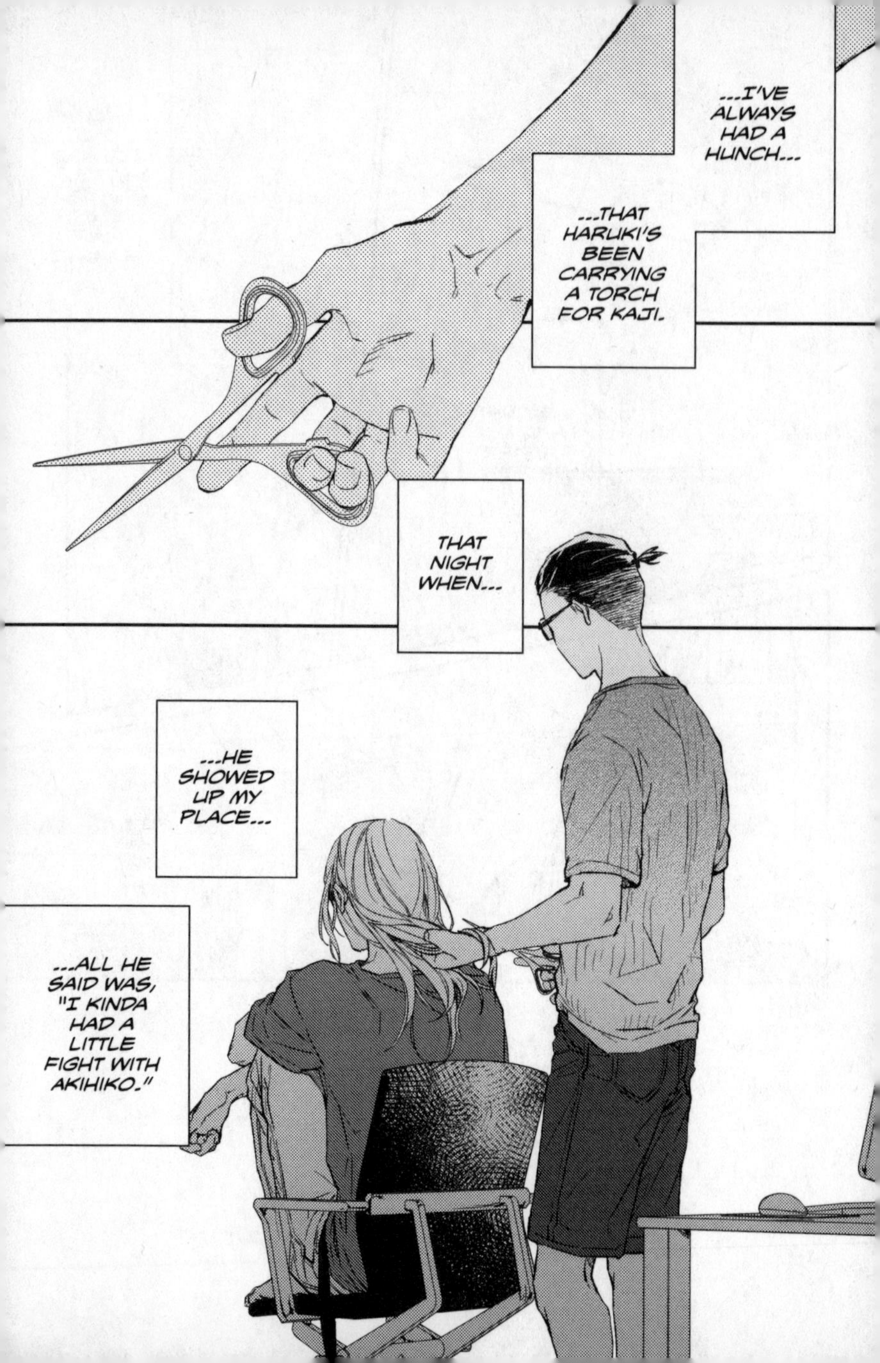
...I'VE ALWAYS HAD A HUNCH...
...THAT HARUKI'S BEEN CARRYING A TORCH FOR KAJI.
THAT NIGHT WHEN...
...HE SHOWED UP MY PLACE...
...ALL HE SAID WAS, "I KINDA HAD A LITTLE FIGHT WITH AKIHIKO."

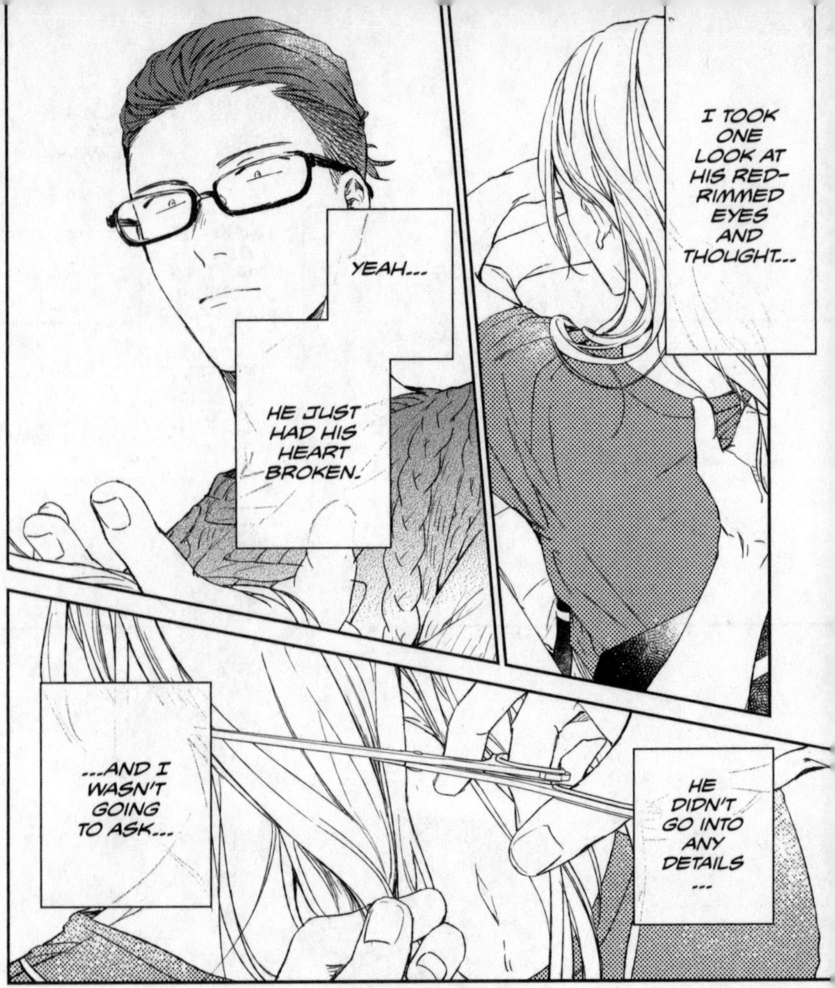
I TOOK ONE LOOK AT HIS RED-RIMMED EYES AND THOUGHT...
YEAH...
HE JUST HAD HIS HEART BROKEN.
HE DIDN'T GO INTO ANY DETAILS...
...AND I WASN'T GOING TO ASK...

...BUT IT SEEMED PRETTY CLEAR THAT SOMETHING MAJOR HAD HAPPENED BETWEEN THEM.

SOMETHING LIKE YEARS AND YEARS OF PENT-UP FEELINGS BEING CRUSHED IN A SINGLE NIGHT.

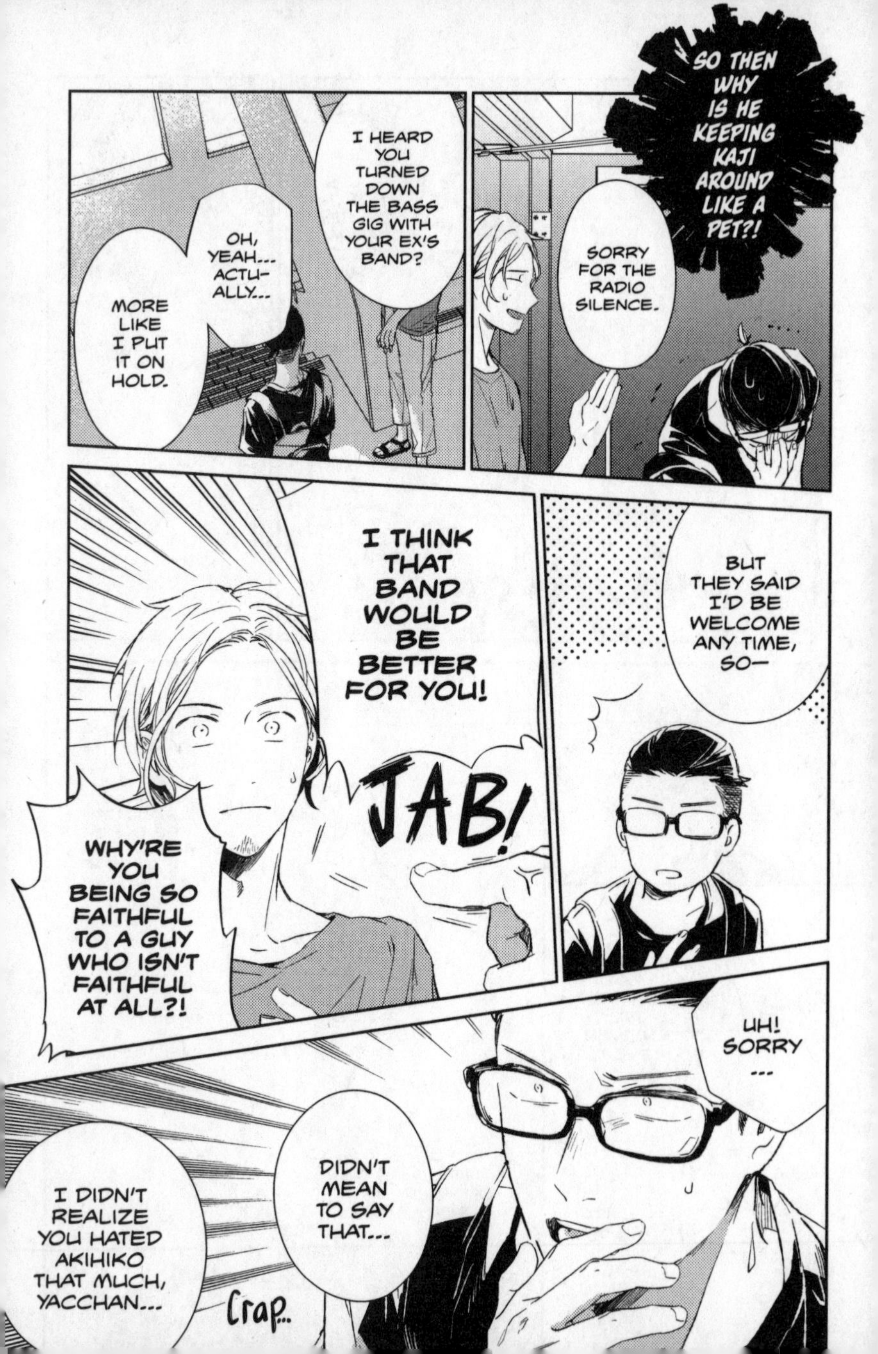
SO THEN WHY IS HE KEEPING KAJI AROUND LIKE A PET?!
SORRY FOR THE RADIO SILENCE.
...
I HEARD YOU TURNED DOWN THE BASS GIG WITH YOUR EX'S BAND?
OH, YEAH... ACTU-ALLY...
MORE LIKE I PUT IT ON HOLD.
BUT THEY SAID I'D BE WELCOME ANY TIME, SO—
I THINK THAT BAND WOULD BE BETTER FOR YOU!
JAB!
WHY'RE YOU BEING SO FAITHFUL TO A GUY WHO ISN'T FAITHFUL AT ALL?!
UH! SORRY ...
DIDN'T MEAN TO SAY THAT...
I DIDN'T REALIZE YOU HATED AKIHIKO THAT MUCH, YACCHAN...
Crap...

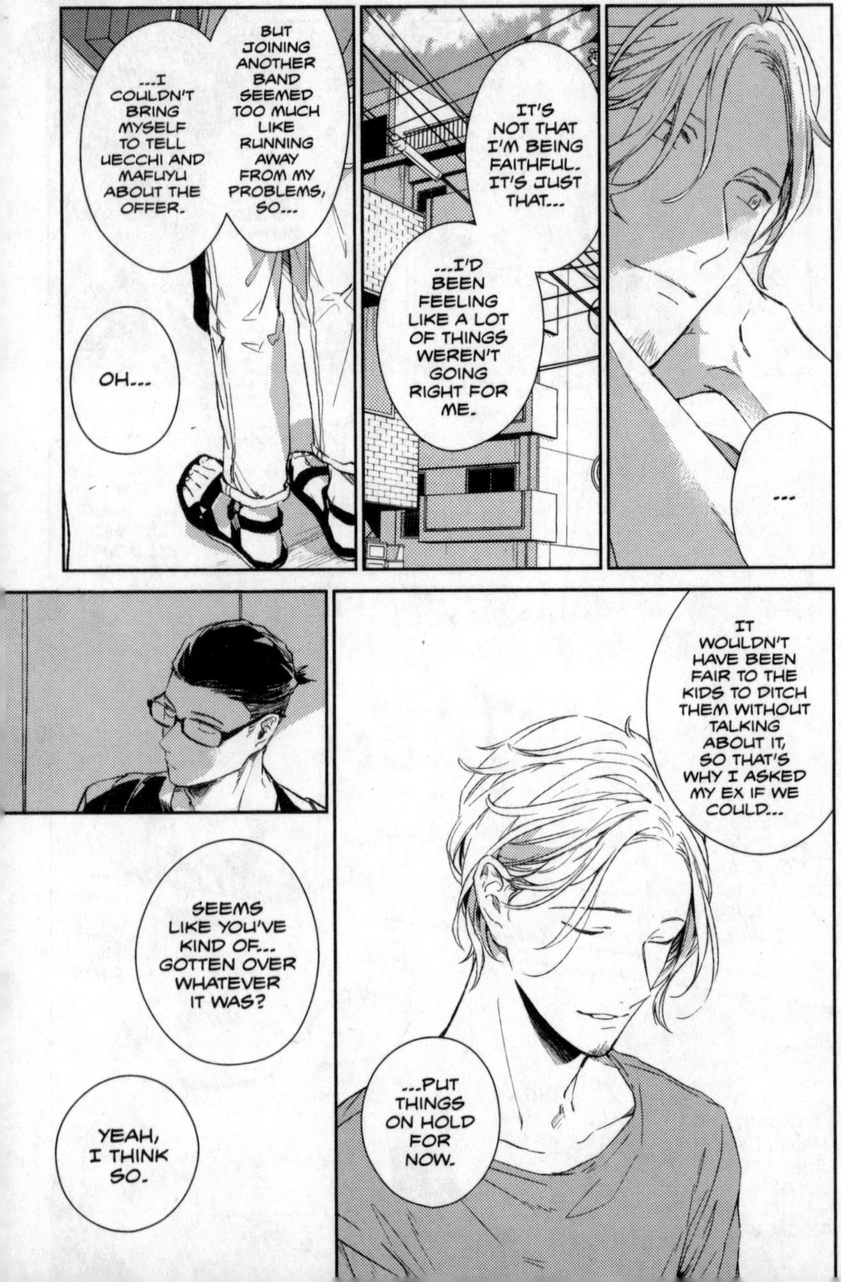
...
IT'S NOT THAT I'M BEING FAITHFUL. IT'S JUST THAT...
...I'D BEEN FEELING LIKE A LOT OF THINGS WEREN'T GOING RIGHT FOR ME.
BUT JOINING ANOTHER BAND SEEMED TOO MUCH LIKE RUNNING AWAY FROM MY PROBLEMS, SO...
...I COULDN'T BRING MYSELF TO TELL UECCHI AND MAFUYU ABOUT THE OFFER.
OH...
IT WOULDN'T HAVE BEEN FAIR TO THE KIDS TO DITCH THEM WITHOUT TALKING ABOUT IT, SO THAT'S WHY I ASKED MY EX IF WE COULD...
...PUT THINGS ON HOLD FOR NOW.
SEEMS LIKE YOU'VE KIND OF... GOTTEN OVER WHATEVER IT WAS?
YEAH, I THINK SO.

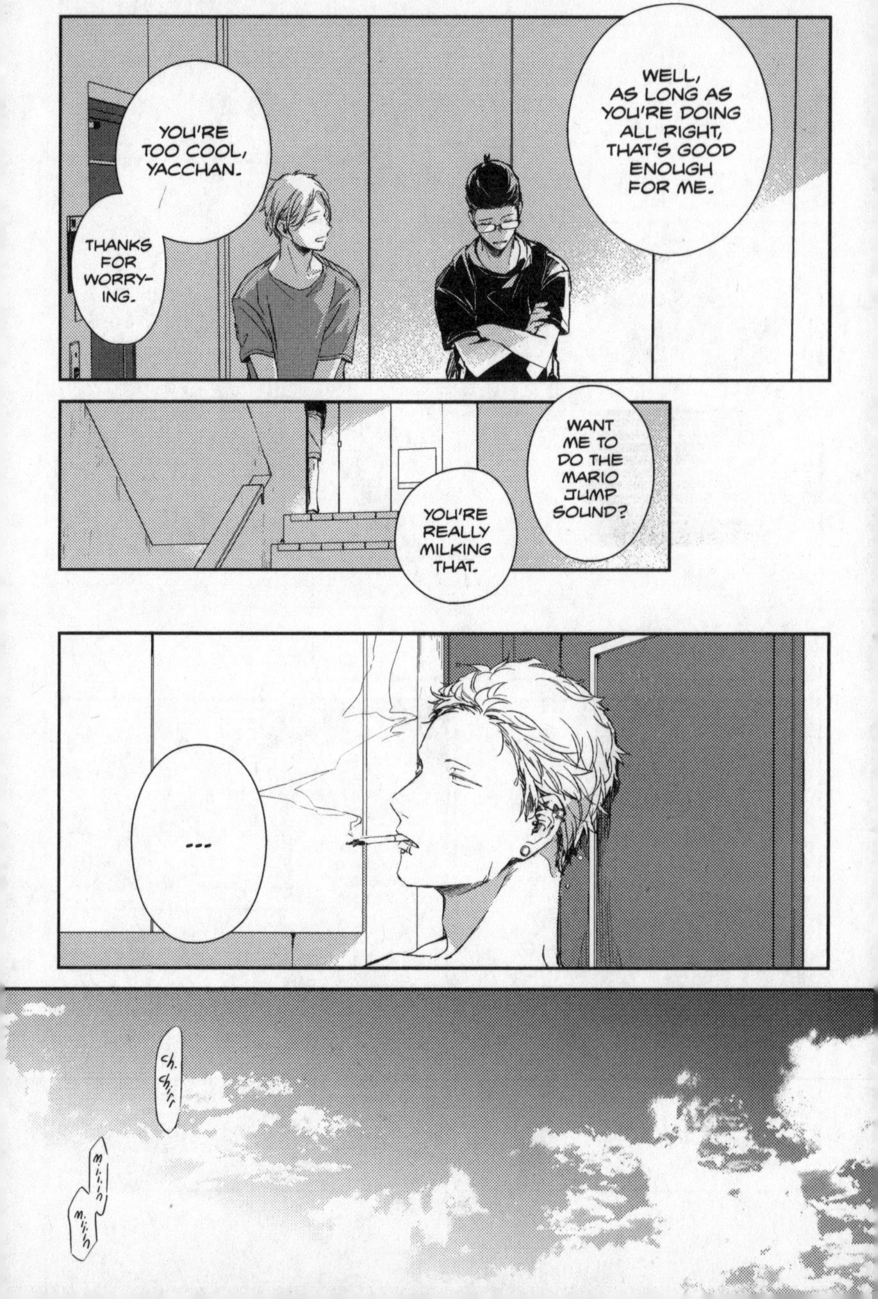
WELL, AS LONG AS YOU'RE DOING ALL RIGHT, THAT'S GOOD ENOUGH FOR ME.
YOU'RE TOO COOL, YACCHAN.
THANKS FOR WORRYING.
WANT ME TO DO THE MARIO JUMP SOUND?
YOU'RE REALLY MILKING THAT.
...
ch. chirr
m.i.i.n m.i.i.n

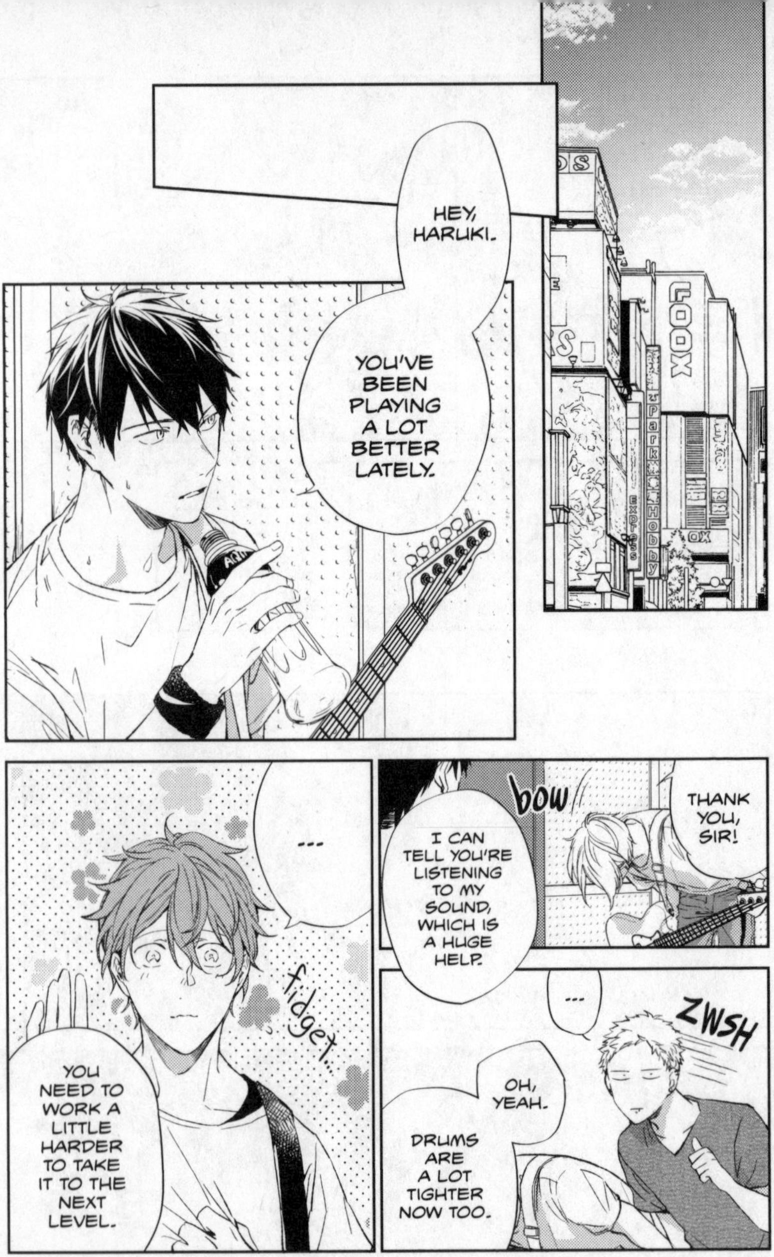
HEY, HARUKI...
YOU'VE BEEN PLAYING A LOT BETTER LATELY.
I CAN TELL YOU'RE LISTENING TO MY SOUND, WHICH IS A HUGE HELP.
bow
THANK YOU, SIR!
...
ZWSH
OH, YEAH.
DRUMS ARE A LOT TIGHTER NOW TOO.
...
fidget...
YOU NEED TO WORK A LITTLE HARDER TO TAKE IT TO THE NEXT LEVEL.

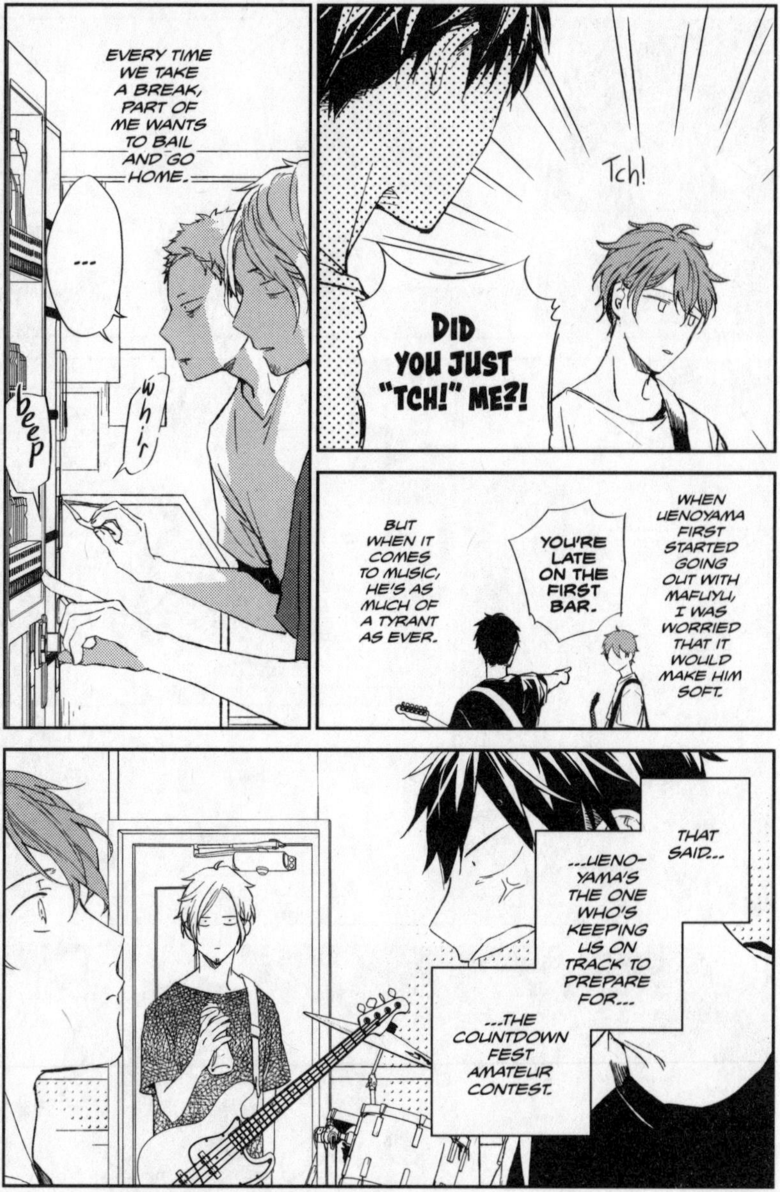
Tch!
DID YOU JUST "TCH!" ME?!
WHEN UENOYAMA FIRST STARTED GOING OUT WITH MAFUYU, I WAS WORRIED THAT IT WOULD MAKE HIM SOFT.
YOU'RE LATE ON THE FIRST BAR.
BUT WHEN IT COMES TO MUSIC, HE'S AS MUCH OF A TYRANT AS EVER.
EVERY TIME WE TAKE A BREAK, PART OF ME WANTS TO BAIL AND GO HOME.
...
whir
beep
THAT SAID...
...UENOYAMA'S THE ONE WHO'S KEEPING US ON TRACK TO PREPARE FOR...
...THE COUNTDOWN FEST AMATEUR CONTEST.

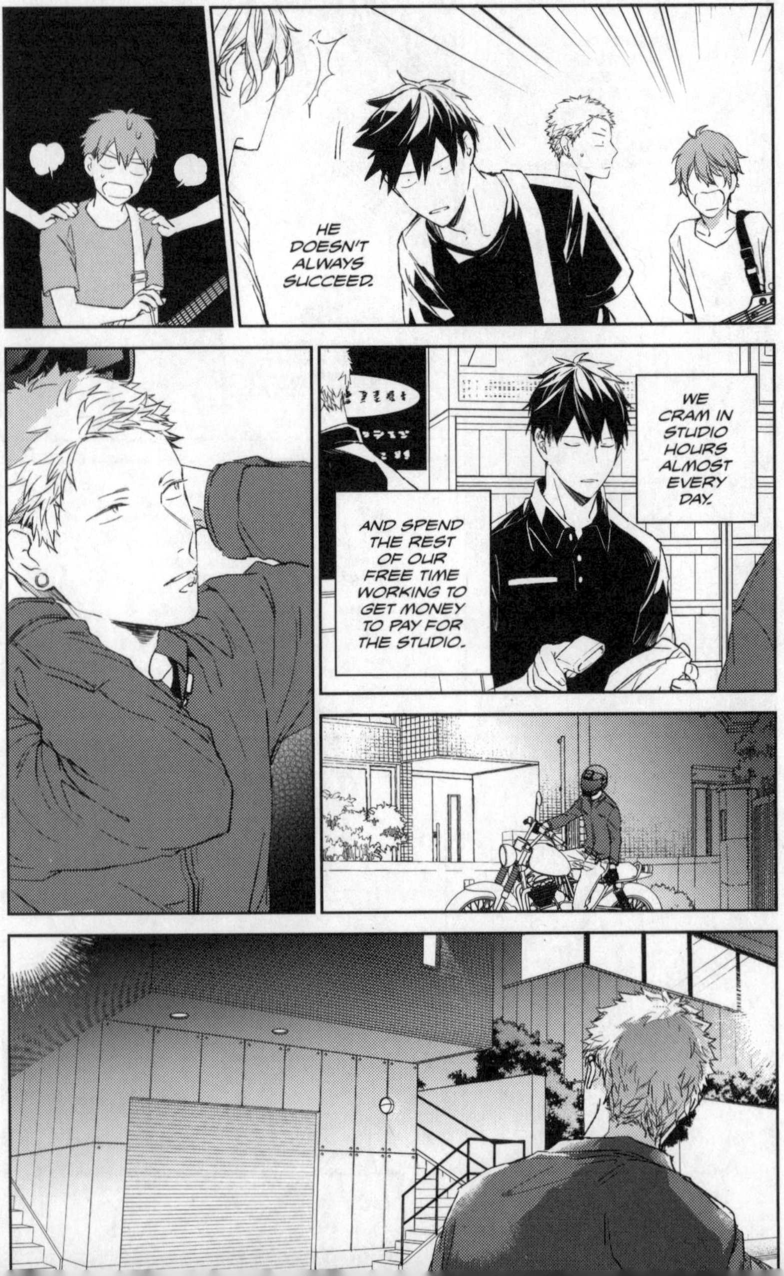
HE DOESN'T ALWAYS SUCCEED.
WE CRAM IN STUDIO HOURS ALMOST EVERY DAY.
AND SPEND THE REST OF OUR FREE TIME WORKING TO GET MONEY TO PAY FOR THE STUDIO.

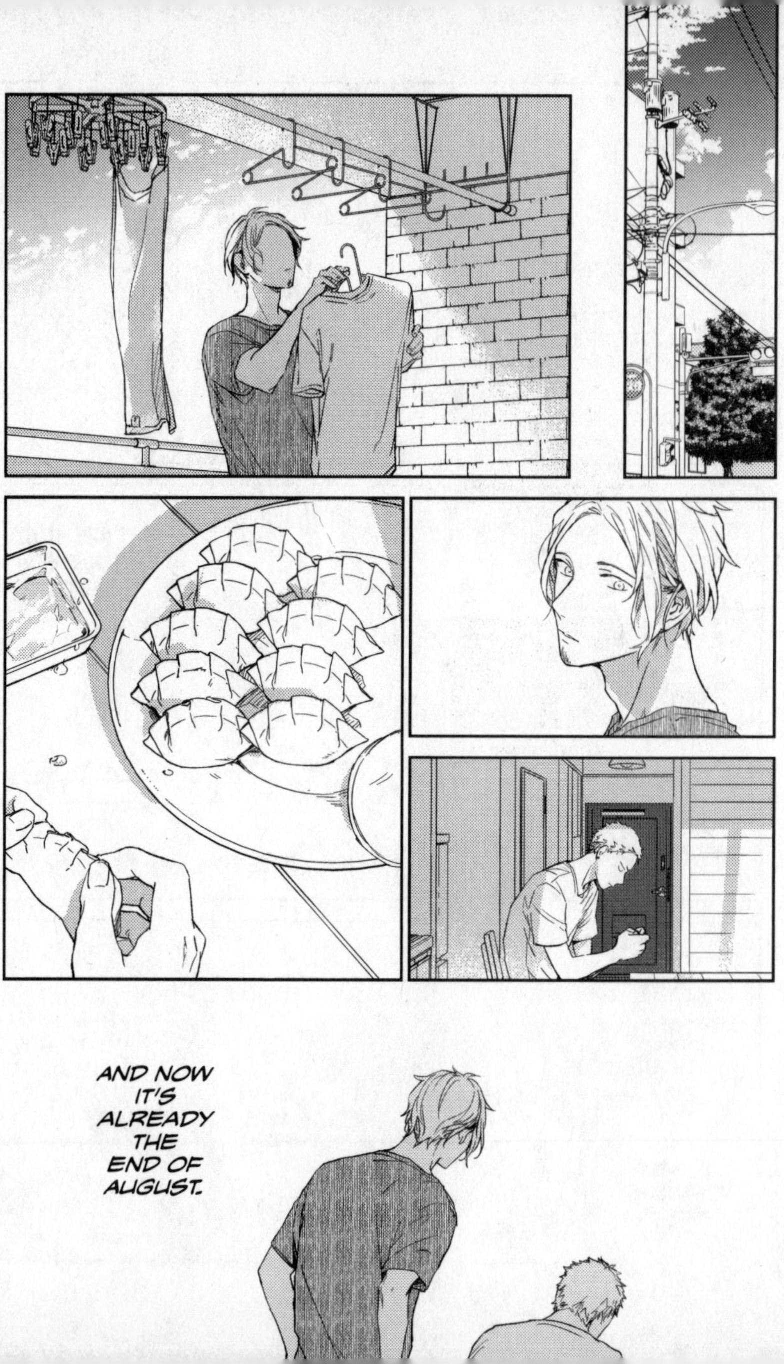
AND NOW IT'S ALREADY THE END OF AUGUST.

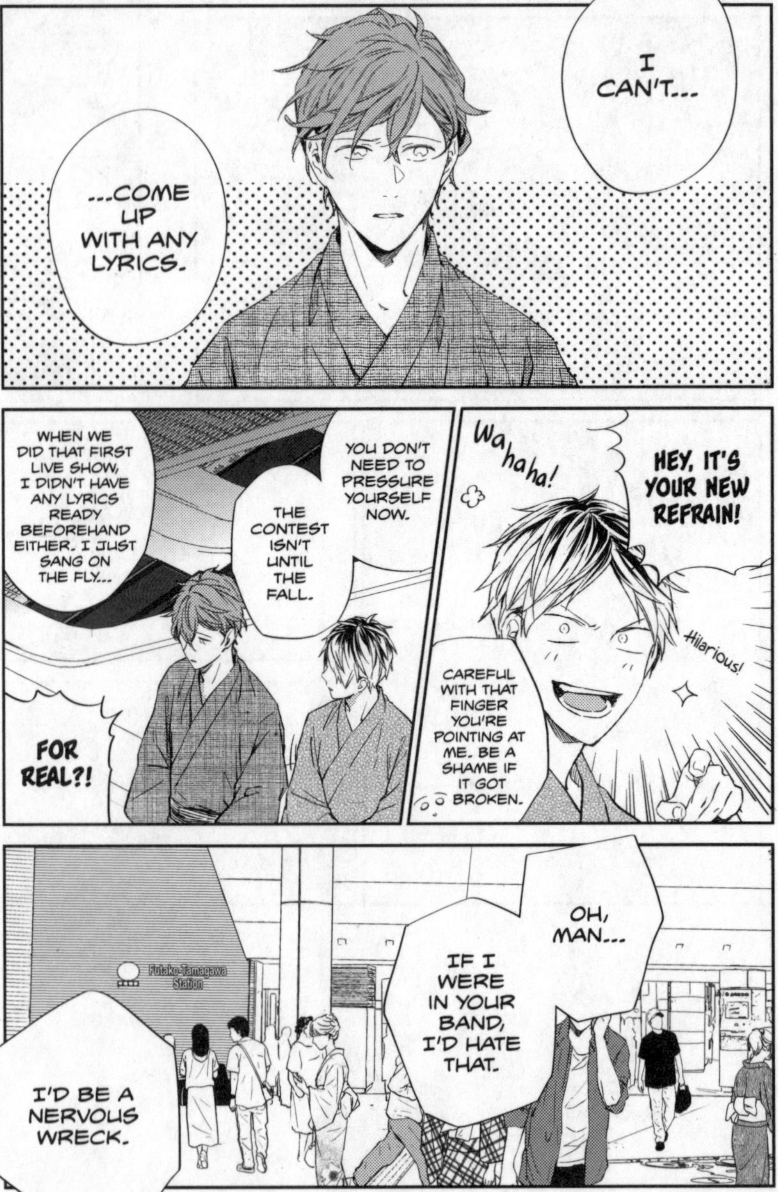
I CAN'T...
...COME UP WITH ANY LYRICS.
Wahaha!
HEY, IT'S YOUR NEW REFRAIN!
Hilarious!
CAREFUL WITH THAT FINGER YOU'RE POINTING AT ME. BE A SHAME IF IT GOT BROKEN.
YOU DON'T NEED TO PRESSURE YOURSELF NOW.
THE CONTEST ISN'T UNTIL THE FALL.
WHEN WE DID THAT FIRST LIVE SHOW, I DIDN'T HAVE ANY LYRICS READY BEFOREHAND EITHER. I JUST SANG ON THE FLY...
FOR REAL?!
OH, MAN...
IF I WERE IN YOUR BAND, I'D HATE THAT.
Futako-Tamagawa Station
I'D BE A NERVOUS WRECK.

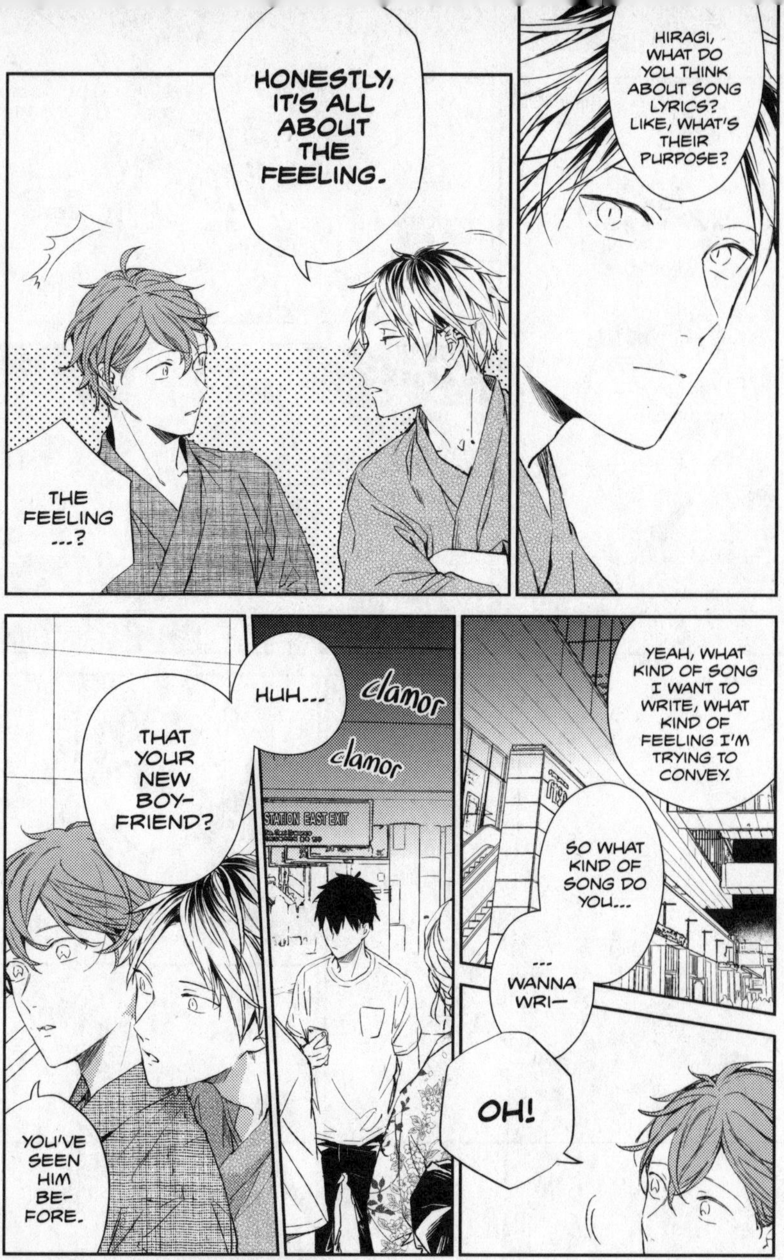
HIRAGI, WHAT DO YOU THINK ABOUT SONG LYRICS? LIKE, WHAT'S THEIR PURPOSE?
HONESTLY, IT'S ALL ABOUT THE FEELING.
THE FEELING ...?
YEAH, WHAT KIND OF SONG I WANT TO WRITE, WHAT KIND OF FEELING I'M TRYING TO CONVEY.
SO WHAT KIND OF SONG DO YOU...
... WANNA WRI—
OH!
clamor
clamor
STATION EAST EXIT
HUH... THAT YOUR NEW BOY-FRIEND?
YOU'VE SEEN HIM BE-FORE.

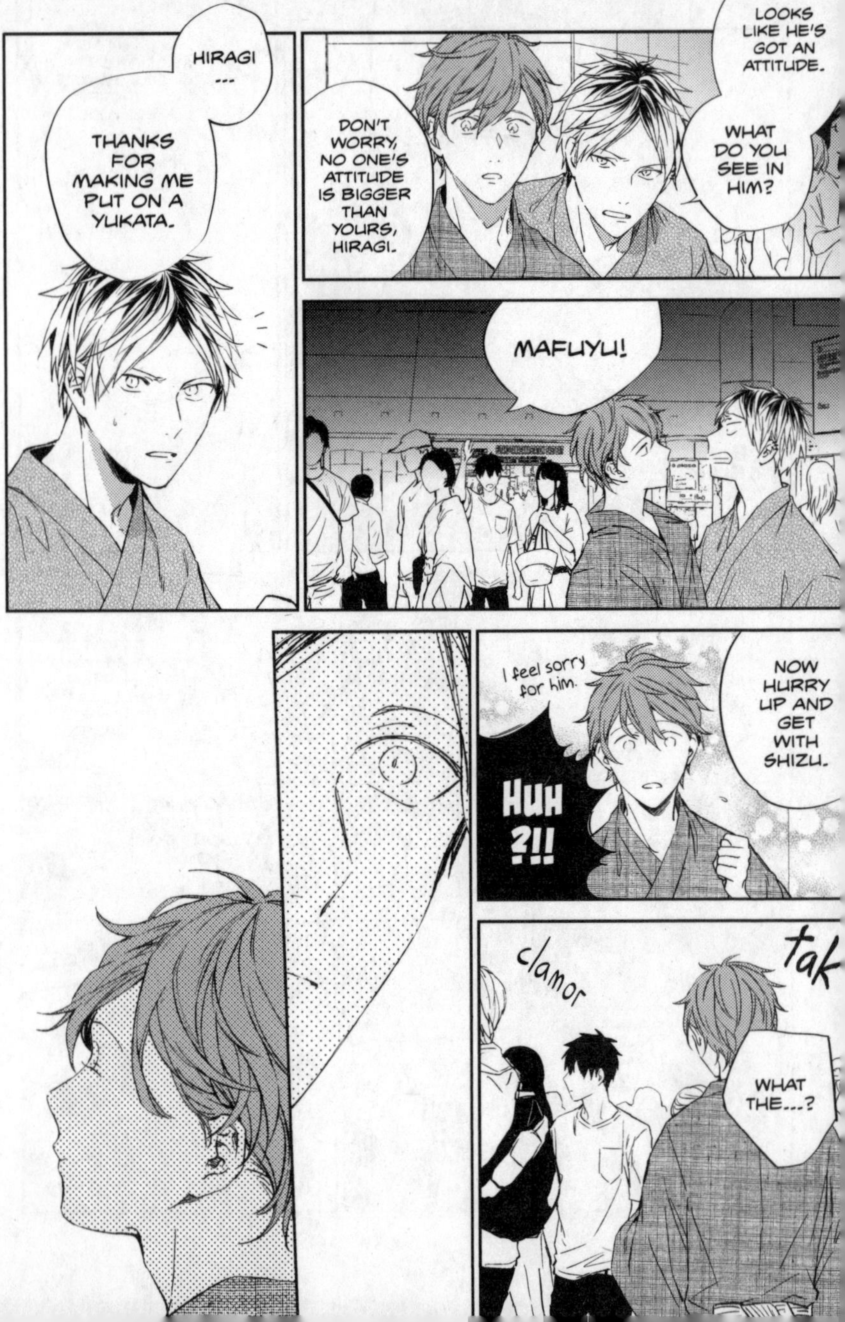
LOOKS LIKE HE'S GOT AN ATTITUDE.
WHAT DO YOU SEE IN HIM?
DON'T WORRY, NO ONE'S ATTITUDE IS BIGGER THAN YOURS, HIRAGI.
MAFUYU!
HIRAGI...
THANKS FOR MAKING ME PUT ON A YUKATA.
NOW HURRY UP AND GET WITH SHIZU.
I feel sorry for him.
HUH ?!!
tak
clamor
WHAT THE...?

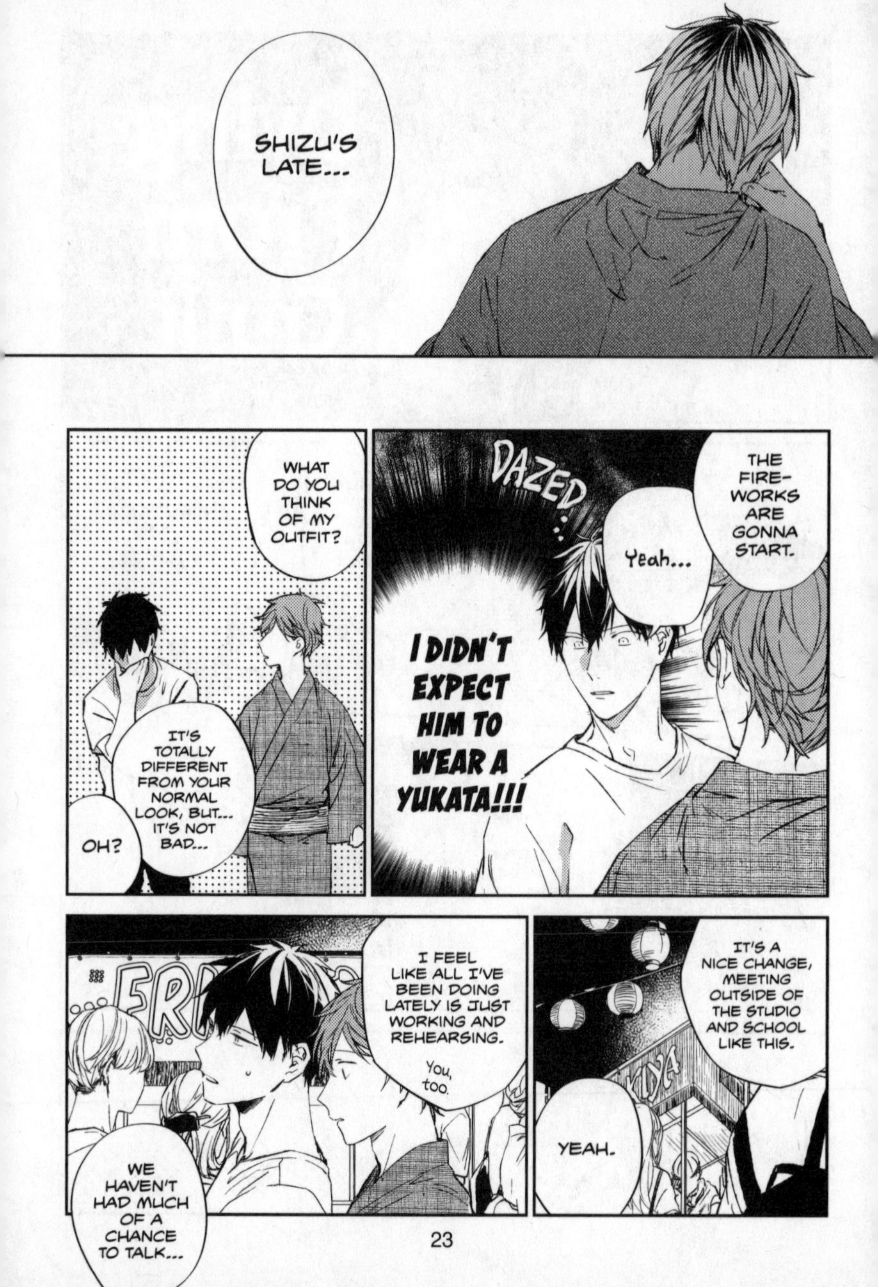
SHIZU'S LATE...
THE FIRE-WORKS ARE GONNA START.
Yeah...
DAZED
I DIDN'T EXPECT HIM TO WEAR A YUKATA!!!
WHAT DO YOU THINK OF MY OUTFIT?
IT'S TOTALLY DIFFERENT FROM YOUR NORMAL LOOK, BUT... IT'S NOT BAD...
OH?
IT'S A NICE CHANGE, MEETING OUTSIDE OF THE STUDIO AND SCHOOL LIKE THIS.
YEAH.
I FEEL LIKE ALL I'VE BEEN DOING LATELY IS JUST WORKING AND REHEARSING.
You, too.
WE HAVEN'T HAD MUCH OF A CHANCE TO TALK...

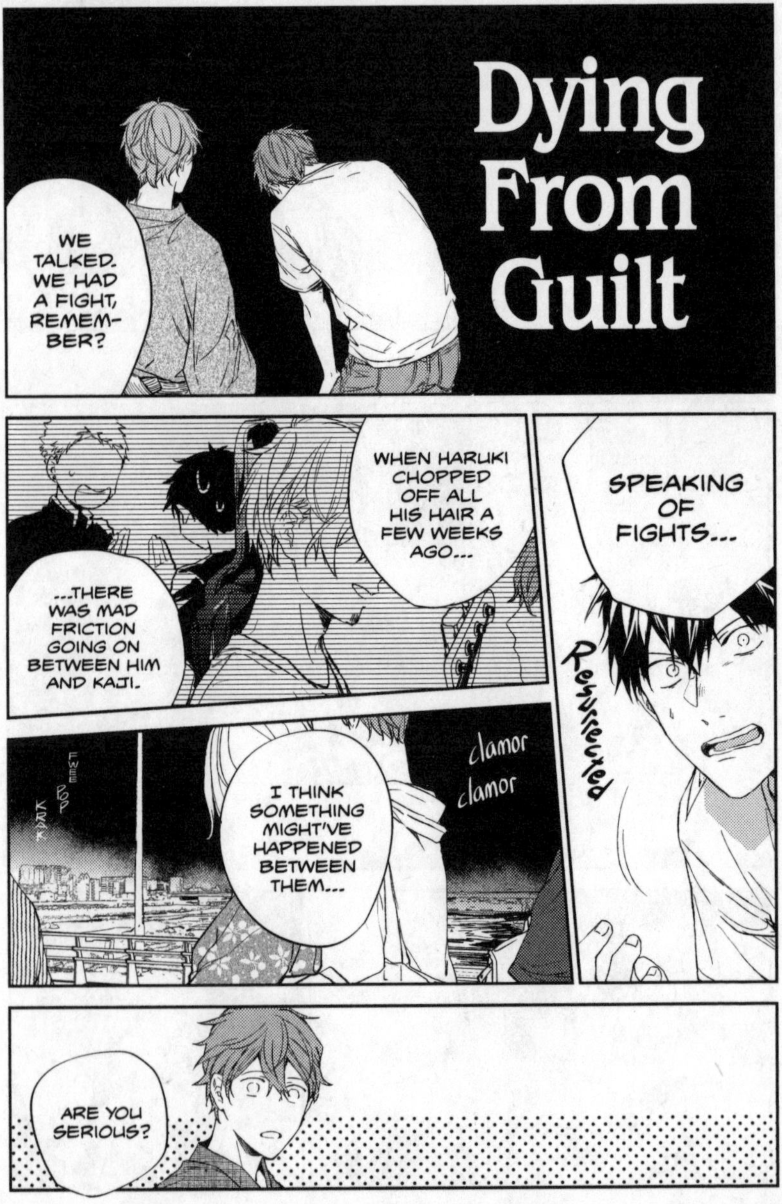
Dying From Guilt
WE TALKED. WE HAD A FIGHT, REMEMBER?
SPEAKING OF FIGHTS...
Resurrected
WHEN HARUKI CHOPPED OFF ALL HIS HAIR A FEW WEEKS AGO...
...THERE WAS MAD FRICTION GOING ON BETWEEN HIM AND KAJI.
clamor clamor
I THINK SOMETHING MIGHT'VE HAPPENED BETWEEN THEM...
FWEE
POP
KRAK
ARE YOU SERIOUS?

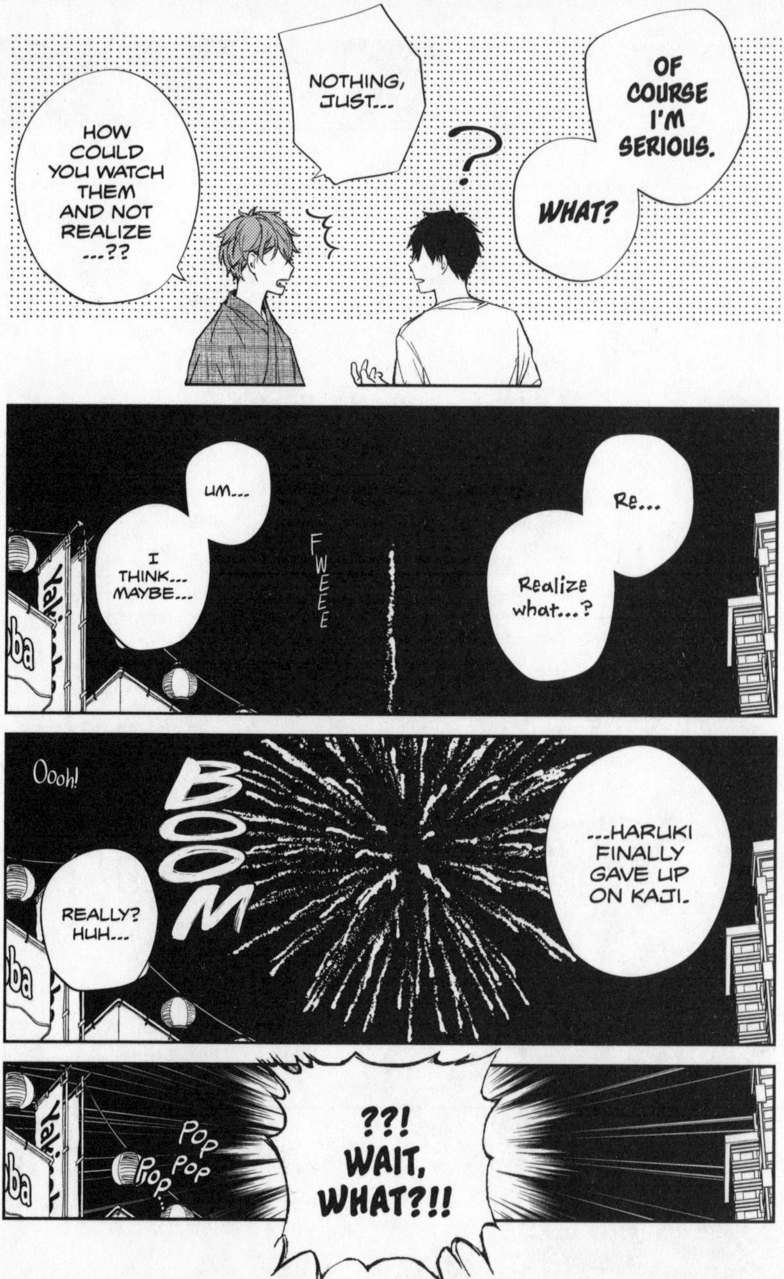
OF COURSE I'M SERIOUS.
WHAT?
NOTHING, JUST...
HOW COULD YOU WATCH THEM AND NOT REALIZE ...??
Re...
Realize what...?
FWEEE
UM...
I THINK... MAYBE...
...HARUKI FINALLY GAVE UP ON KAJI.
BOOM
Oooh!
REALLY? HUH...
??! WAIT, WHAT?!!
POP POP POP...

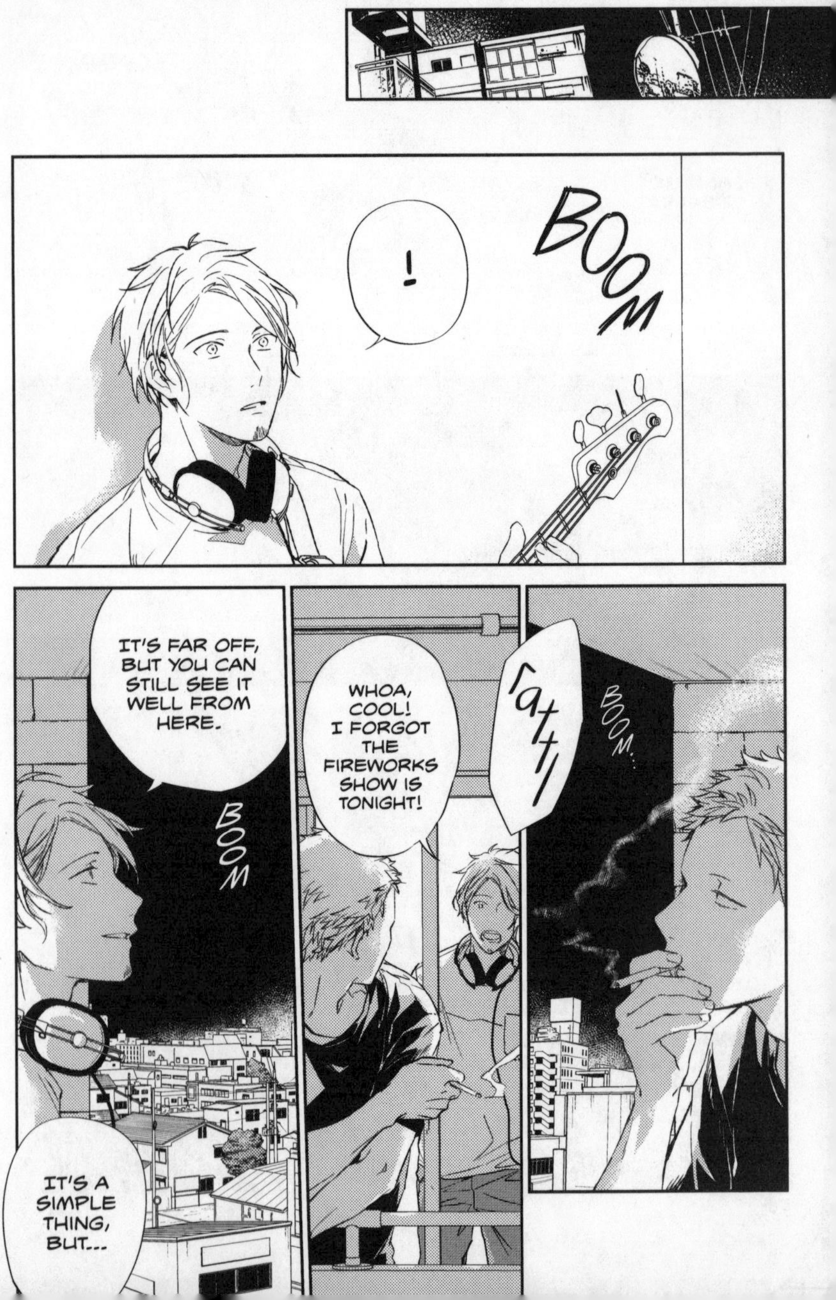
!
BOOM
BOOM...
WHOA, COOL! I FORGOT THE FIREWORKS SHOW IS TONIGHT!
IT'S FAR OFF, BUT YOU CAN STILL SEE IT WELL FROM HERE.
BOOM
IT'S A SIMPLE THING, BUT...

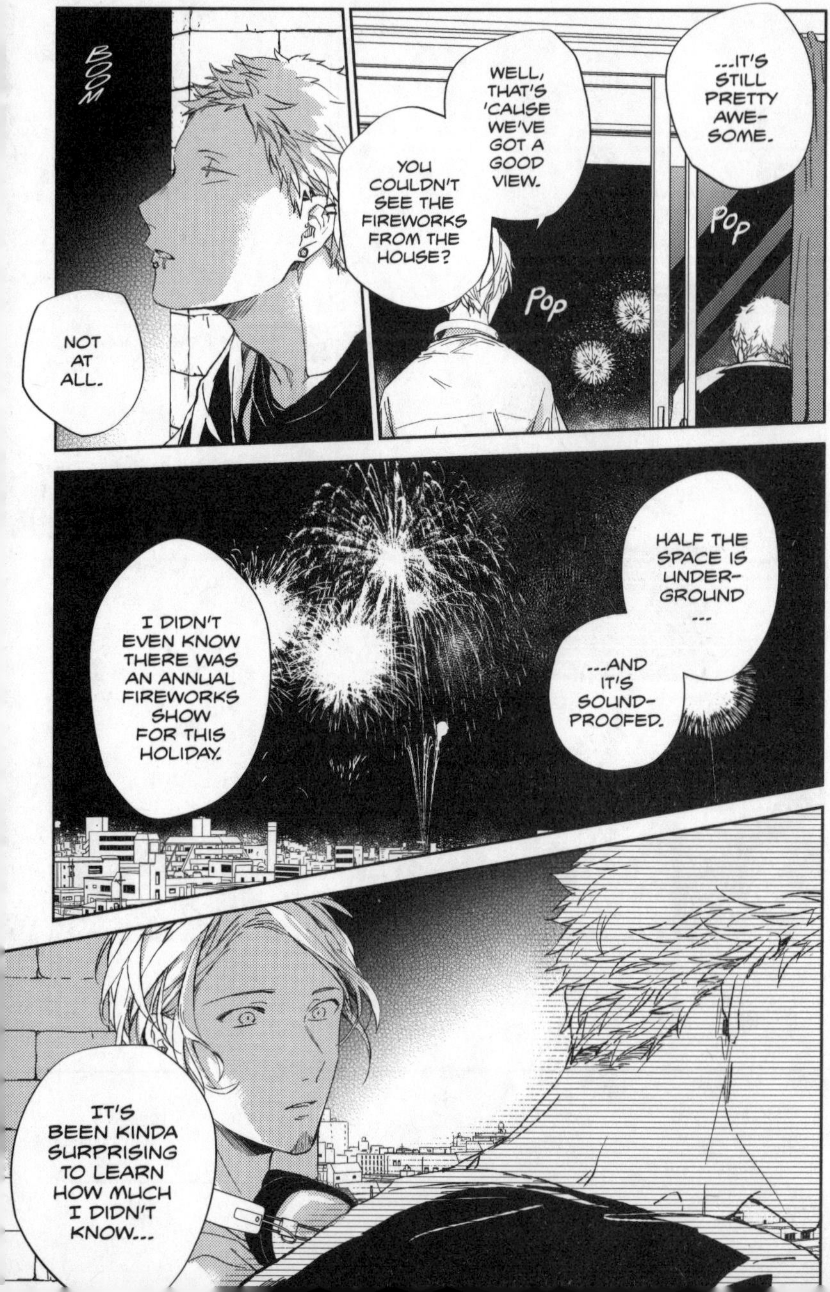
...IT'S STILL PRETTY AWE-SOME.
POP
WELL, THAT'S 'CAUSE WE'VE GOT A GOOD VIEW.
YOU COULDN'T SEE THE FIREWORKS FROM THE HOUSE?
POP
BOOM
NOT AT ALL.
HALF THE SPACE IS UNDER-GROUND ...
...AND IT'S SOUND-PROOFED.
I DIDN'T EVEN KNOW THERE WAS AN ANNUAL FIREWORKS SHOW FOR THIS HOLIDAY.
IT'S BEEN KINDA SURPRISING TO LEARN HOW MUCH I DIDN'T KNOW...

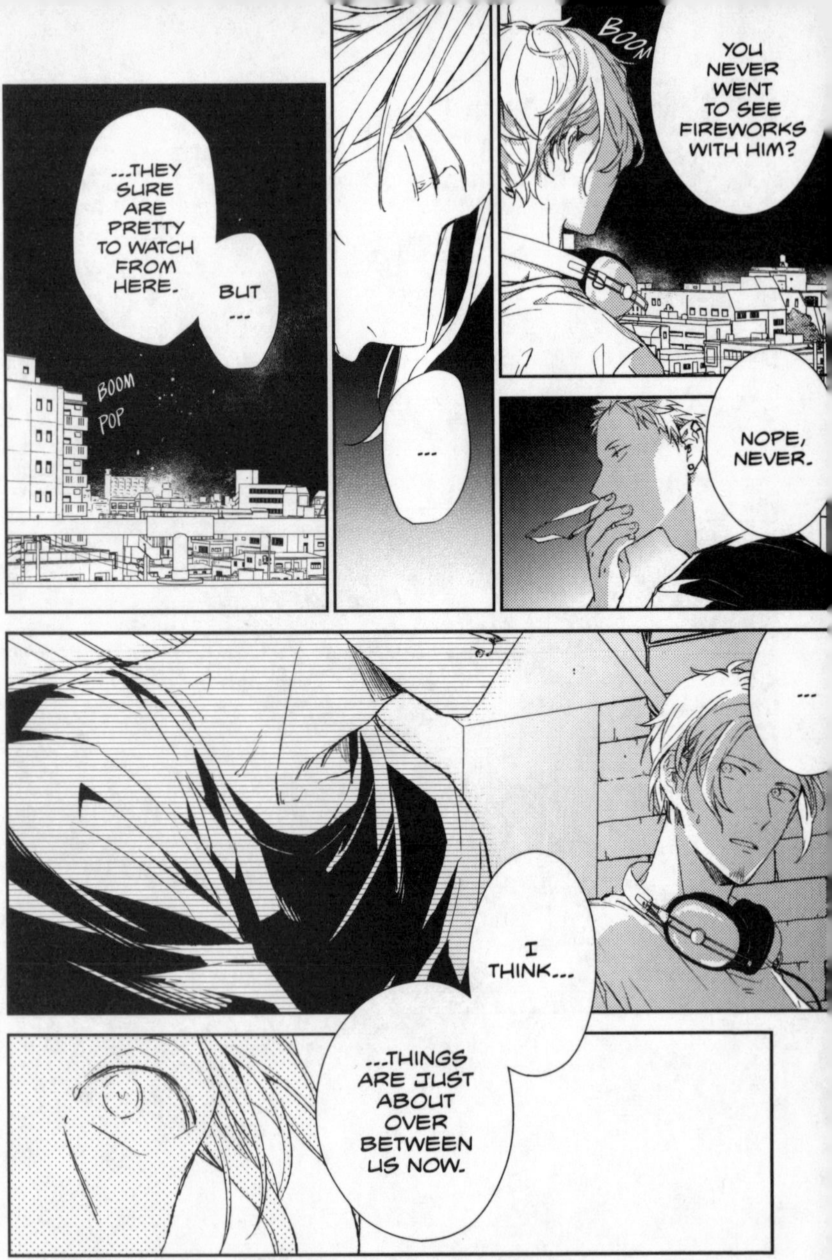
BOOM
YOU NEVER WENT TO SEE FIREWORKS WITH HIM?
NOPE, NEVER.
...
...THEY SURE ARE PRETTY TO WATCH FROM HERE.
BUT ...
BOOM
POP
...
I THINK...
...THINGS ARE JUST ABOUT OVER BETWEEN US NOW.

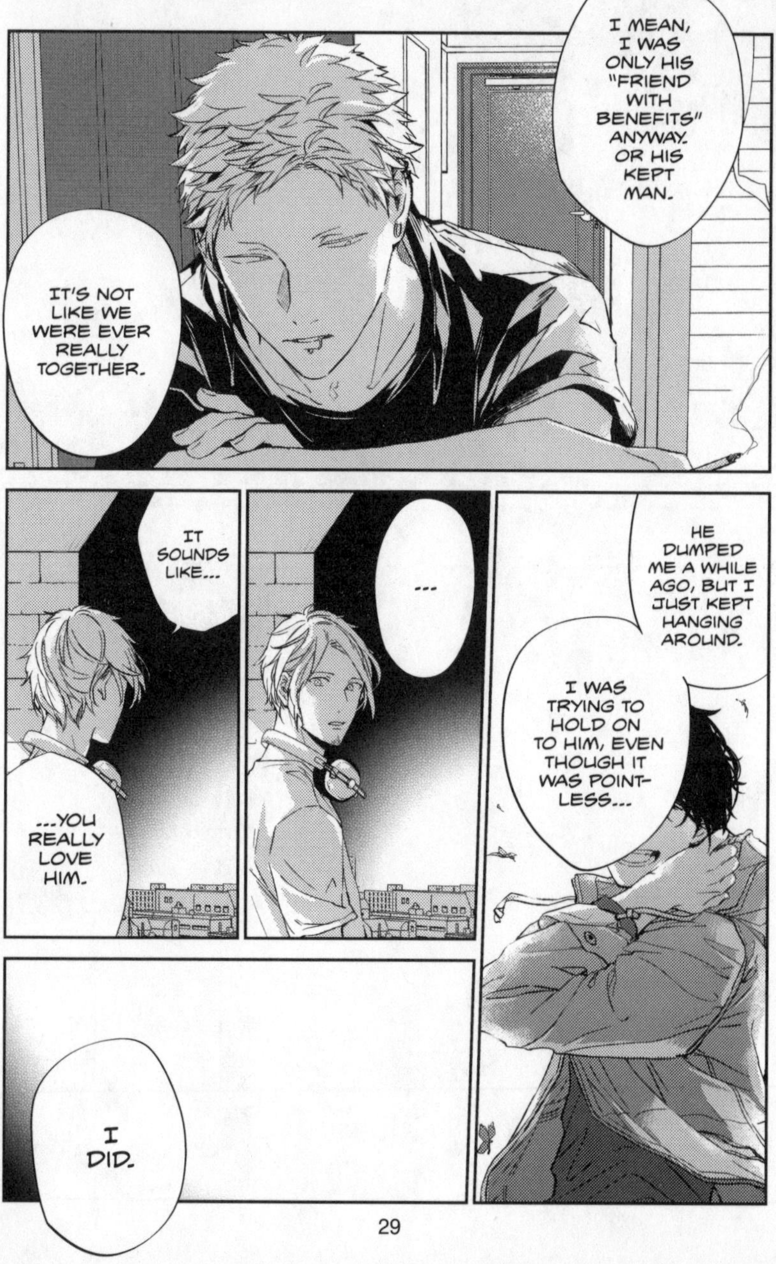
I MEAN, I WAS ONLY HIS "FRIEND WITH BENEFITS" ANYWAY. OR HIS KEPT MAN.
IT'S NOT LIKE WE WERE EVER REALLY TOGETHER.
HE DUMPED ME A WHILE AGO, BUT I JUST KEPT HANGING AROUND.
I WAS TRYING TO HOLD ON TO HIM, EVEN THOUGH IT WAS POINT-LESS...
...
IT SOUNDS LIKE...
...YOU REALLY LOVE HIM.
I DID.

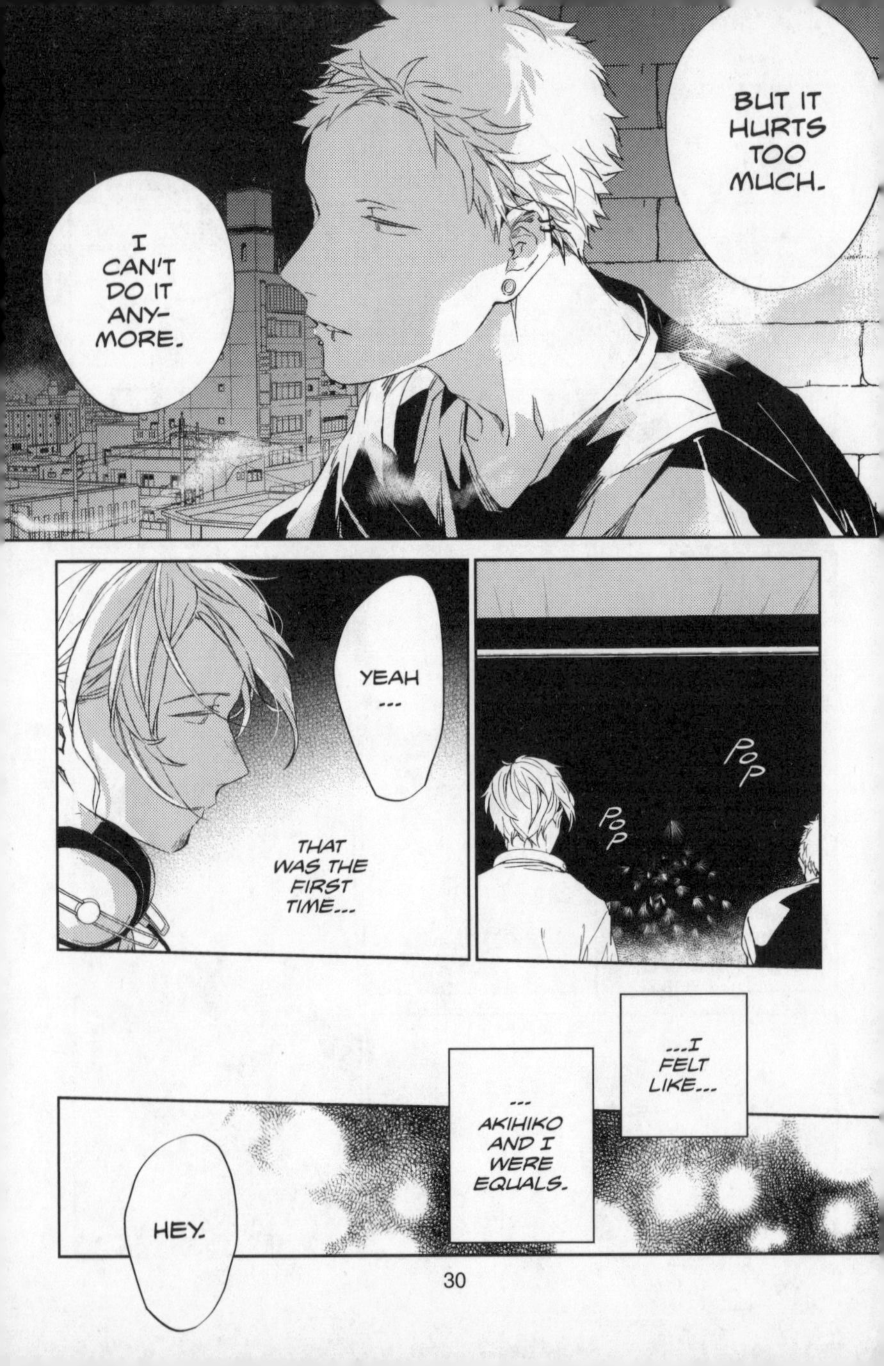
BUT IT HURTS TOO MUCH.
I CAN'T DO IT ANYMORE.
POP
POP
YEAH ...
THAT WAS THE FIRST TIME...
...I FELT LIKE...
...AKIHIKO AND I WERE EQUALS.
HEY.

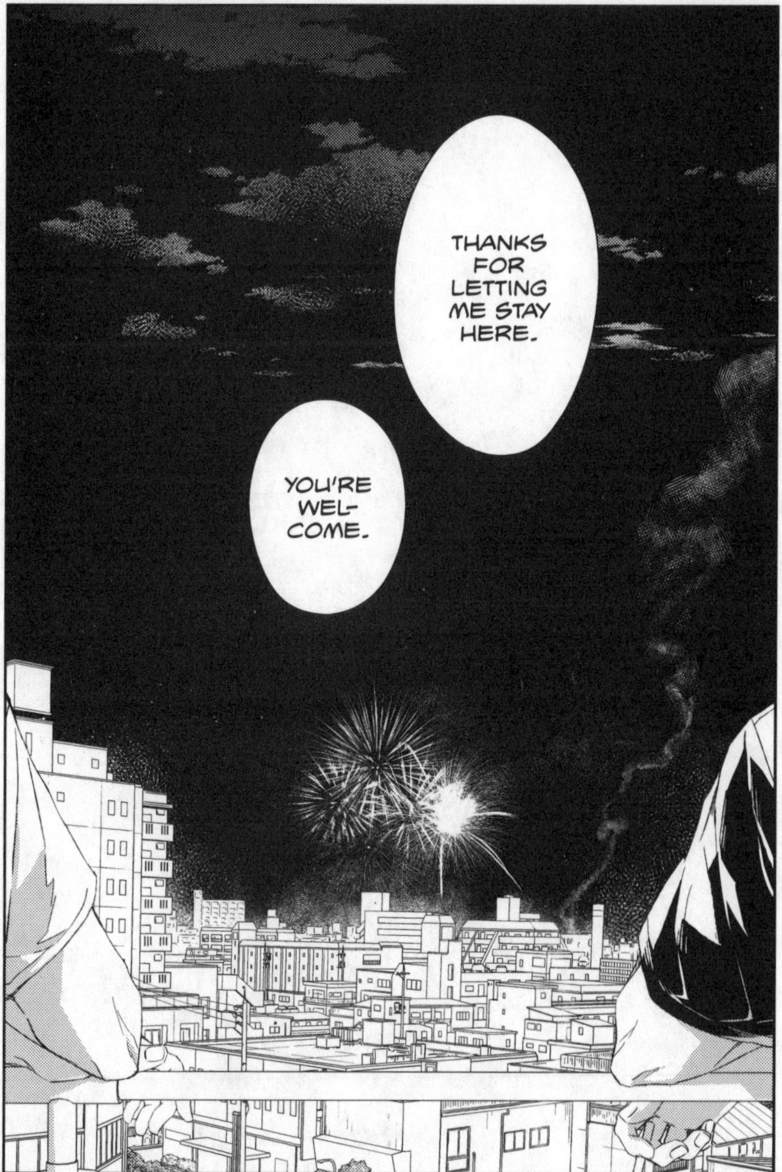
THANKS FOR LETTING ME STAY HERE.
YOU'RE WEL-COME.

given

by Natsuki Kizu

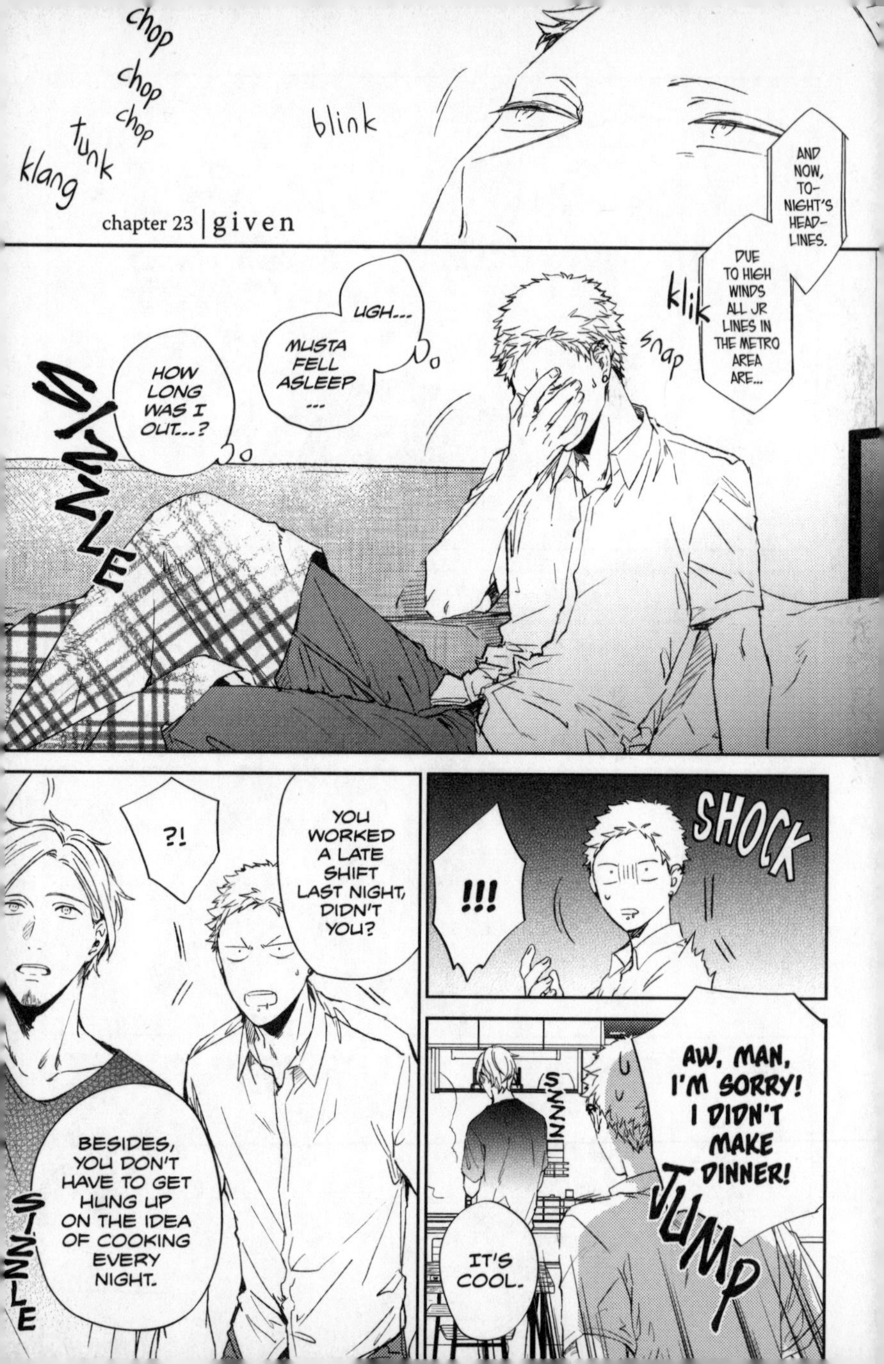
chapter 23 | given
AND NOW, TO-NIGHT'S HEAD-LINES.
blink
chop chop chop
tunk
klang
DUE TO HIGH WINDS ALL JR LINES IN THE METRO AREA ARE...
klik
snap
UGH... MUSTA FELL ASLEEP...
HOW LONG WAS I OUT...?
SIZZLE
SHOCK
!!!
AW, MAN, I'M SORRY! I DIDN'T MAKE DINNER!
JUMP
SNNN
IT'S COOL.
YOU WORKED A LATE SHIFT LAST NIGHT, DIDN'T YOU?
?!
BESIDES, YOU DON'T HAVE TO GET HUNG UP ON THE IDEA OF COOKING EVERY NIGHT.
SIZZLE

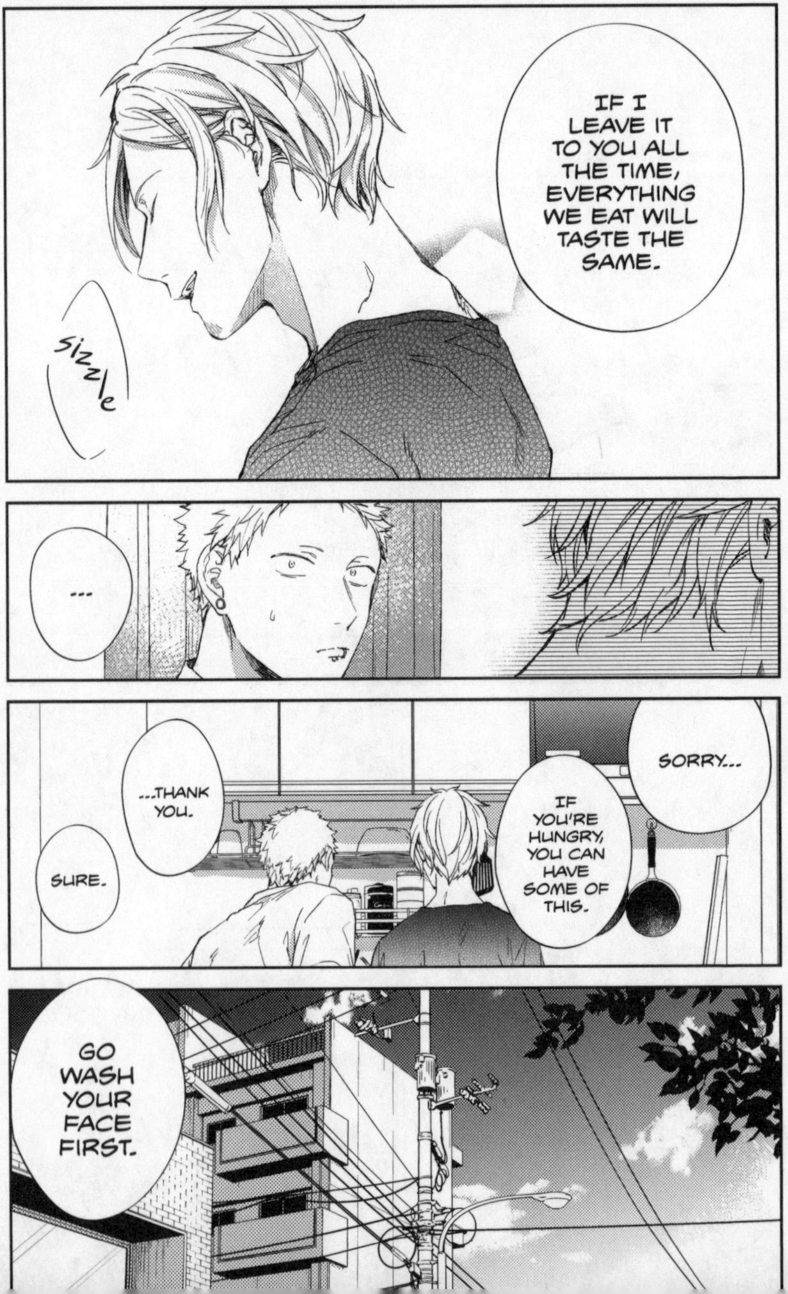
IF I LEAVE IT TO YOU ALL THE TIME, EVERYTHING WE EAT WILL TASTE THE SAME.
sizzle
...
SORRY...
IF YOU'RE HUNGRY, YOU CAN HAVE SOME OF THIS.
...THANK YOU.
SURE.
GO WASH YOUR FACE FIRST.

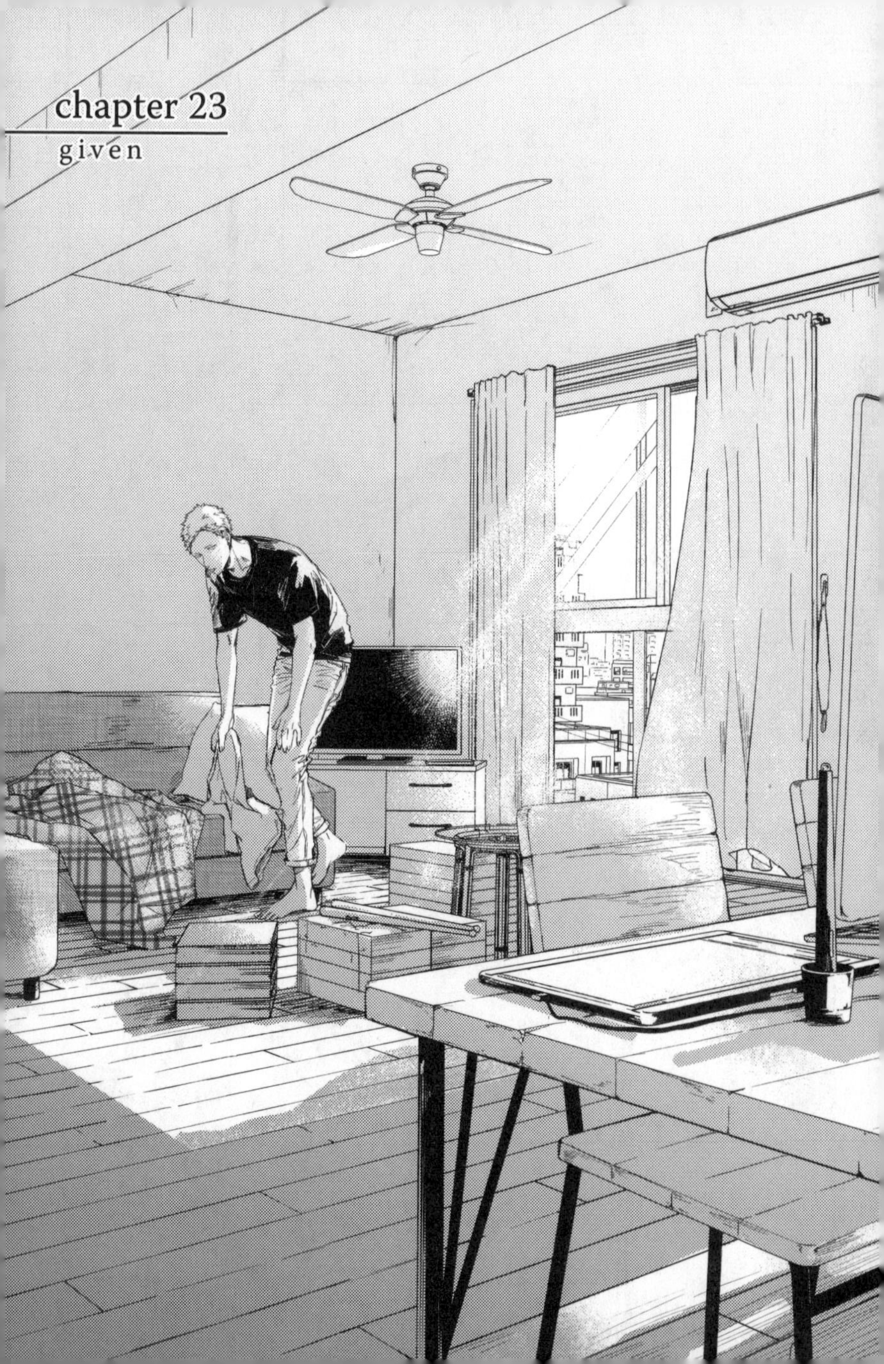
chapter 23
given

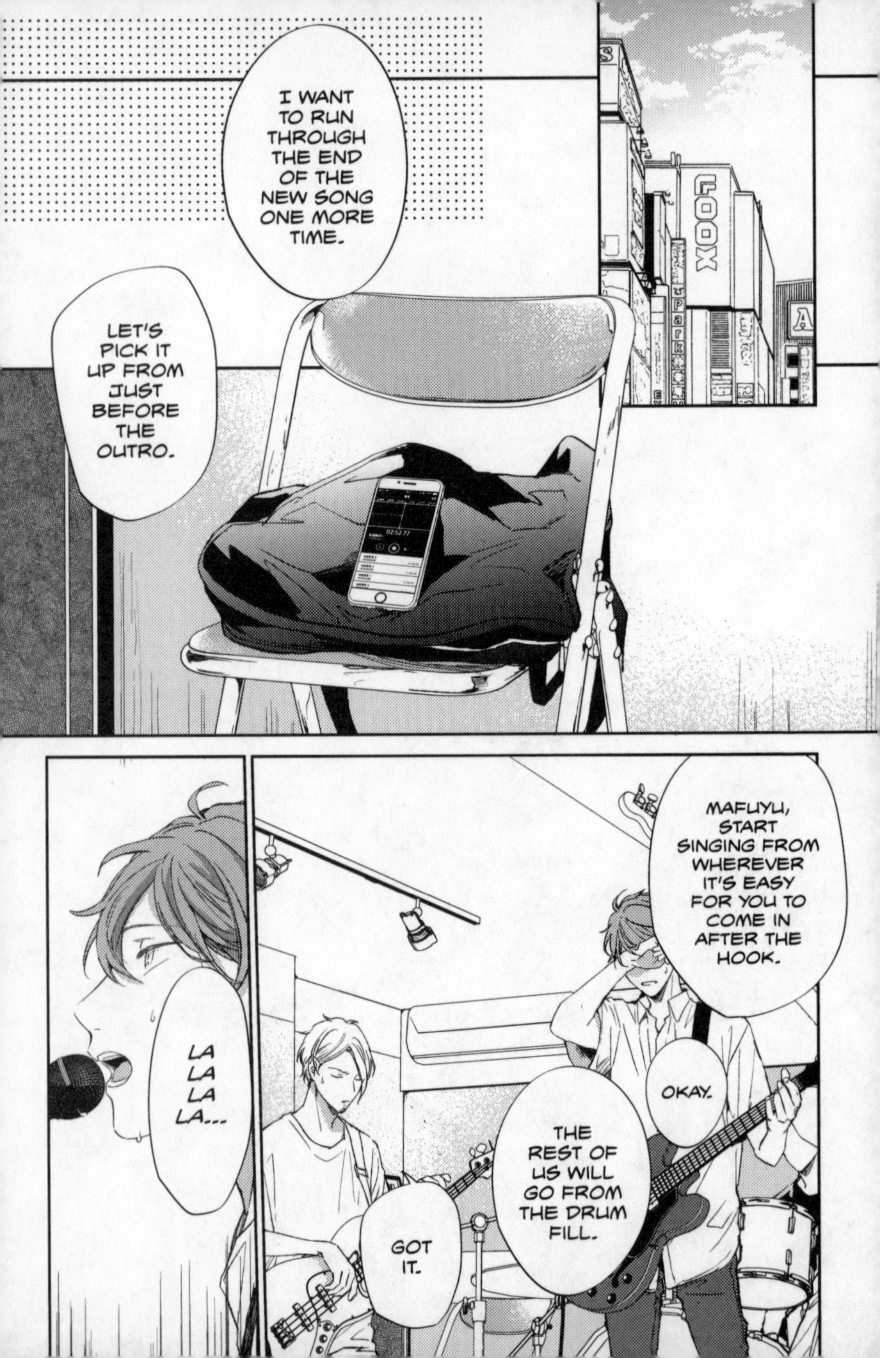
LOOX
I WANT TO RUN THROUGH THE END OF THE NEW SONG ONE MORE TIME.
LET'S PICK IT UP FROM JUST BEFORE THE OUTRO.
MAFUYU, START SINGING FROM WHEREVER IT'S EASY FOR YOU TO COME IN AFTER THE HOOK.
OKAY.
THE REST OF US WILL GO FROM THE DRUM FILL.
GOT IT.
LA LA LA LA...

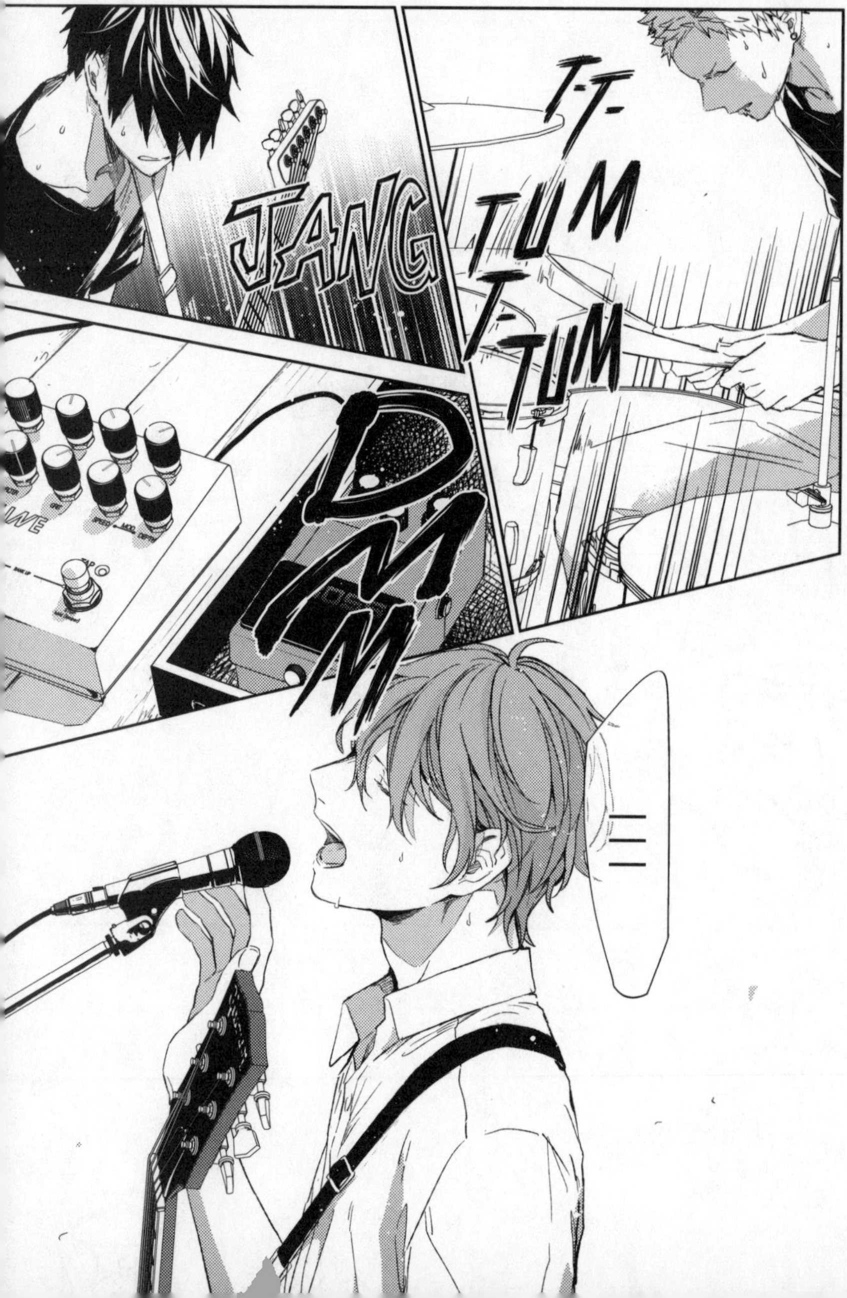
T-T-TUM
T-TUM
JANG
DMM
...

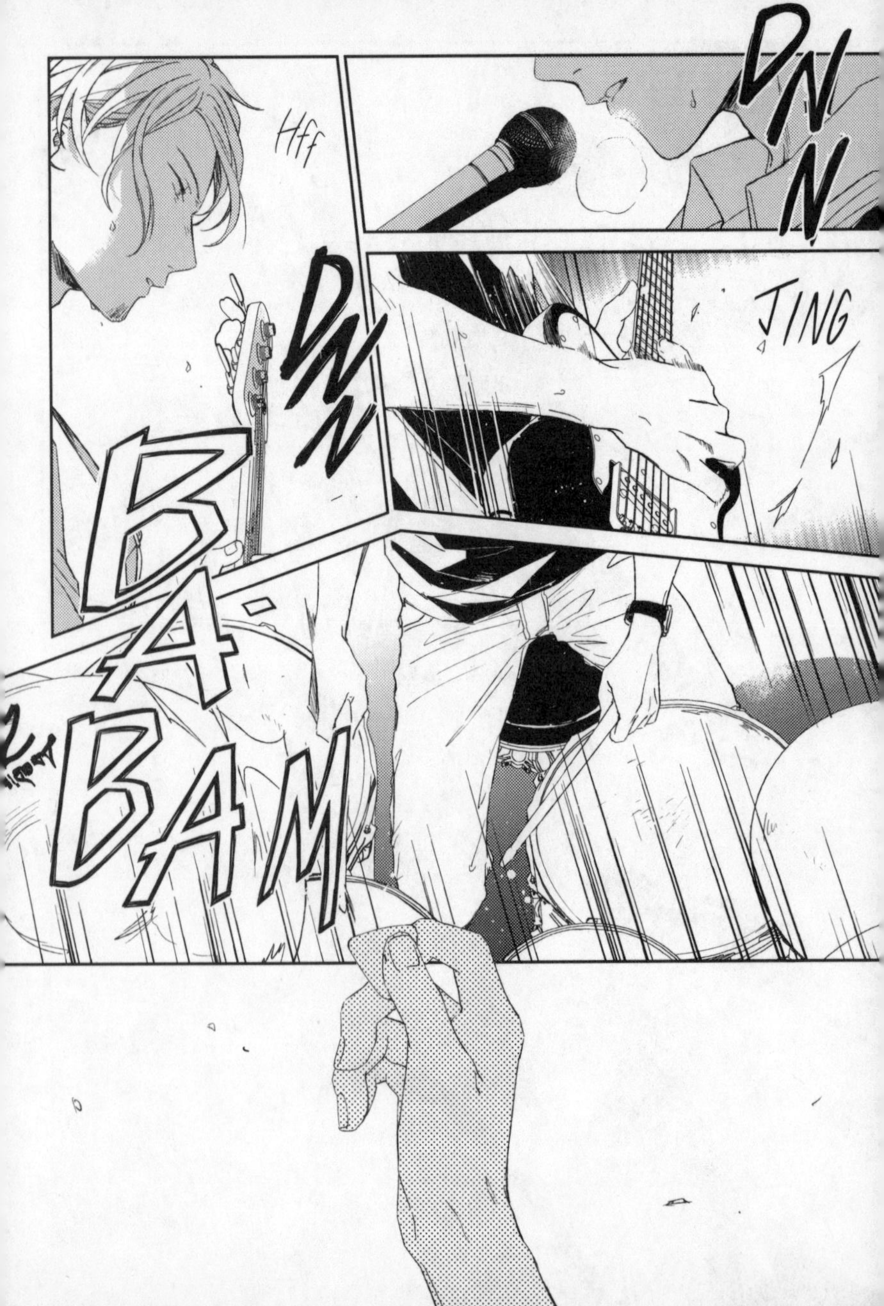
DNN
Hff
DNN
JING
BA-BAM

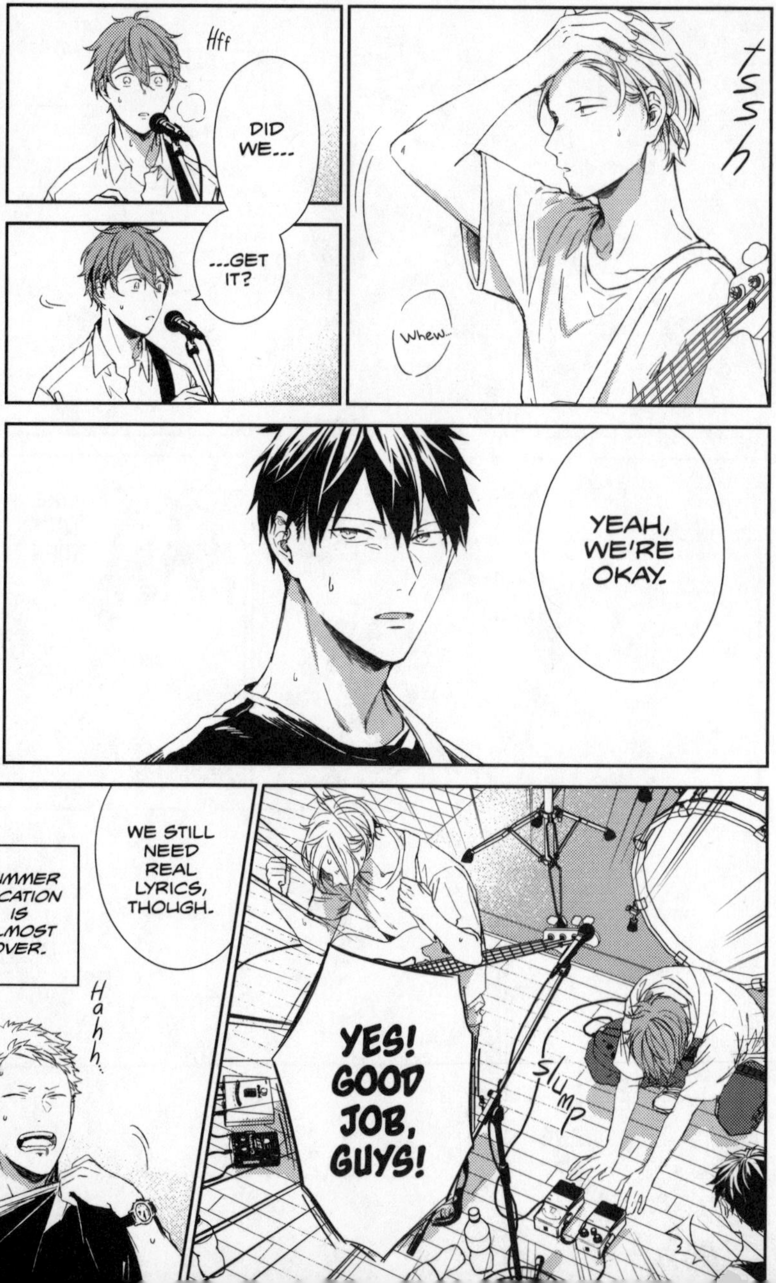
tssh
Whew...
Hff
DID WE...
...GET IT?
YEAH, WE'RE OKAY.
WE STILL NEED REAL LYRICS, THOUGH.
YES! GOOD JOB, GUYS!
slump
SUMMER VACATION IS ALMOST OVER.
Hahh...

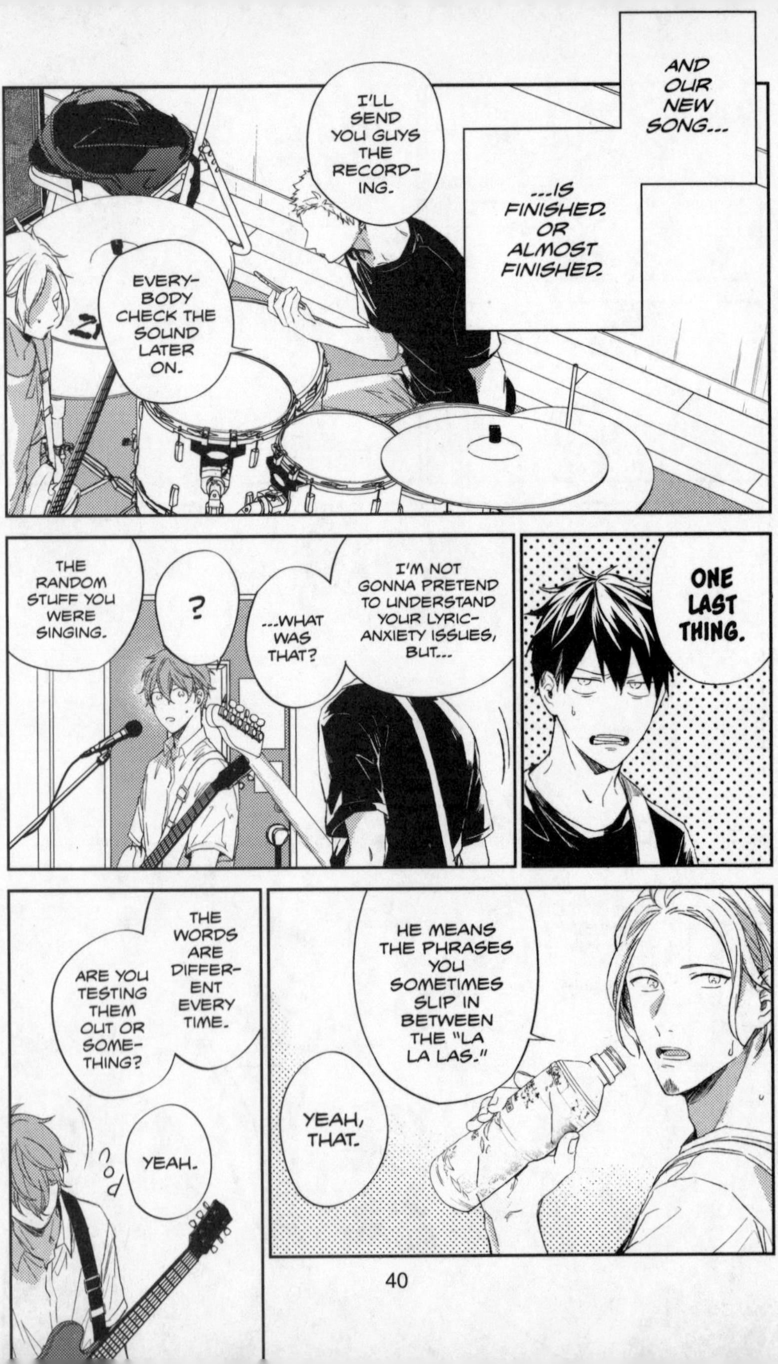
AND OUR NEW SONG...
...IS FINISHED. OR ALMOST FINISHED.
I'LL SEND YOU GUYS THE RECORDING.
EVERYBODY CHECK THE SOUND LATER ON.
ONE LAST THING.
I'M NOT GONNA PRETEND TO UNDERSTAND YOUR LYRIC-ANXIETY ISSUES, BUT...
...WHAT WAS THAT?
?
THE RANDOM STUFF YOU WERE SINGING.
HE MEANS THE PHRASES YOU SOMETIMES SLIP IN BETWEEN THE "LA LA LAS."
YEAH, THAT.
THE WORDS ARE DIFFERENT EVERY TIME.
ARE YOU TESTING THEM OUT OR SOMETHING?
POP
YEAH.

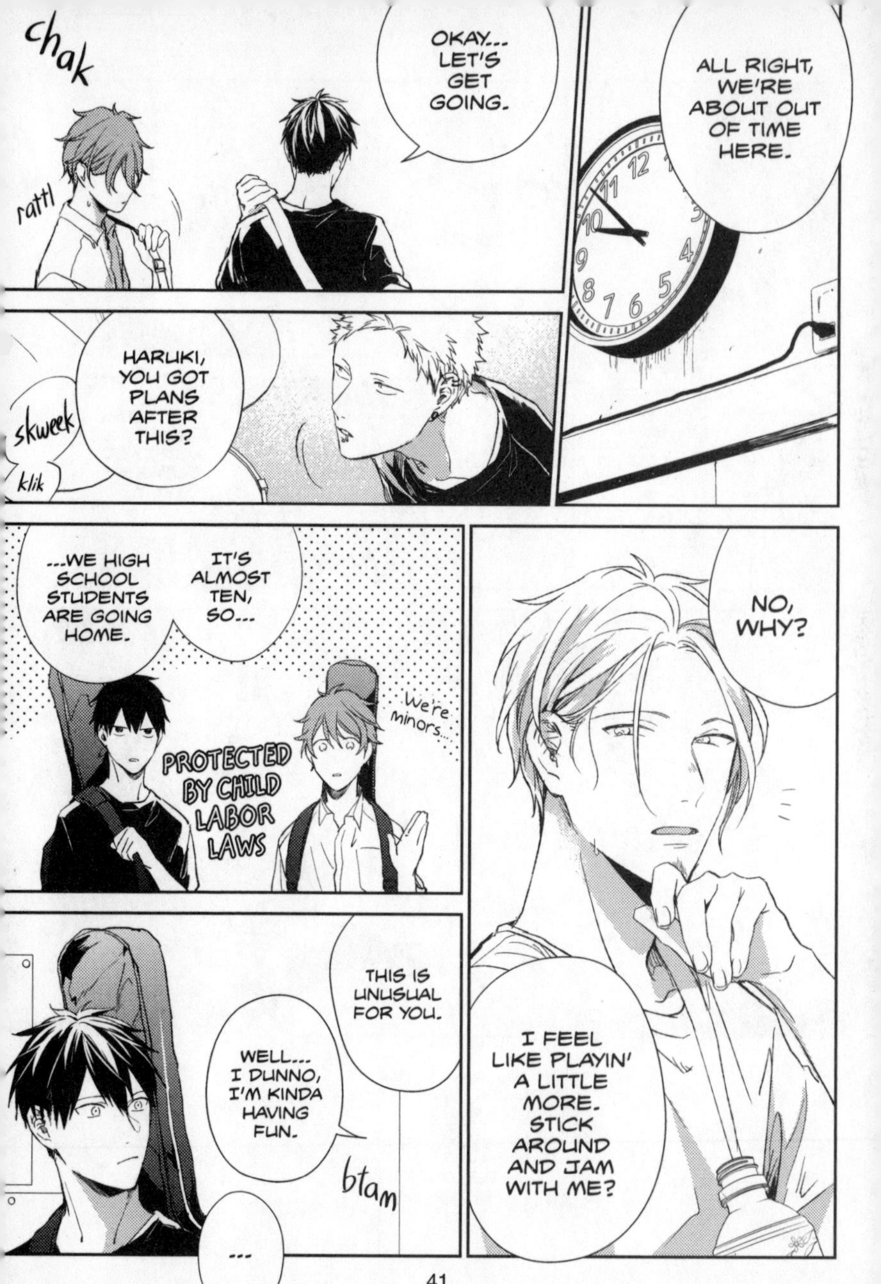
ALL RIGHT, WE'RE ABOUT OUT OF TIME HERE.
OKAY... LET'S GET GOING.
chak
rattl
HARUKI, YOU GOT PLANS AFTER THIS?
skweek
klik
NO, WHY?
I FEEL LIKE PLAYIN' A LITTLE MORE. STICK AROUND AND JAM WITH ME?
IT'S ALMOST TEN, SO...
...WE HIGH SCHOOL STUDENTS ARE GOING HOME.
We're minors...
PROTECTED BY CHILD LABOR LAWS
THIS IS UNUSUAL FOR YOU.
WELL... I DUNNO, I'M KINDA HAVING FUN.
btam
...

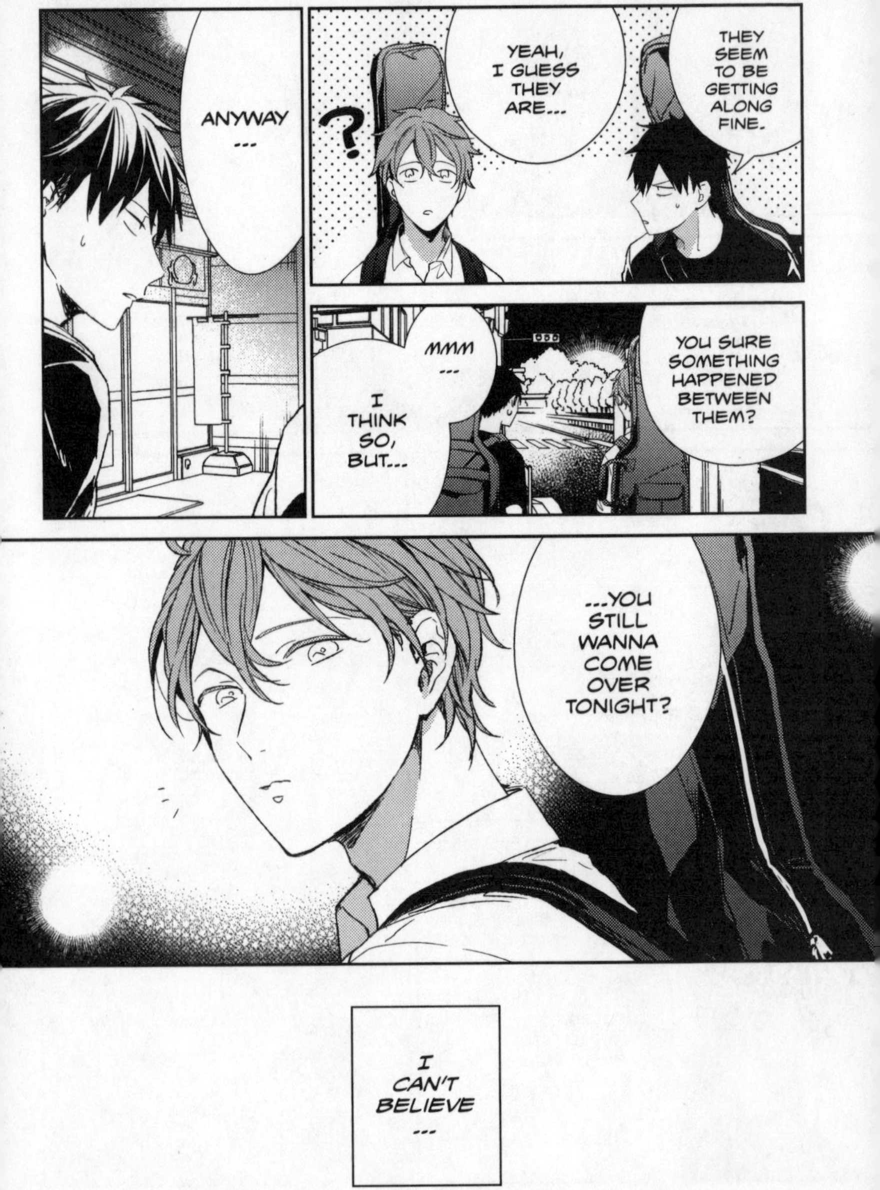
THEY SEEM TO BE GETTING ALONG FINE.
YEAH, I GUESS THEY ARE...
YOU SURE SOMETHING HAPPENED BETWEEN THEM?
MMM ... I THINK SO, BUT...
ANYWAY ...
...YOU STILL WANNA COME OVER TONIGHT?
I CAN'T BELIEVE ...

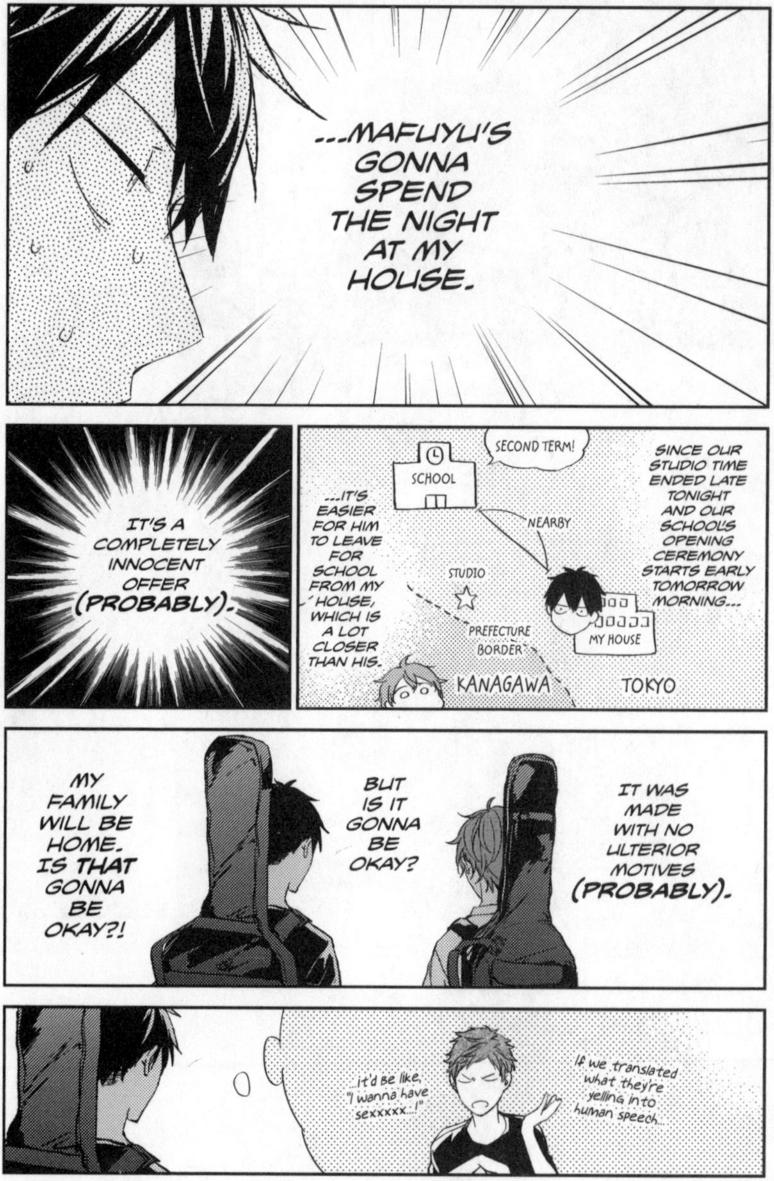
...MAFUYU'S GONNA SPEND THE NIGHT AT MY HOUSE.
SINCE OUR STUDIO TIME ENDED LATE TONIGHT AND OUR SCHOOL'S OPENING CEREMONY STARTS EARLY TOMORROW MORNING...
SECOND TERM!
SCHOOL
NEARBY
...IT'S EASIER FOR HIM TO LEAVE FOR SCHOOL FROM MY HOUSE, WHICH IS A LOT CLOSER THAN HIS.
STUDIO
MY HOUSE
PREFECTURE BORDER
TOKYO
KANAGAWA
IT'S A COMPLETELY INNOCENT OFFER (PROBABLY).
IT WAS MADE WITH NO ULTERIOR MOTIVES (PROBABLY).
BUT IS IT GONNA BE OKAY?
MY FAMILY WILL BE HOME. IS THAT GONNA BE OKAY?!
If we translated what they're yelling into human speech...
it'd be like, "I wanna have sexxxxx...!"

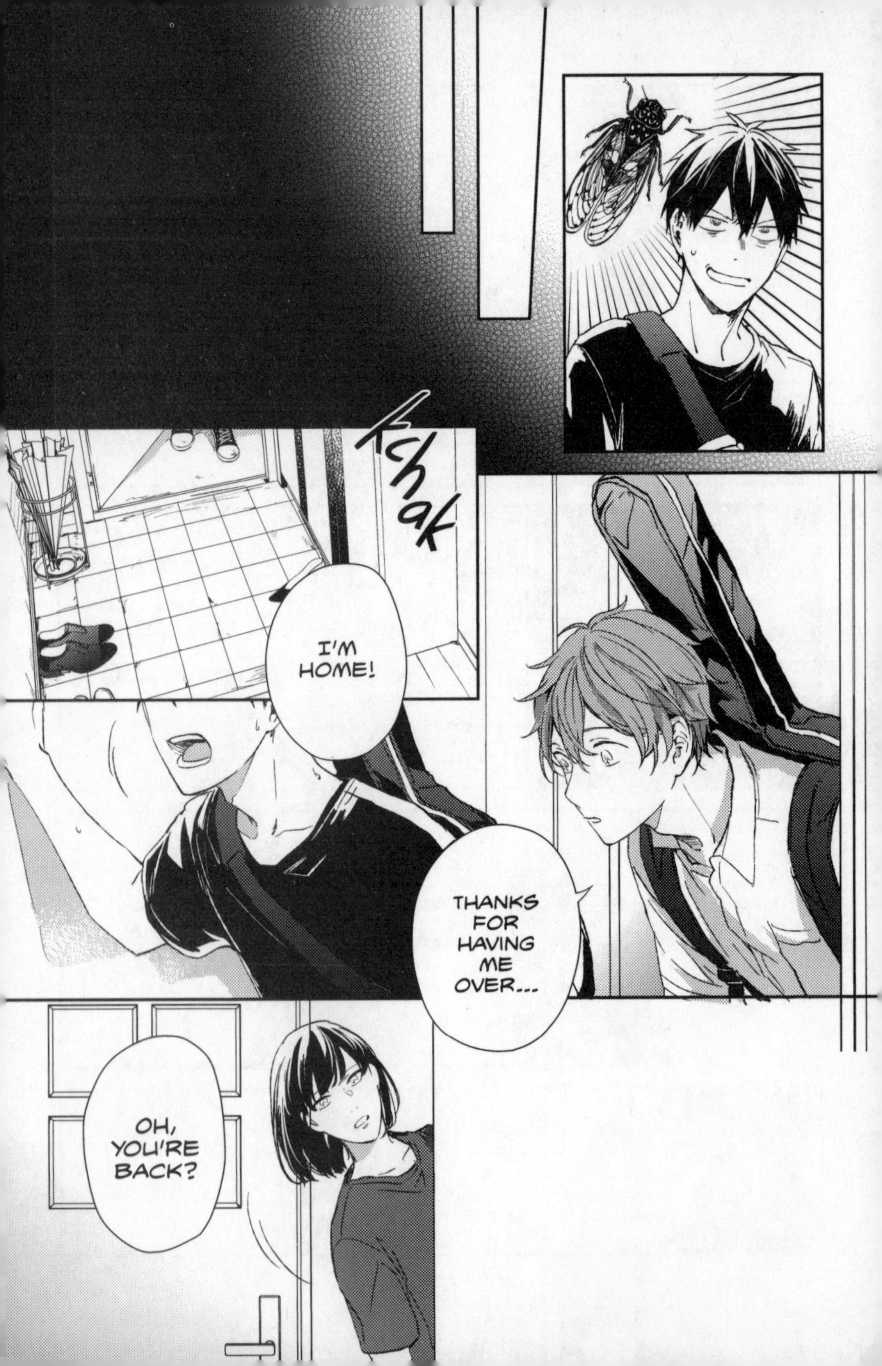
kchak
I'M HOME!
THANKS FOR HAVING ME OVER...
OH, YOU'RE BACK?

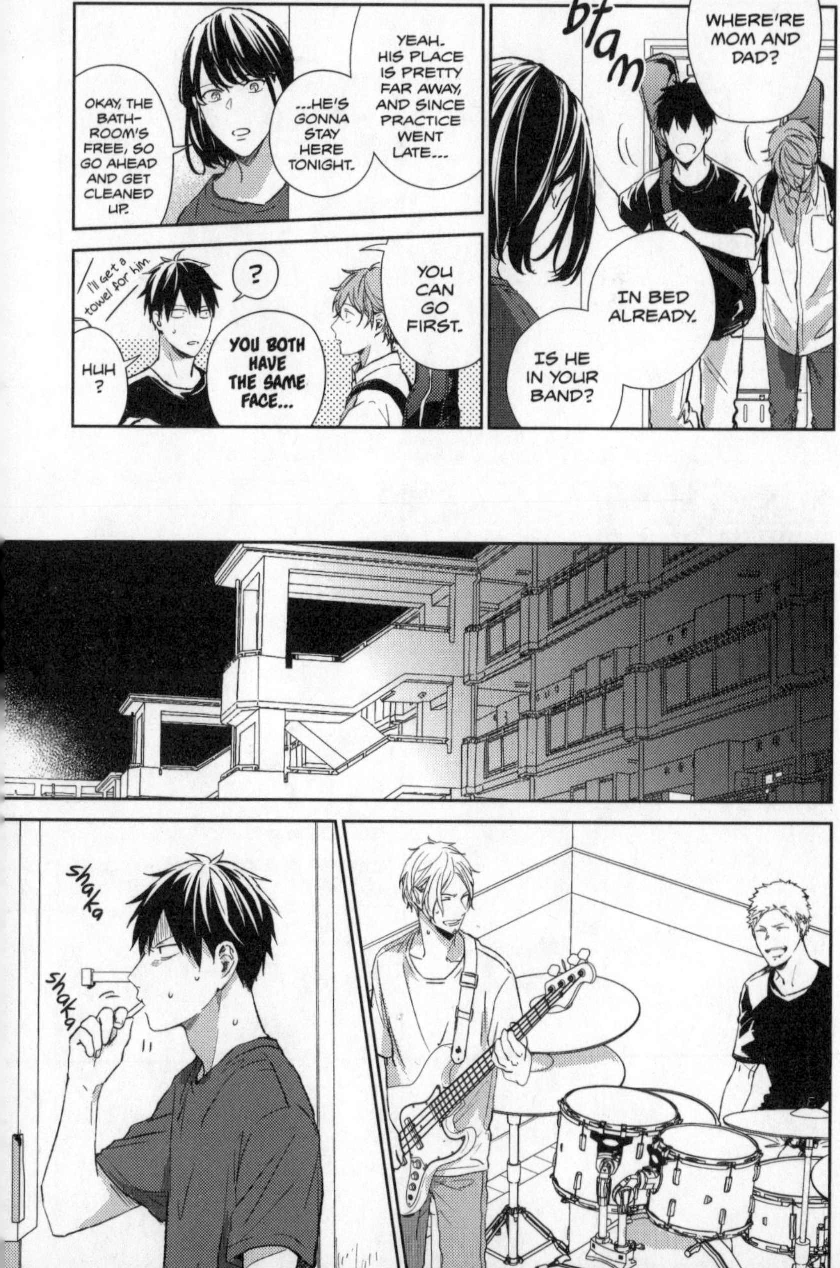
btam
WHERE'RE MOM AND DAD?
IN BED ALREADY.
IS HE IN YOUR BAND?
YEAH. HIS PLACE IS PRETTY FAR AWAY, AND SINCE PRACTICE WENT LATE...
...HE'S GONNA STAY HERE TONIGHT.
OKAY, THE BATH-ROOM'S FREE, SO GO AHEAD AND GET CLEANED UP.
YOU CAN GO FIRST.
YOU BOTH HAVE THE SAME FACE...
?
HUH?
I'll get a towel for him.
shaka
shaka

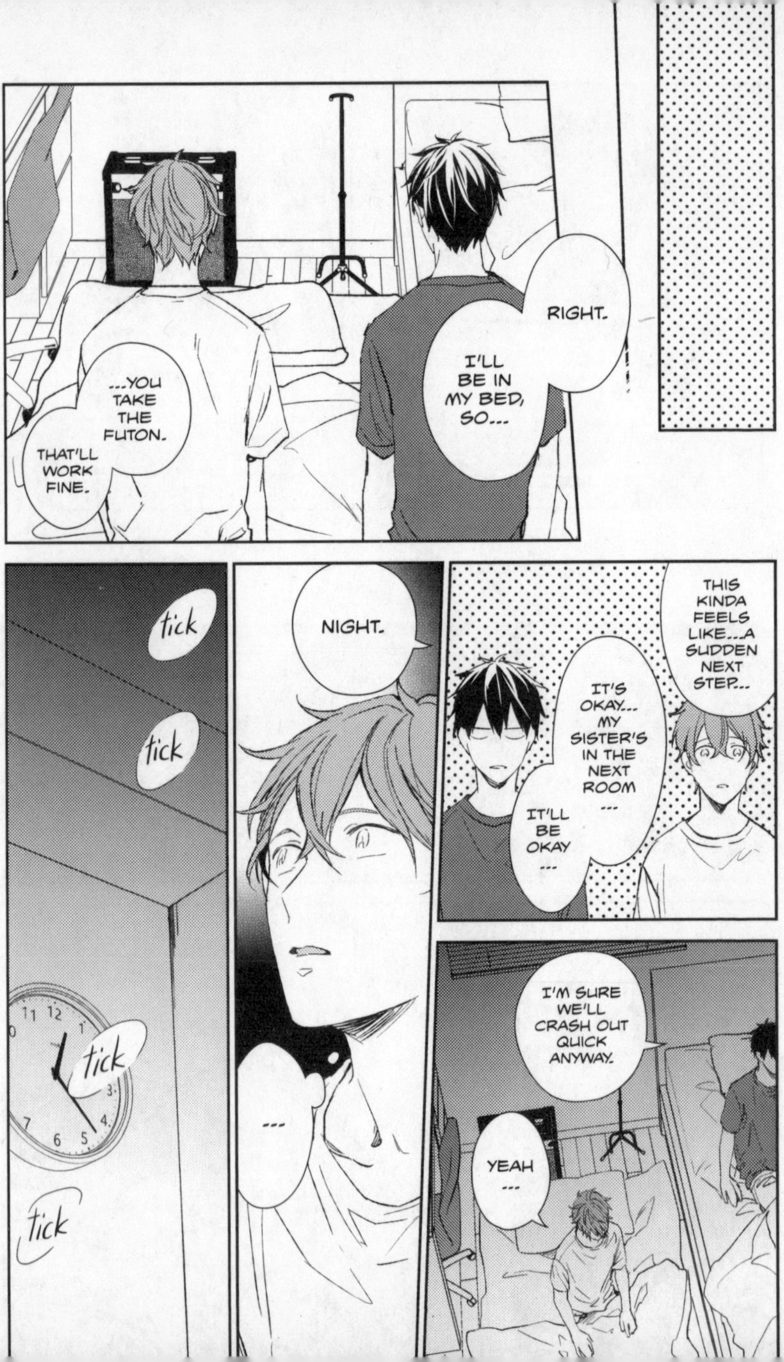
RIGHT.
I'LL BE IN MY BED, SO...
...YOU TAKE THE FUTON.
THAT'LL WORK FINE.
THIS KINDA FEELS LIKE...A SUDDEN NEXT STEP...
IT'S OKAY... MY SISTER'S IN THE NEXT ROOM...
IT'LL BE OKAY...
I'M SURE WE'LL CRASH OUT QUICK ANYWAY.
YEAH...
NIGHT.
...
tick
tick
tick
tick

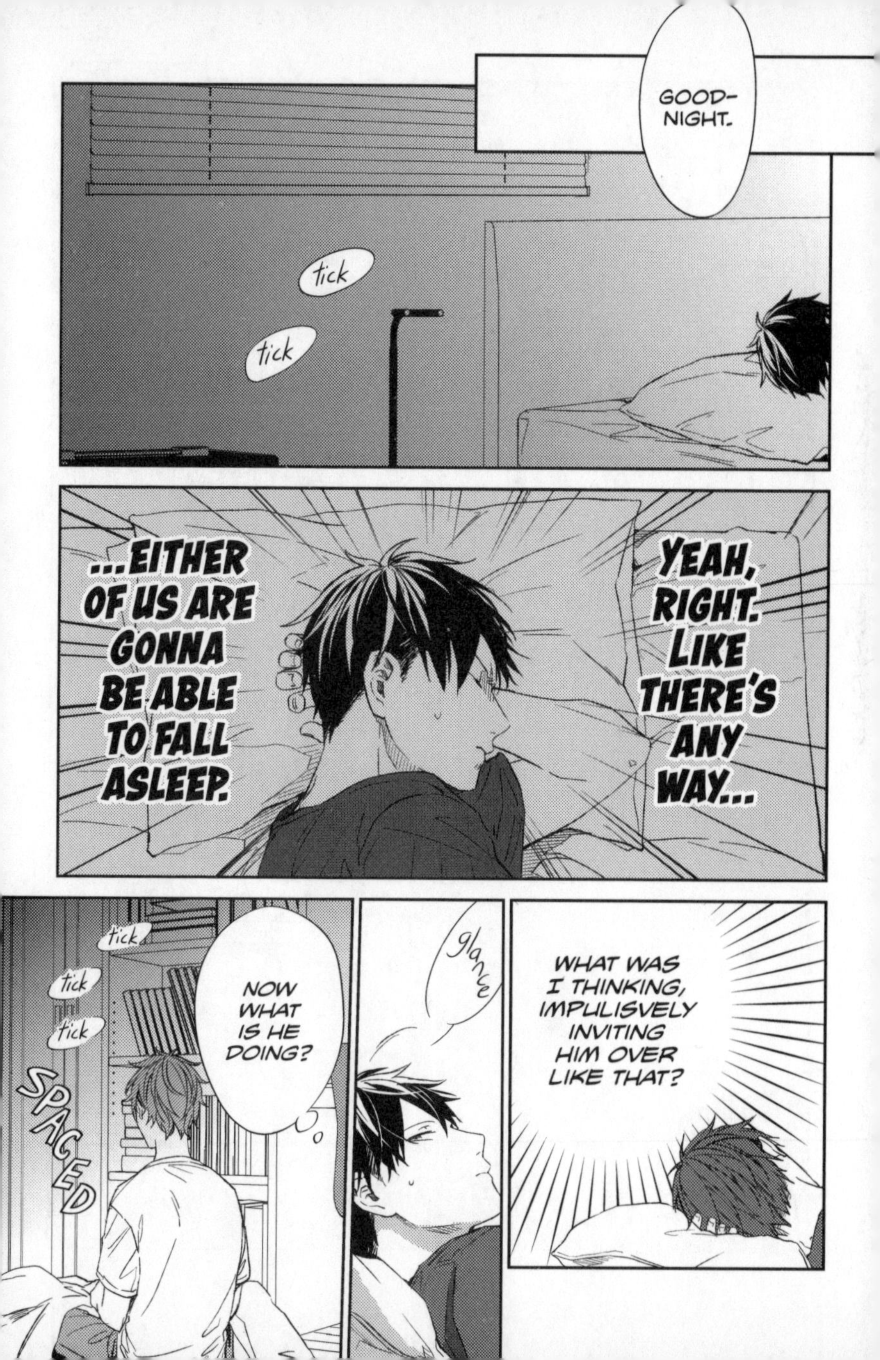
GOOD-NIGHT.
tick
tick
YEAH, RIGHT. LIKE THERE'S ANY WAY...
...EITHER OF US ARE GONNA BE ABLE TO FALL ASLEEP.
WHAT WAS I THINKING, IMPULISVELY INVITING HIM OVER LIKE THAT?
glance
NOW WHAT IS HE DOING?
tick
tick
tick
SPACED

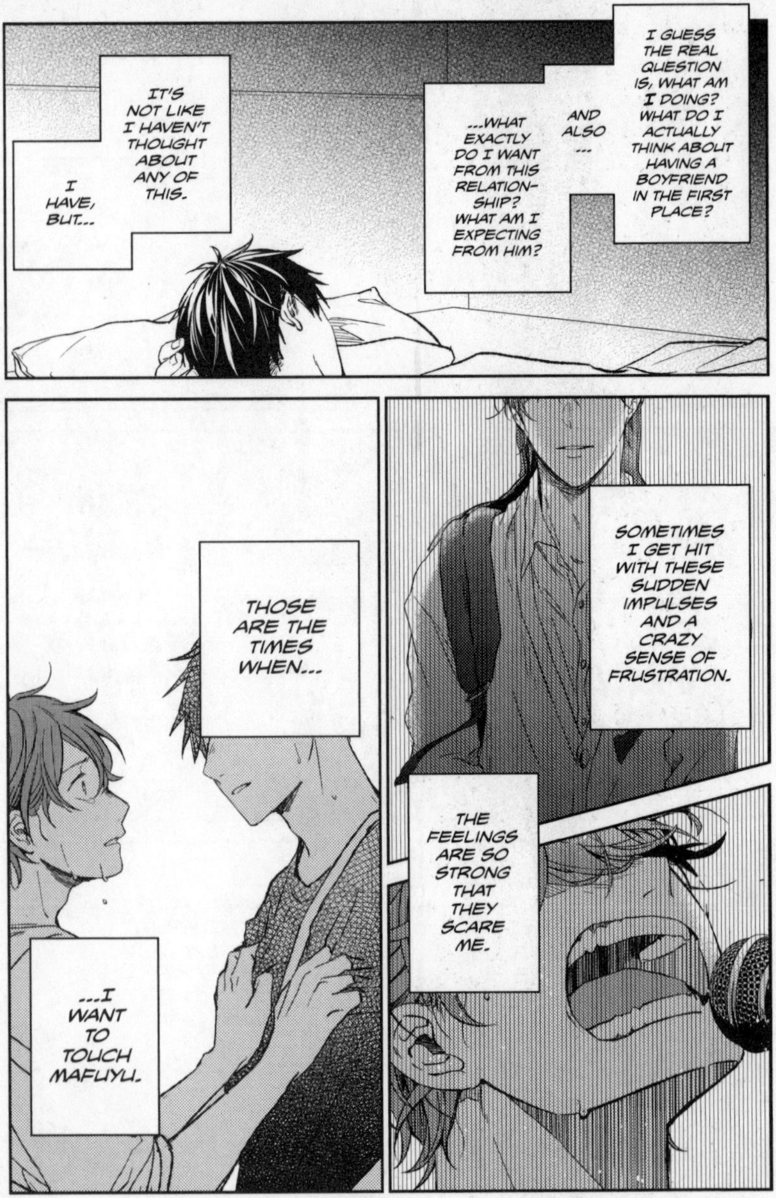
I GUESS THE REAL QUESTION IS, WHAT AM I DOING? WHAT DO I ACTUALLY THINK ABOUT HAVING A BOYFRIEND IN THE FIRST PLACE?
AND ALSO ...
...WHAT EXACTLY DO I WANT FROM THIS RELATION-SHIP? WHAT AM I EXPECTING FROM HIM?
IT'S NOT LIKE I HAVEN'T THOUGHT ABOUT ANY OF THIS.
I HAVE, BUT...
SOMETIMES I GET HIT WITH THESE SUDDEN IMPULSES AND A CRAZY SENSE OF FRUSTRATION.
THE FEELINGS ARE SO STRONG THAT THEY SCARE ME.
THOSE ARE THE TIMES WHEN...
...I WANT TO TOUCH MAFUYU.

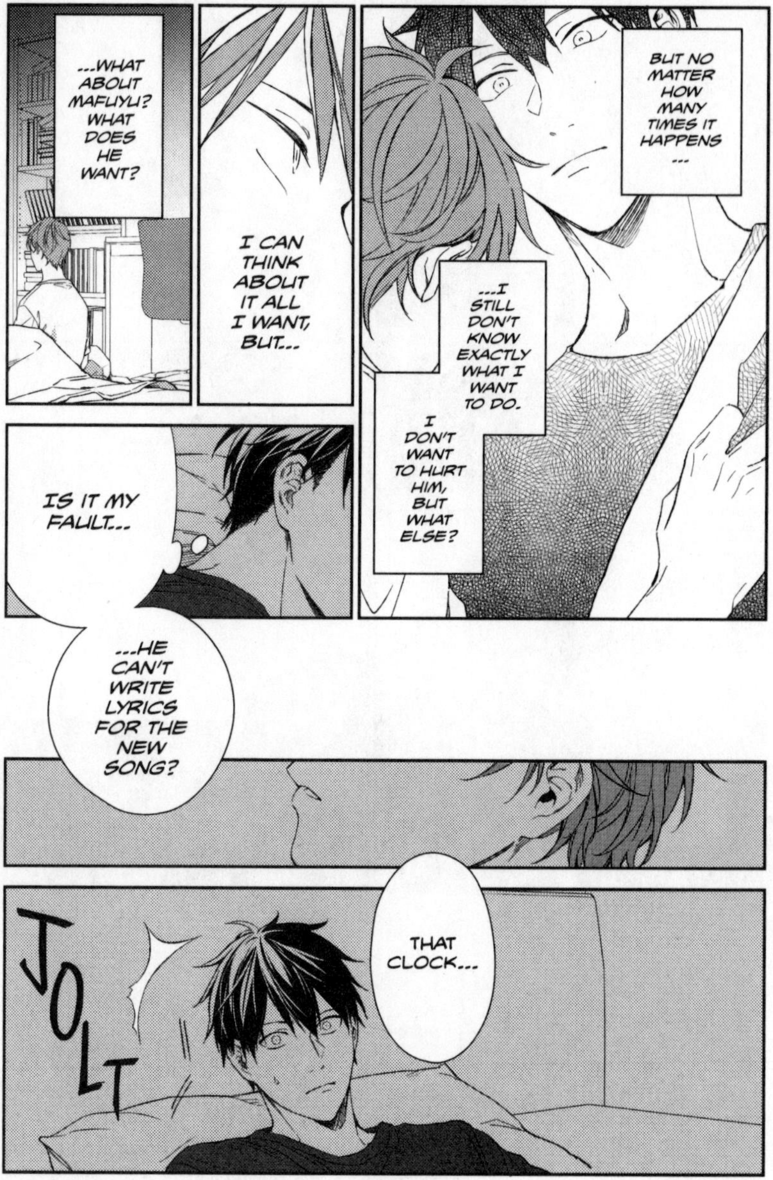
BUT NO MATTER HOW MANY TIMES IT HAPPENS...
...I STILL DON'T KNOW EXACTLY WHAT I WANT TO DO.
I DON'T WANT TO HURT HIM, BUT WHAT ELSE?
I CAN THINK ABOUT IT ALL I WANT, BUT...
...WHAT ABOUT MAFUYU? WHAT DOES HE WANT?
IS IT MY FAULT...
...HE CAN'T WRITE LYRICS FOR THE NEW SONG?
THAT CLOCK...
JOLT

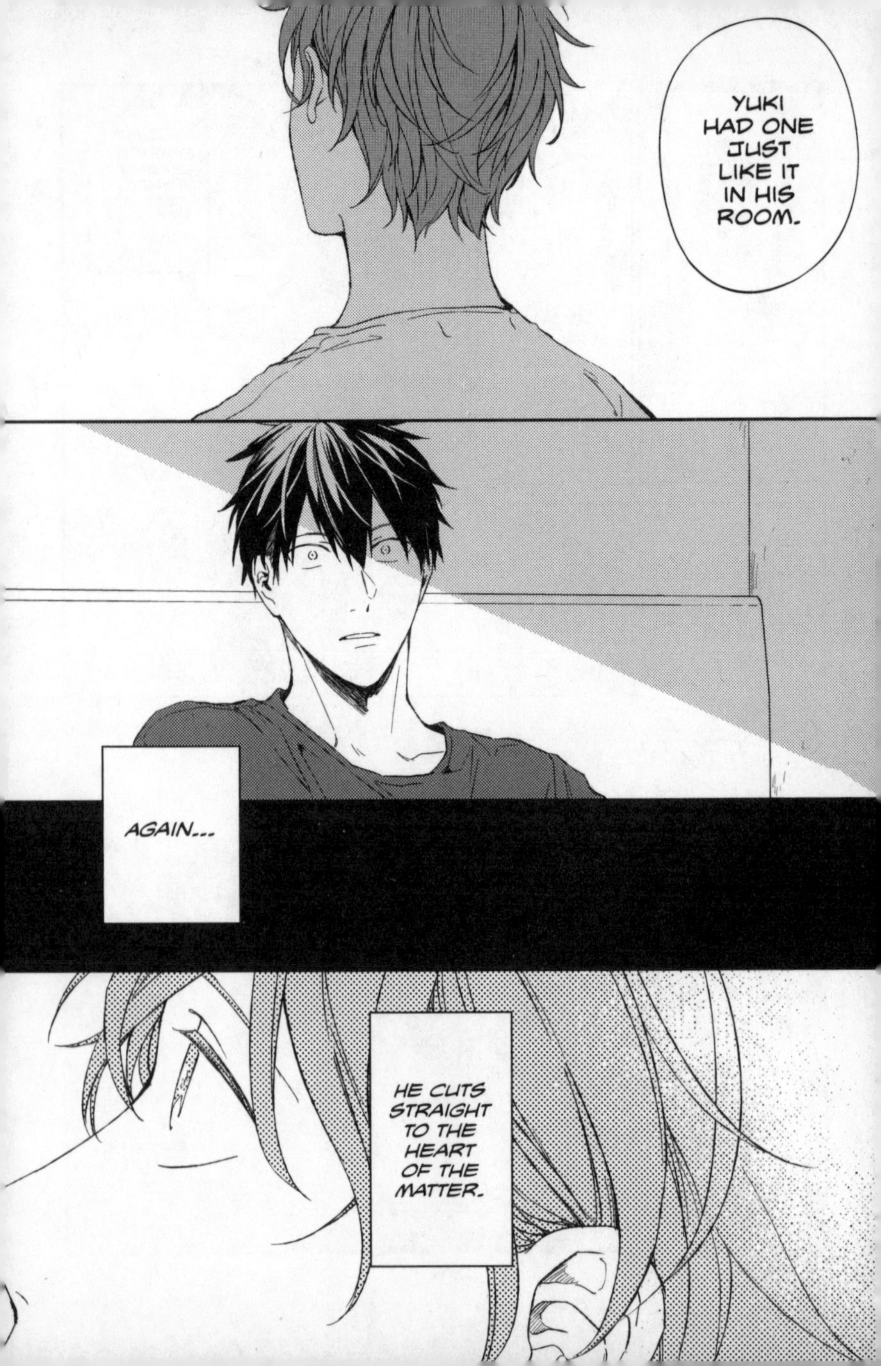
YUKI HAD ONE JUST LIKE IT IN HIS ROOM.
AGAIN...
HE CUTS STRAIGHT TO THE HEART OF THE MATTER.

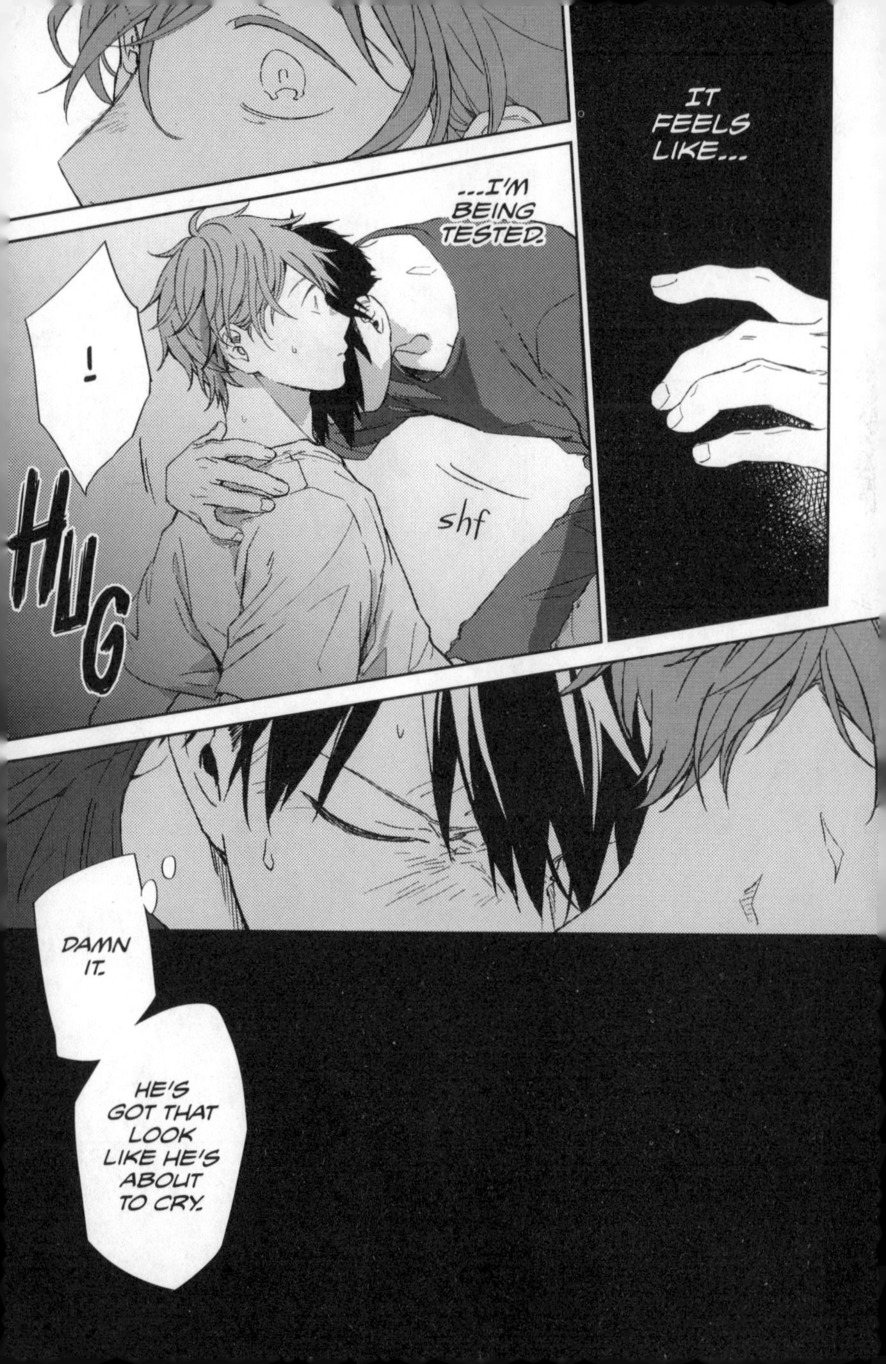
IT FEELS LIKE...
...I'M BEING TESTED.
!
shf
HUG
DAMN IT.
HE'S GOT THAT LOOK LIKE HE'S ABOUT TO CRY.

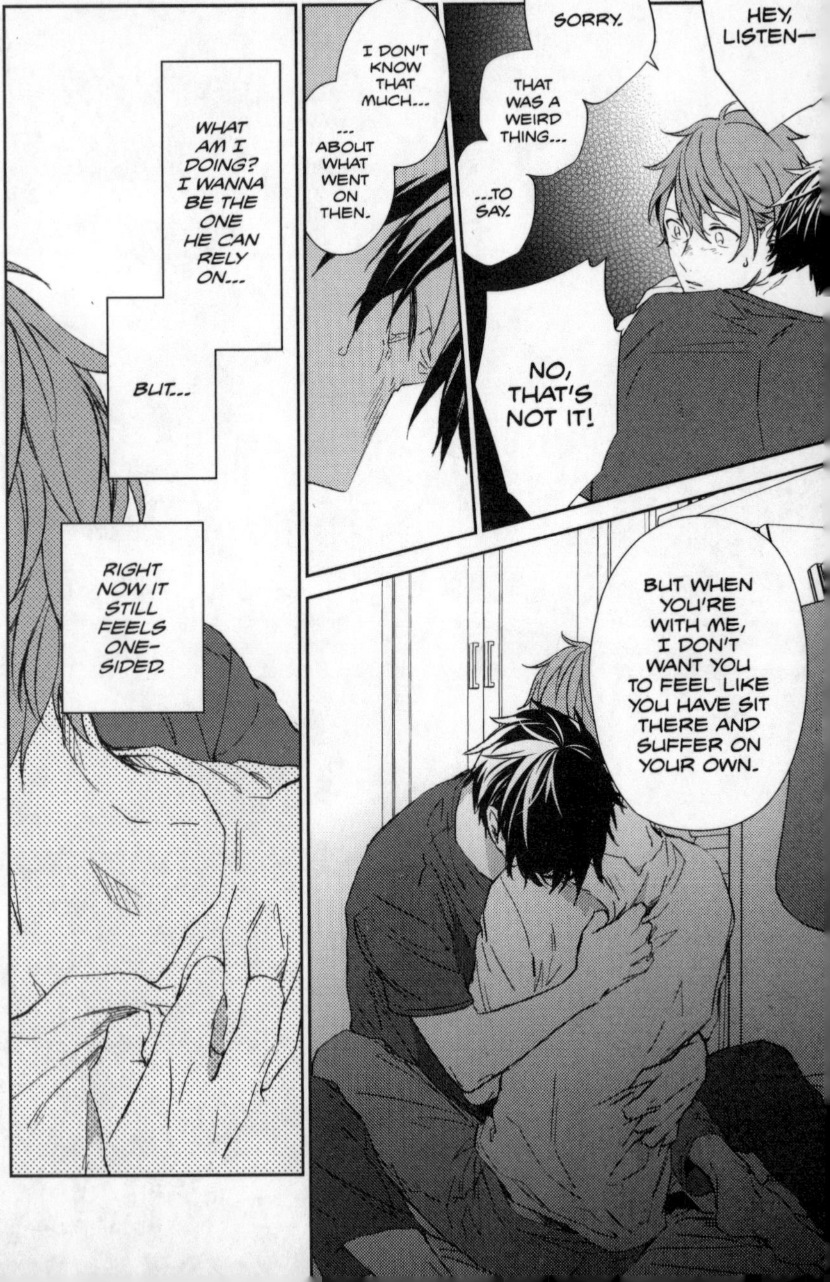
HEY, LISTEN—
SORRY.
THAT WAS A WEIRD THING...
...TO SAY.
NO, THAT'S NOT IT!
I DON'T KNOW THAT MUCH...
...ABOUT WHAT WENT ON THEN.
BUT WHEN YOU'RE WITH ME, I DON'T WANT YOU TO FEEL LIKE YOU HAVE SIT THERE AND SUFFER ON YOUR OWN.
WHAT AM I DOING? I WANNA BE THE ONE HE CAN RELY ON...
BUT...
RIGHT NOW IT STILL FEELS ONE-SIDED.

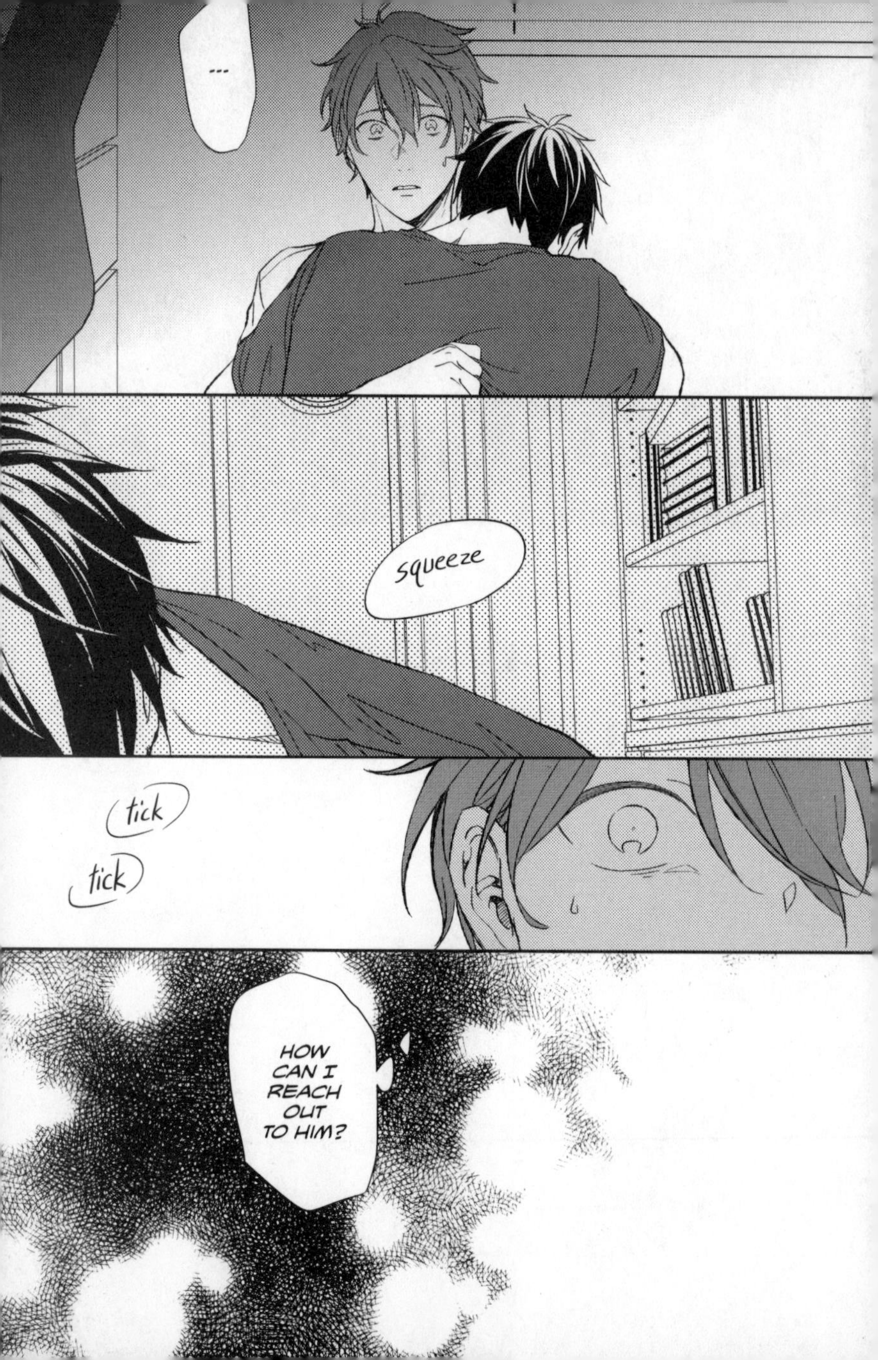
...
squeeze
tick
tick
HOW CAN I REACH OUT TO HIM?

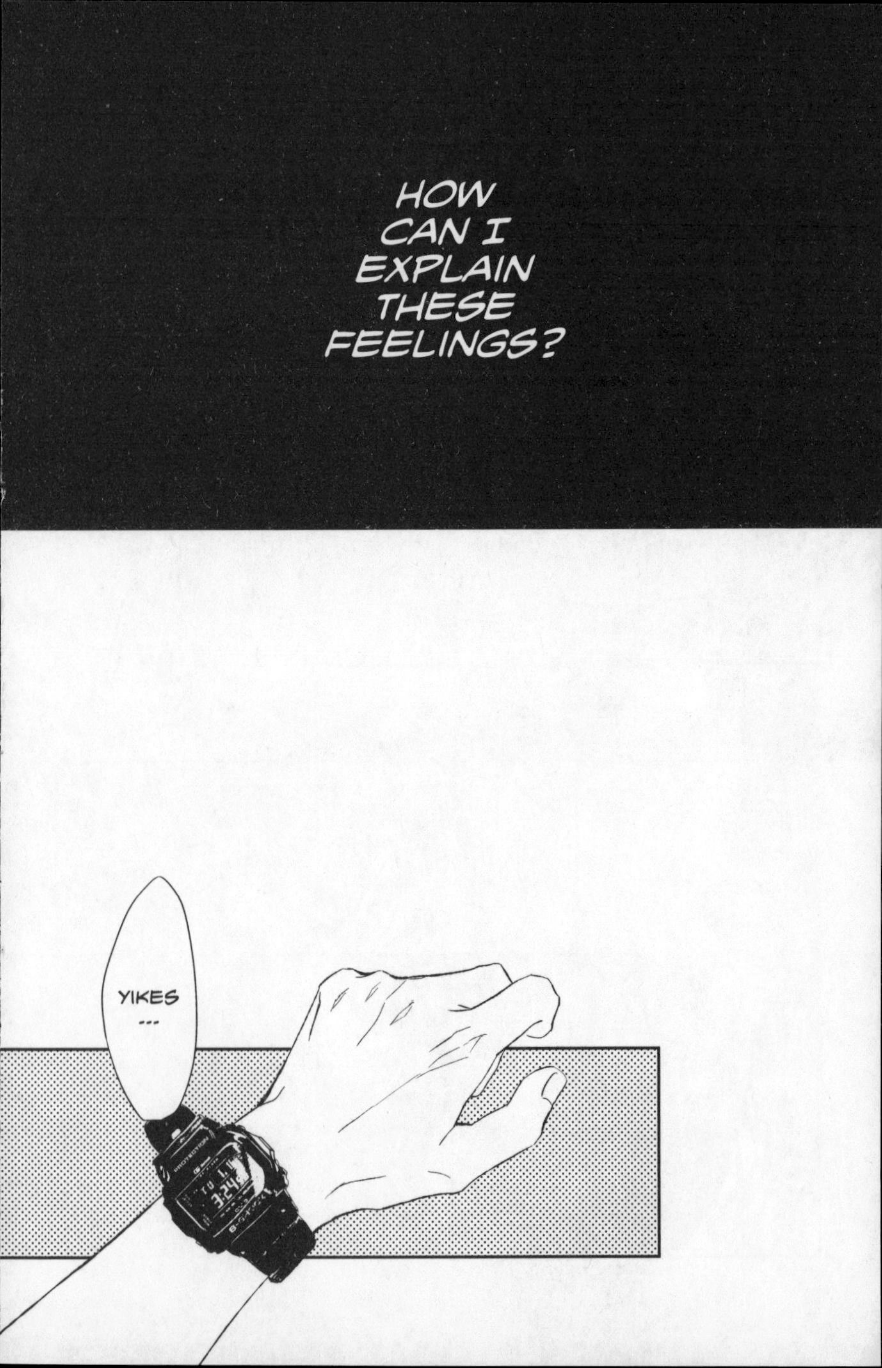
HOW CAN I EXPLAIN THESE FEELINGS?
YIKES ...

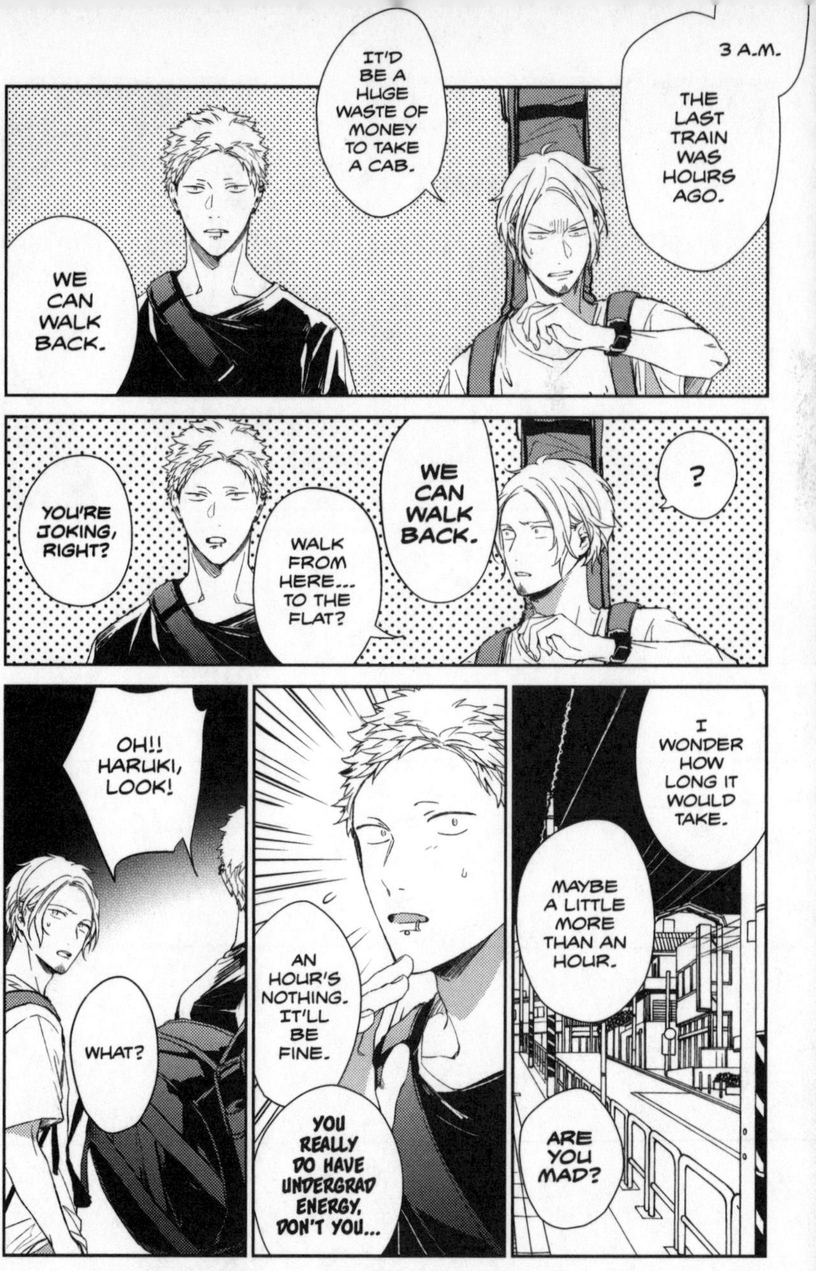
3 A.M.
THE LAST TRAIN WAS HOURS AGO.
IT'D BE A HUGE WASTE OF MONEY TO TAKE A CAB.
WE CAN WALK BACK.
?
WE CAN WALK BACK.
WALK FROM HERE... TO THE FLAT?
YOU'RE JOKING, RIGHT?
I WONDER HOW LONG IT WOULD TAKE.
MAYBE A LITTLE MORE THAN AN HOUR.
ARE YOU MAD?
AN HOUR'S NOTHING. IT'LL BE FINE.
YOU REALLY DO HAVE UNDERGRAD ENERGY, DON'T YOU...
OH!! HARUKI, LOOK!
WHAT?

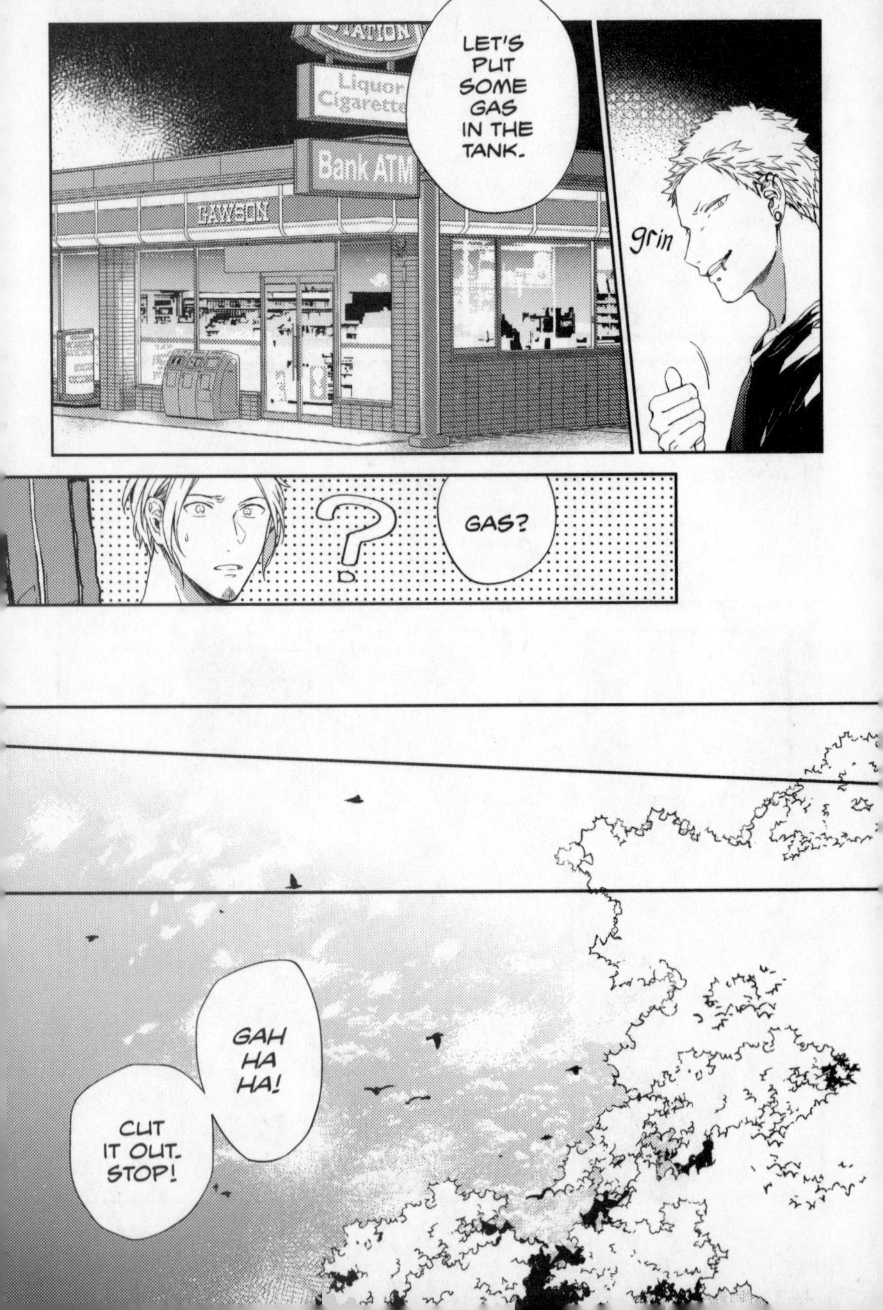
grin
LET'S PUT SOME GAS IN THE TANK.
STATION
Liquor Cigarette
Bank ATM
LAWSON
GAS?
GAH HA HA!
CUT IT OUT. STOP!

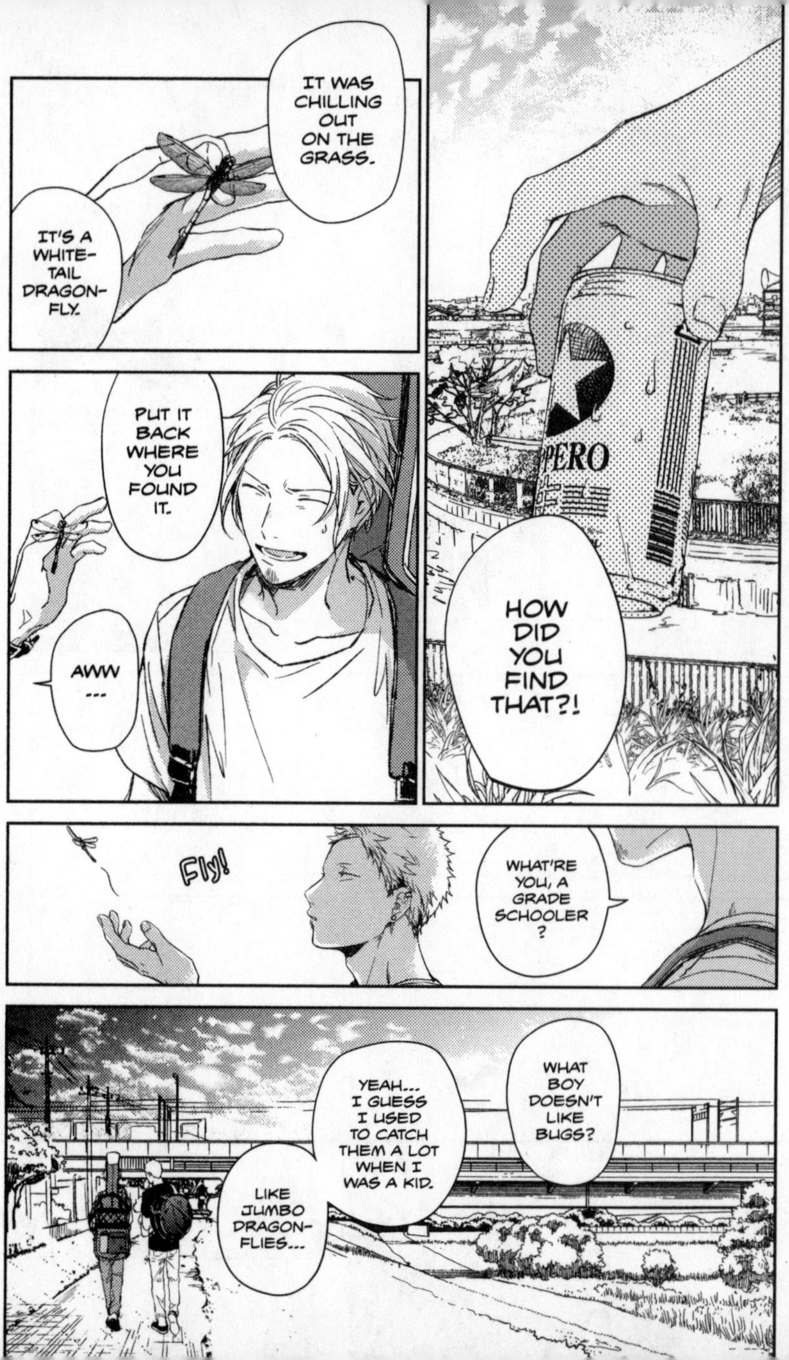
PERO
HOW DID YOU FIND THAT?!
IT WAS CHILLING OUT ON THE GRASS.
IT'S A WHITE-TAIL DRAGON-FLY.
PUT IT BACK WHERE YOU FOUND IT.
AWW...
WHAT'RE YOU, A GRADE SCHOOLER?
Fly!
WHAT BOY DOESN'T LIKE BUGS?
YEAH... I GUESS I USED TO CATCH THEM A LOT WHEN I WAS A KID.
LIKE JUMBO DRAGON-FLIES...

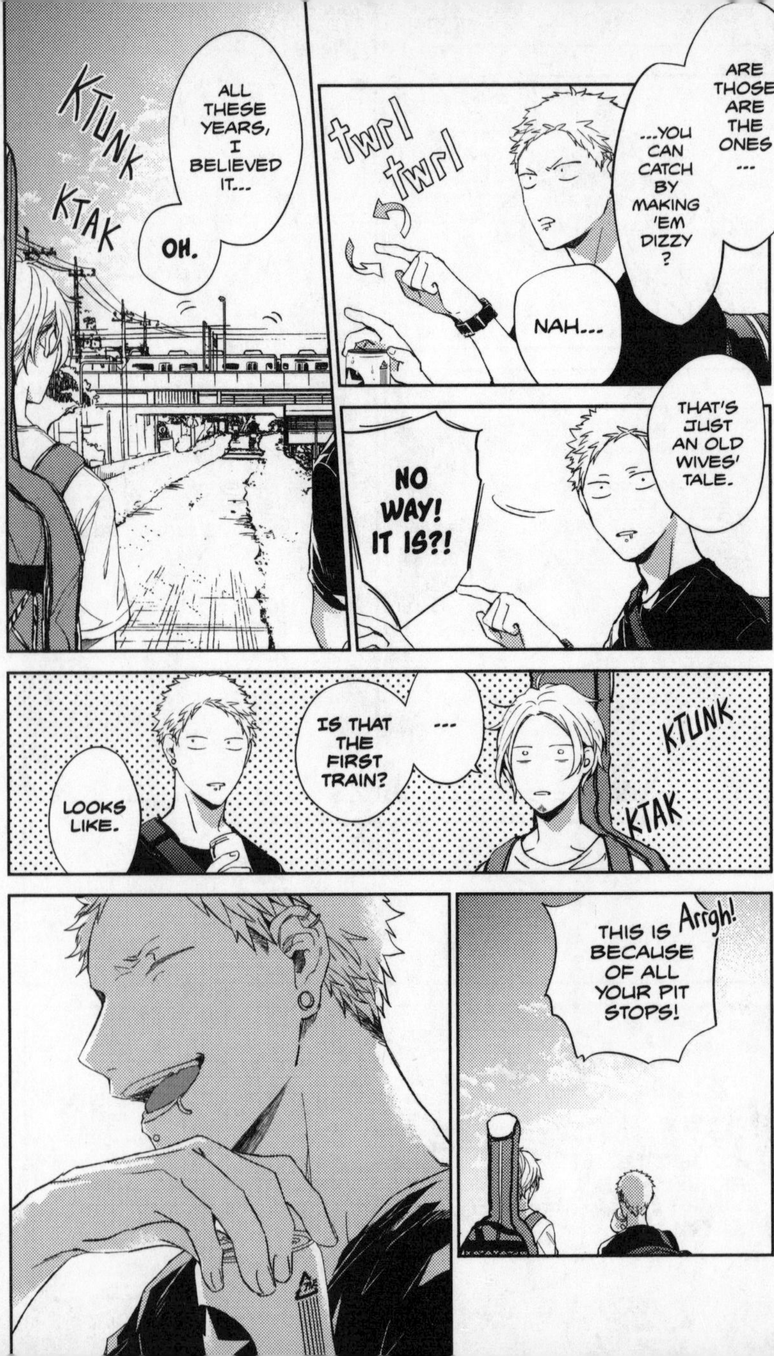
ARE THOSE ARE THE ONES ---
...YOU CAN CATCH BY MAKING 'EM DIZZY?
twrl twrl
NAH...
THAT'S JUST AN OLD WIVES' TALE.
NO WAY! IT IS?!
ALL THESE YEARS, I BELIEVED IT...
OH.
KTUNK
KTAK
KTUNK
KTAK
IS THAT THE FIRST TRAIN? ---
LOOKS LIKE.
Arrgh!
THIS IS BECAUSE OF ALL YOUR PIT STOPS!

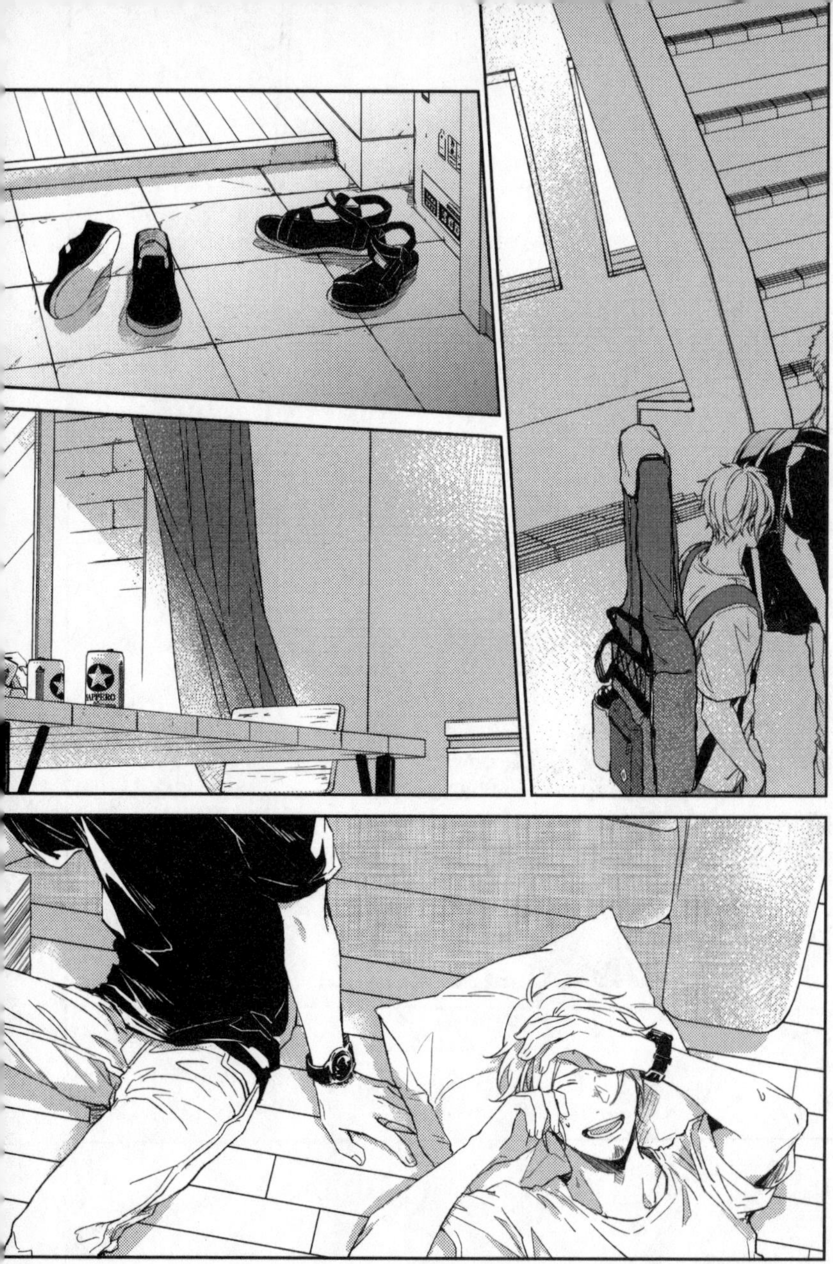

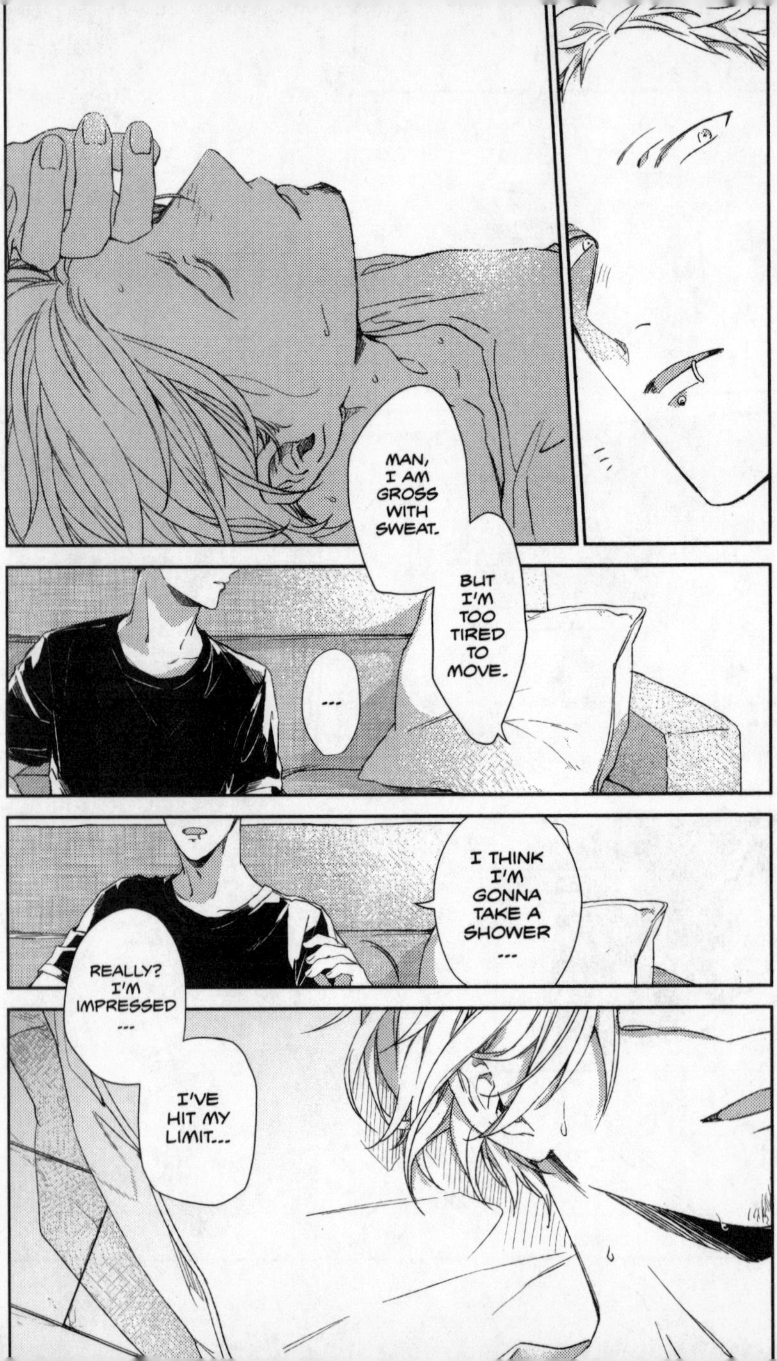
MAN, I AM GROSS WITH SWEAT.
BUT I'M TOO TIRED TO MOVE.
...
I THINK I'M GONNA TAKE A SHOWER...
REALLY? I'M IMPRESSED...
I'VE HIT MY LIMIT...

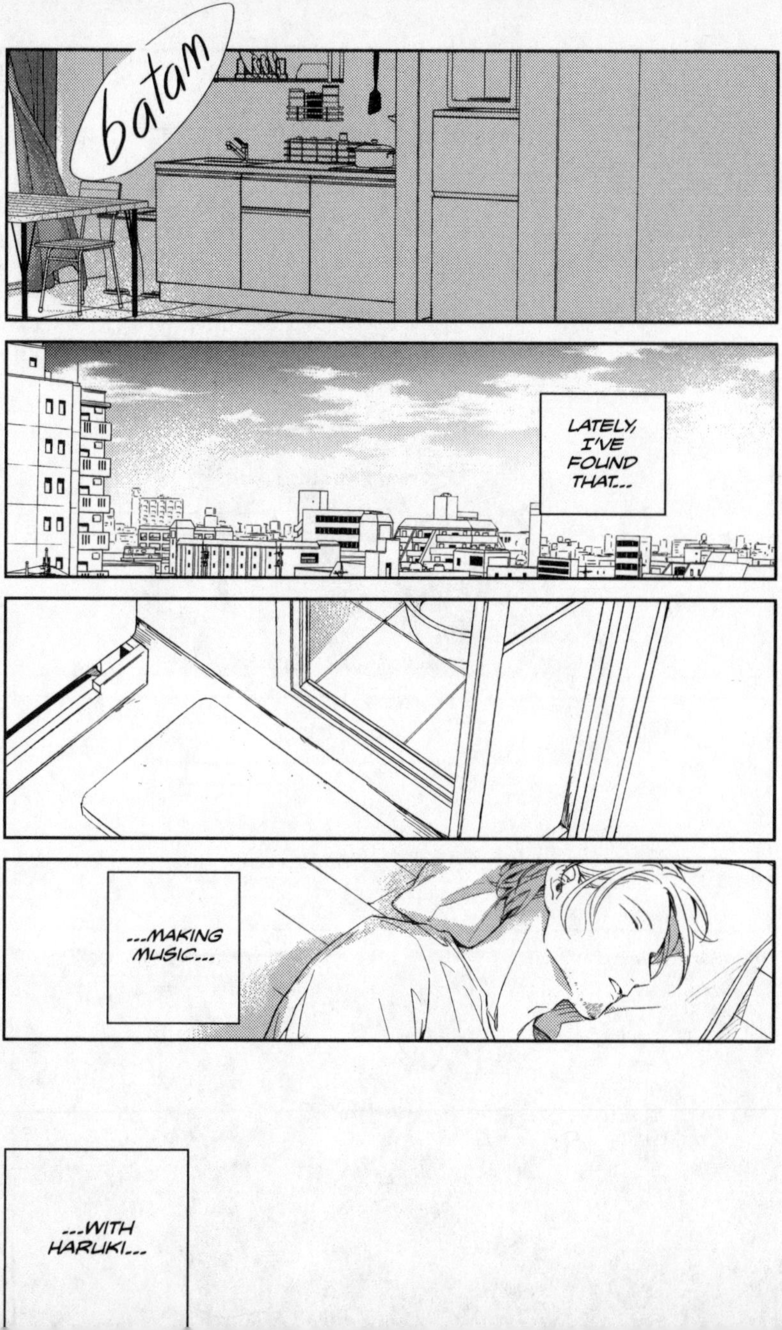
batam
LATELY, I'VE FOUND THAT...
...MAKING MUSIC...
...WITH HARUKI...

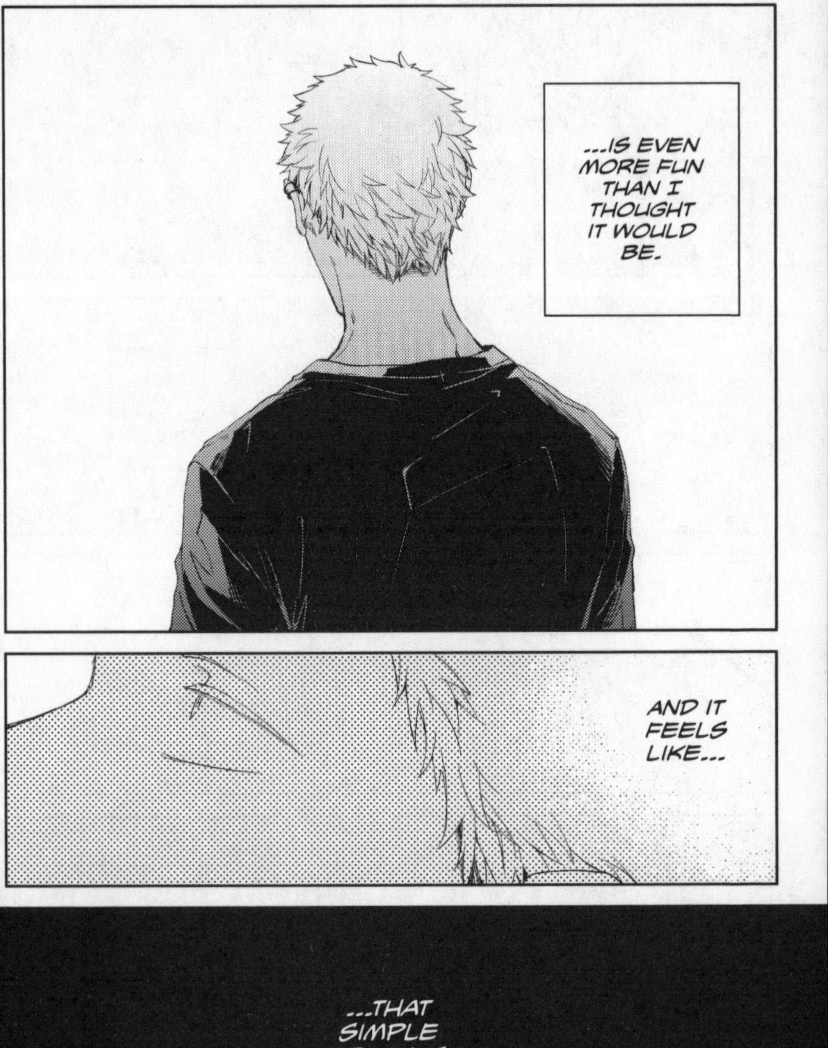
...IS EVEN MORE FUN THAN I THOUGHT IT WOULD BE.
AND IT FEELS LIKE...
...THAT SIMPLE

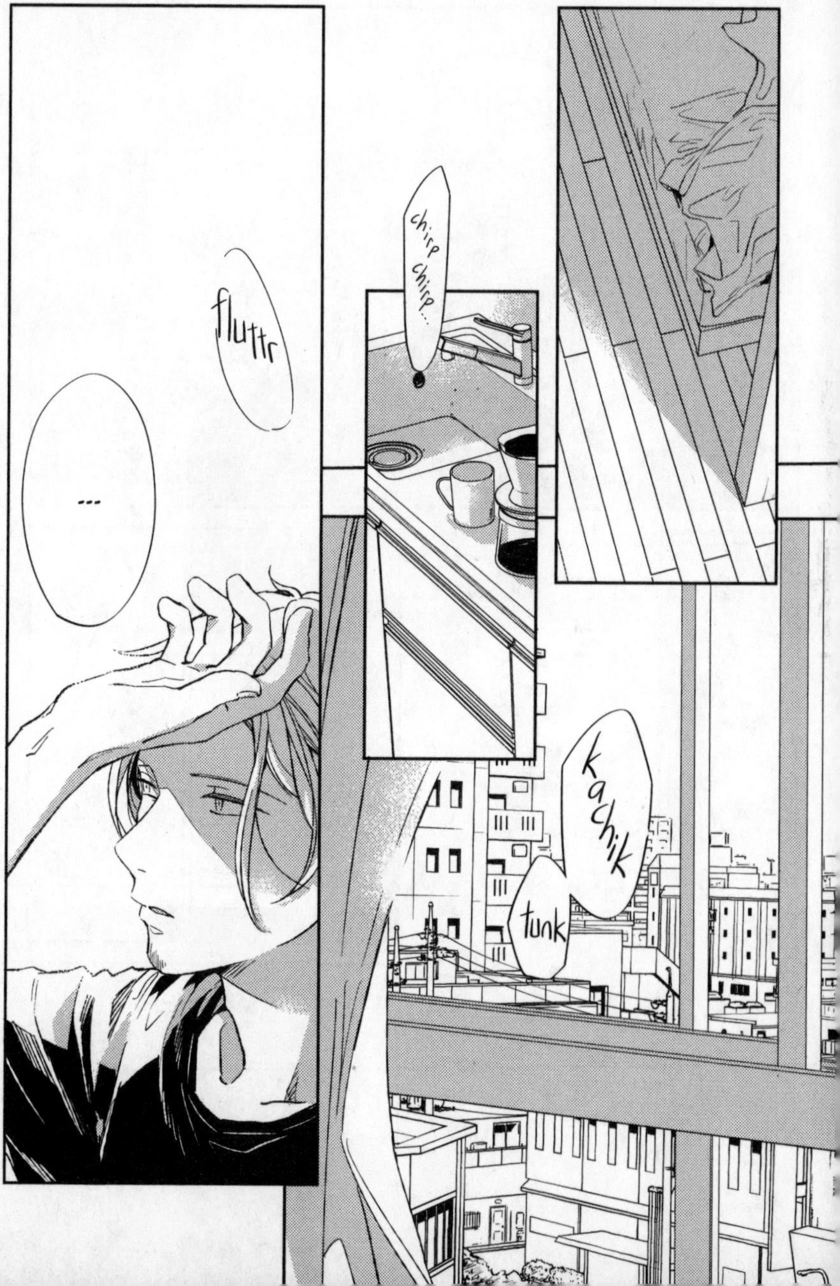
chirp chirp...
kachik
tunk
fluttr
...

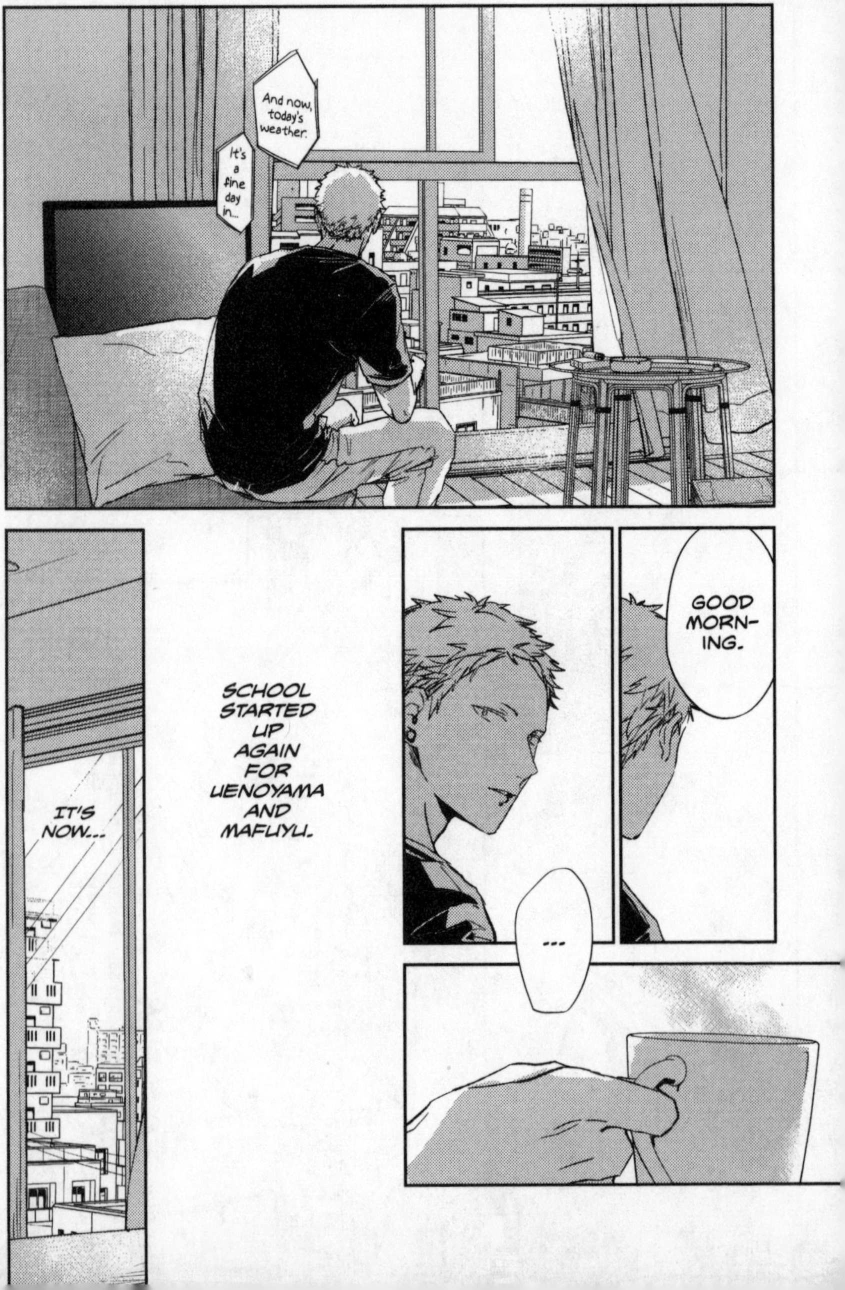
And now, today's weather.
It's a fine day in...
GOOD MORNING.
...
SCHOOL STARTED UP AGAIN FOR UENOYAMA AND MAFUYU.
IT'S NOW...

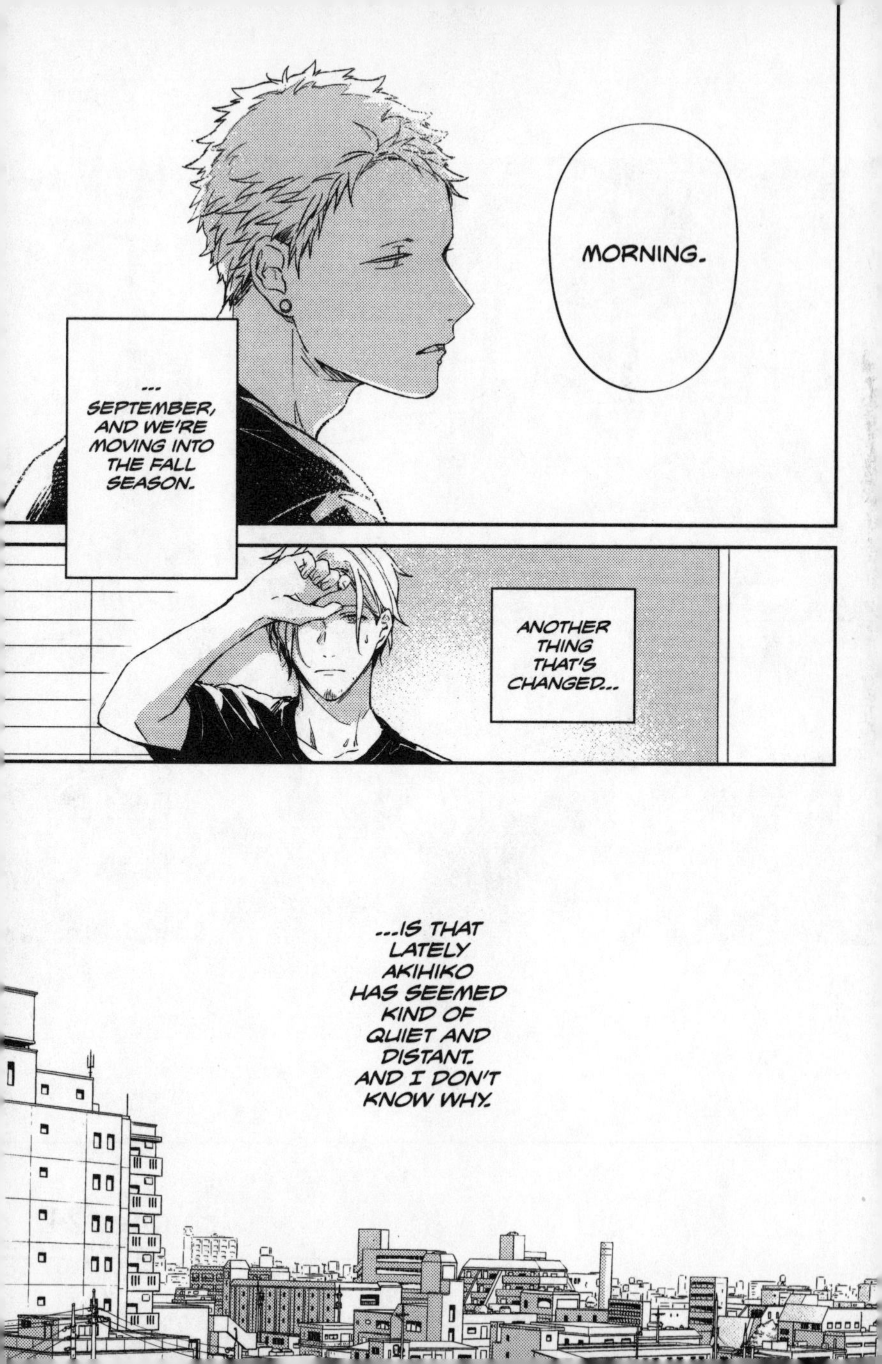
MORNING.
... SEPTEMBER, AND WE'RE MOVING INTO THE FALL SEASON.
ANOTHER THING THAT'S CHANGED...
...IS THAT LATELY AKIHIKO HAS SEEMED KIND OF QUIET AND DISTANT. AND I DON'T KNOW WHY.

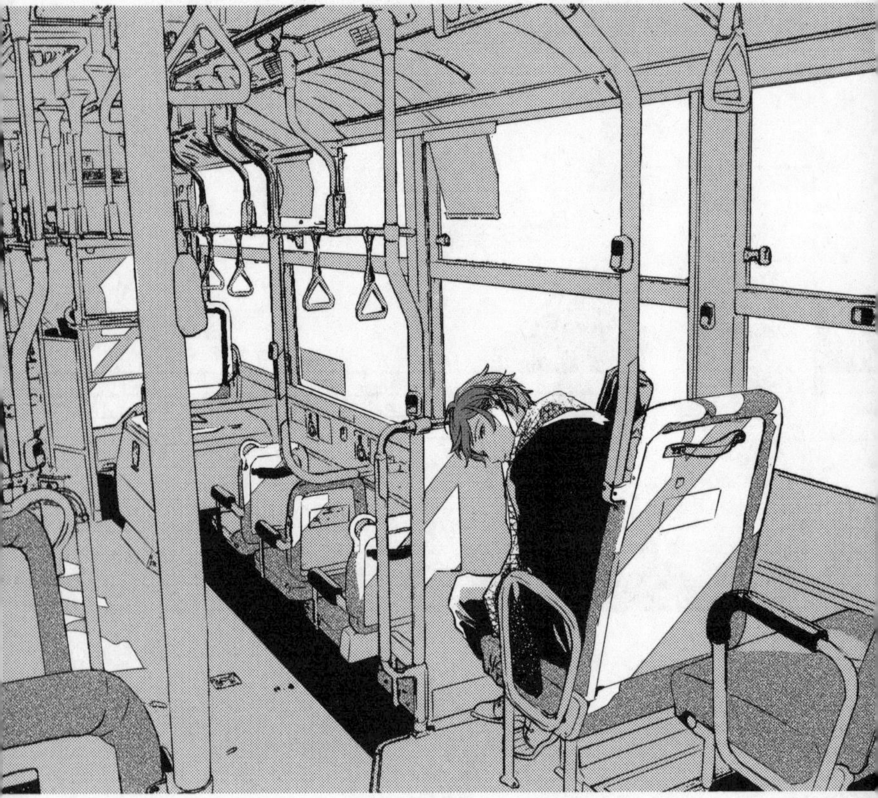

chapter 24

given

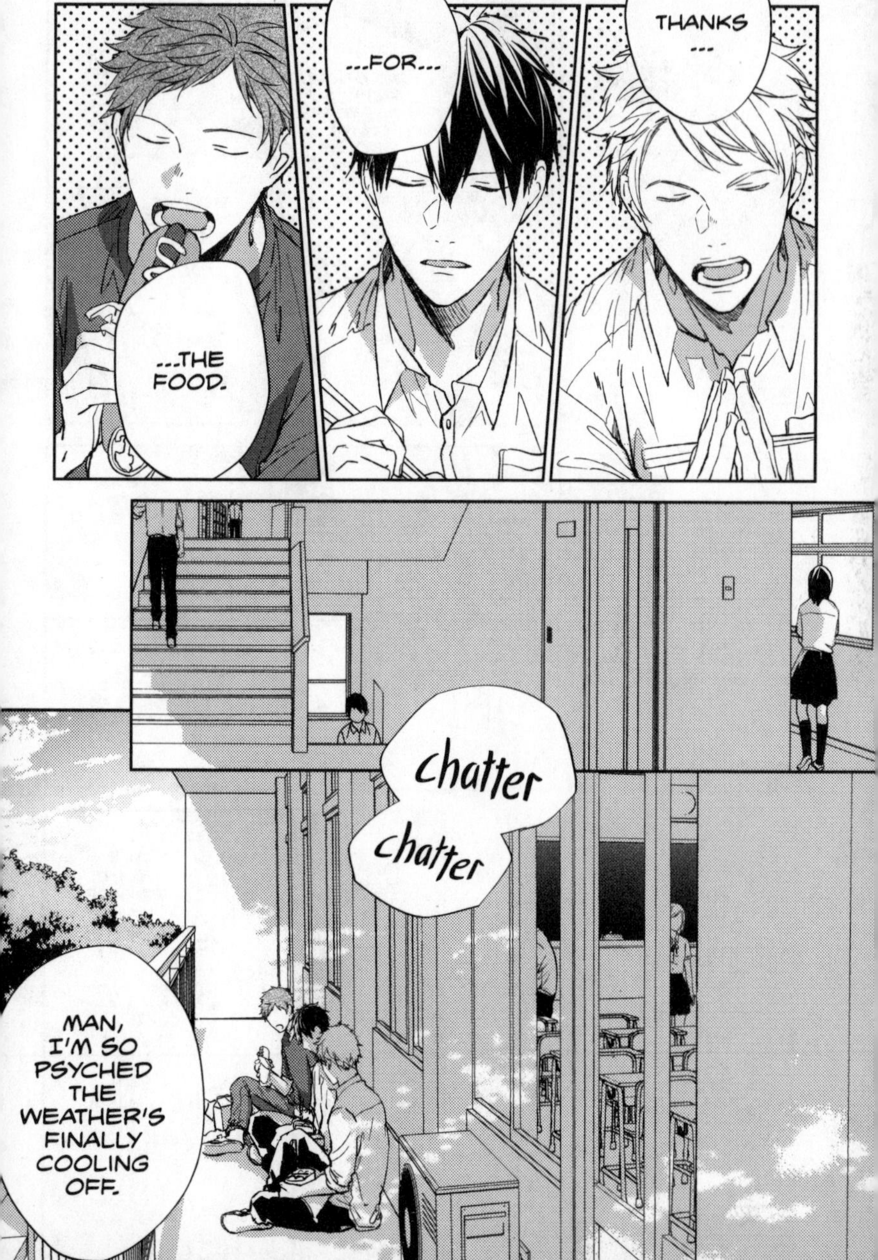
THANKS ---
...FOR...
...THE FOOD.
chatter
chatter
MAN, I'M SO PSYCHED THE WEATHER'S FINALLY COOLING OFF.

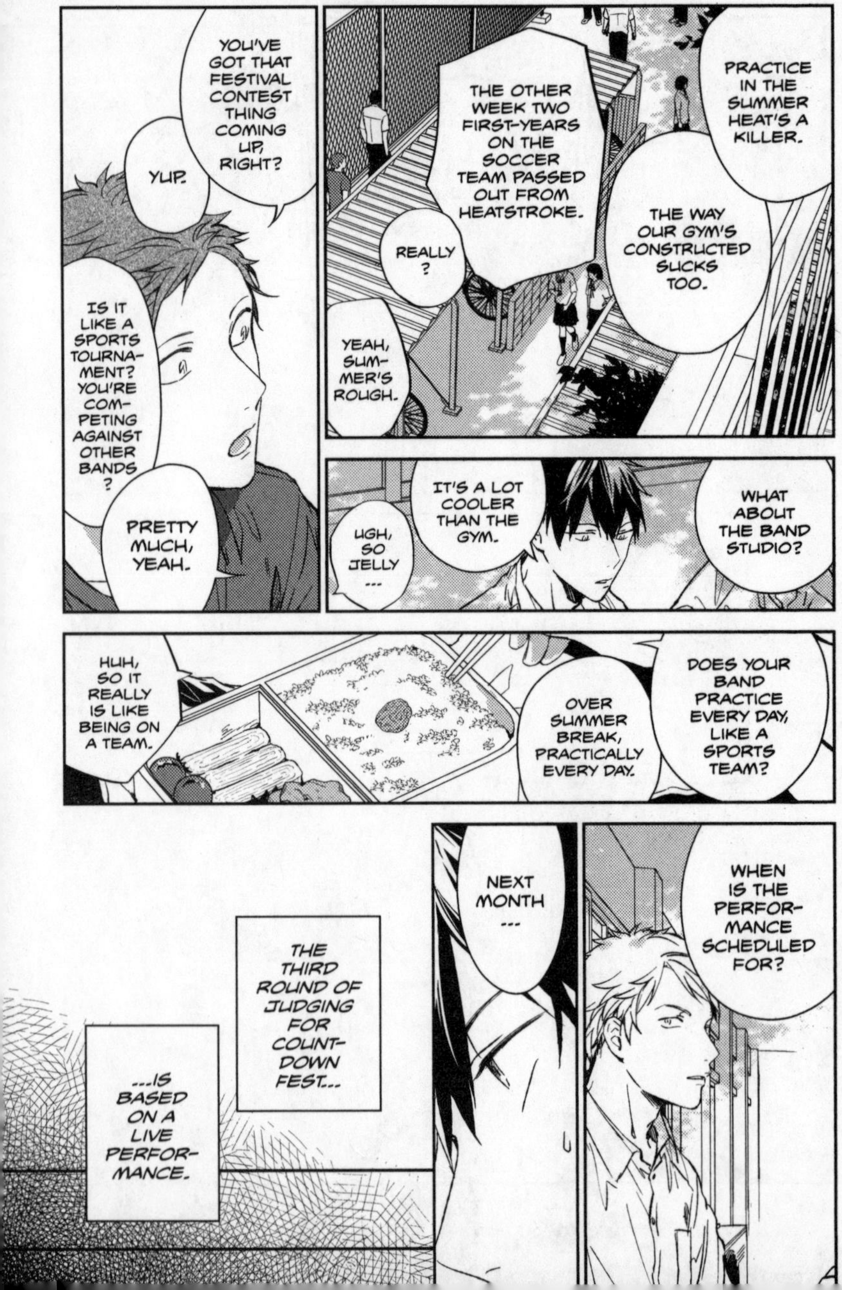
PRACTICE IN THE SUMMER HEAT'S A KILLER.
THE WAY OUR GYM'S CONSTRUCTED SUCKS TOO.
THE OTHER WEEK TWO FIRST-YEARS ON THE SOCCER TEAM PASSED OUT FROM HEATSTROKE.
REALLY?
YEAH, SUMMER'S ROUGH.
WHAT ABOUT THE BAND STUDIO?
IT'S A LOT COOLER THAN THE GYM.
UGH, SO JELLY...
YOU'VE GOT THAT FESTIVAL CONTEST THING COMING UP, RIGHT?
YUP.
IS IT LIKE A SPORTS TOURNAMENT? YOU'RE COMPETING AGAINST OTHER BANDS?
PRETTY MUCH, YEAH.
DOES YOUR BAND PRACTICE EVERY DAY, LIKE A SPORTS TEAM?
OVER SUMMER BREAK, PRACTICALLY EVERY DAY.
HUH, SO IT REALLY IS LIKE BEING ON A TEAM.
WHEN IS THE PERFORMANCE SCHEDULED FOR?
NEXT MONTH...
THE THIRD ROUND OF JUDGING FOR COUNTDOWN FEST...
...IS BASED ON A LIVE PERFORMANCE.

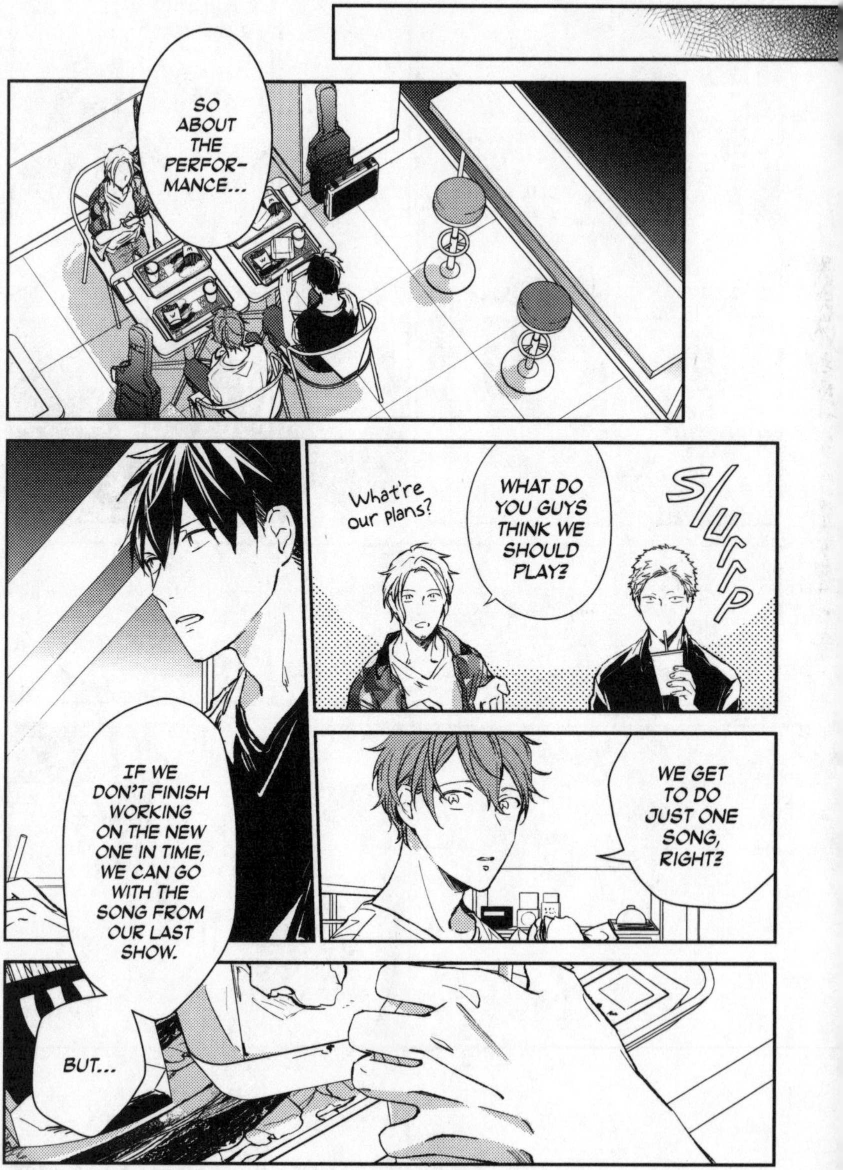
SO ABOUT THE PERFORMANCE...
SLURRP
WHAT DO YOU GUYS THINK WE SHOULD PLAY?
What're our plans?
WE GET TO DO JUST ONE SONG, RIGHT?
IF WE DON'T FINISH WORKING ON THE NEW ONE IN TIME, WE CAN GO WITH THE SONG FROM OUR LAST SHOW.
BUT...

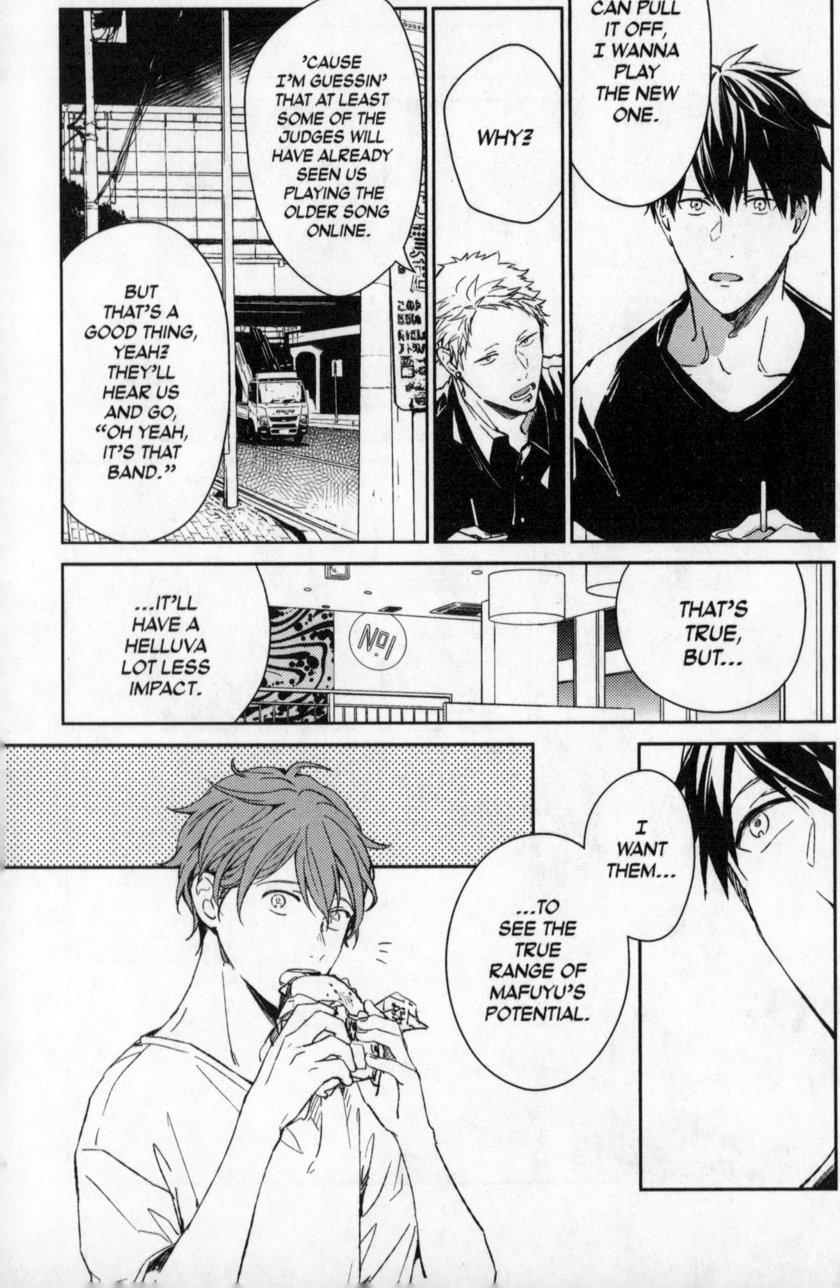
...IF WE CAN PULL IT OFF, I WANNA PLAY THE NEW ONE.
WHY?
'CAUSE I'M GUESSIN' THAT AT LEAST SOME OF THE JUDGES WILL HAVE ALREADY SEEN US PLAYING THE OLDER SONG ONLINE.
BUT THAT'S A GOOD THING, YEAH? THEY'LL HEAR US AND GO, "OH YEAH, IT'S THAT BAND."
THAT'S TRUE, BUT...
...IT'LL HAVE A HELLUVA LOT LESS IMPACT.
I WANT THEM...
...TO SEE THE TRUE RANGE OF MAFUYU'S POTENTIAL.

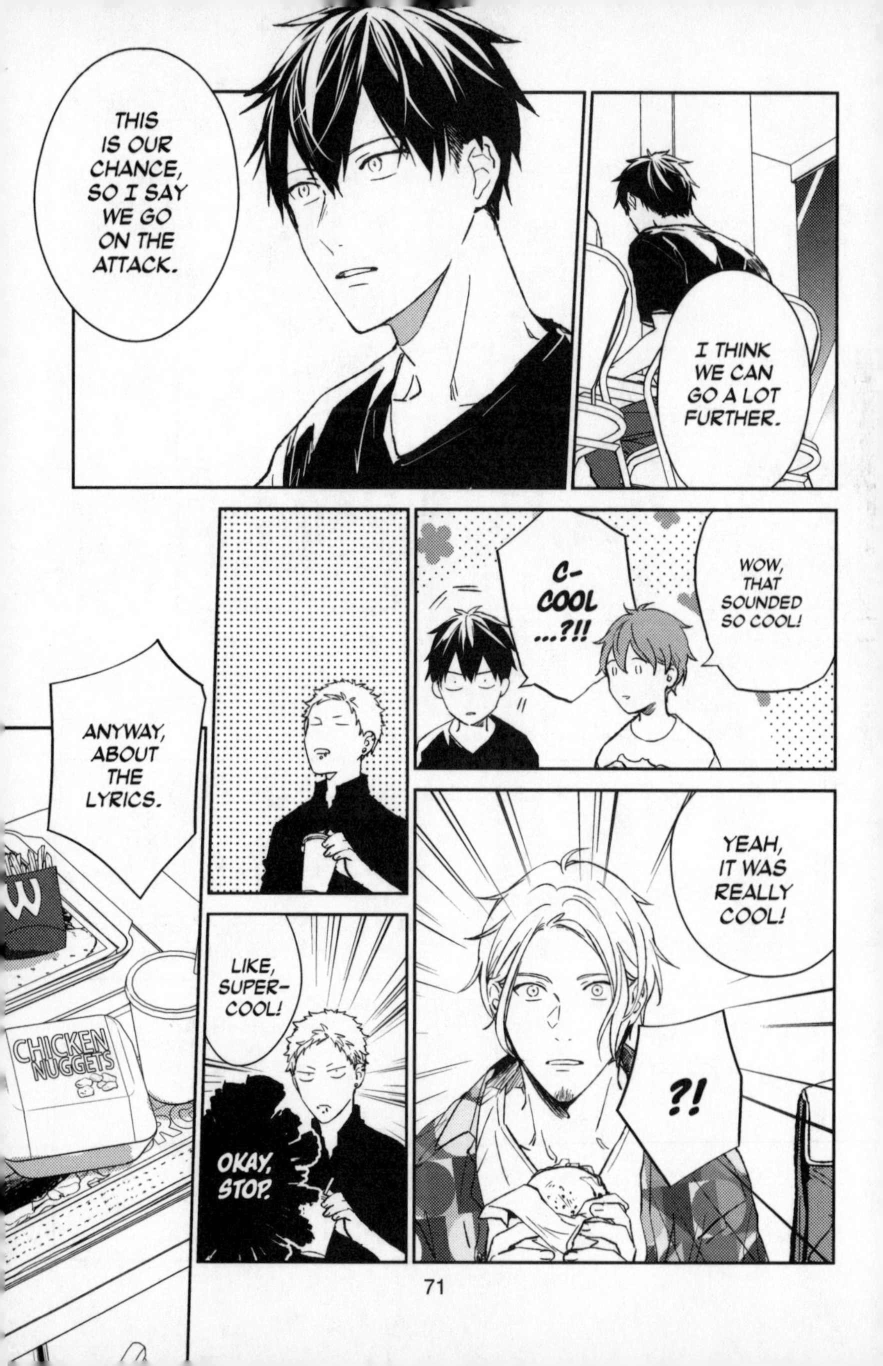
I THINK WE CAN GO A LOT FURTHER.
THIS IS OUR CHANCE, SO I SAY WE GO ON THE ATTACK.
WOW, THAT SOUNDED SO COOL!
C-COOL ...?!!
ANYWAY, ABOUT THE LYRICS.
YEAH, IT WAS REALLY COOL!
?!
LIKE, SUPER-COOL!
OKAY, STOP.
CHICKEN NUGGETS

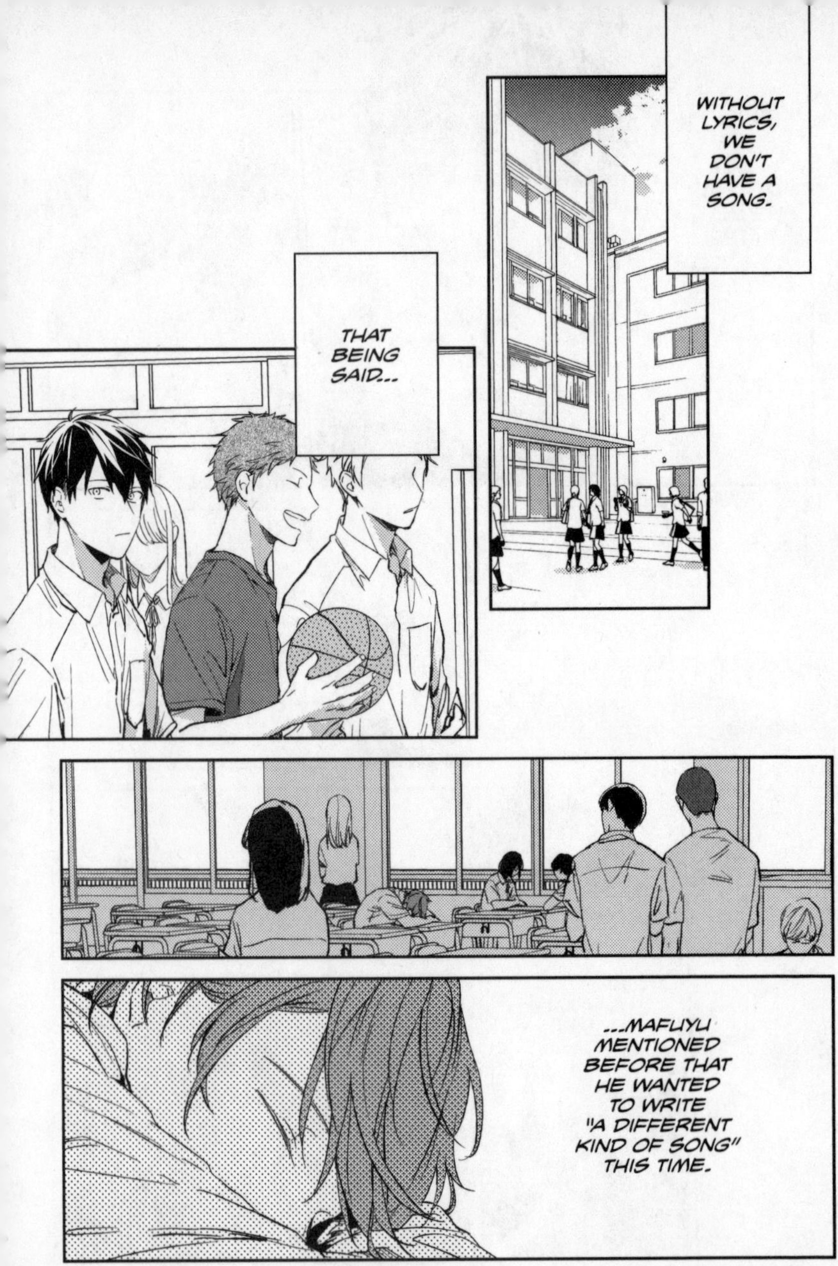
WITHOUT LYRICS, WE DON'T HAVE A SONG.
THAT BEING SAID...
...MAFUYU MENTIONED BEFORE THAT HE WANTED TO WRITE "A DIFFERENT KIND OF SONG" THIS TIME.

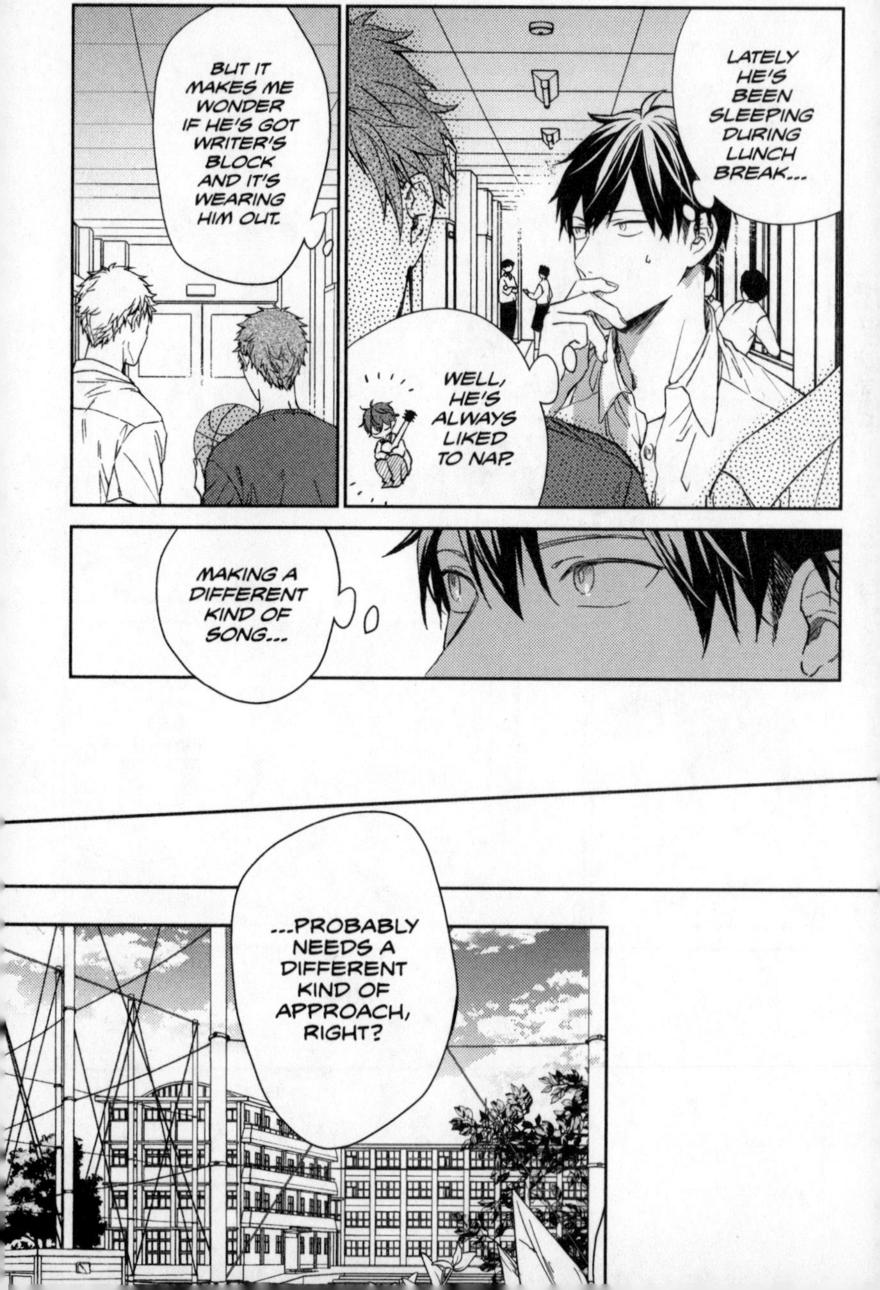
LATELY HE'S BEEN SLEEPING DURING LUNCH BREAK...
WELL, HE'S ALWAYS LIKED TO NAP.
BUT IT MAKES ME WONDER IF HE'S GOT WRITER'S BLOCK AND IT'S WEARING HIM OUT.
MAKING A DIFFERENT KIND OF SONG...
...PROBABLY NEEDS A DIFFERENT KIND OF APPROACH, RIGHT?

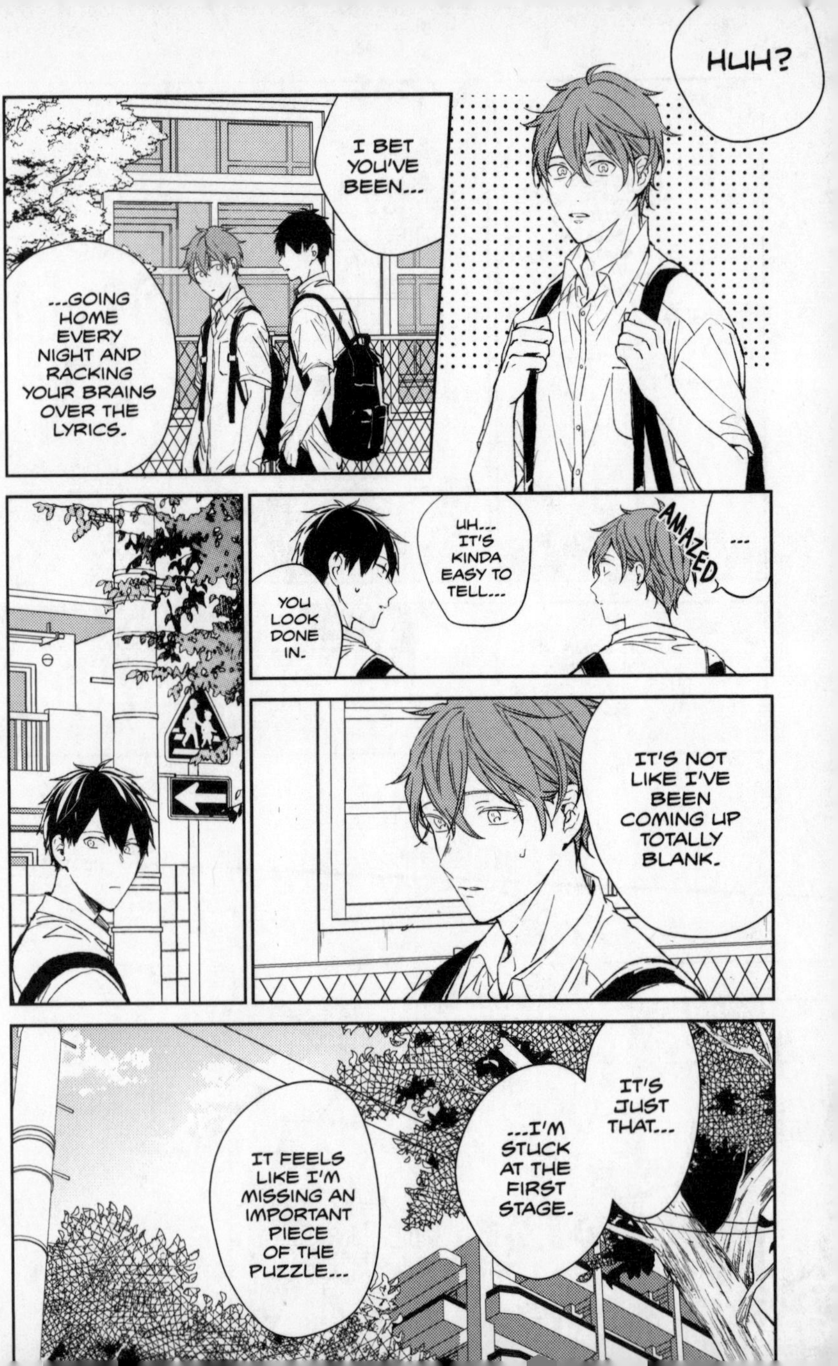
HUH?
I BET YOU'VE BEEN...
...GOING HOME EVERY NIGHT AND RACKING YOUR BRAINS OVER THE LYRICS.
AMAZED
...
UH... IT'S KINDA EASY TO TELL...
YOU LOOK DONE IN.
IT'S NOT LIKE I'VE BEEN COMING UP TOTALLY BLANK.
IT'S JUST THAT...
...I'M STUCK AT THE FIRST STAGE.
IT FEELS LIKE I'M MISSING AN IMPORTANT PIECE OF THE PUZZLE...

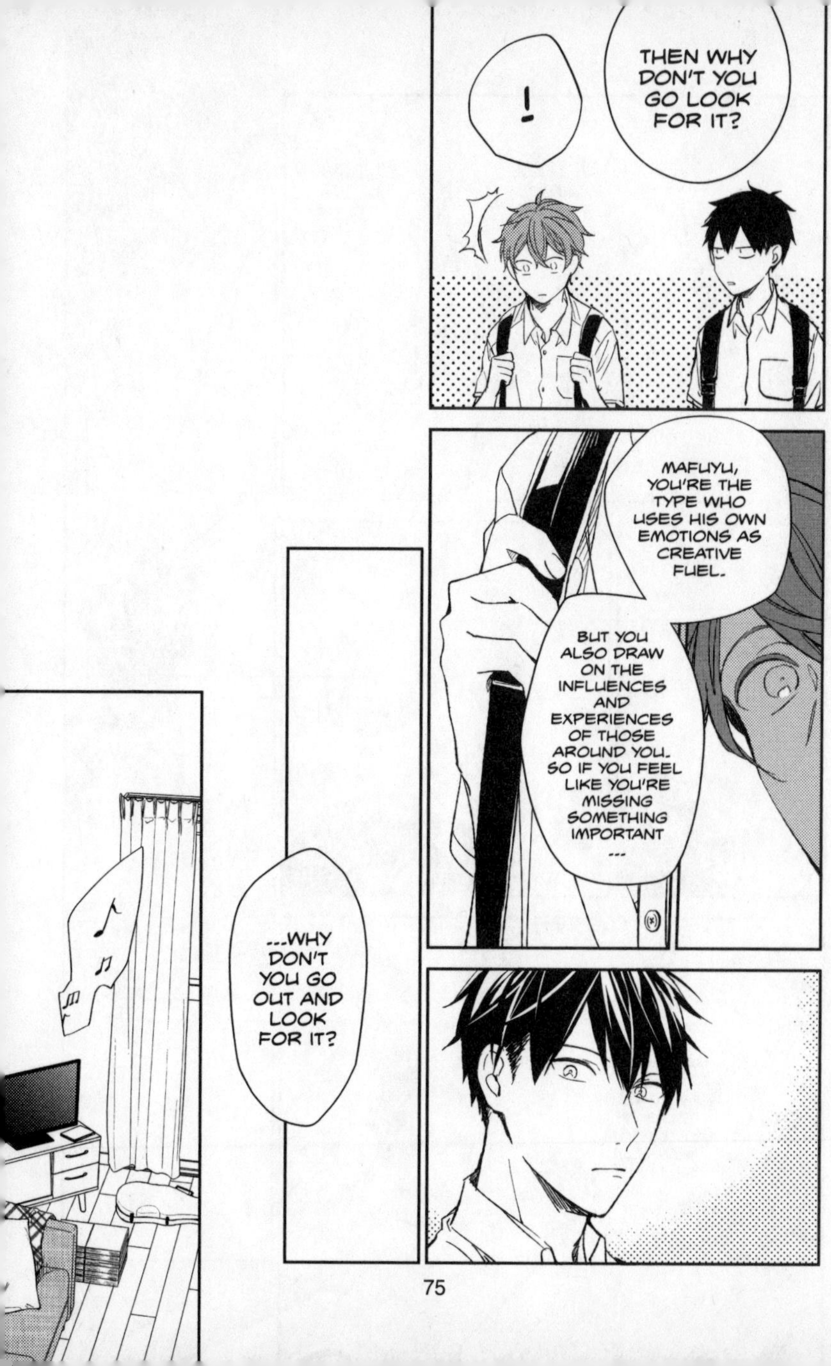
THEN WHY DON'T YOU GO LOOK FOR IT?
!
MAFUYU, YOU'RE THE TYPE WHO USES HIS OWN EMOTIONS AS CREATIVE FUEL.
BUT YOU ALSO DRAW ON THE INFLUENCES AND EXPERIENCES OF THOSE AROUND YOU. SO IF YOU FEEL LIKE YOU'RE MISSING SOMETHING IMPORTANT ...
...WHY DON'T YOU GO OUT AND LOOK FOR IT?

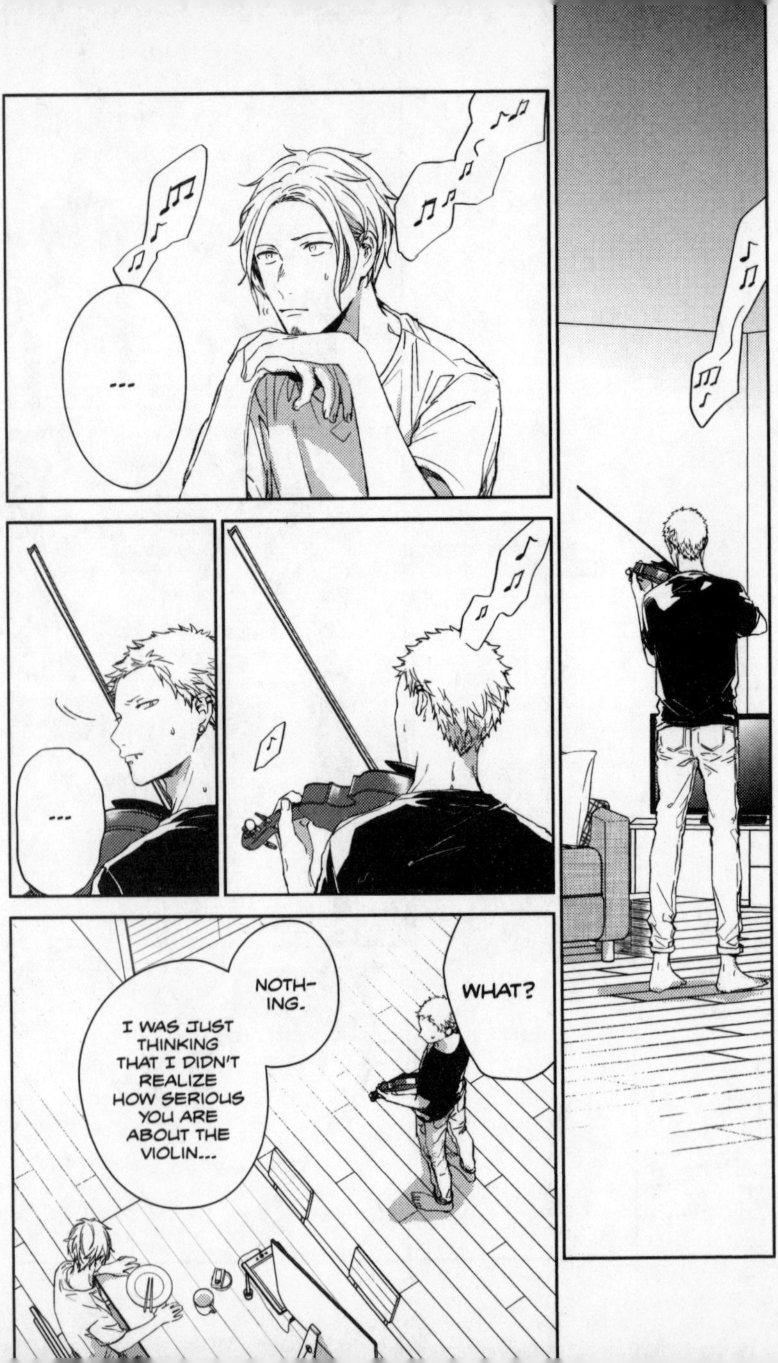
...
...
WHAT?
NOTH-ING.
I WAS JUST THINKING THAT I DIDN'T REALIZE HOW SERIOUS YOU ARE ABOUT THE VIOLIN...

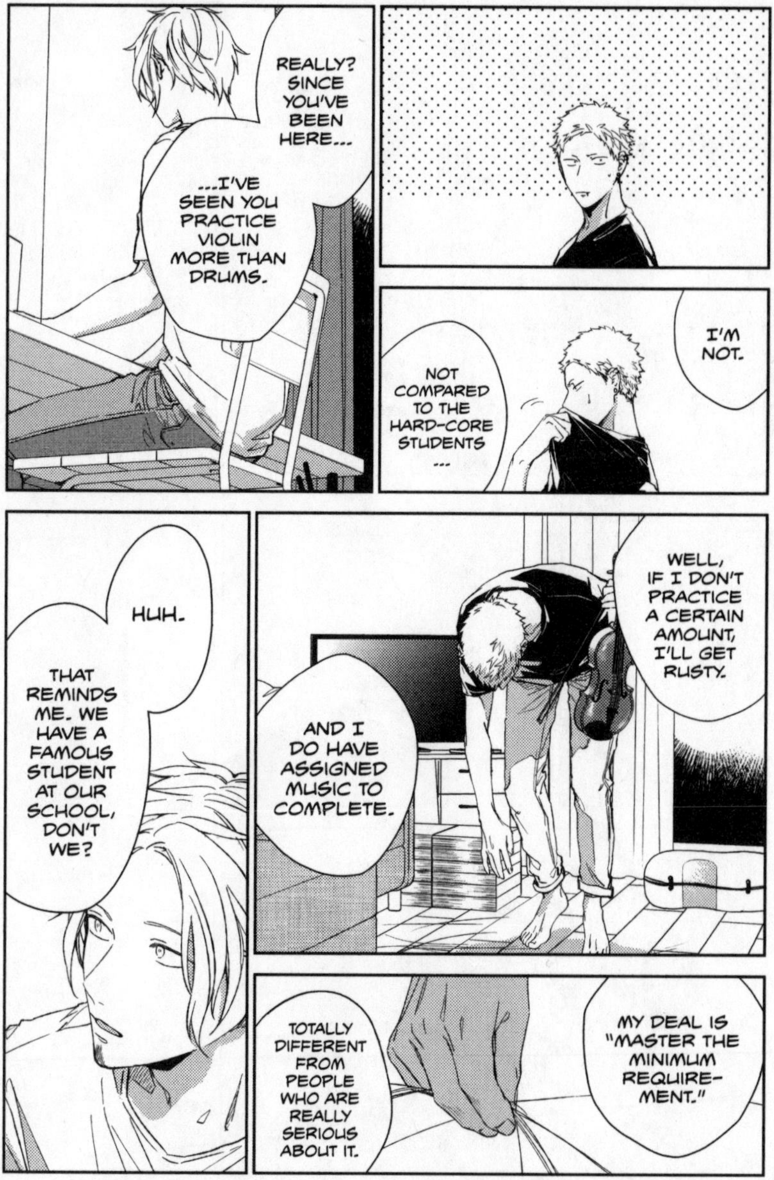
I'M NOT.
NOT COMPARED TO THE HARD-CORE STUDENTS...
REALLY? SINCE YOU'VE BEEN HERE...
...I'VE SEEN YOU PRACTICE VIOLIN MORE THAN DRUMS.
WELL, IF I DON'T PRACTICE A CERTAIN AMOUNT, I'LL GET RUSTY.
AND I DO HAVE ASSIGNED MUSIC TO COMPLETE.
MY DEAL IS "MASTER THE MINIMUM REQUIRE-MENT."
TOTALLY DIFFERENT FROM PEOPLE WHO ARE REALLY SERIOUS ABOUT IT.
HUH.
THAT REMINDS ME. WE HAVE A FAMOUS STUDENT AT OUR SCHOOL, DON'T WE?

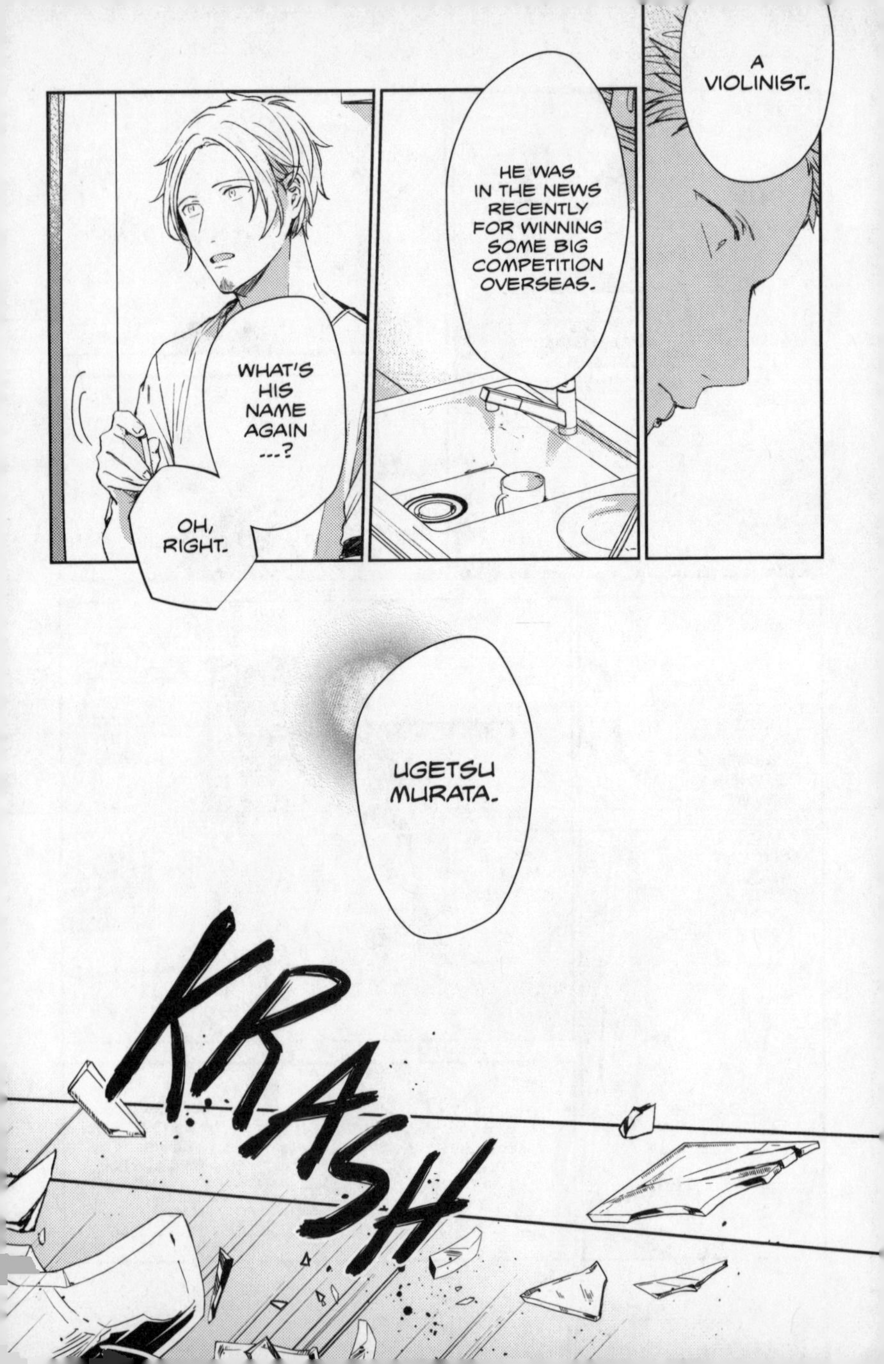
A VIOLINIST.
HE WAS IN THE NEWS RECENTLY FOR WINNING SOME BIG COMPETITION OVERSEAS.
WHAT'S HIS NAME AGAIN...?
OH, RIGHT.
UGETSU MURATA.
KRASH

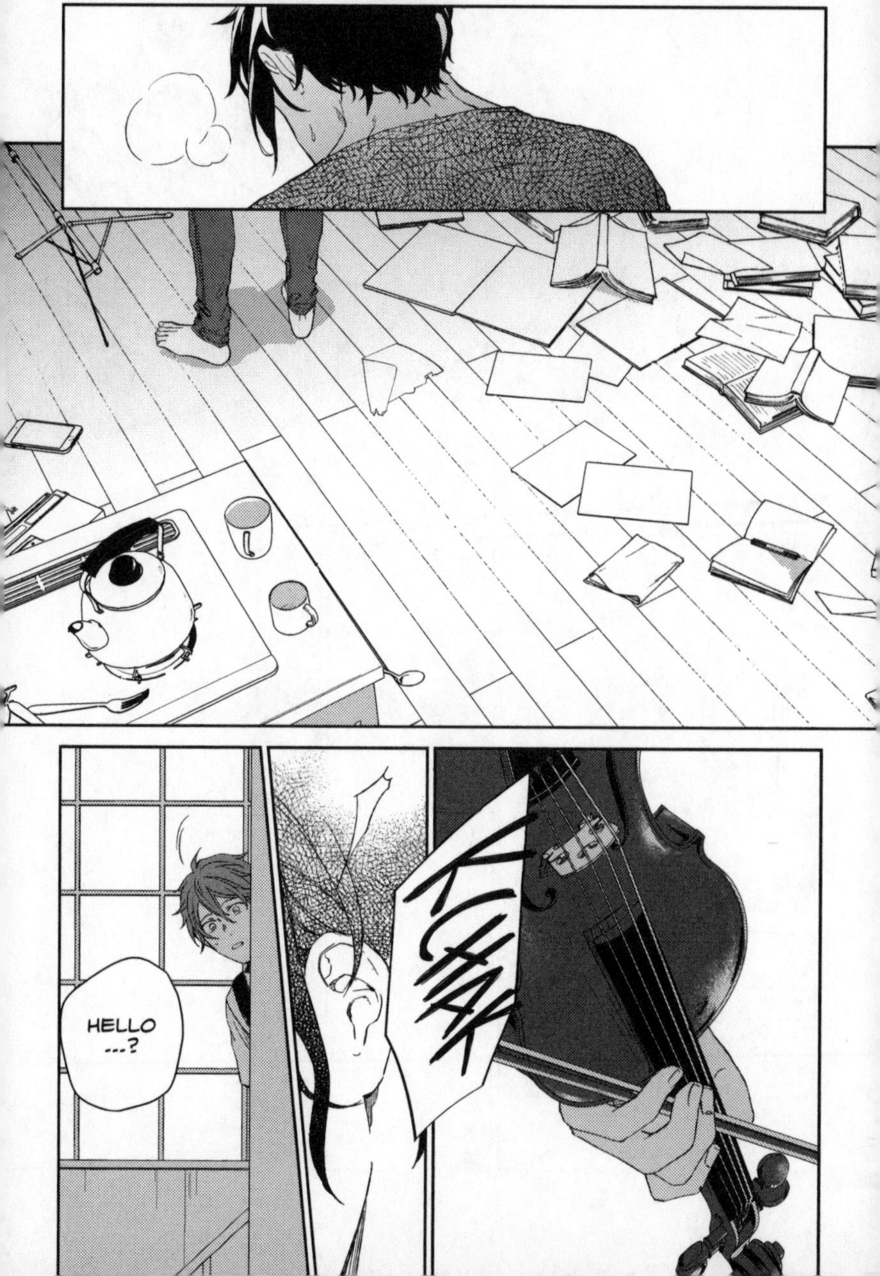
KCHAK
HELLO ...?

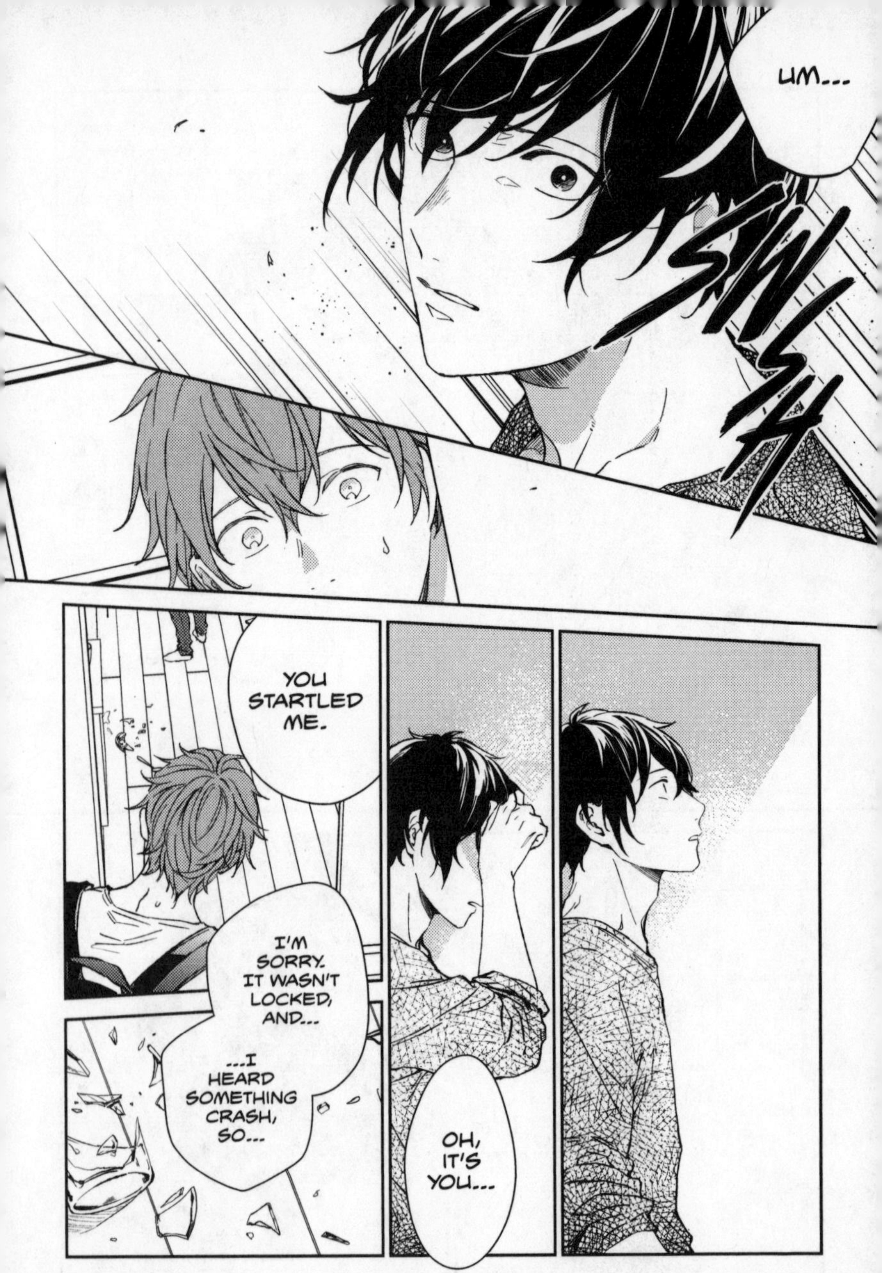
UM...
SWISH
OH, IT'S YOU...
YOU STARTLED ME.
I'M SORRY. IT WASN'T LOCKED, AND...
...I HEARD SOMETHING CRASH, SO...

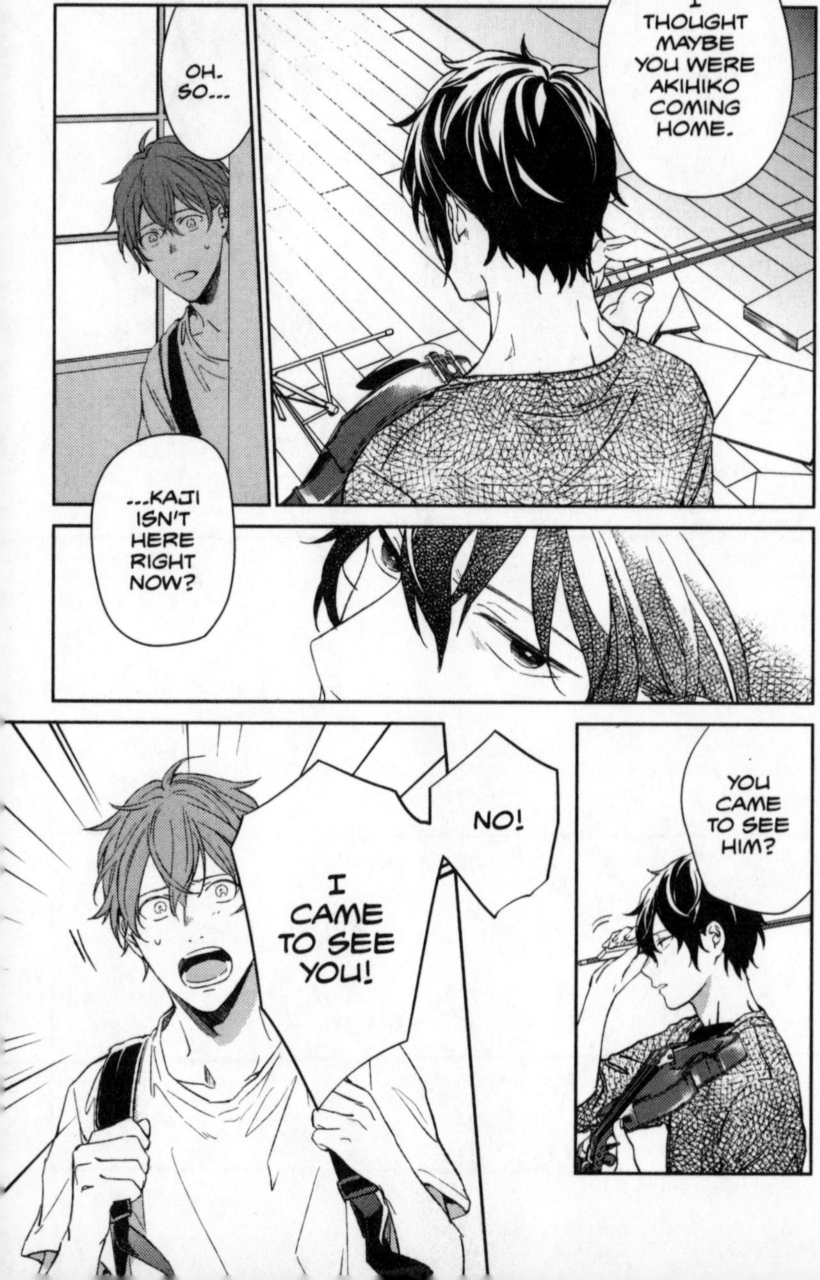
I THOUGHT MAYBE YOU WERE AKIHIKO COMING HOME.
OH. SO...
...KAJI ISN'T HERE RIGHT NOW?
YOU CAME TO SEE HIM?
NO!
I CAME TO SEE YOU!

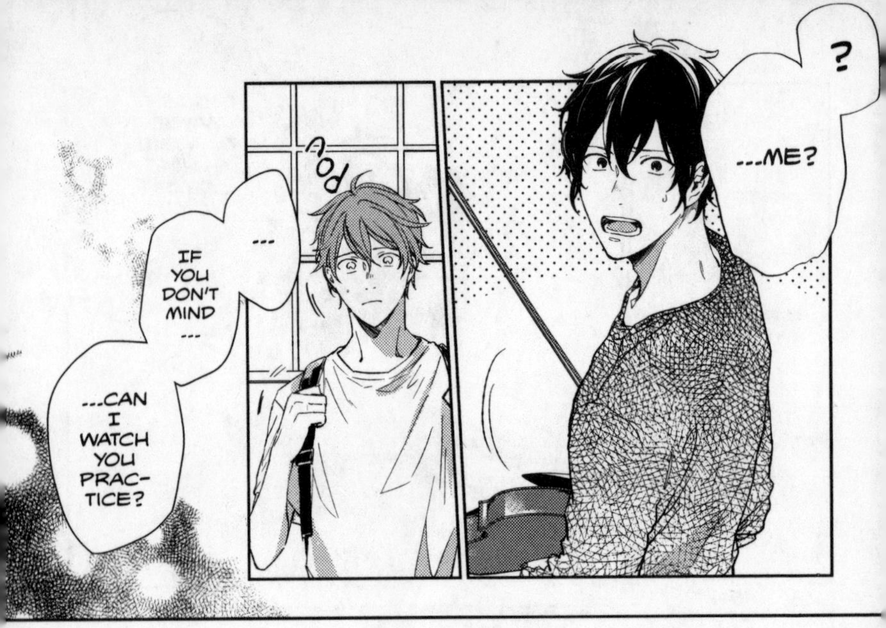
?
...ME?
...
IF YOU DON'T MIND ...
...CAN I WATCH YOU PRACTICE?

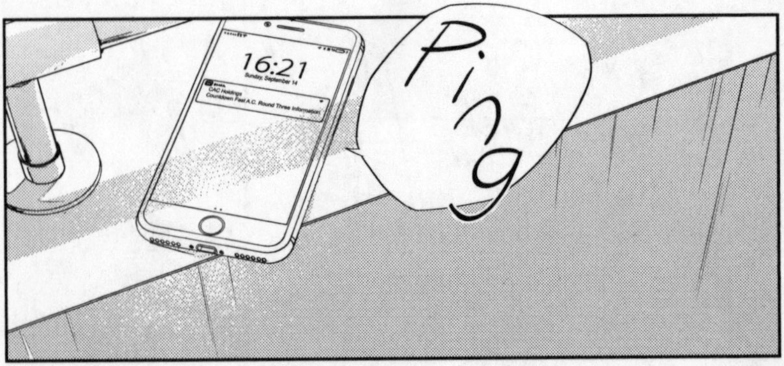
16:21
Sunday, September 14
CAC Holdings
Countdown Fest A.C. Round Three Information
Ping

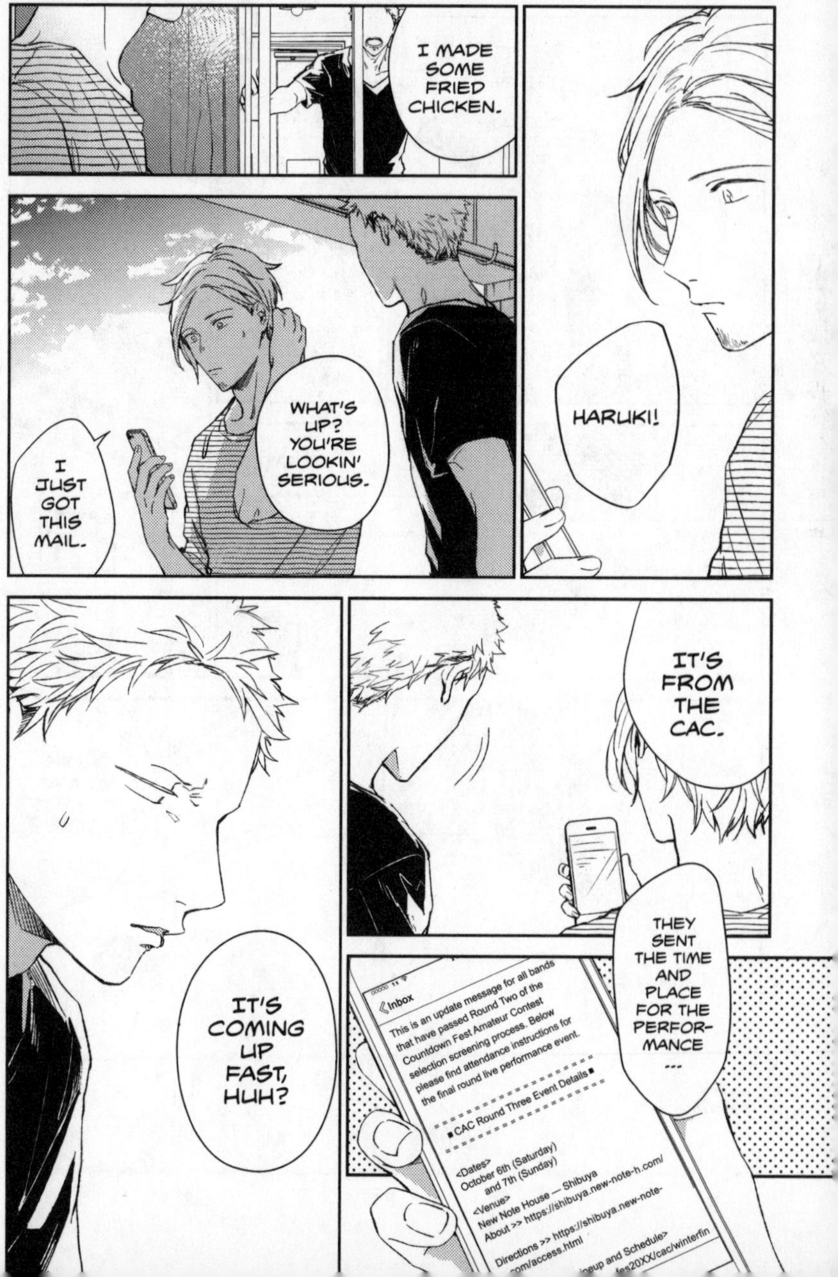
HARUKI!
I MADE SOME FRIED CHICKEN.
WHAT'S UP? YOU'RE LOOKIN' SERIOUS.
I JUST GOT THIS MAIL.
IT'S FROM THE CAC.
THEY SENT THE TIME AND PLACE FOR THE PERFORMANCE ...
Inbox
This is an update message for all bands that have passed Round Two of the Countdown Fest Amateur Contest selection screening process. Below please find attendance instructions for the final round live performance event.
■CAC Round Three Event Details■
<Dates>
October 6th (Saturday) and 7th (Sunday)
<Venue>
New Note House — Shibuya
About >> https://shibuya.new-note-h.com/
Directions >> https://shibuya.new-note-
com/access.html
IT'S COMING UP FAST, HUH?

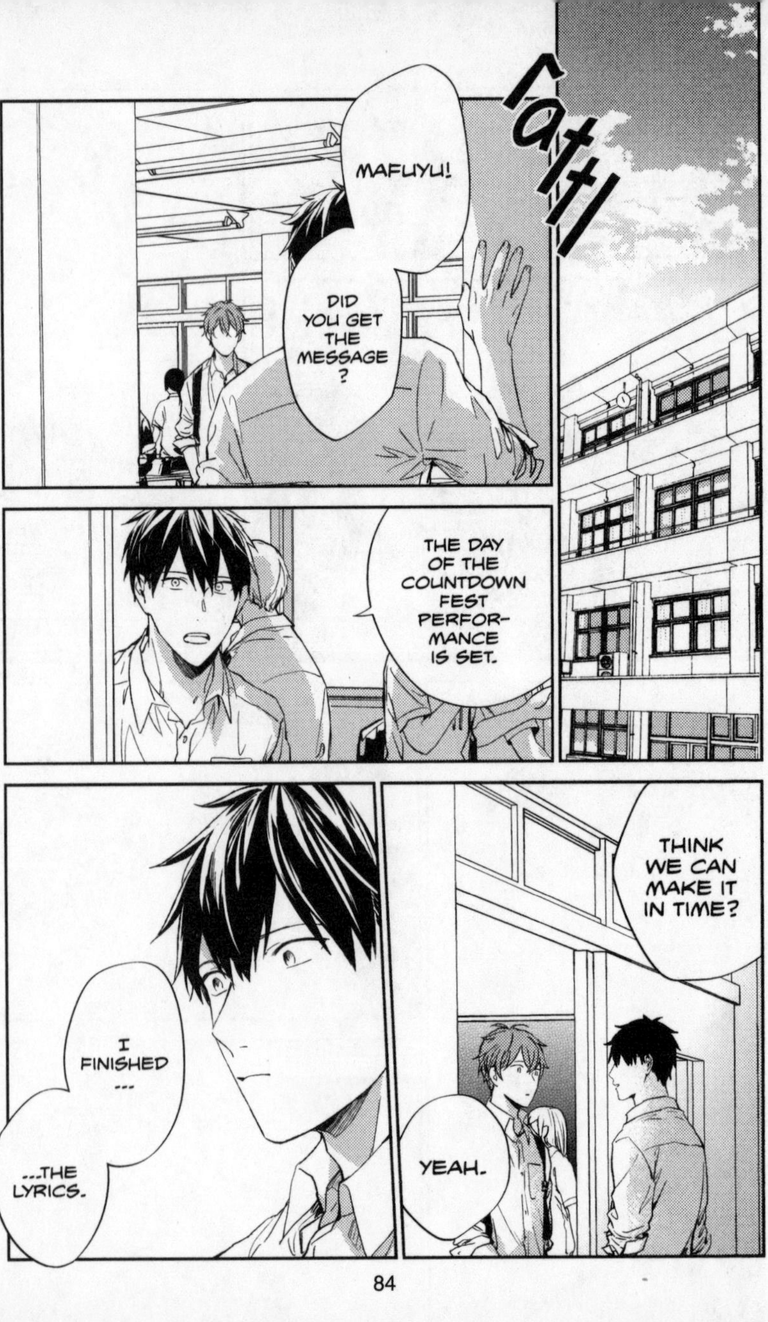
RATT!!
MAFUYU!
DID YOU GET THE MESSAGE?
THE DAY OF THE COUNTDOWN FEST PERFORMANCE IS SET.
THINK WE CAN MAKE IT IN TIME?
YEAH.
I FINISHED...
...THE LYRICS.

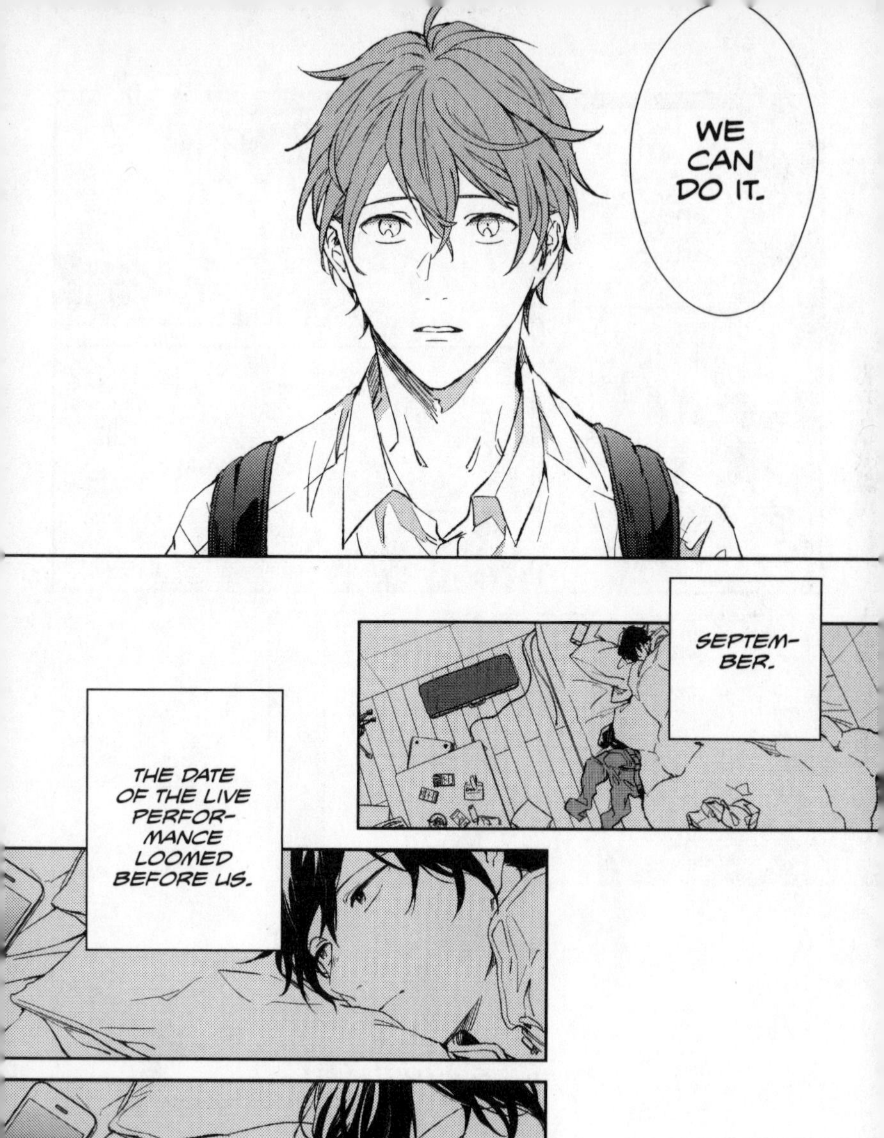
WE CAN DO IT.
SEPTEMBER.
THE DATE OF THE LIVE PERFORMANCE LOOMED BEFORE US.

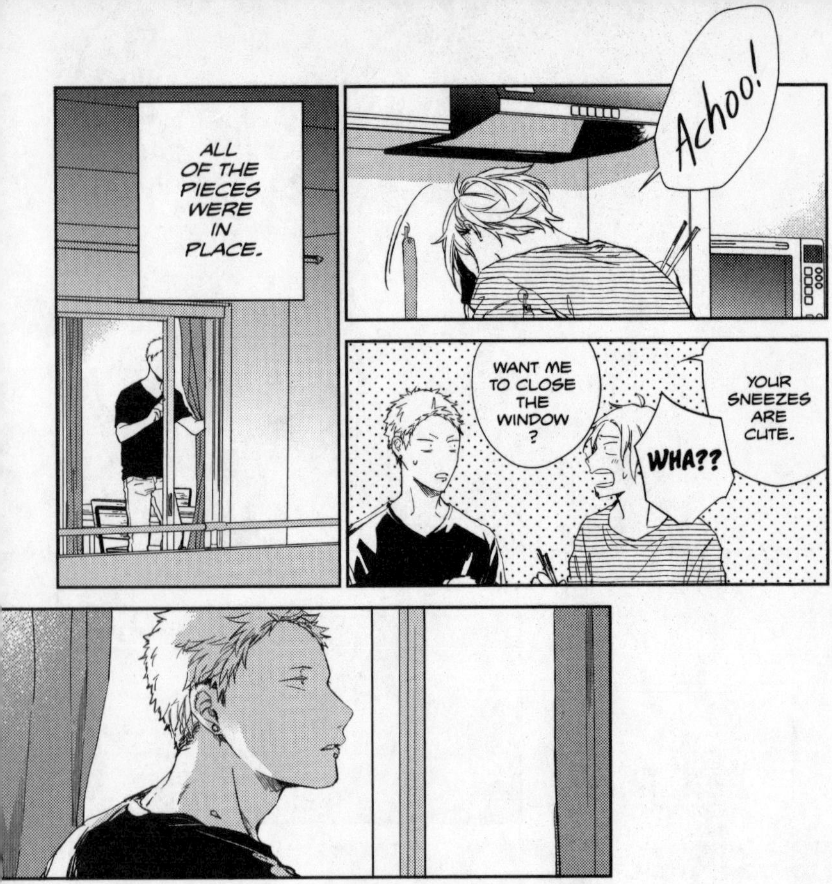
Achoo!
YOUR SNEEZES ARE CUTE.
WANT ME TO CLOSE THE WINDOW ?
WHA??
ALL OF THE PIECES WERE IN PLACE.

FALL HAD STARTED AND THERE WAS NO GOING BACK.

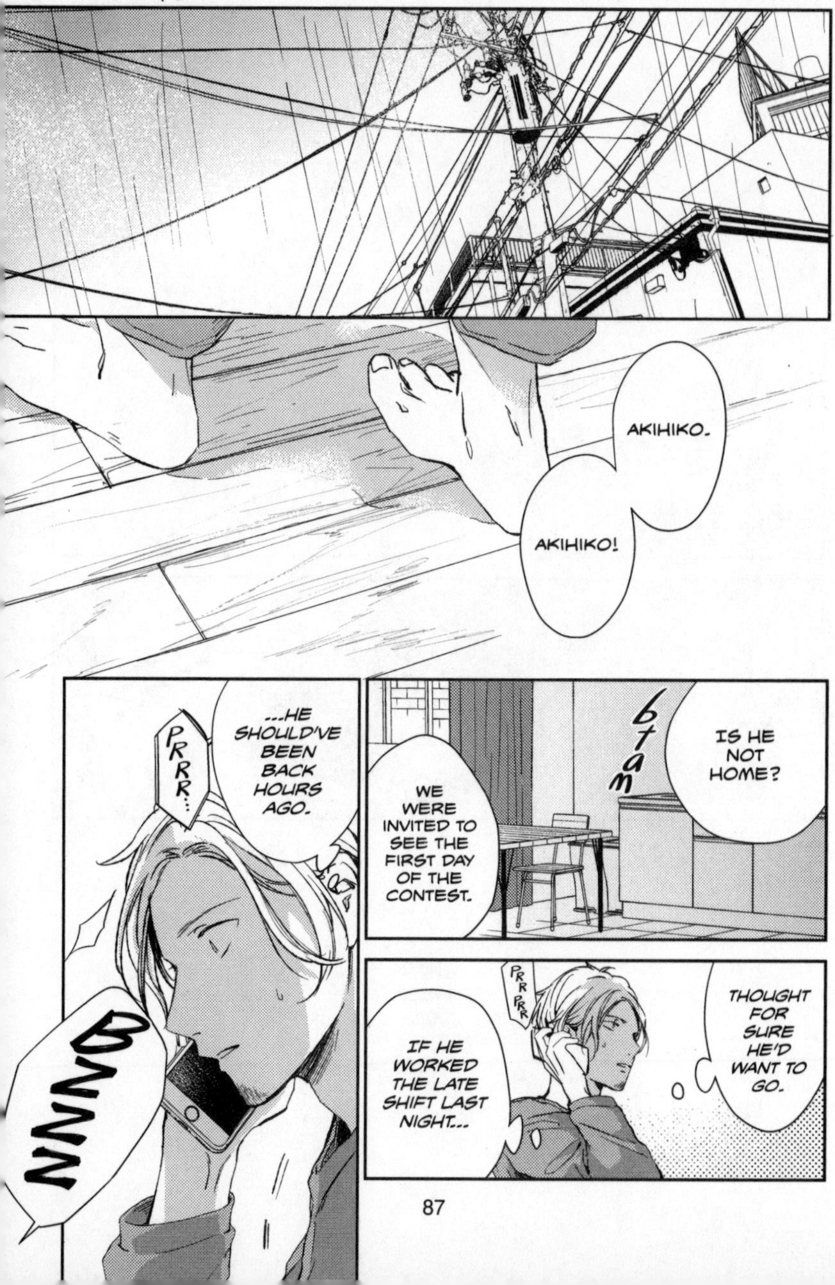
AKIHIKO.
AKIHIKO!
btam
IS HE NOT HOME?
WE WERE INVITED TO SEE THE FIRST DAY OF THE CONTEST.
THOUGHT FOR SURE HE'D WANT TO GO.
PRRR PRRR
IF HE WORKED THE LATE SHIFT LAST NIGHT...
...HE SHOULD'VE BEEN BACK HOURS AGO.
PRRR...

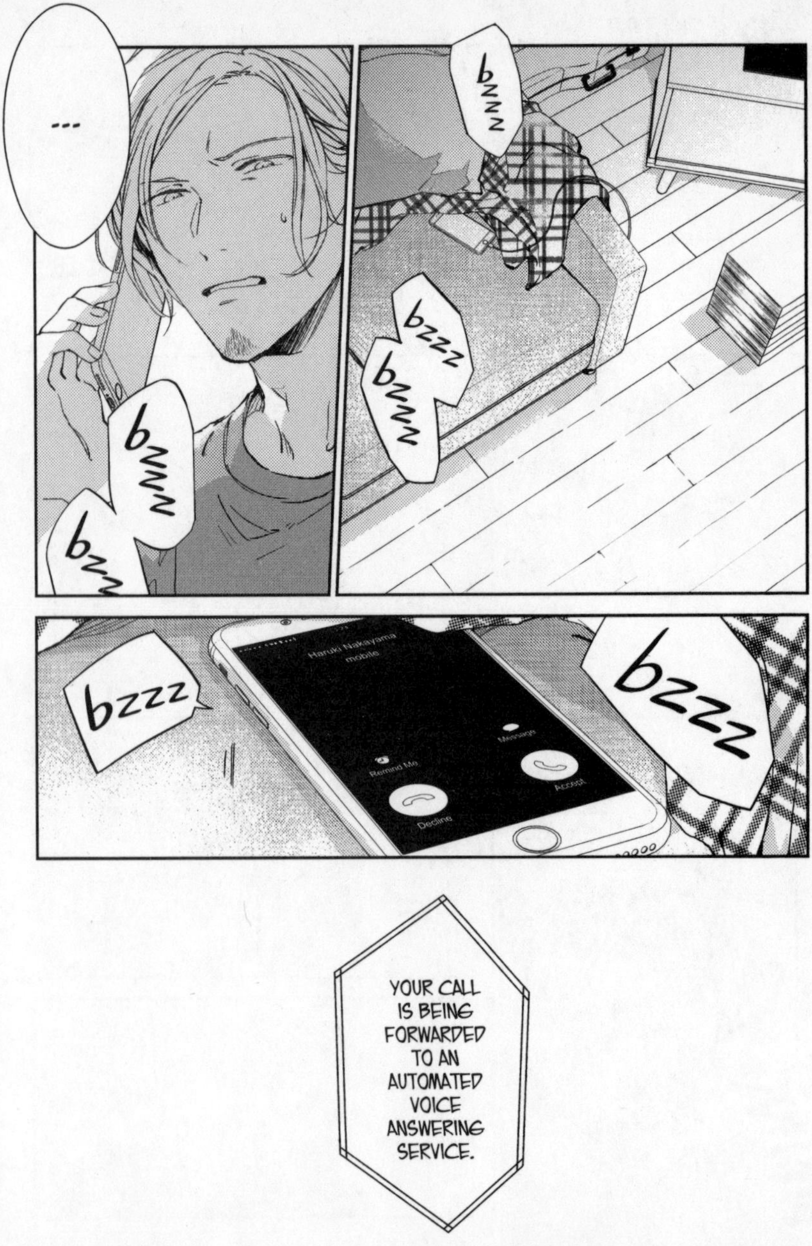
bzzz
bzzz
bzzz
...
bzzz
bzz
bzzz
Haruki Nakayama
mobile
Message
Remind Me
Accept
Decline
bzzz
YOUR CALL IS BEING FORWARDED TO AN AUTOMATED VOICE ANSWERING SERVICE.

chapter 25
given

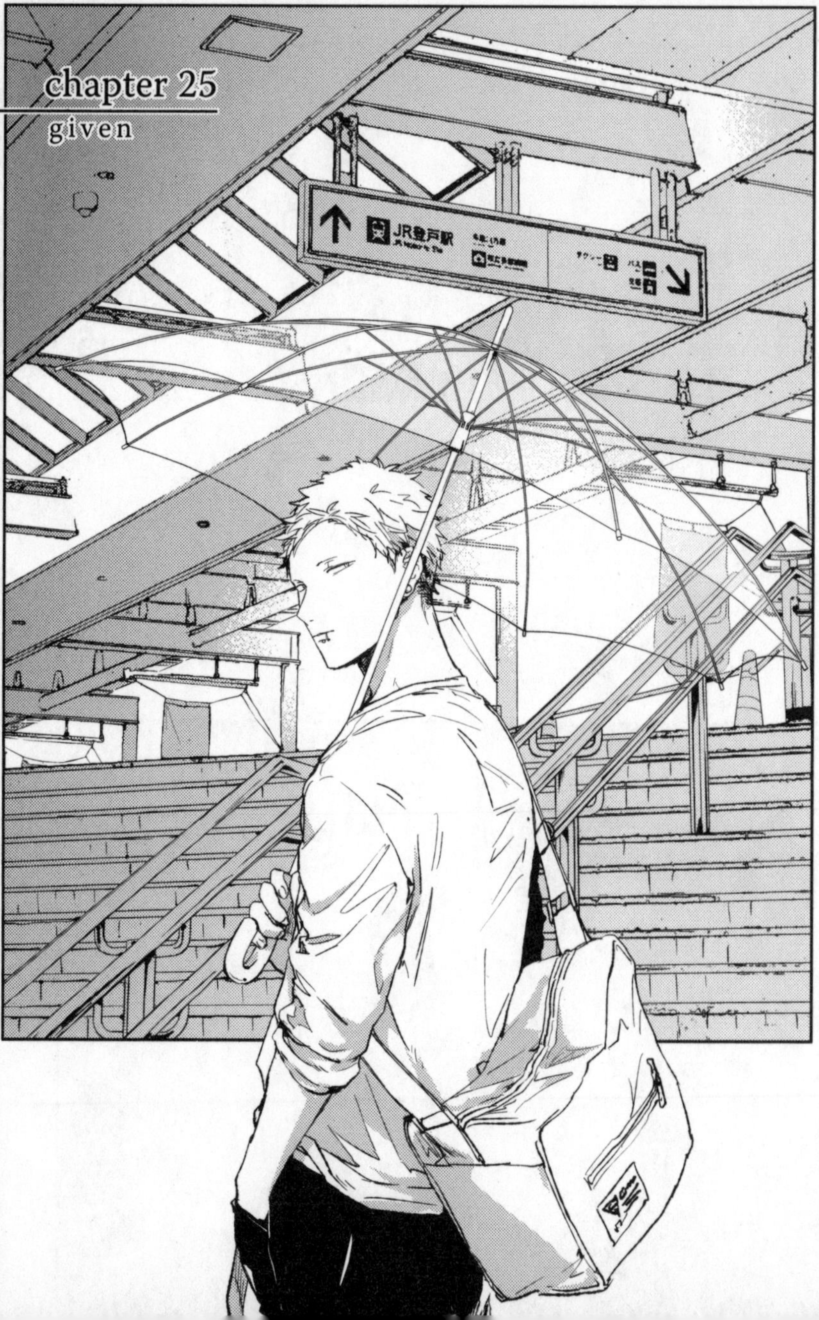
JR登戸駅

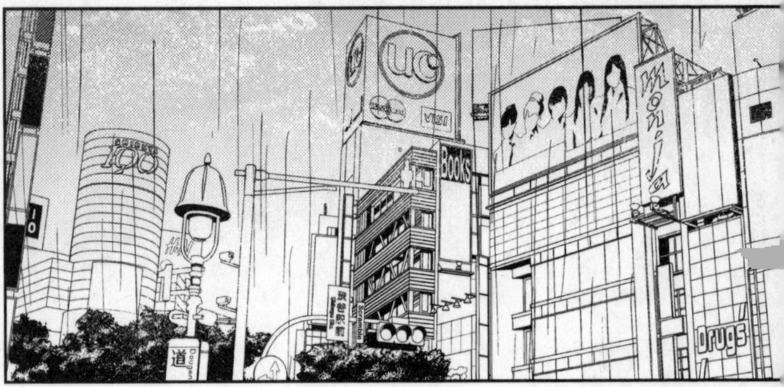
UC
Books
Drugs
道

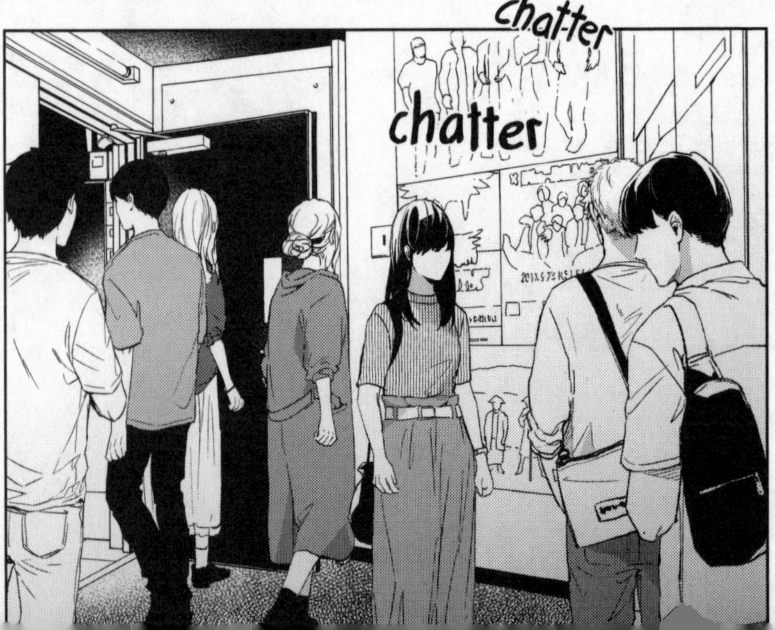
chatter
chatter

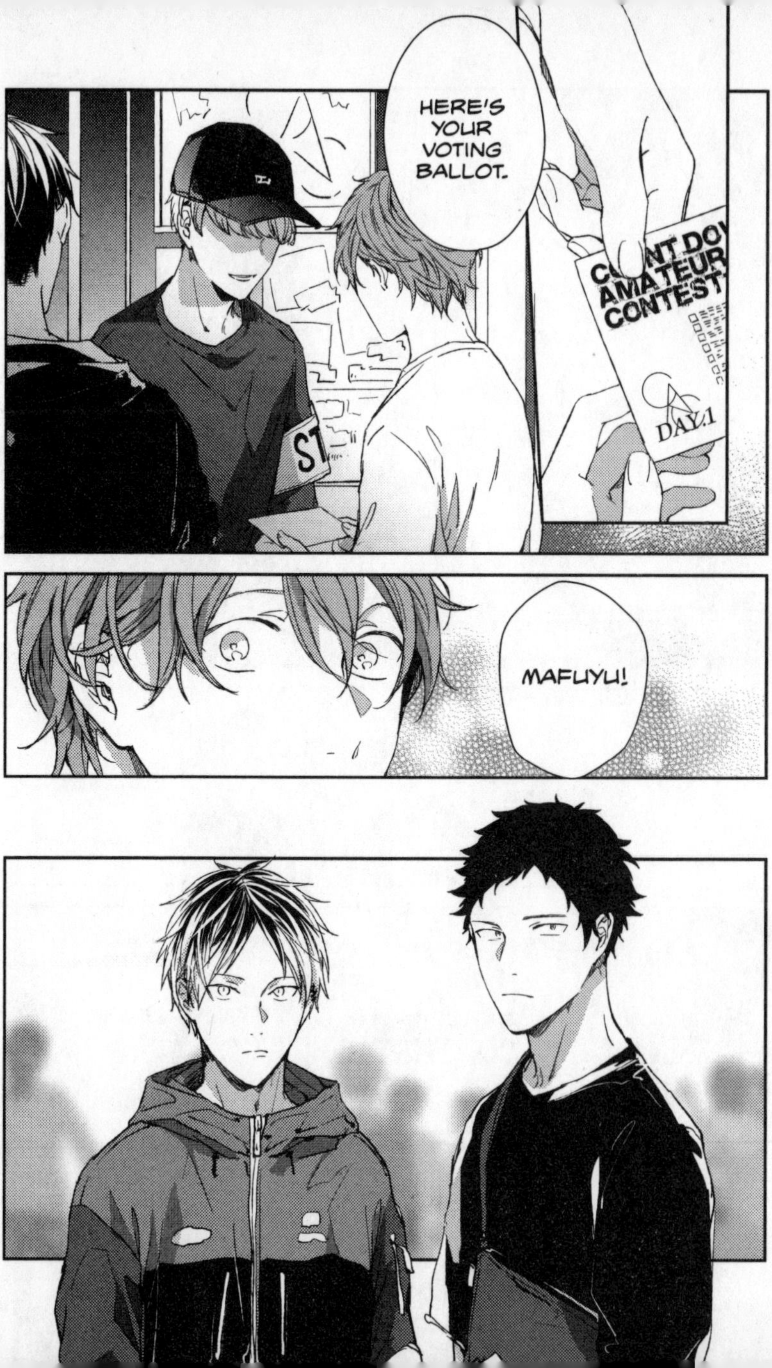
HERE'S YOUR VOTING BALLOT.
AMATEUR
CONTEST
DAY.1
MAFUYU!

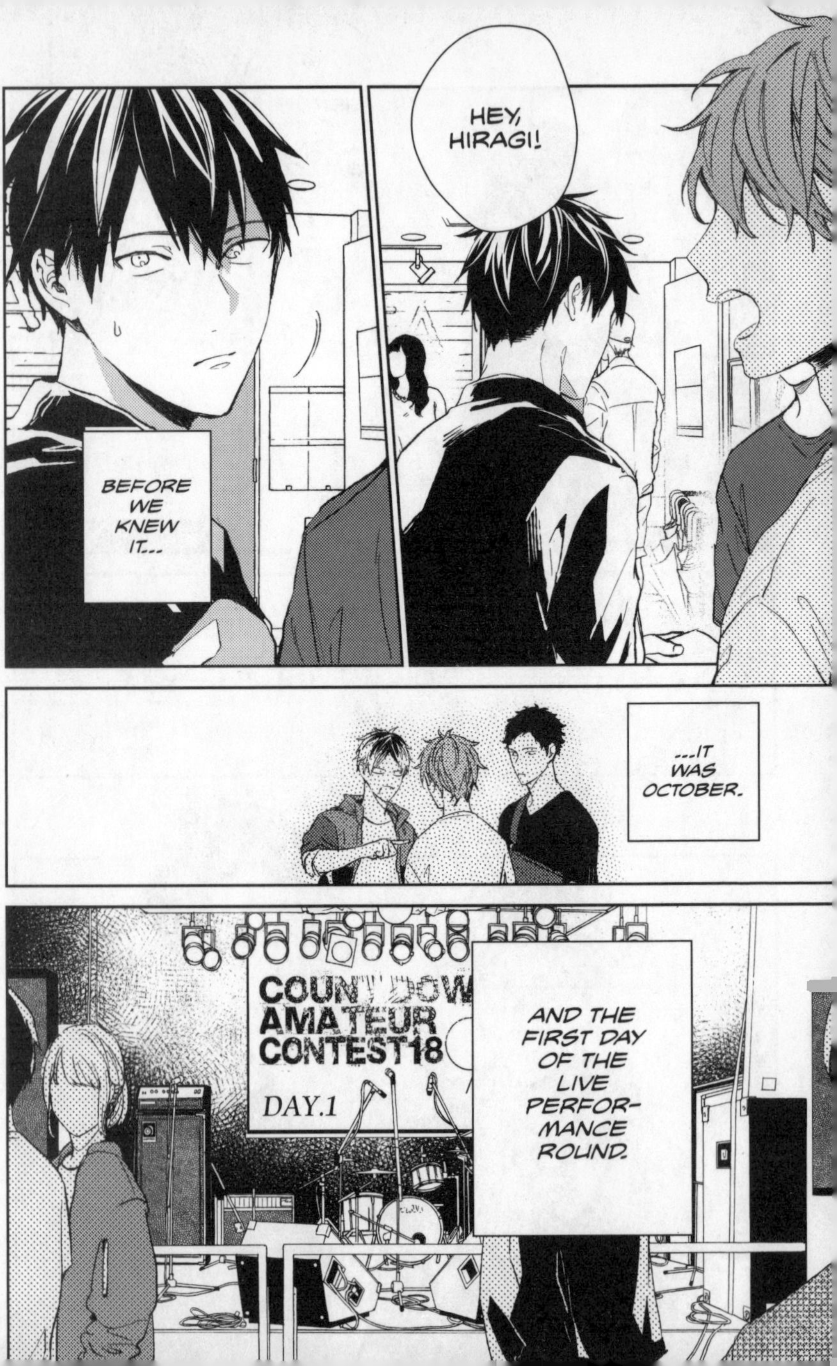
HEY, HIRAGI!
BEFORE WE KNEW IT...
...IT WAS OCTOBER.
AND THE FIRST DAY OF THE LIVE PERFORMANCE ROUND.
COUN DOW
AMATEUR
CONTEST18
DAY.1

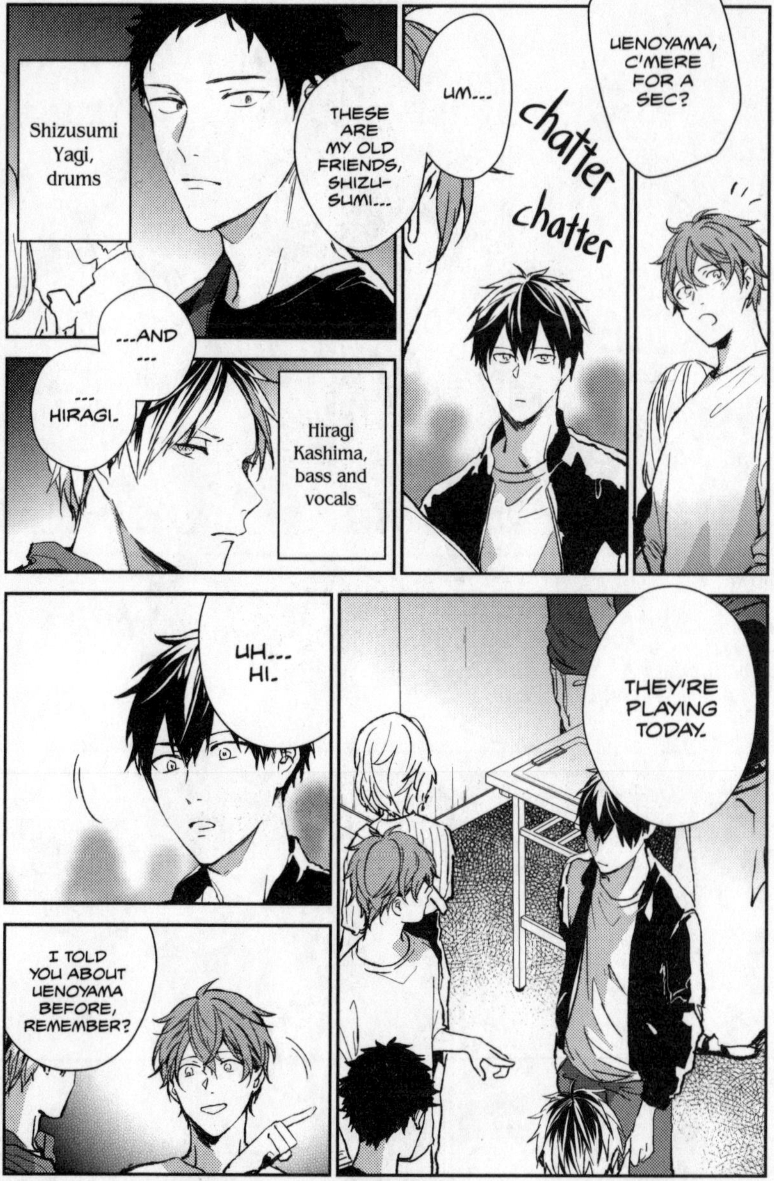
UENOYAMA, C'MERE FOR A SEC?
UM...
chatter chatter
THESE ARE MY OLD FRIENDS, SHIZUSUMI...
Shizusumi Yagi, drums
...AND... ...HIRAGI.
Hiragi Kashima, bass and vocals
THEY'RE PLAYING TODAY.
UH... HI.
I TOLD YOU ABOUT UENOYAMA BEFORE, REMEMBER?

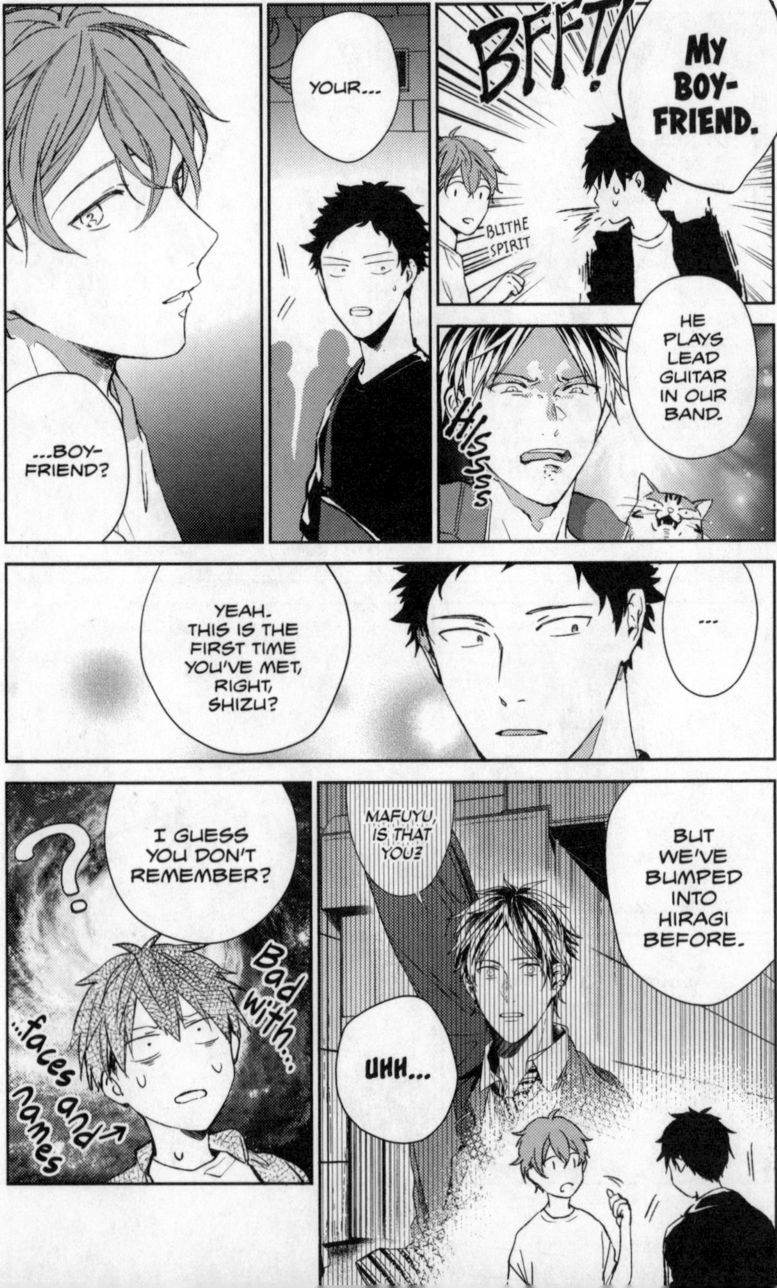

BFFT!
MY BOY-FRIEND.
BLITHE SPIRIT
HE PLAYS LEAD GUITAR IN OUR BAND.
HISSSS
YOUR...
...BOY-FRIEND?
...
YEAH. THIS IS THE FIRST TIME YOU'VE MET, RIGHT, SHIZU?
BUT WE'VE BUMPED INTO HIRAGI BEFORE.
MAFUYU, IS THAT YOU?
UHH...
I GUESS YOU DON'T REMEMBER?
Bad with... ...faces and names

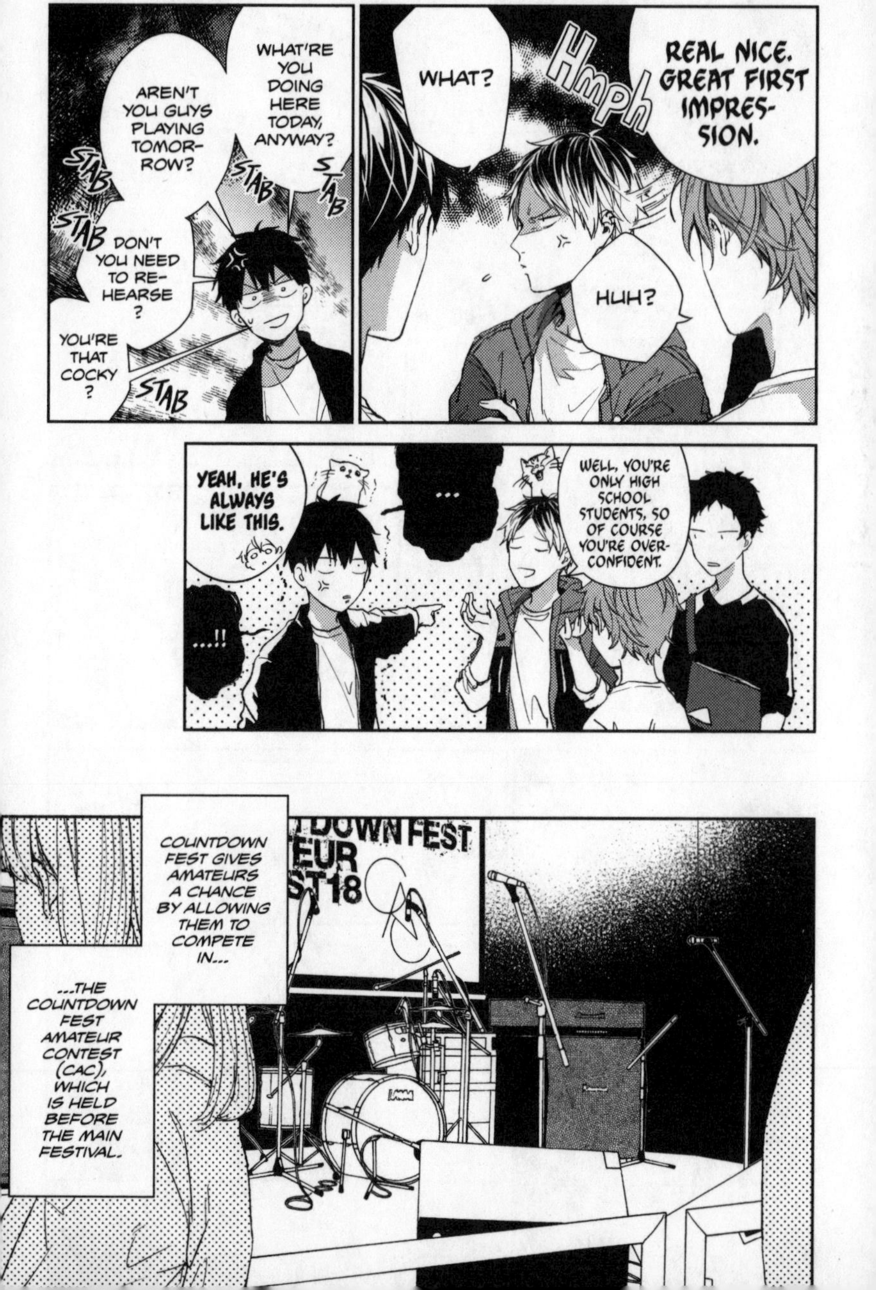
Hmph
REAL NICE. GREAT FIRST IMPRES-SION.
WHAT?
HUH?
WHAT'RE YOU DOING HERE TODAY, ANYWAY?
AREN'T YOU GUYS PLAYING TOMOR-ROW?
STAB STAB STAB STAB
DON'T YOU NEED TO RE-HEARSE?
YOU'RE THAT COCKY?
STAB
WELL, YOU'RE ONLY HIGH SCHOOL STUDENTS, SO OF COURSE YOU'RE OVER-CONFIDENT.
...
YEAH, HE'S ALWAYS LIKE THIS.
...!!
COUNTDOWN FEST GIVES AMATEURS A CHANCE BY ALLOWING THEM TO COMPETE IN...
...THE COUNTDOWN FEST AMATEUR CONTEST (CAC), WHICH IS HELD BEFORE THE MAIN FESTIVAL.

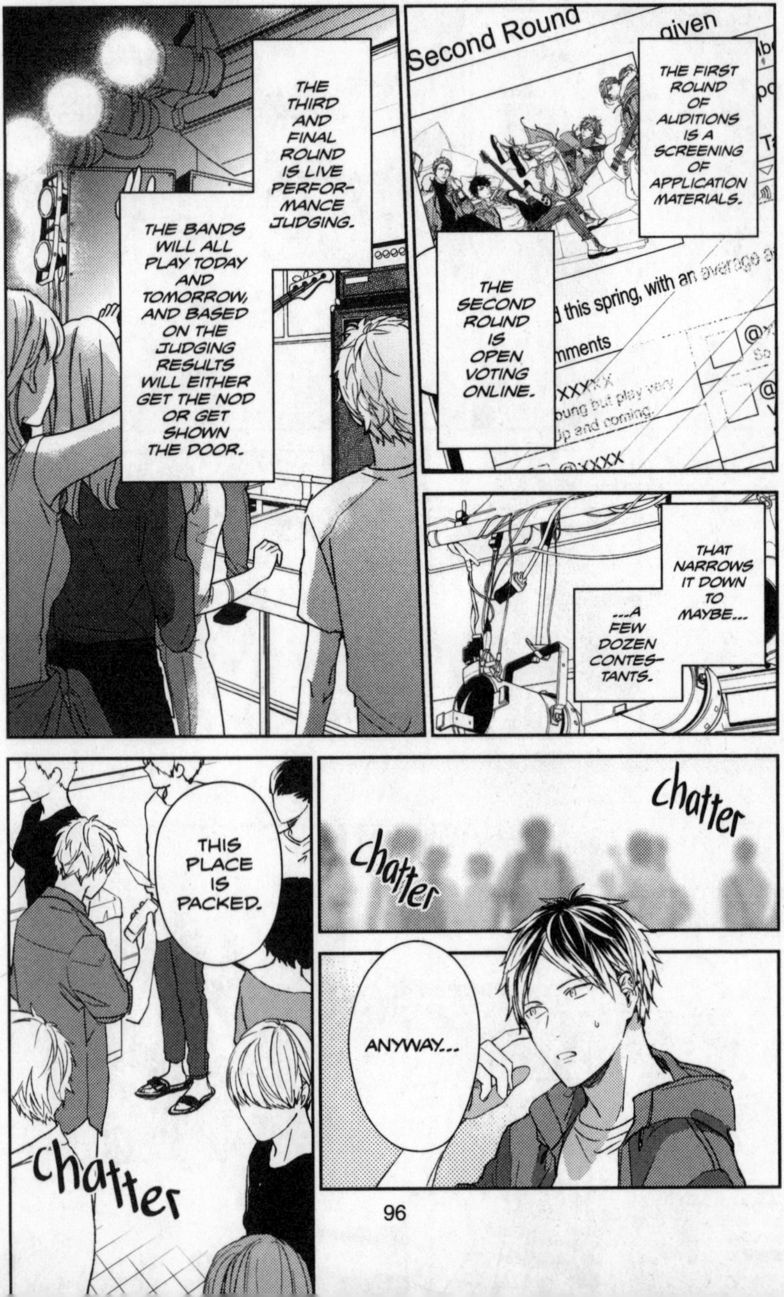
Second Round
THE FIRST ROUND OF AUDITIONS IS A SCREENING OF APPLICATION MATERIALS.
THE SECOND ROUND IS OPEN VOTING ONLINE.
THAT NARROWS IT DOWN TO MAYBE...
...A FEW DOZEN CONTESTANTS.
THE THIRD AND FINAL ROUND IS LIVE PERFORMANCE JUDGING.
THE BANDS WILL ALL PLAY TODAY AND TOMORROW, AND BASED ON THE JUDGING RESULTS WILL EITHER GET THE NOD OR GET SHOWN THE DOOR.
chatter
chatter
ANYWAY...
THIS PLACE IS PACKED.
chatter

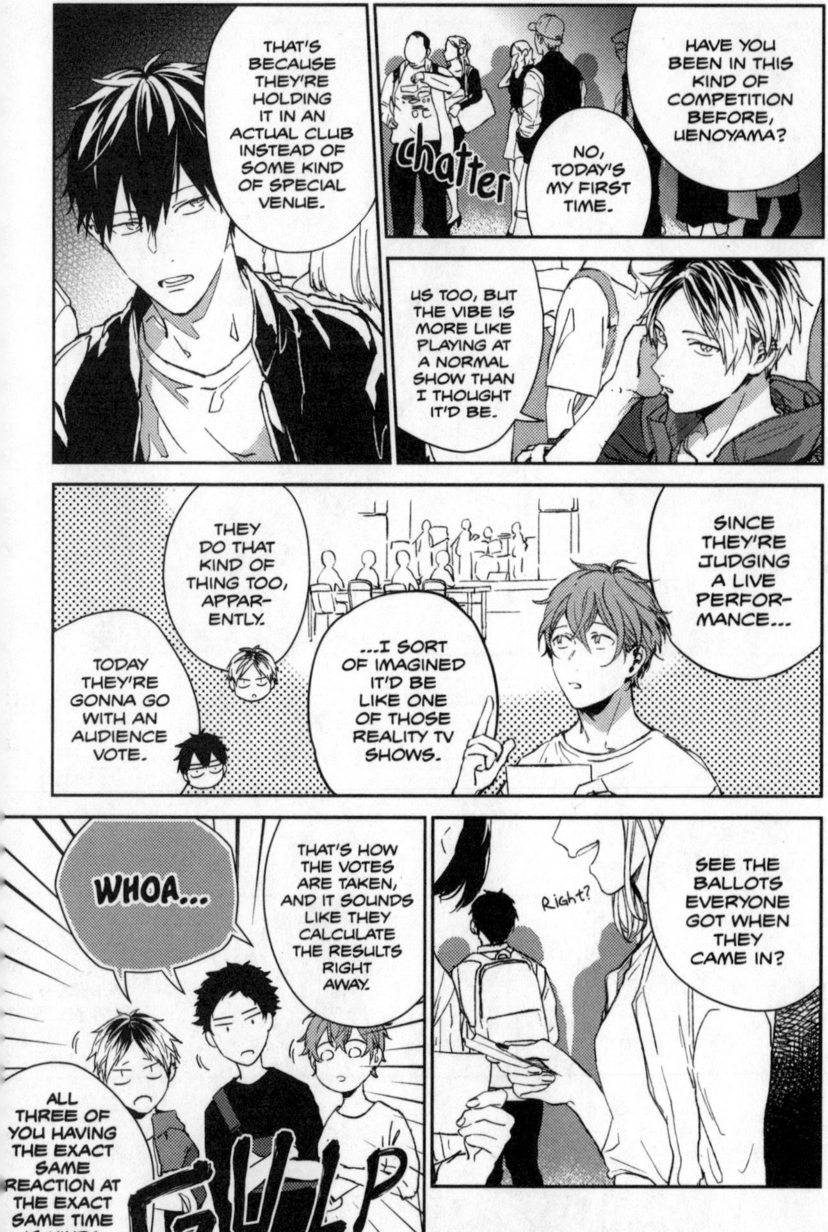
HAVE YOU BEEN IN THIS KIND OF COMPETITION BEFORE, UENOYAMA?
NO, TODAY'S MY FIRST TIME.
chatter
US TOO, BUT THE VIBE IS MORE LIKE PLAYING AT A NORMAL SHOW THAN I THOUGHT IT'D BE.
THAT'S BECAUSE THEY'RE HOLDING IT IN AN ACTUAL CLUB INSTEAD OF SOME KIND OF SPECIAL VENUE.
SINCE THEY'RE JUDGING A LIVE PERFORMANCE...
...I SORT OF IMAGINED IT'D BE LIKE ONE OF THOSE REALITY TV SHOWS.
THEY DO THAT KIND OF THING TOO, APPARENTLY.
TODAY THEY'RE GONNA GO WITH AN AUDIENCE VOTE.
SEE THE BALLOTS EVERYONE GOT WHEN THEY CAME IN?
Right?
THAT'S HOW THE VOTES ARE TAKEN, AND IT SOUNDS LIKE THEY CALCULATE THE RESULTS RIGHT AWAY.
WHOA...
GULP
ALL THREE OF YOU HAVING THE EXACT SAME REACTION AT THE EXACT SAME TIME IS KINDA CREEPY.

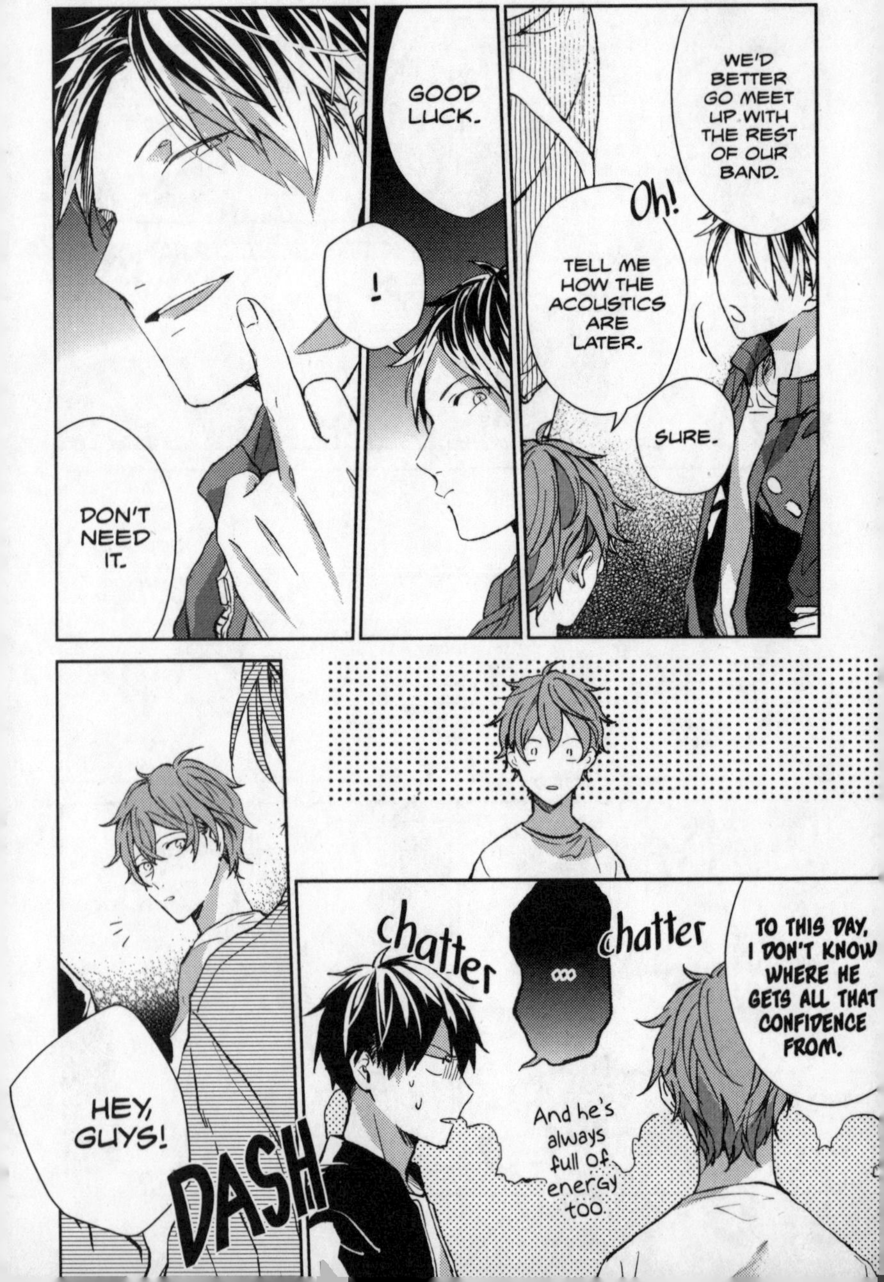
WE'D BETTER GO MEET UP WITH THE REST OF OUR BAND.
Oh!
TELL ME HOW THE ACOUSTICS ARE LATER.
SURE.
GOOD LUCK.
!
DON'T NEED IT.
TO THIS DAY, I DON'T KNOW WHERE HE GETS ALL THAT CONFIDENCE FROM.
chatter
chatter
...
And he's always full of energy too
HEY, GUYS!
DASH

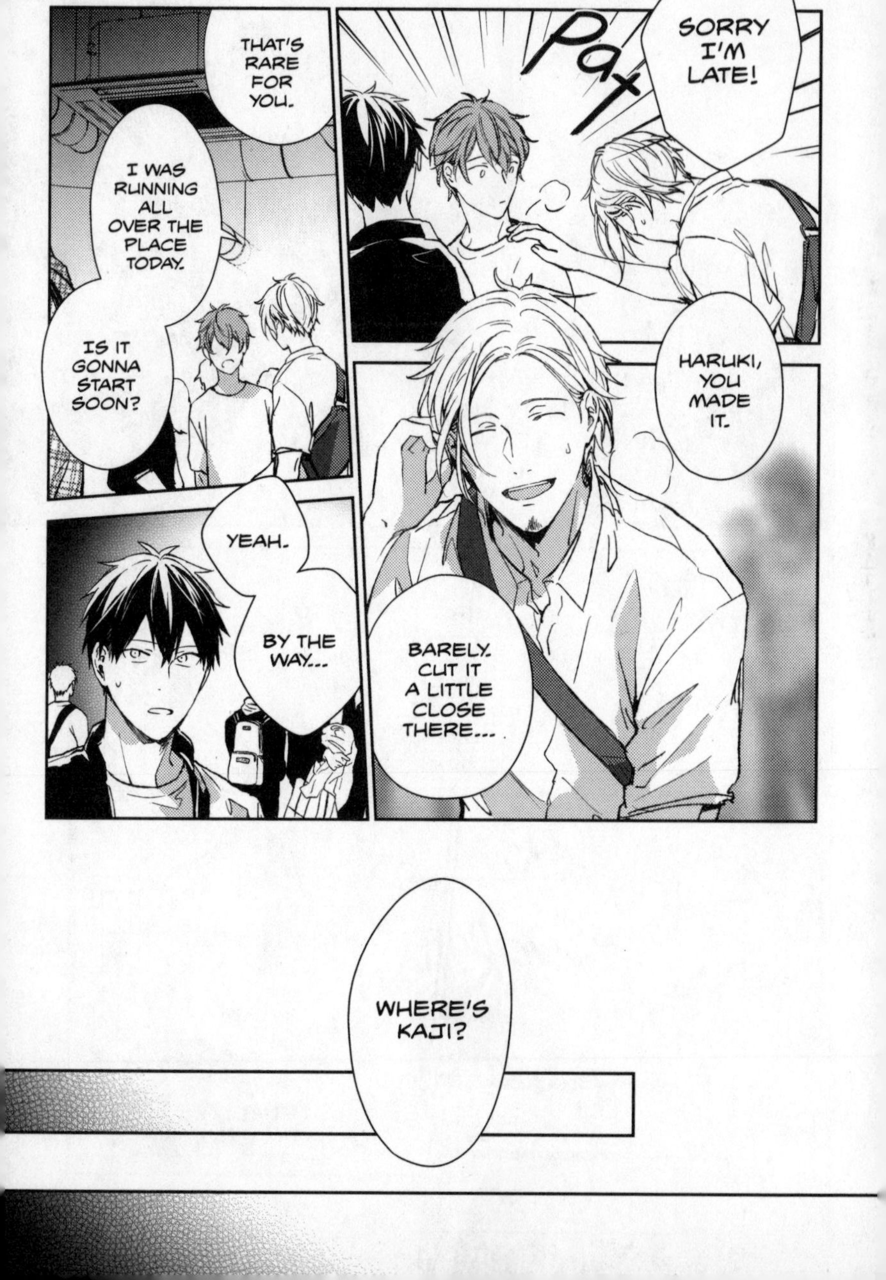
Pat
SORRY I'M LATE!
HARUKI, YOU MADE IT.
BARELY. CUT IT A LITTLE CLOSE THERE...
THAT'S RARE FOR YOU.
I WAS RUNNING ALL OVER THE PLACE TODAY.
IS IT GONNA START SOON?
YEAH.
BY THE WAY...
WHERE'S KAJI?

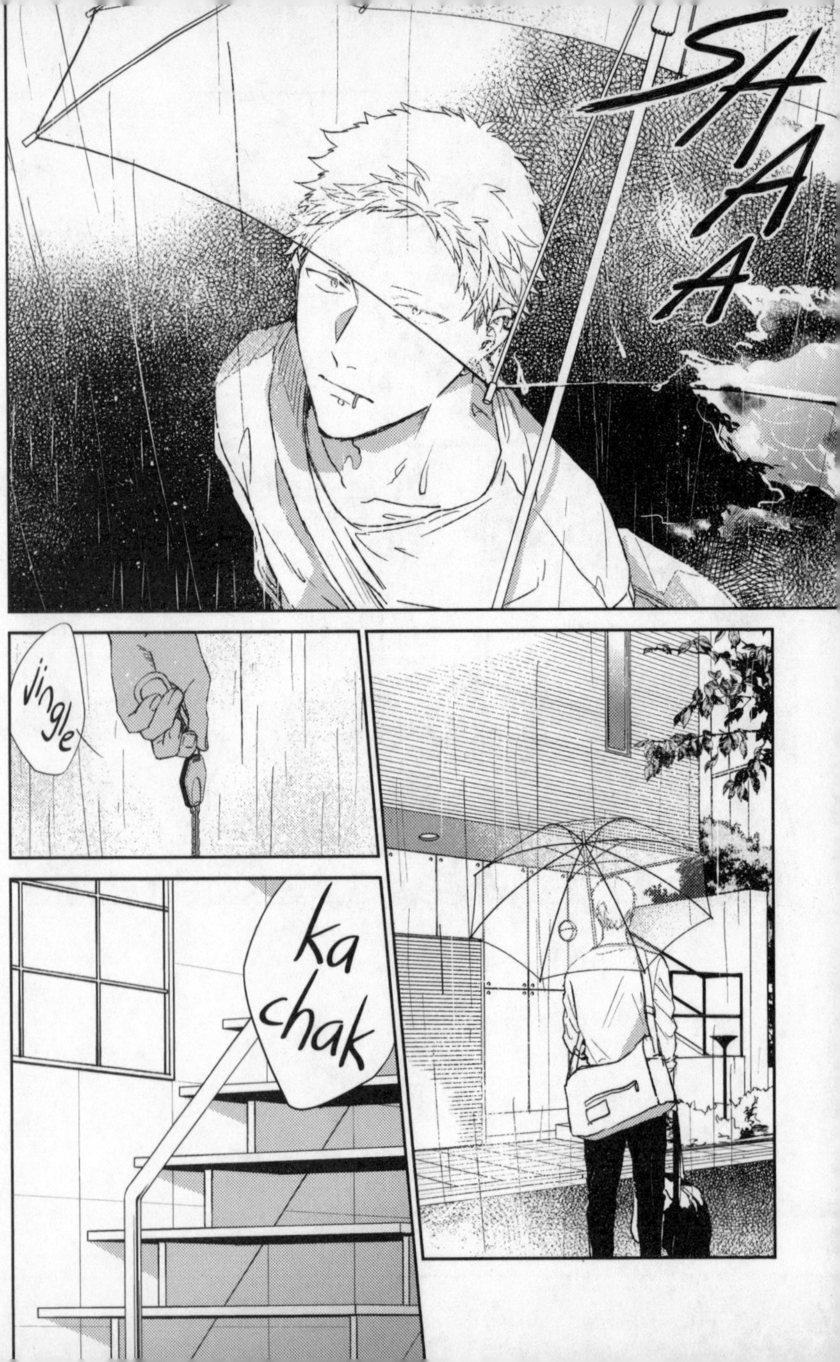
SHAAA
jingle
ka chak

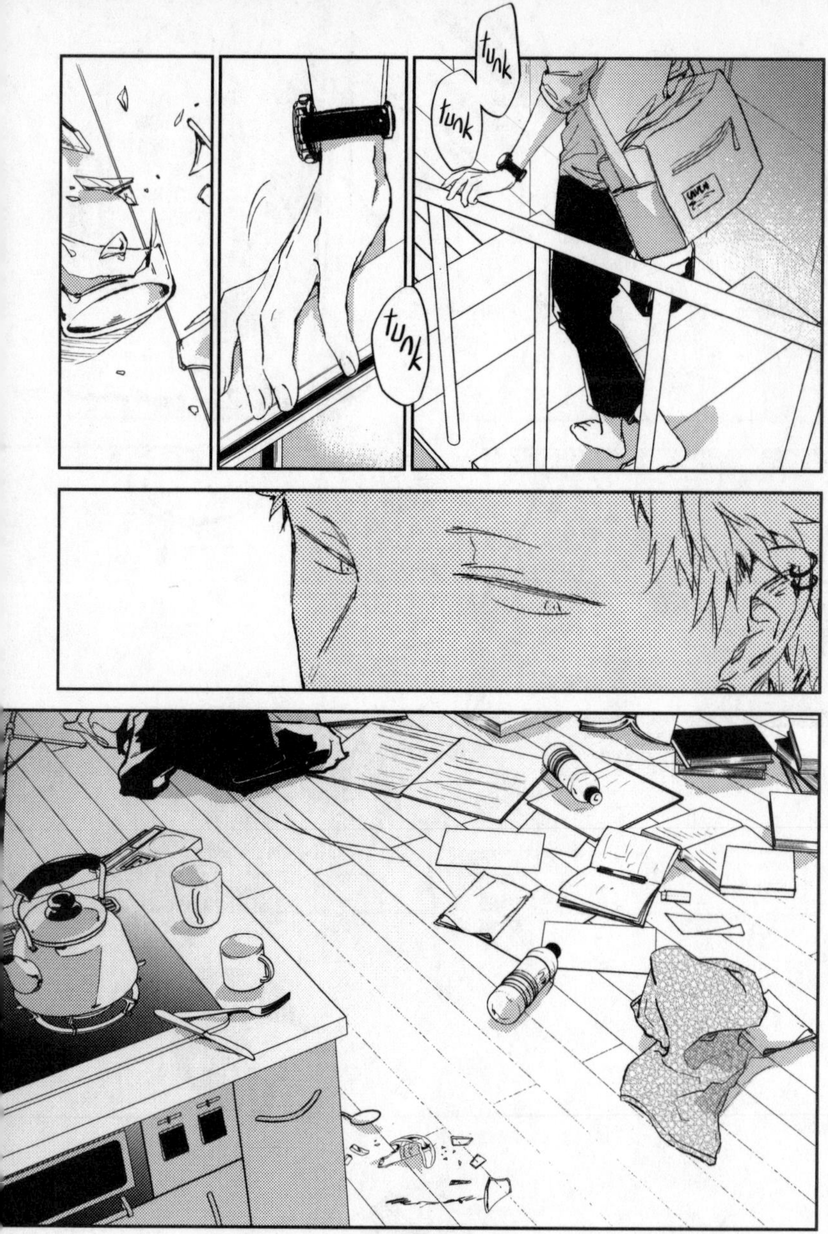
tunk
tunk
tunk

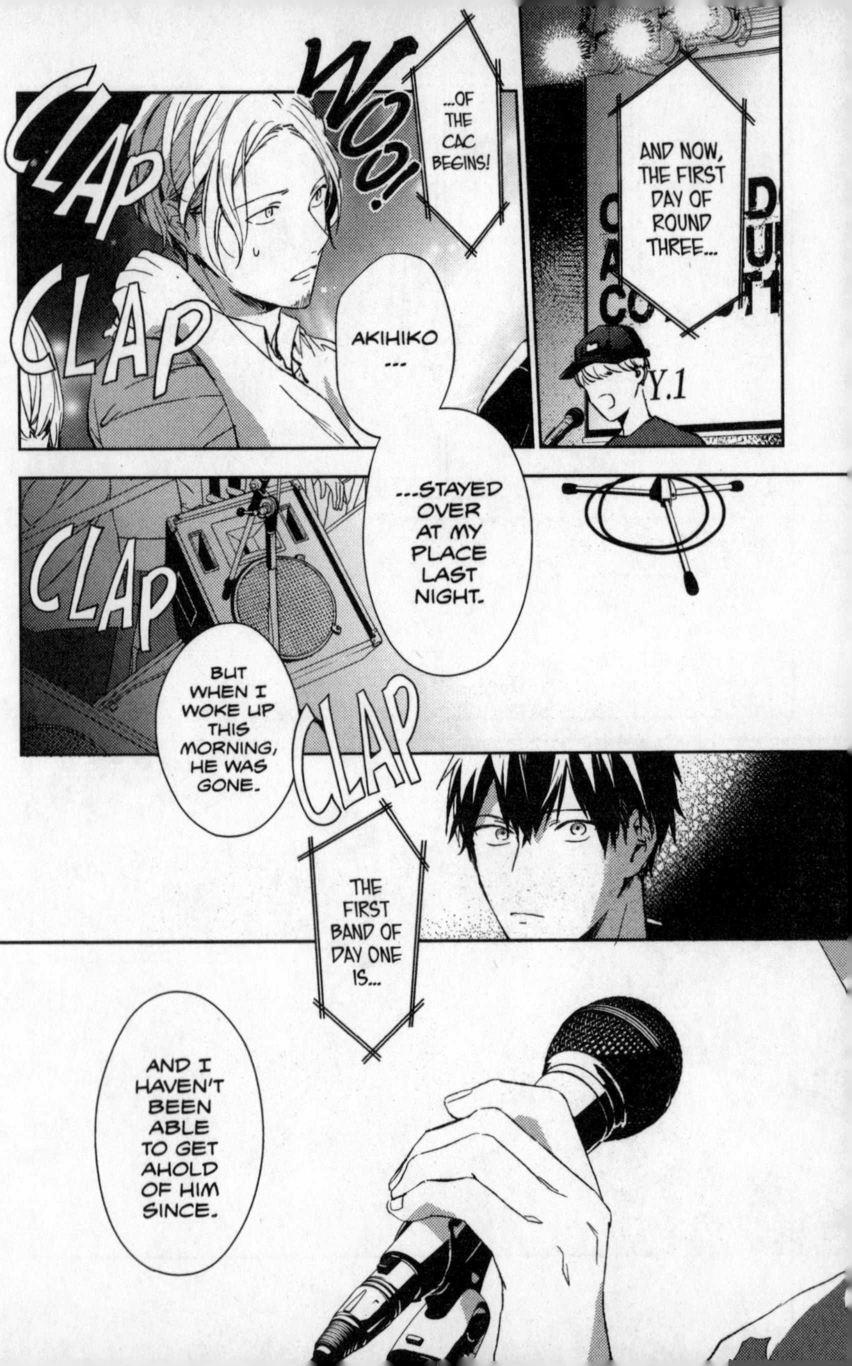
AND NOW, THE FIRST DAY OF ROUND THREE...
...OF THE CAC BEGINS!
WOO!!
CLAP
CLAP
AKIHIKO ---
---STAYED OVER AT MY PLACE LAST NIGHT.
CLAP
BUT WHEN I WOKE UP THIS MORNING, HE WAS GONE.
CLAP
THE FIRST BAND OF DAY ONE IS...
AND I HAVEN'T BEEN ABLE TO GET AHOLD OF HIM SINCE.

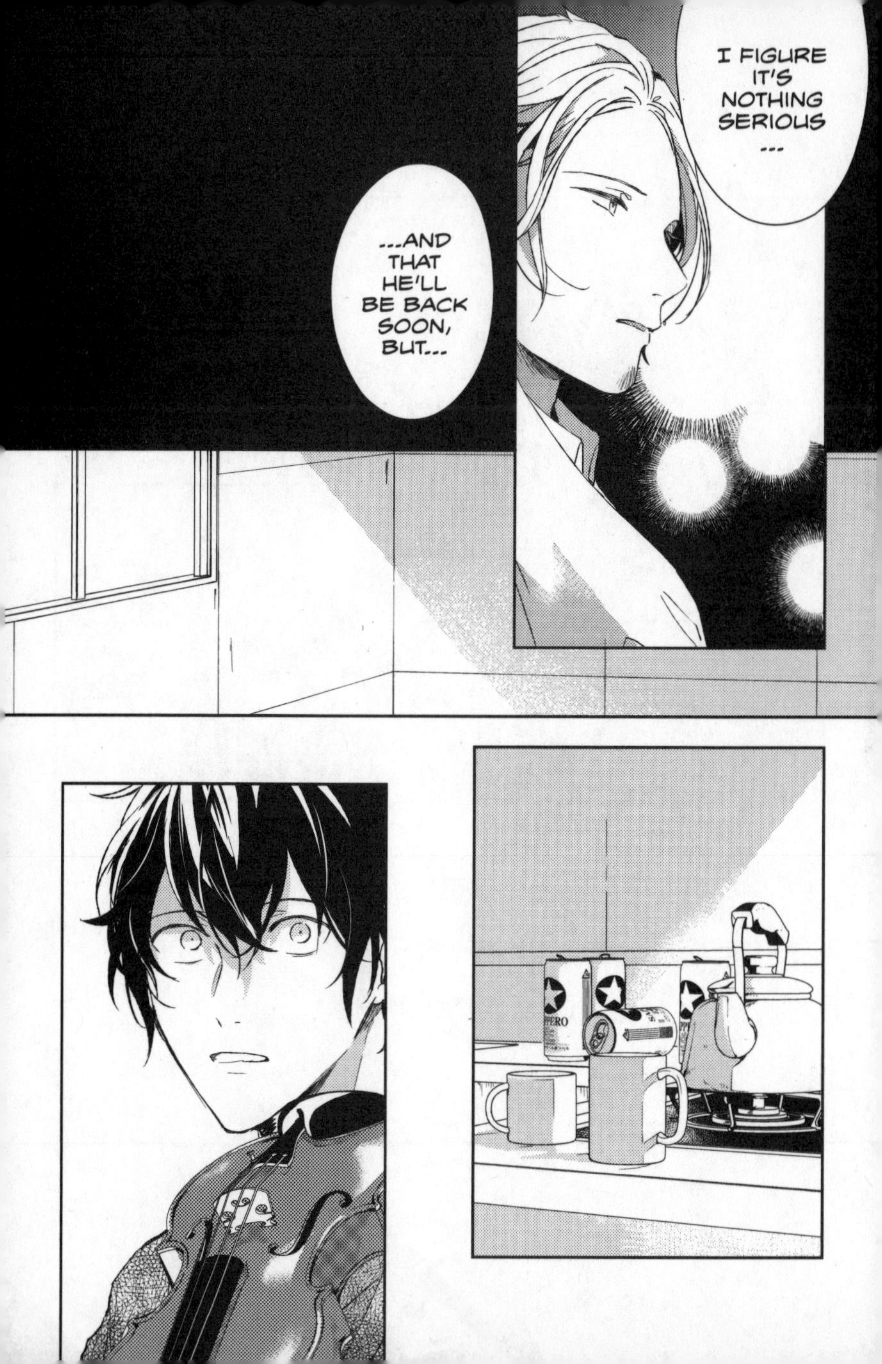
I FIGURE IT'S NOTHING SERIOUS ...
...AND THAT HE'LL BE BACK SOON, BUT...

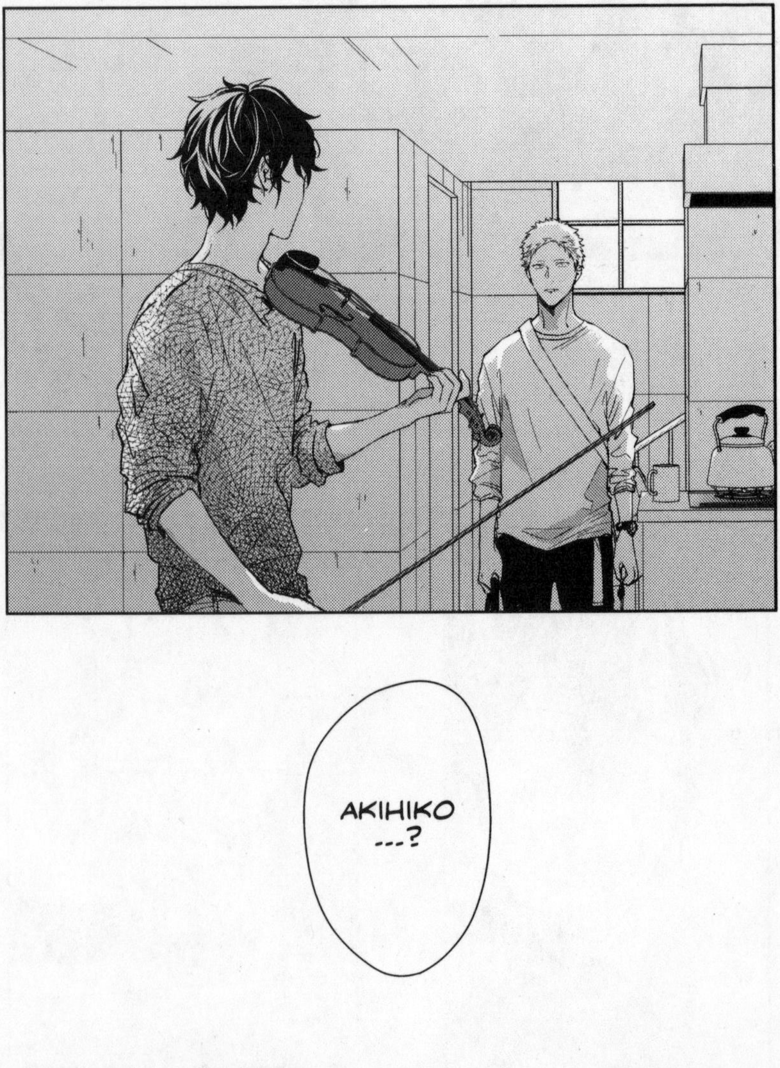
AKIHIKO ---?

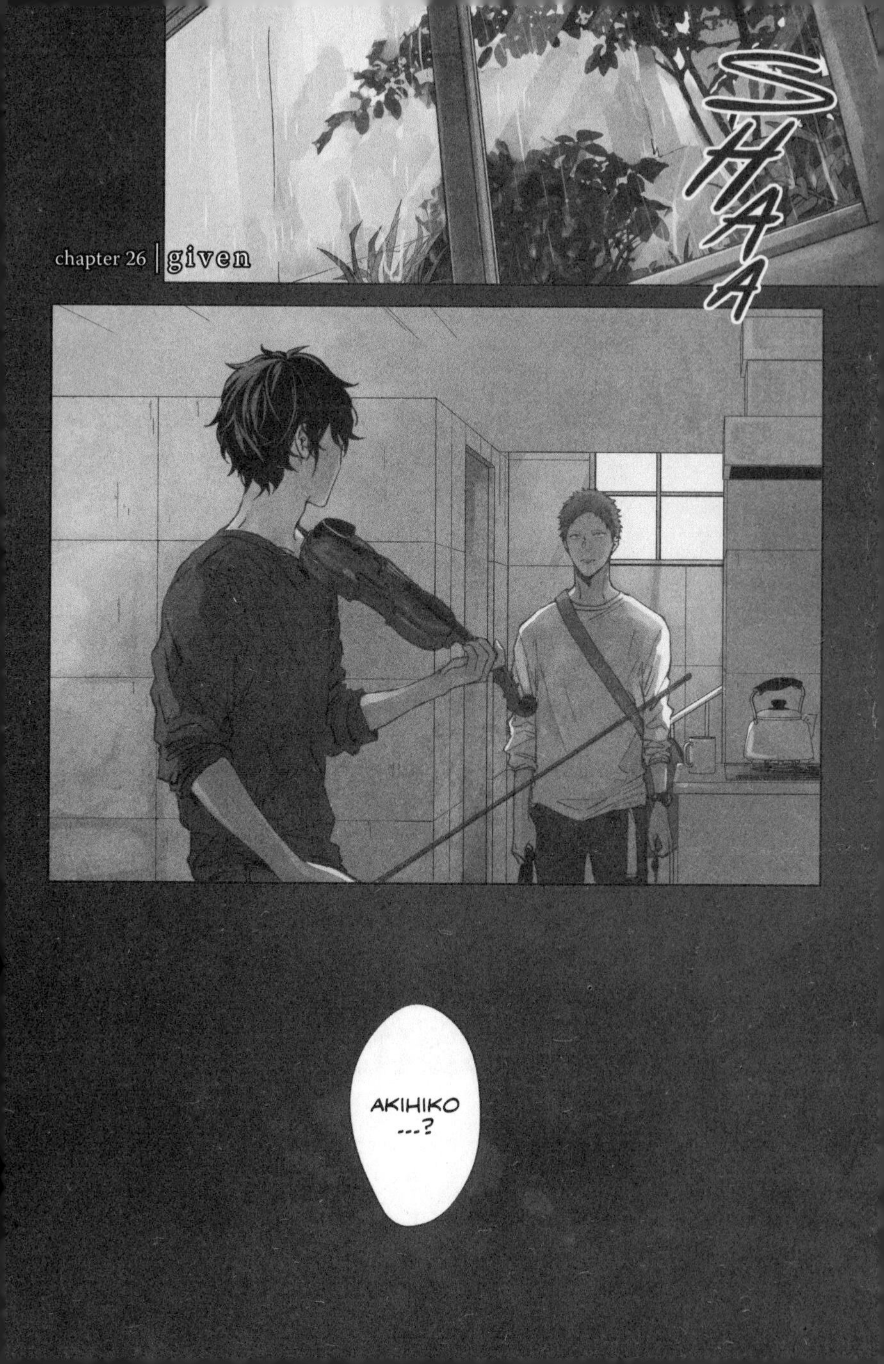
chapter 26 | given
SHAA
AKIHIKO
---?

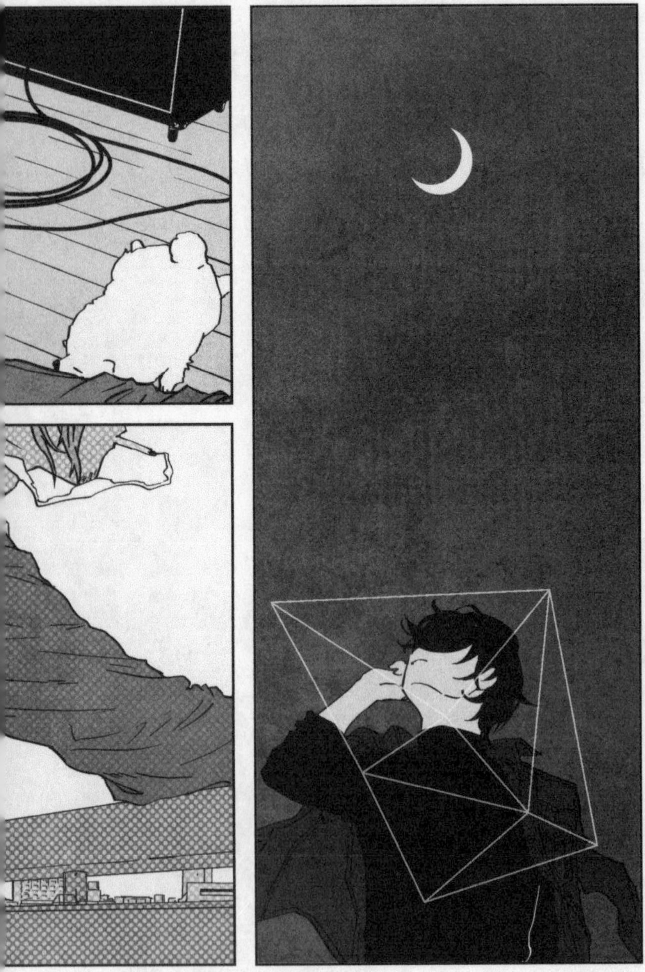

chapter 26

given

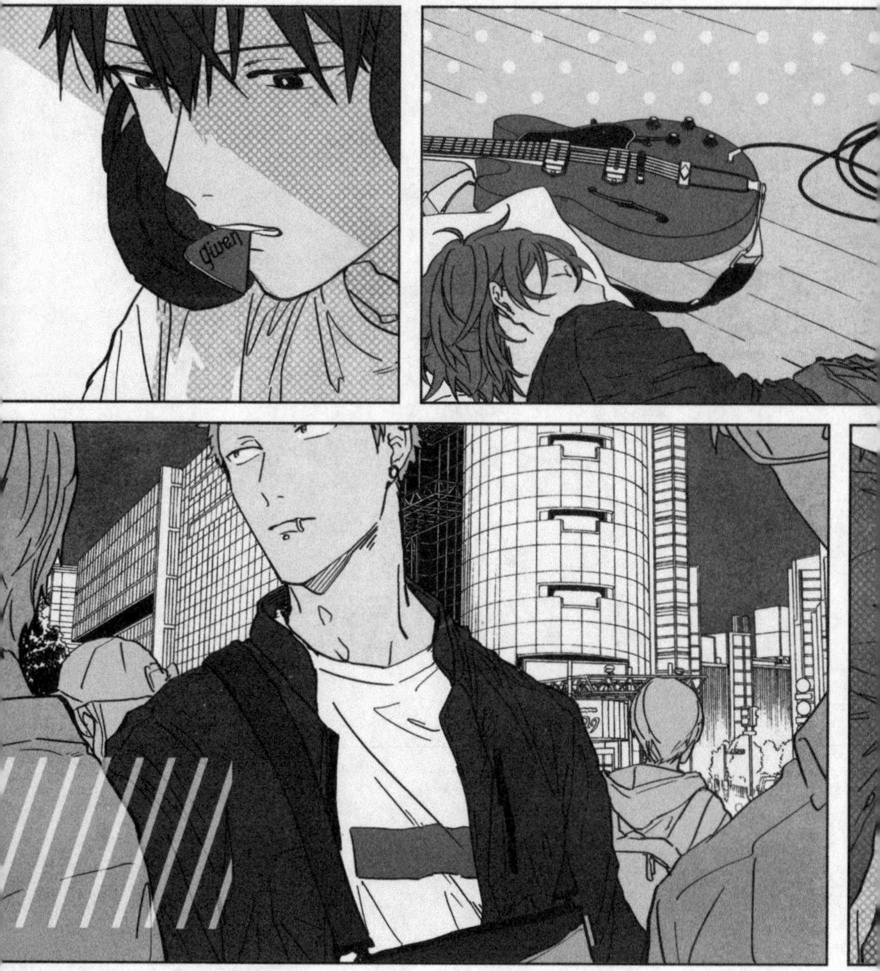
given

given

by Natsuki Kizu

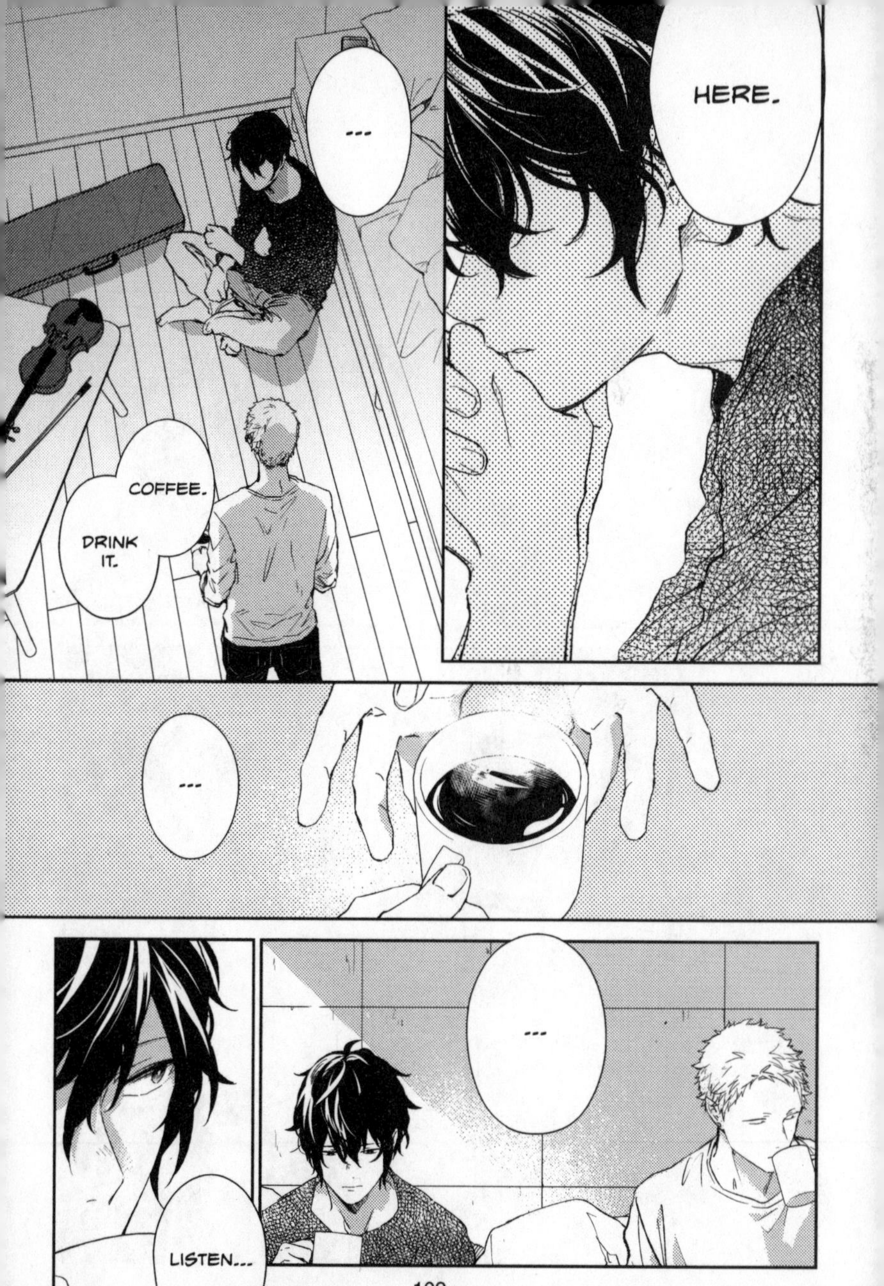
HERE.
...
COFFEE.
DRINK IT.
...
...
LISTEN...

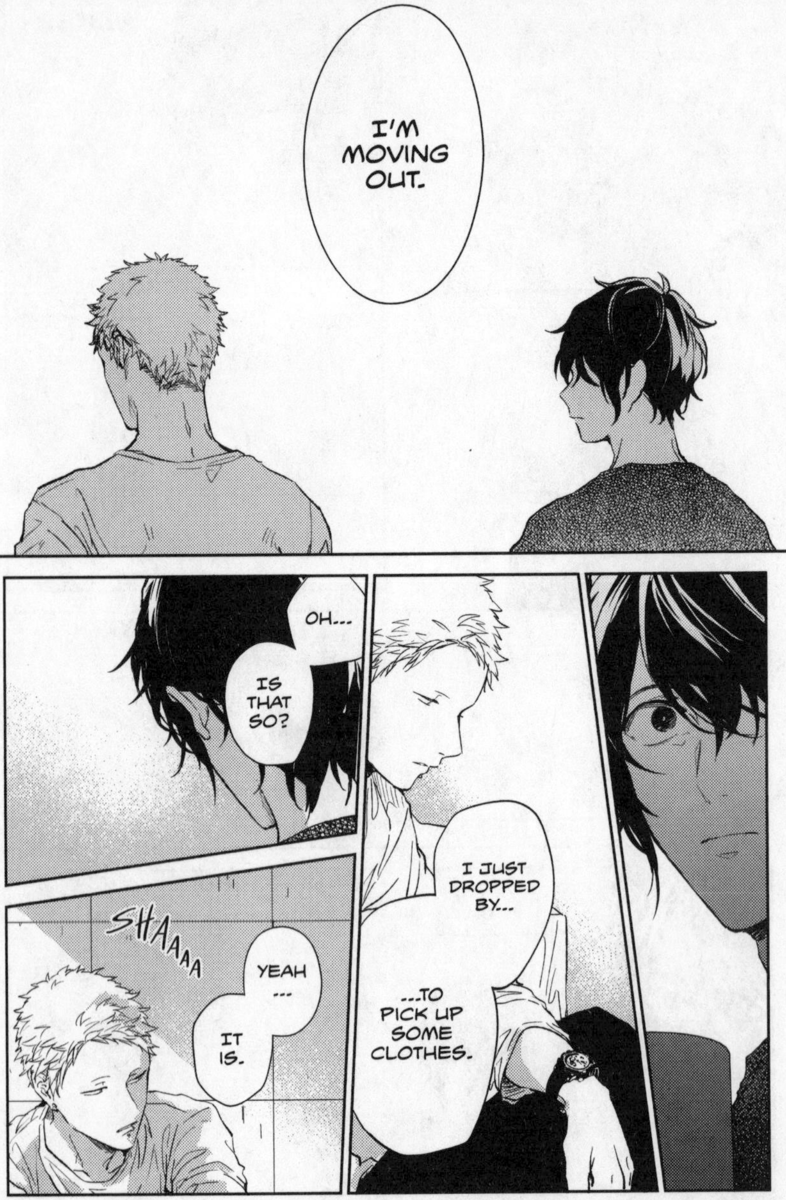
I'M MOVING OUT.
I JUST DROPPED BY...
...TO PICK UP SOME CLOTHES.
OH...
IS THAT SO?
SHAAAA
YEAH...
IT IS.

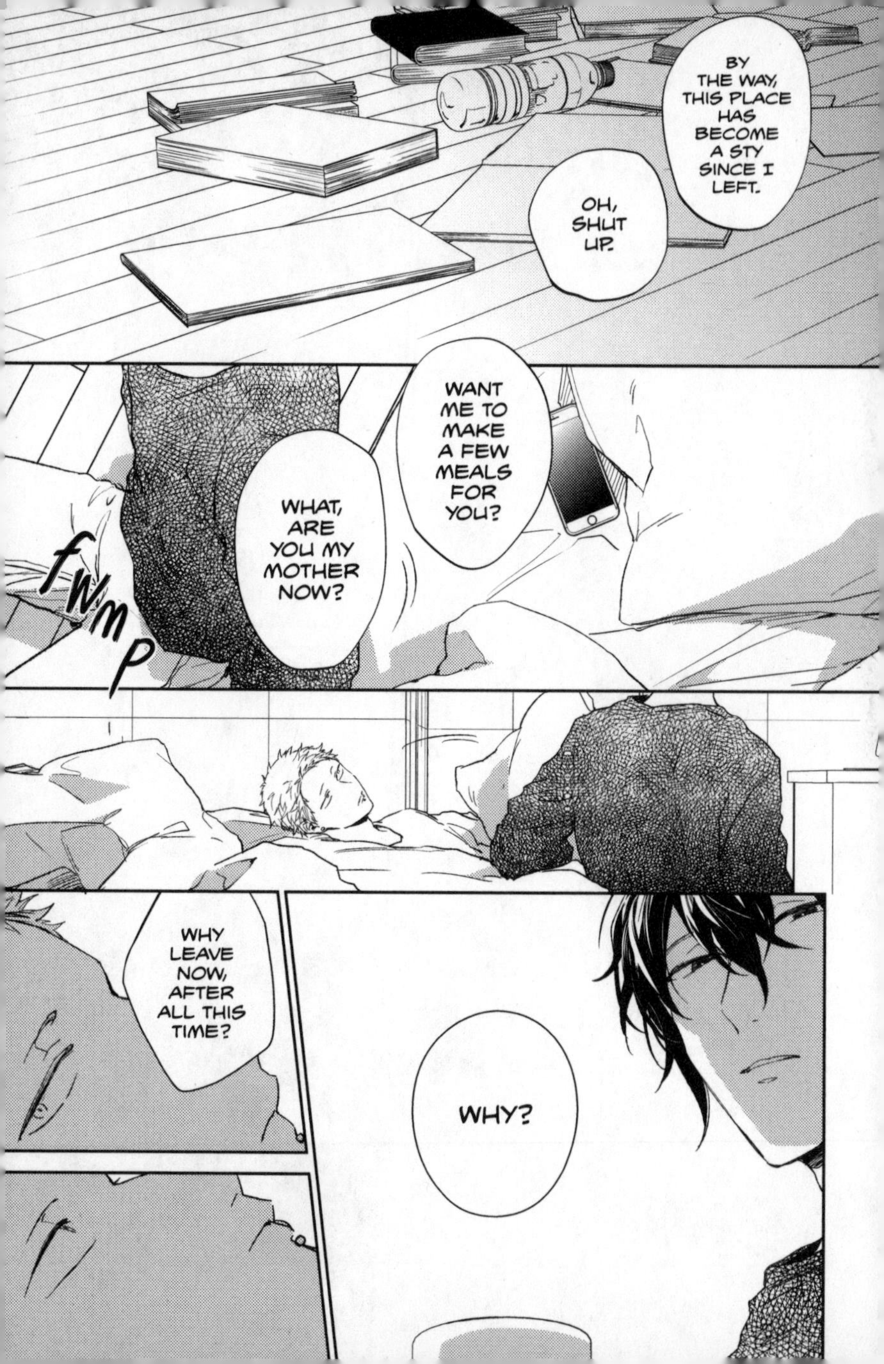
BY THE WAY, THIS PLACE HAS BECOME A STY SINCE I LEFT.
OH, SHUT UP.
WANT ME TO MAKE A FEW MEALS FOR YOU?
WHAT, ARE YOU MY MOTHER NOW?
fwmp
WHY?
WHY LEAVE NOW, AFTER ALL THIS TIME?

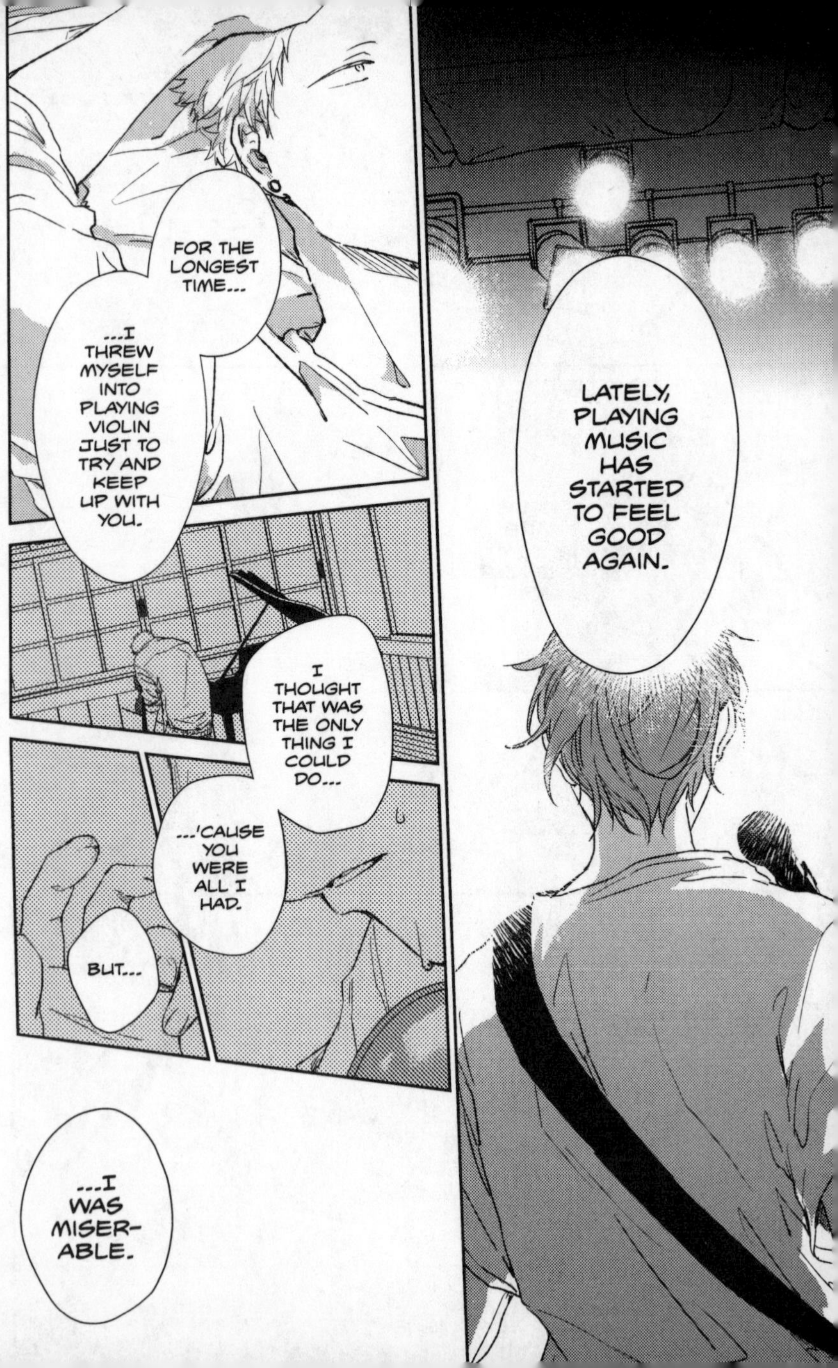
LATELY, PLAYING MUSIC HAS STARTED TO FEEL GOOD AGAIN.
FOR THE LONGEST TIME...
...I THREW MYSELF INTO PLAYING VIOLIN JUST TO TRY AND KEEP UP WITH YOU.
I THOUGHT THAT WAS THE ONLY THING I COULD DO...
...'CAUSE YOU WERE ALL I HAD.
BUT...
...I WAS MISER-ABLE.

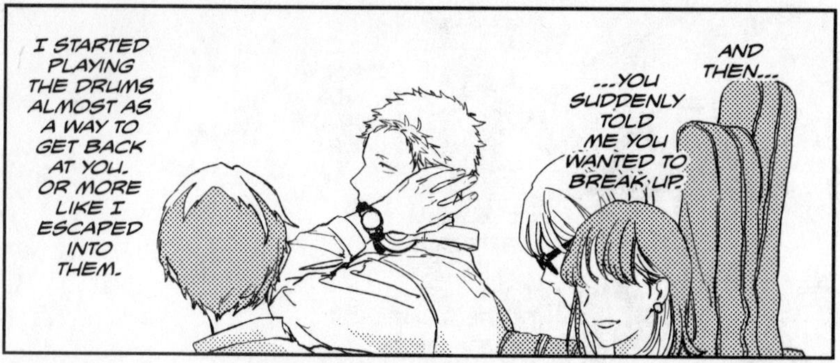
AND THEN...
...YOU SUDDENLY TOLD ME YOU WANTED TO BREAK UP.
I STARTED PLAYING THE DRUMS ALMOST AS A WAY TO GET BACK AT YOU. OR MORE LIKE I ESCAPED INTO THEM.

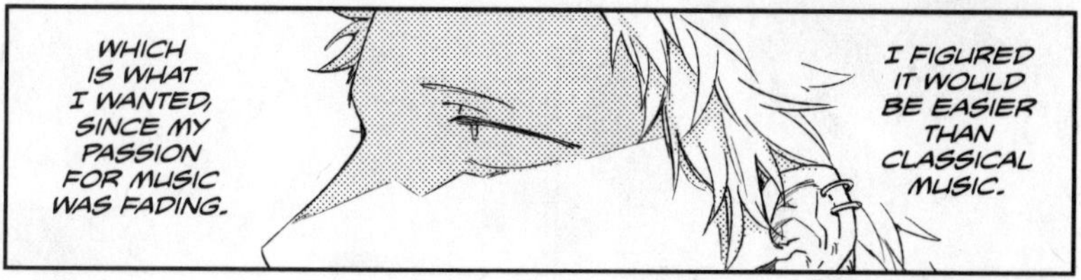
I FIGURED IT WOULD BE EASIER THAN CLASSICAL MUSIC.
WHICH IS WHAT I WANTED, SINCE MY PASSION FOR MUSIC WAS FADING.

BUT...

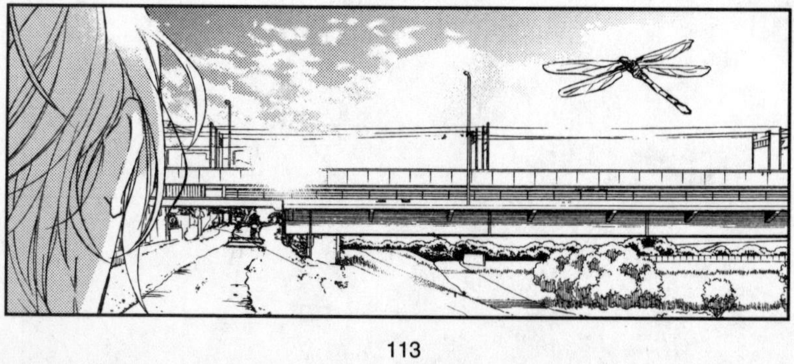

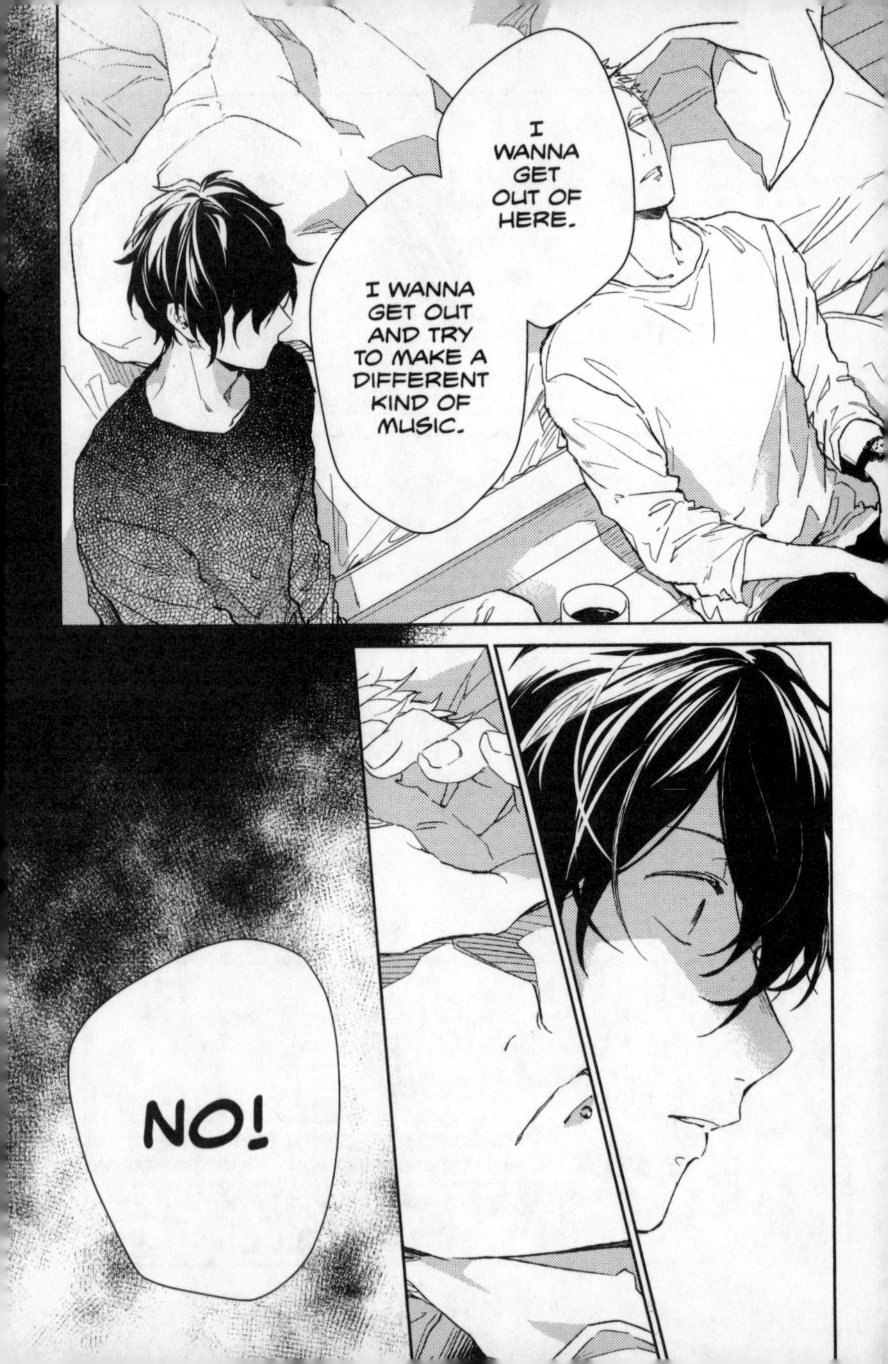
I WANNA GET OUT OF HERE.
I WANNA GET OUT AND TRY TO MAKE A DIFFERENT KIND OF MUSIC.
NO!

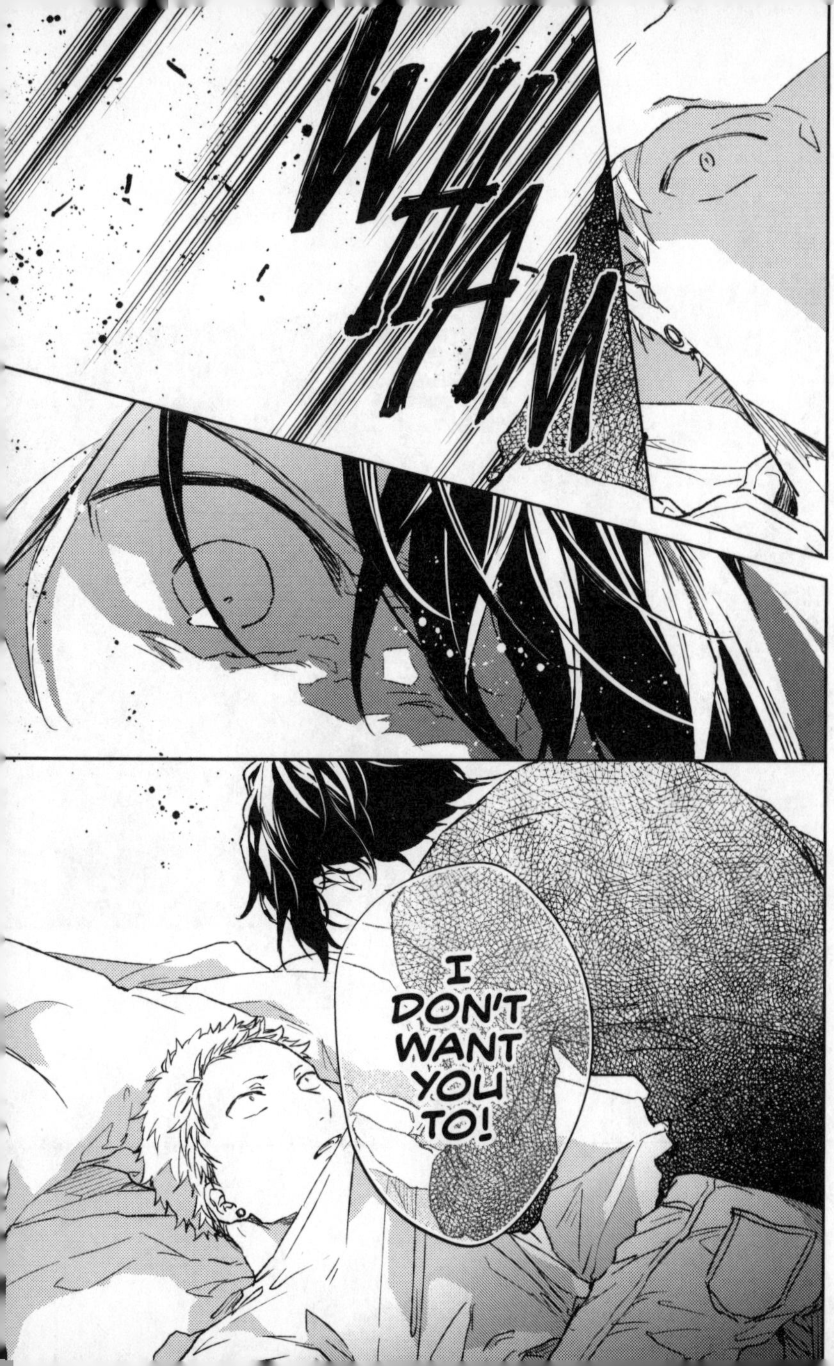
WHAM
I DON'T WANT YOU TO!

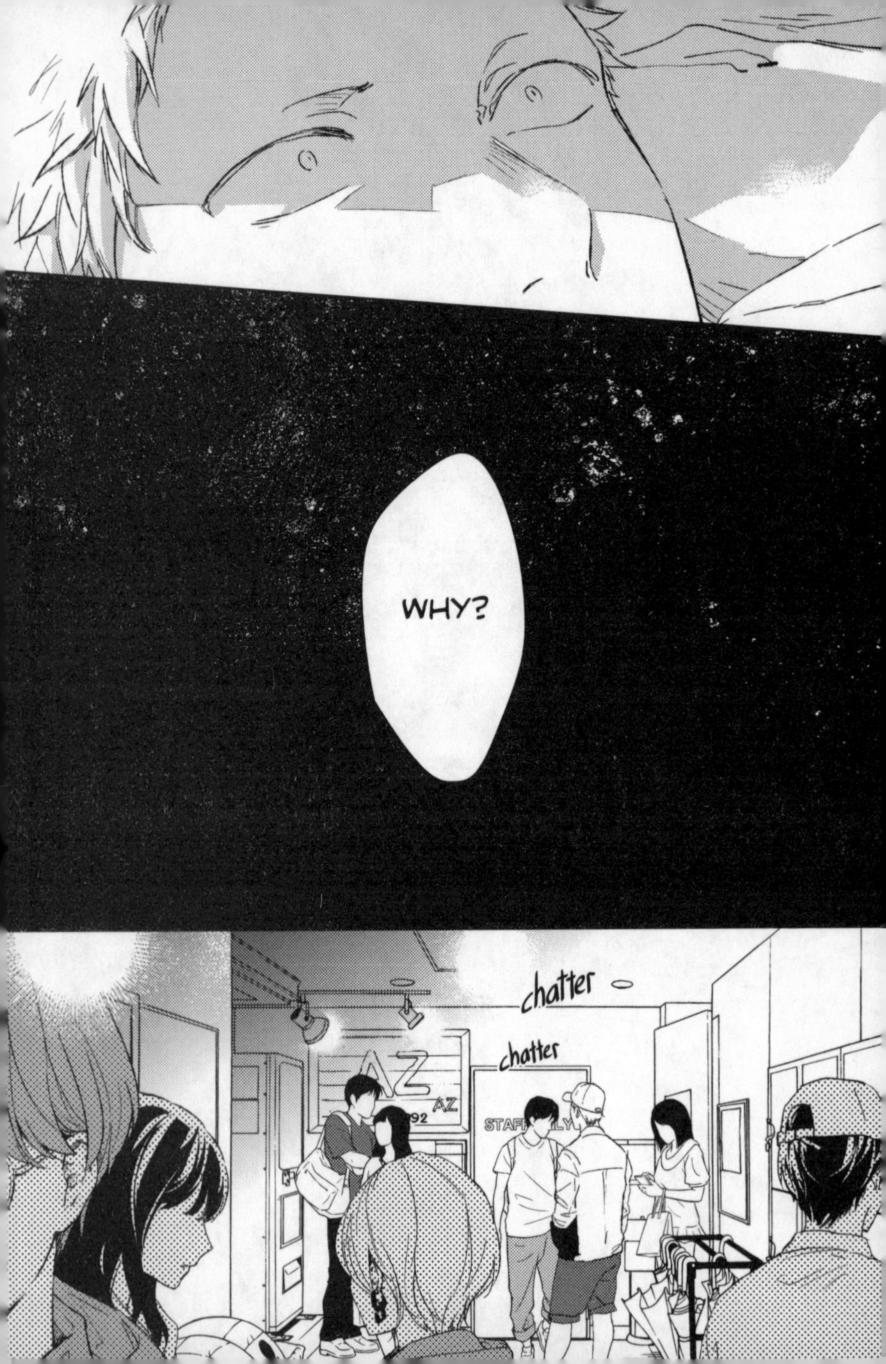
WHY?
chatter
chatter
AZ
AZ

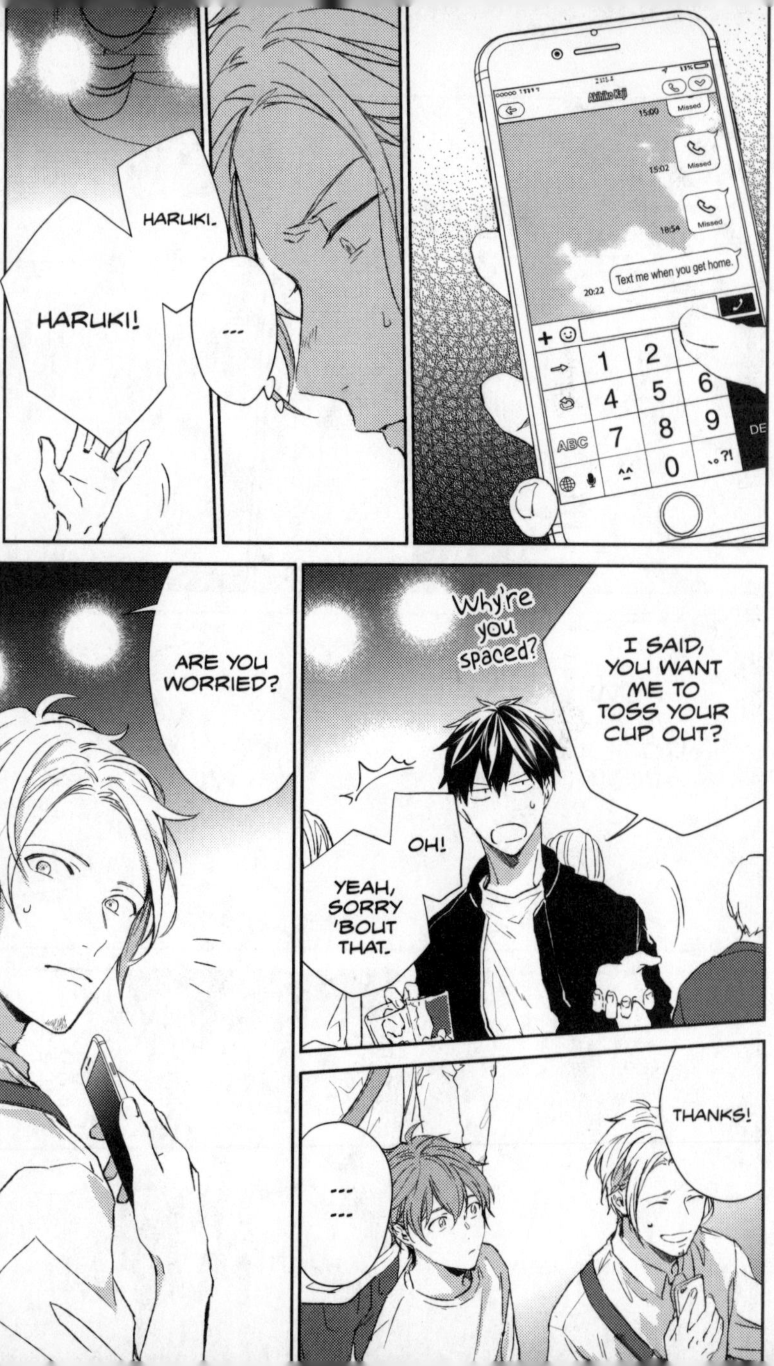

Akihiko Kaji
15:00
Missed
15:02
Missed
18:54
Missed
20:22
Text me when you get home.
...
HARUKI.
HARUKI!
Why're you spaced?
I SAID, YOU WANT ME TO TOSS YOUR CUP OUT?
OH!
YEAH, SORRY 'BOUT THAT.
THANKS!
...
...
ARE YOU WORRIED?

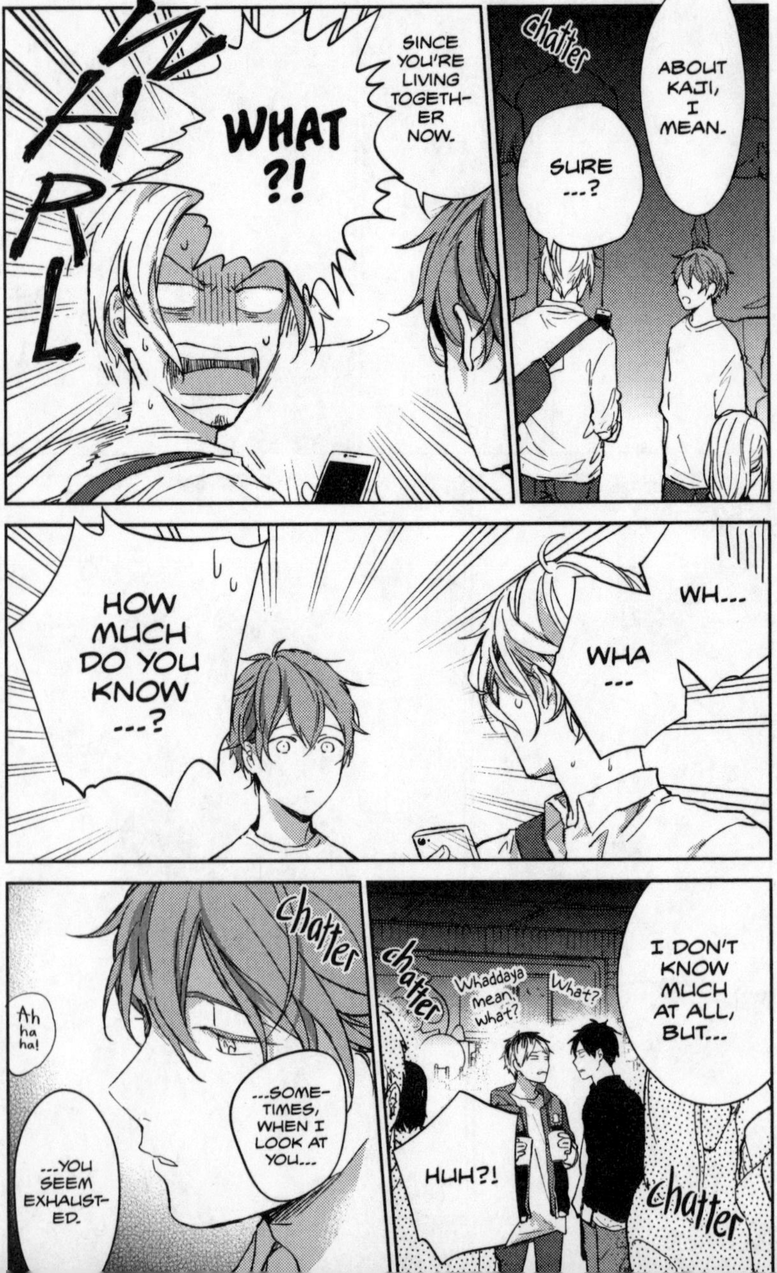
chatter
ABOUT KAJI, I MEAN.
SURE...?
SINCE YOU'RE LIVING TOGETHER NOW.
WHAT?!
WHRL
WH...
WHA...
HOW MUCH DO YOU KNOW...?
I DON'T KNOW MUCH AT ALL, BUT...
What?
Whaddaya mean, what?
chatter
chatter
HUH?!
chatter
...SOMETIMES, WHEN I LOOK AT YOU...
Ah ha ha!
...YOU SEEM EXHAUSTED.

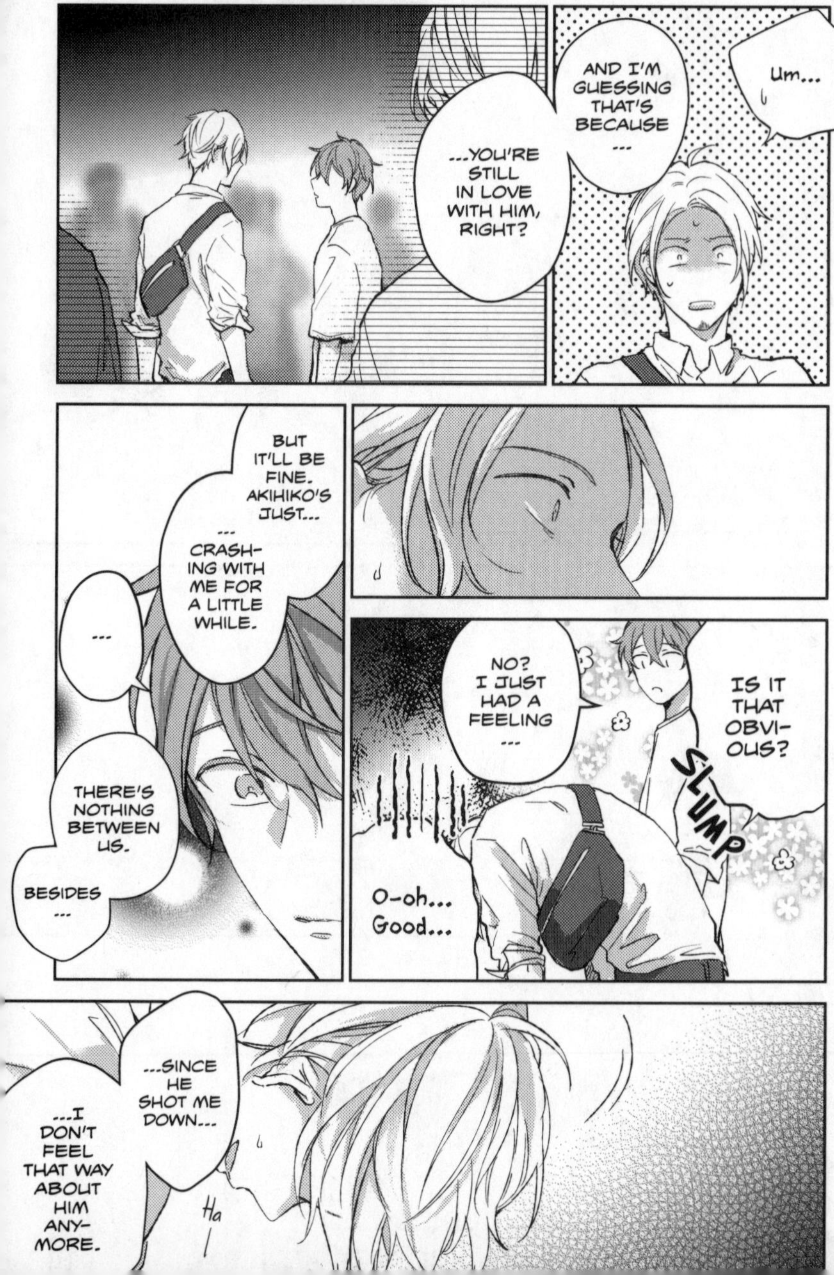
Um...
AND I'M GUESSING THAT'S BECAUSE ...
...YOU'RE STILL IN LOVE WITH HIM, RIGHT?
IS IT THAT OBVIOUS?
NO? I JUST HAD A FEELING ...
SLUMP
O-oh... Good...
BUT IT'LL BE FINE. AKIHIKO'S JUST... ... CRASHING WITH ME FOR A LITTLE WHILE.
...
THERE'S NOTHING BETWEEN US.
BESIDES ...
...SINCE HE SHOT ME DOWN...
...I DON'T FEEL THAT WAY ABOUT HIM ANYMORE.
Ha

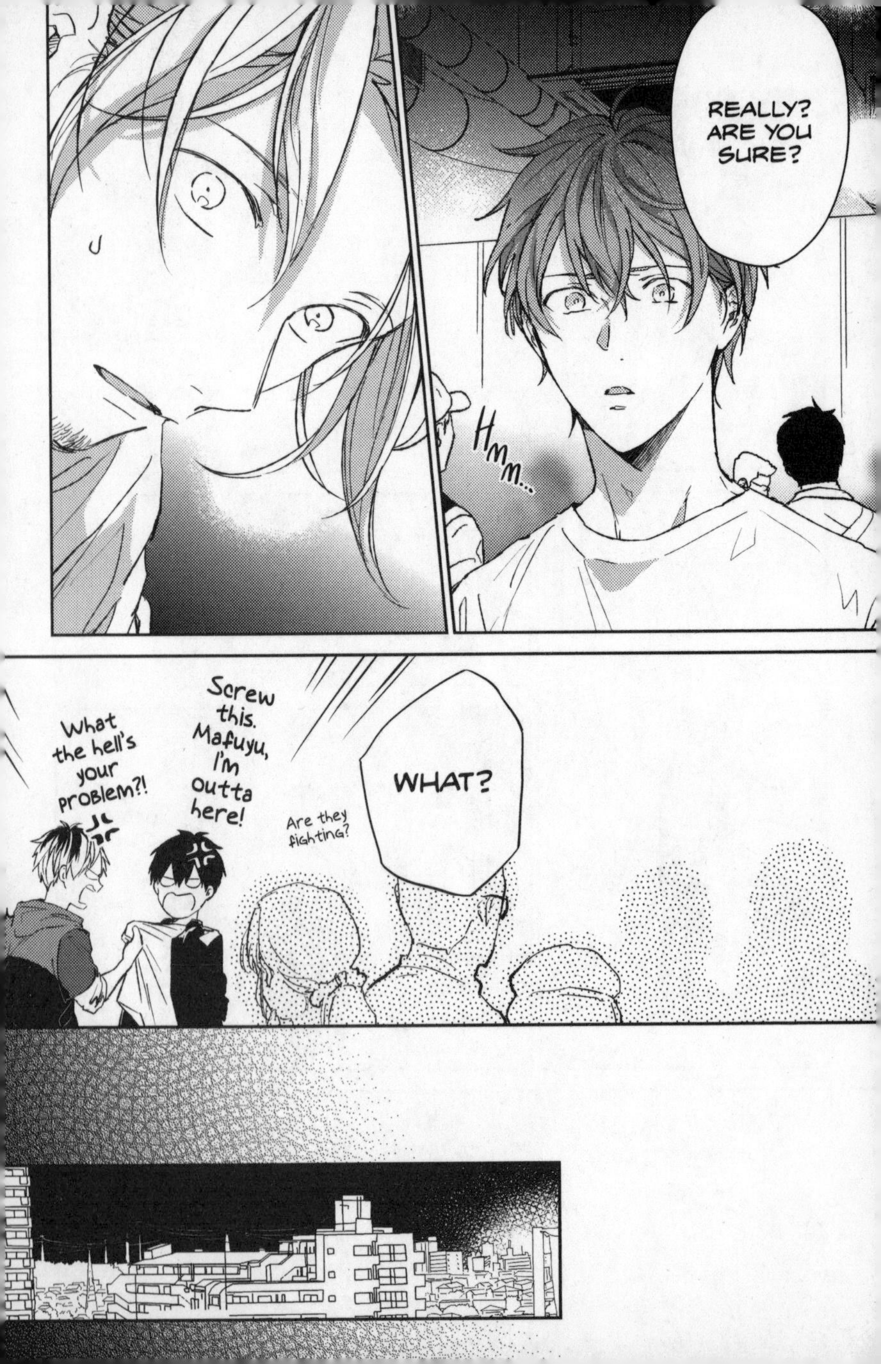
REALLY? ARE YOU SURE?
Hmm...
WHAT?
Are they fighting?
Screw this. Mafuyu, I'm outta here!
What the hell's your problem?!

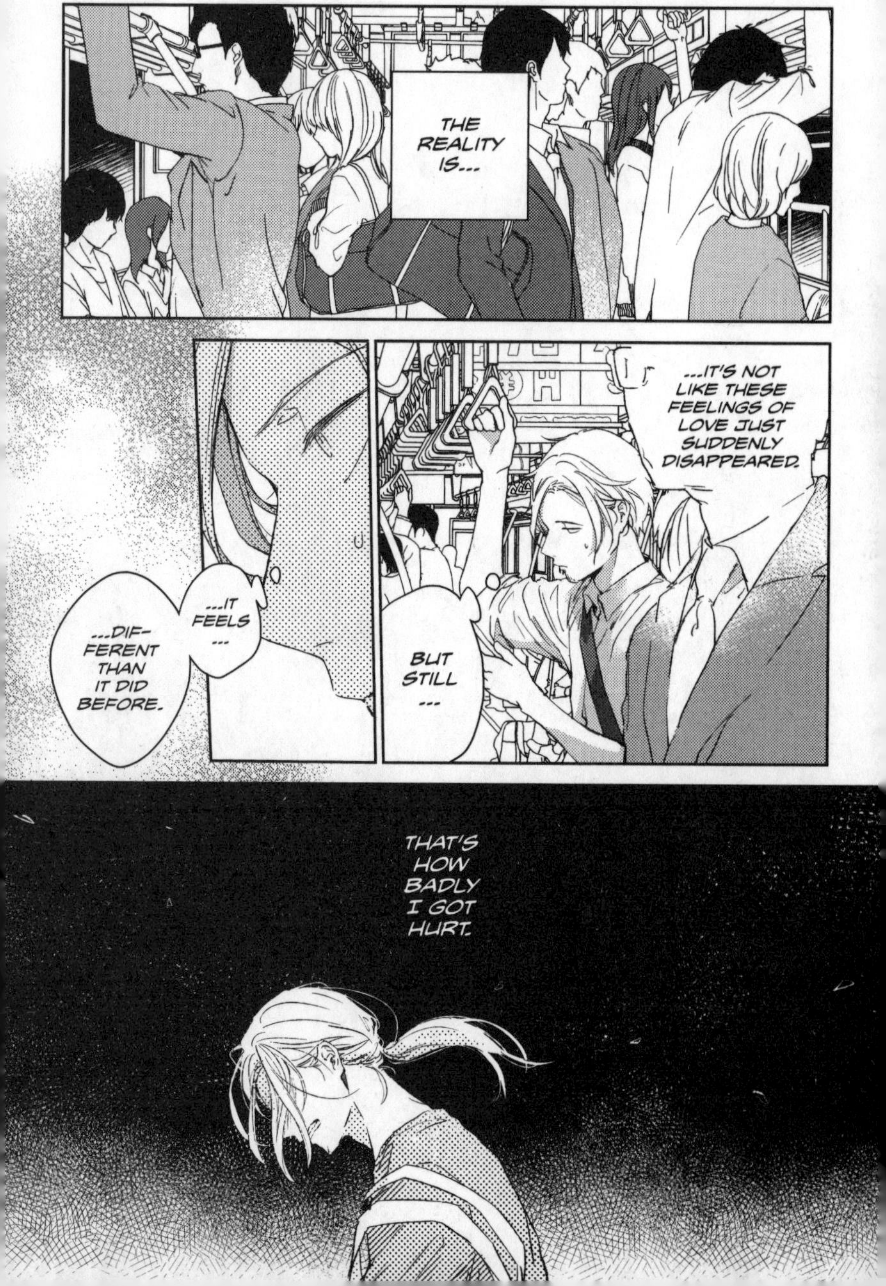
THE REALITY IS...
...IT'S NOT LIKE THESE FEELINGS OF LOVE JUST SUDDENLY DISAPPEARED.
BUT STILL ...
...IT FEELS ...
...DIF-FERENT THAN IT DID BEFORE.
THAT'S HOW BADLY I GOT HURT.

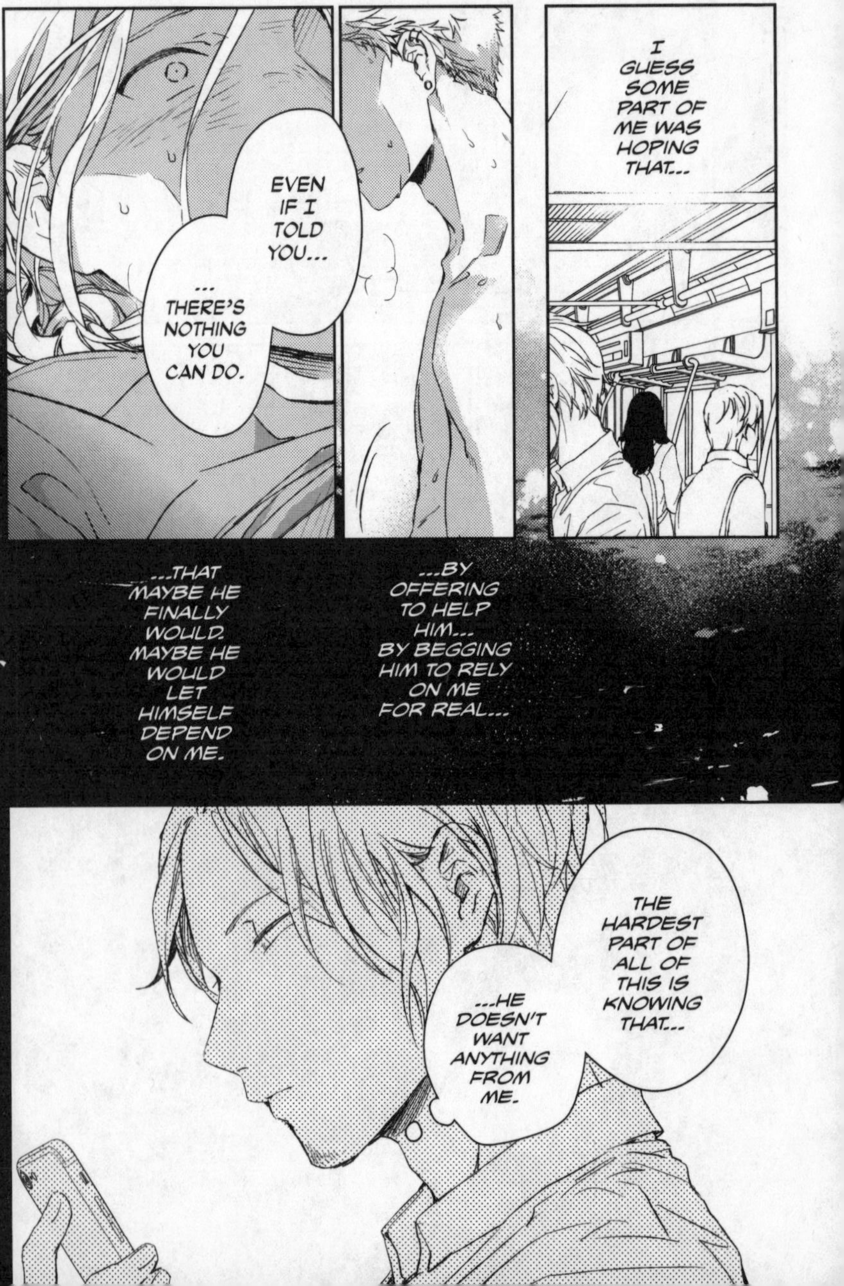
I GUESS SOME PART OF ME WAS HOPING THAT...
EVEN IF I TOLD YOU...
... THERE'S NOTHING YOU CAN DO.
...BY OFFERING TO HELP HIM... BY BEGGING HIM TO RELY ON ME FOR REAL...
...THAT MAYBE HE FINALLY WOULD. MAYBE HE WOULD LET HIMSELF DEPEND ON ME.
THE HARDEST PART OF ALL OF THIS IS KNOWING THAT...
...HE DOESN'T WANT ANYTHING FROM ME.

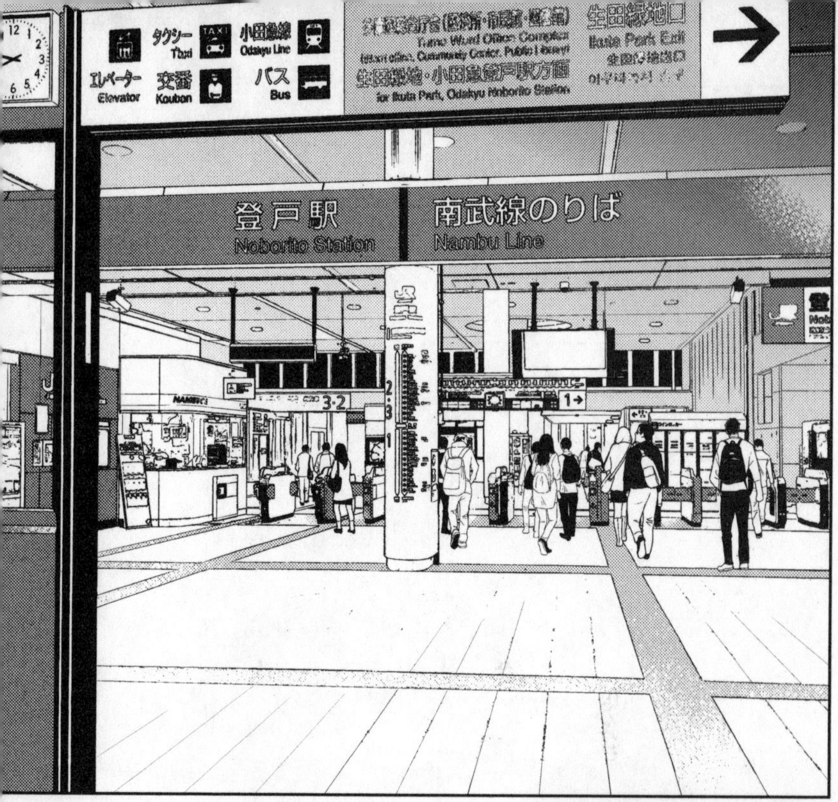
タクシー Taxi
小田急線 Odakyu Line
エレベーター Elevator
交番 Kouban
バス Bus
生田緑地・小田急登戸駅方面
for Ikuta Park, Odakyu Noborito Station
生田緑地口
Ikuta Park Exit
登戸駅
Noborito Station
南武線のりば
Nambu Line

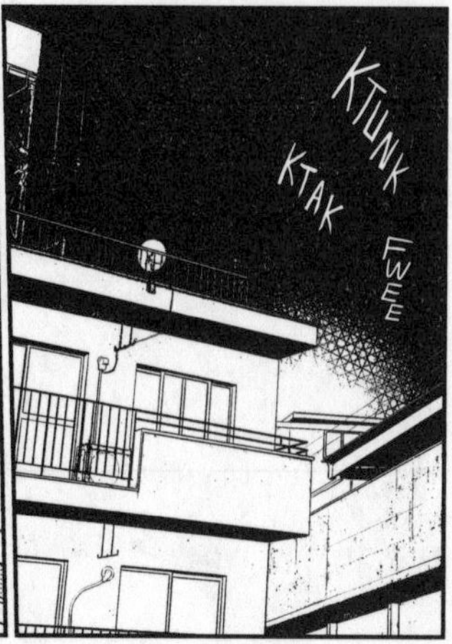
KTUNK
KTAK
FWEE

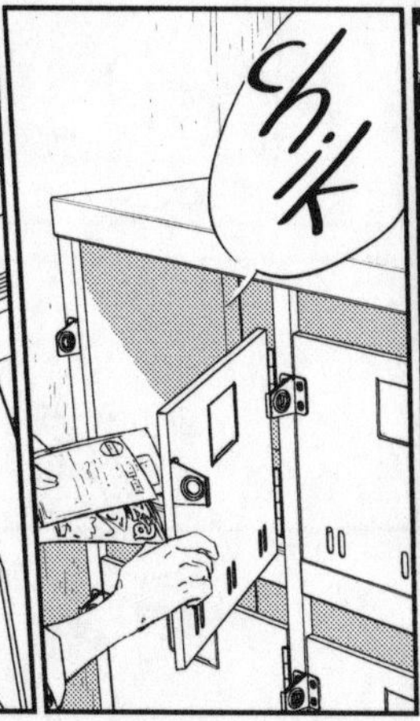
chik

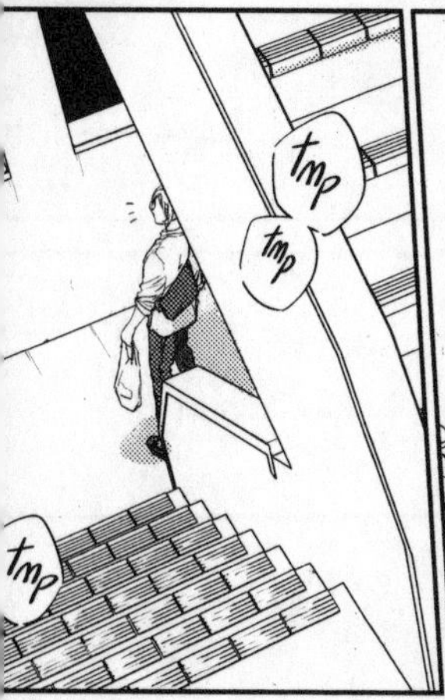
tmp
tmp
tmp

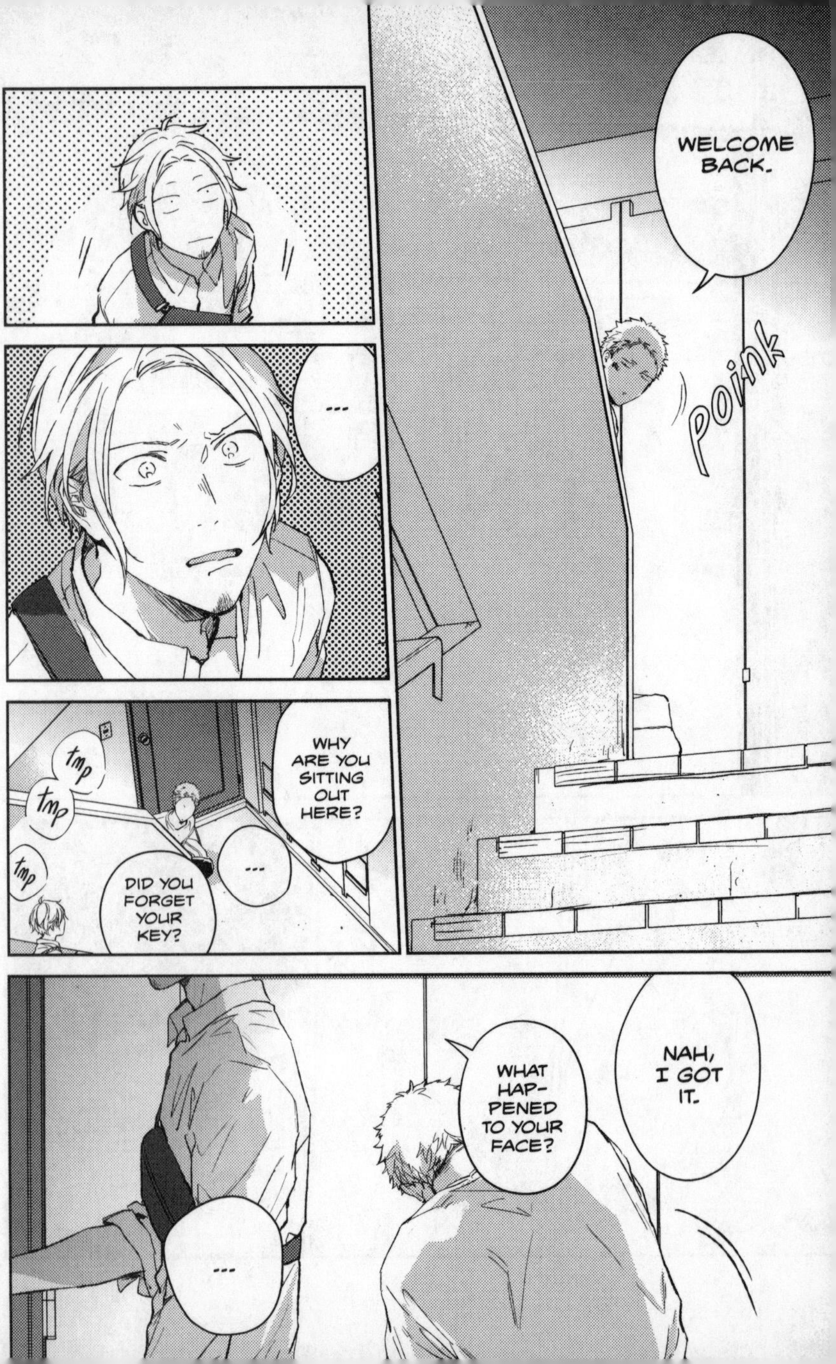

WELCOME BACK.
poink
...
tmp
tmp
tmp
WHY ARE YOU SITTING OUT HERE?
...
DID YOU FORGET YOUR KEY?
NAH, I GOT IT.
WHAT HAP-PENED TO YOUR FACE?
...

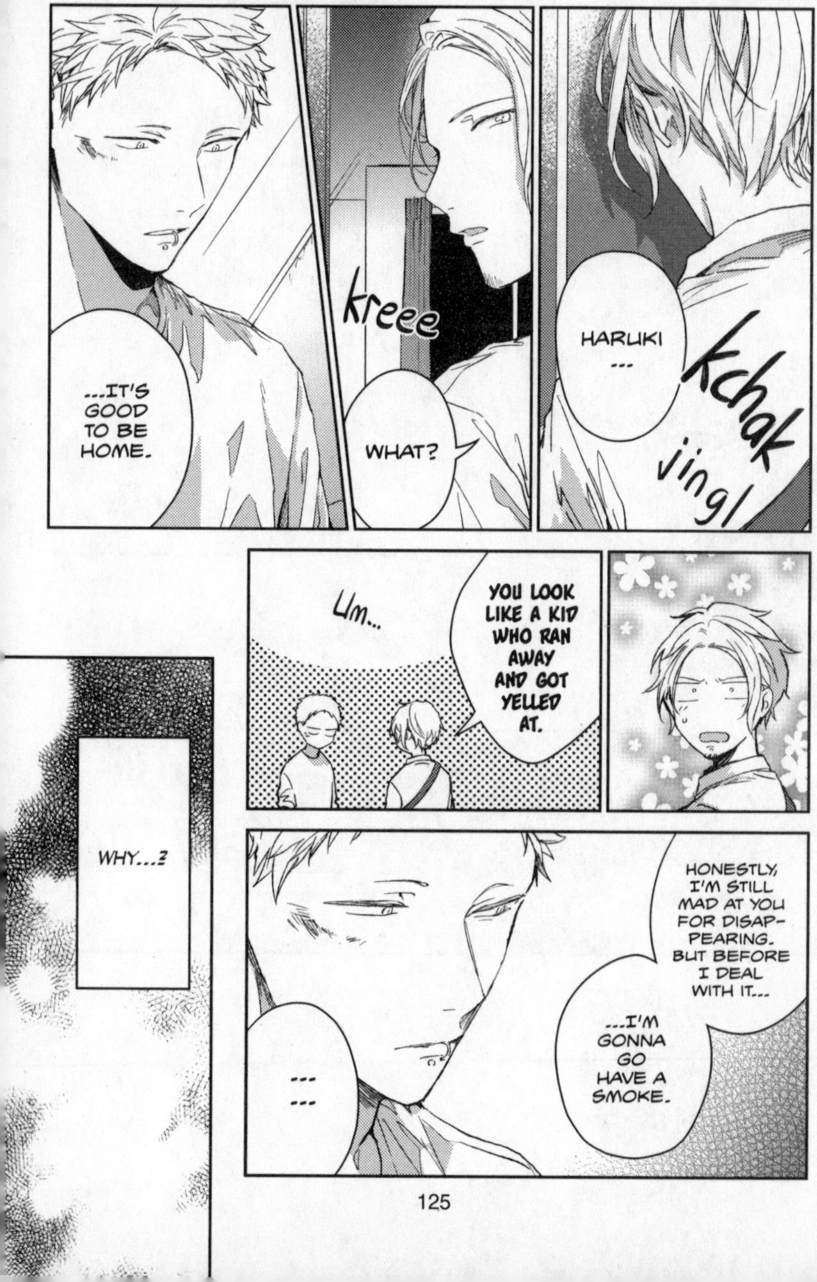
HARUKI ...
kchak
jingl
kreee
WHAT?
...IT'S GOOD TO BE HOME.
YOU LOOK LIKE A KID WHO RAN AWAY AND GOT YELLED AT.
Um...
HONESTLY, I'M STILL MAD AT YOU FOR DISAP-PEARING. BUT BEFORE I DEAL WITH IT...
...I'M GONNA GO HAVE A SMOKE.
... ...
WHY...?

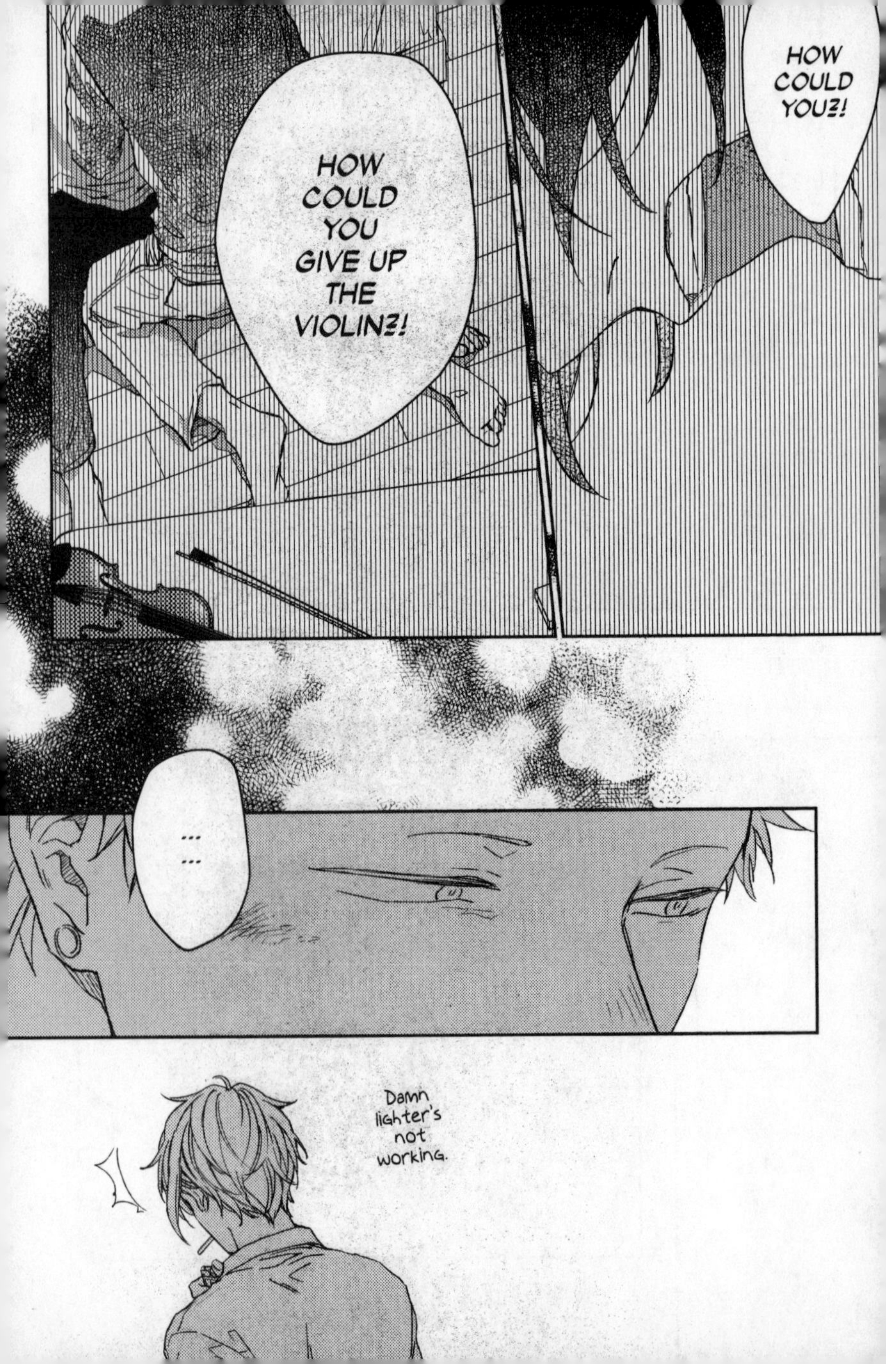
HOW COULD YOU?!
HOW COULD YOU GIVE UP THE VIOLIN?!
...
...
Damn lighter's not working.

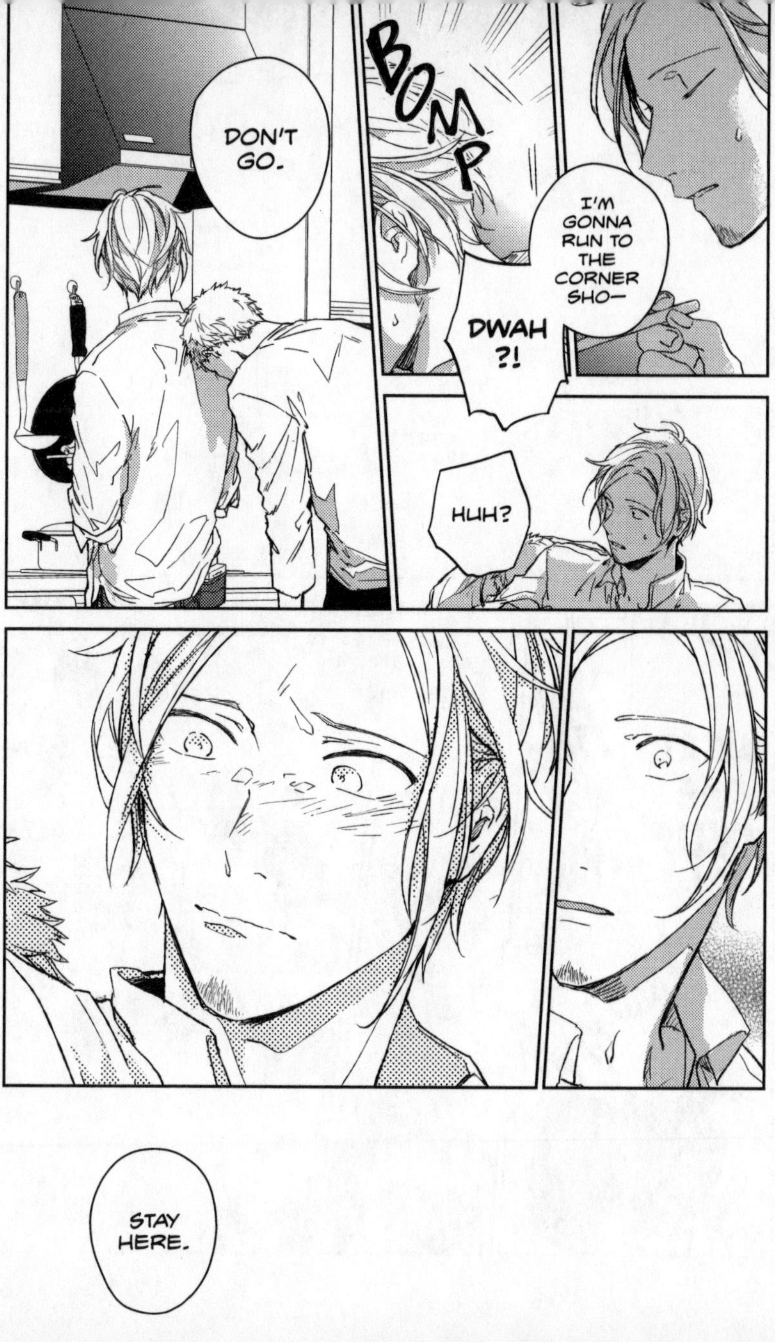
I'M GONNA RUN TO THE CORNER SHO—
BOMP
DWAH?!
HUH?
DON'T GO.
STAY HERE.

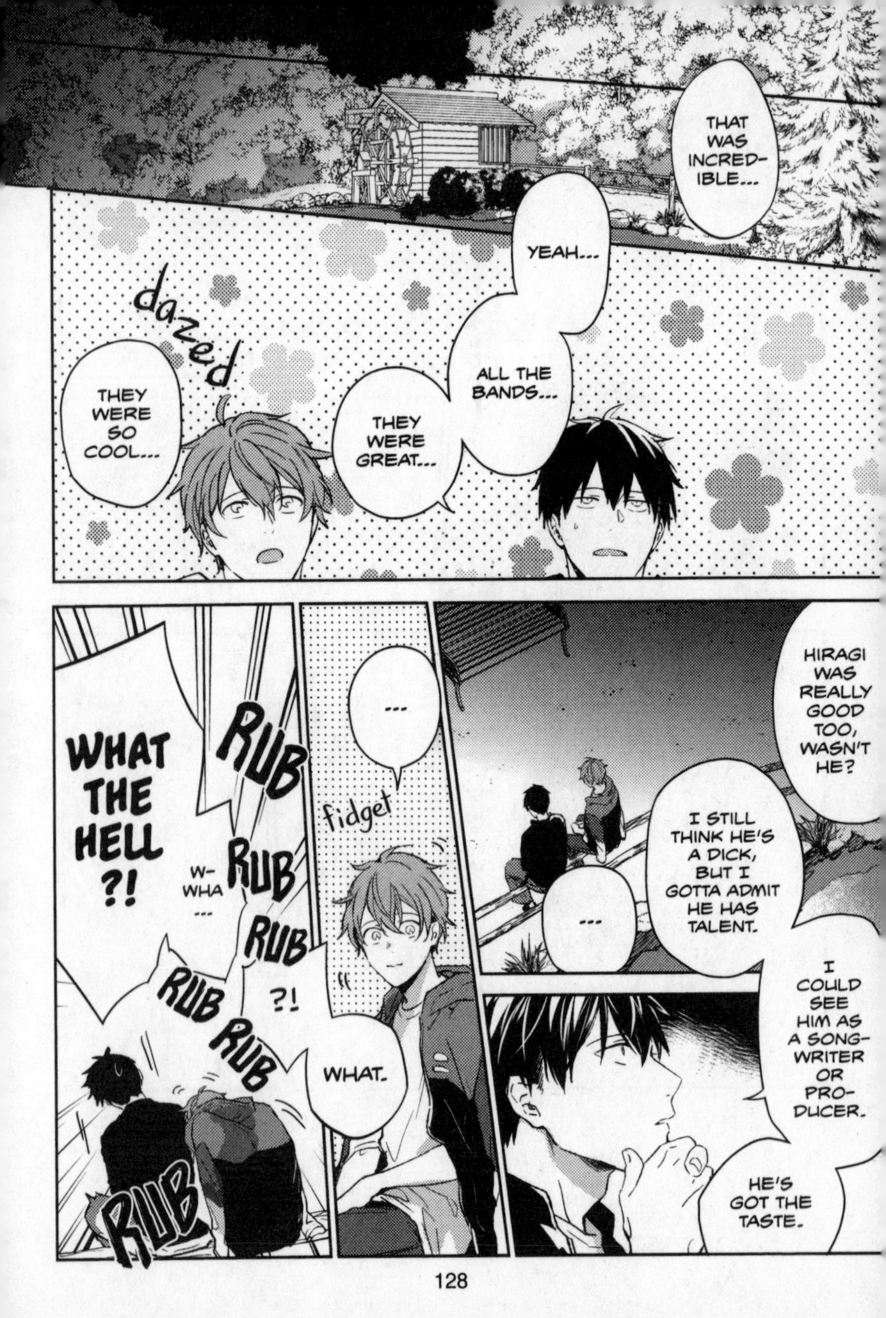
THAT WAS INCREDIBLE...
YEAH...
ALL THE BANDS...
THEY WERE GREAT...
dazed
THEY WERE SO COOL...
HIRAGI WAS REALLY GOOD TOO, WASN'T HE?
I STILL THINK HE'S A DICK, BUT I GOTTA ADMIT HE HAS TALENT.
...
I COULD SEE HIM AS A SONGWRITER OR PRODUCER.
HE'S GOT THE TASTE.
...
fidget
WHAT.
RUB
RUB
RUB
W-WHA...
?!
WHAT THE HELL?!
RUB
RUB
RUB

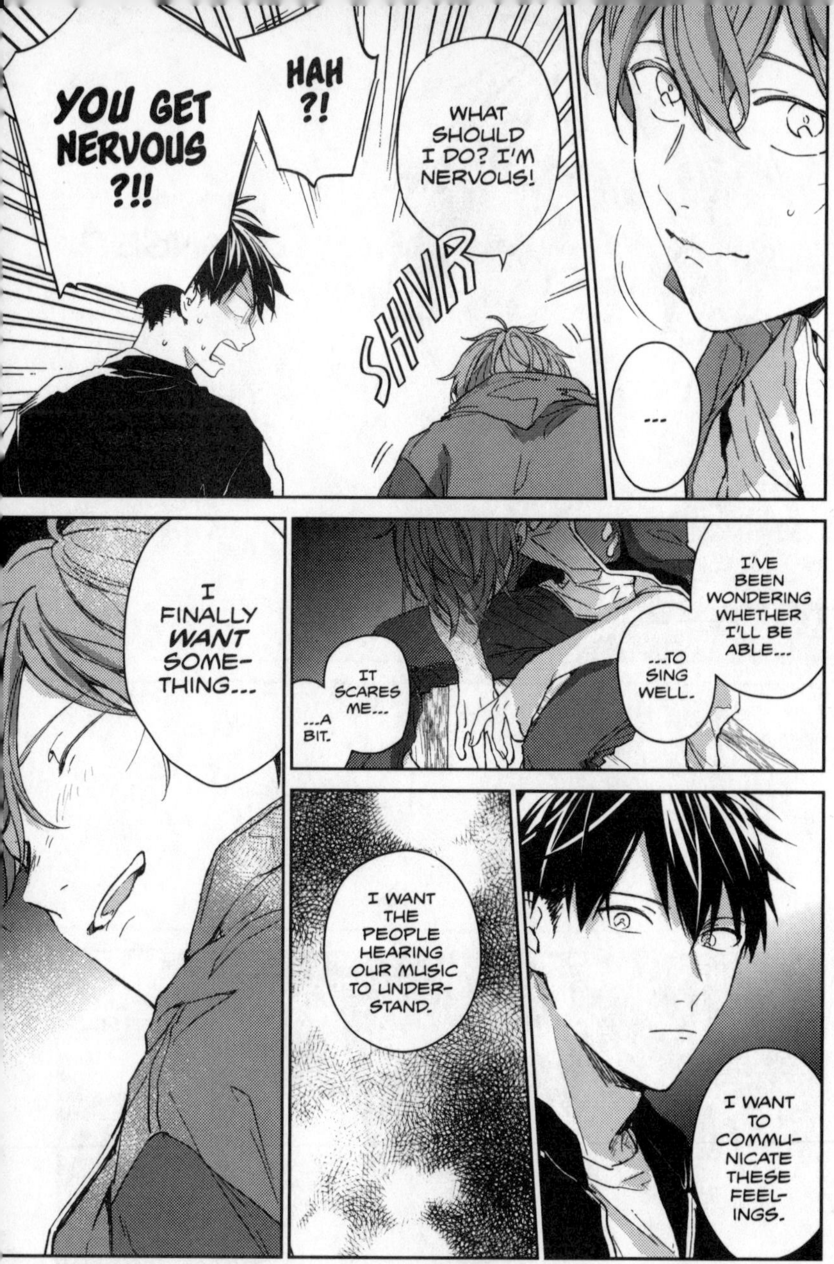
...
WHAT SHOULD I DO? I'M NERVOUS!
SHIVR
HAH ?!
YOU GET NERVOUS ?!!
I'VE BEEN WONDERING WHETHER I'LL BE ABLE...
...TO SING WELL.
IT SCARES ME...
...A BIT.
I WANT TO COMMUNICATE THESE FEELINGS.
I WANT THE PEOPLE HEARING OUR MUSIC TO UNDERSTAND.
I FINALLY *WANT* SOMETHING...

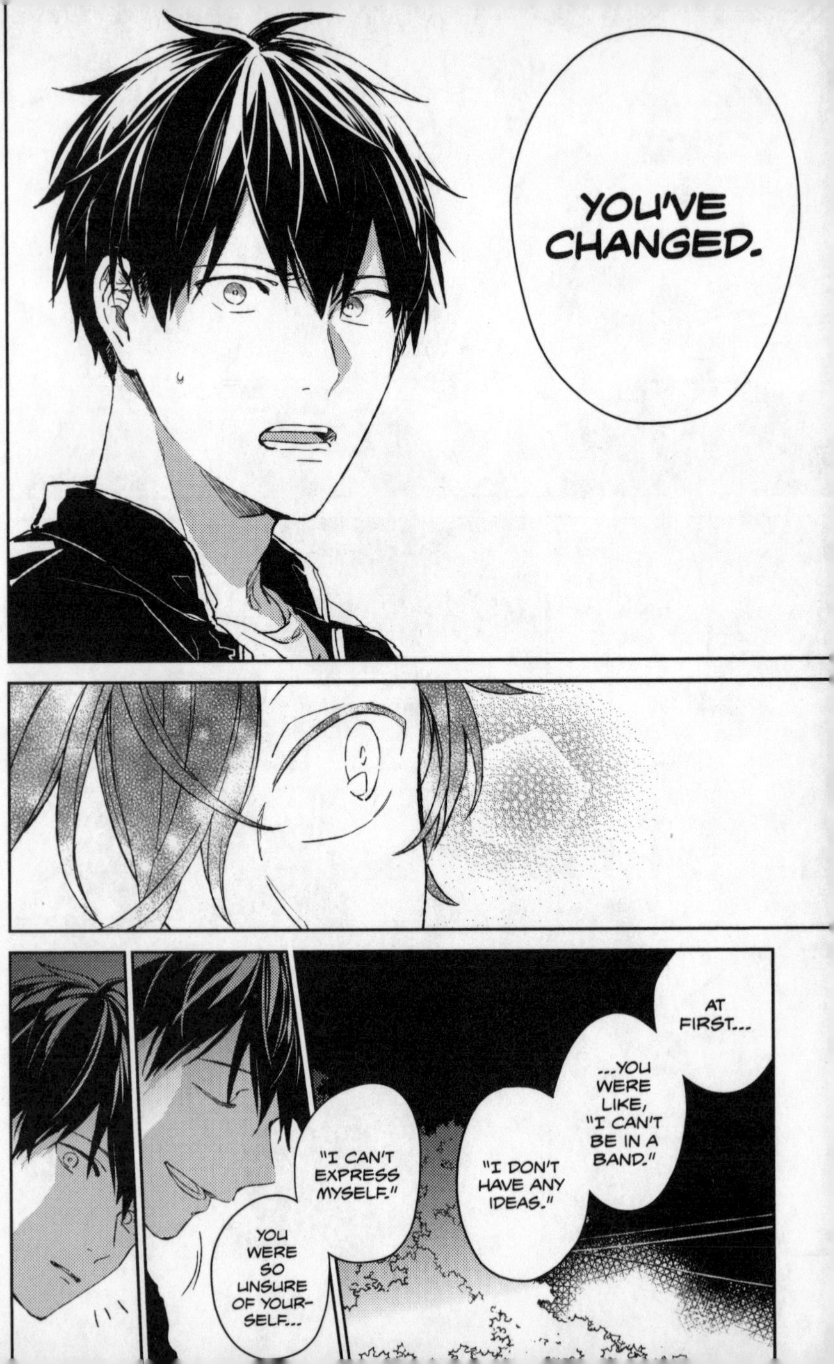
YOU'VE CHANGED.
AT FIRST...
...YOU WERE LIKE, "I CAN'T BE IN A BAND."
"I DON'T HAVE ANY IDEAS."
"I CAN'T EXPRESS MYSELF."
YOU WERE SO UNSURE OF YOURSELF...

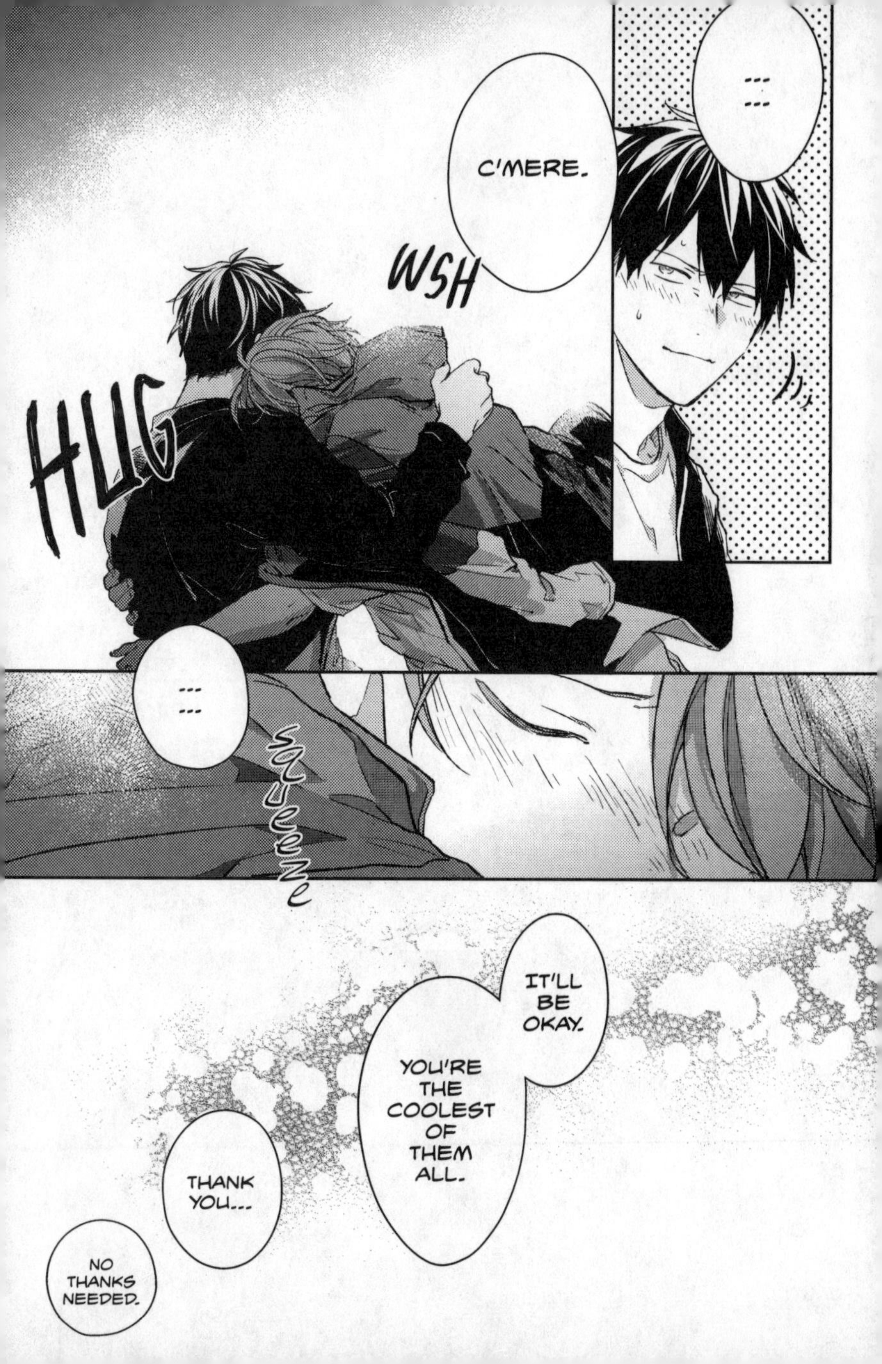
...
C'MERE.
WSH
HUG
...
SQUEEZE
IT'LL BE OKAY.
YOU'RE THE COOLEST OF THEM ALL.
THANK YOU...
NO THANKS NEEDED.

given

by Natsuki Kizu

chapter 27 | given

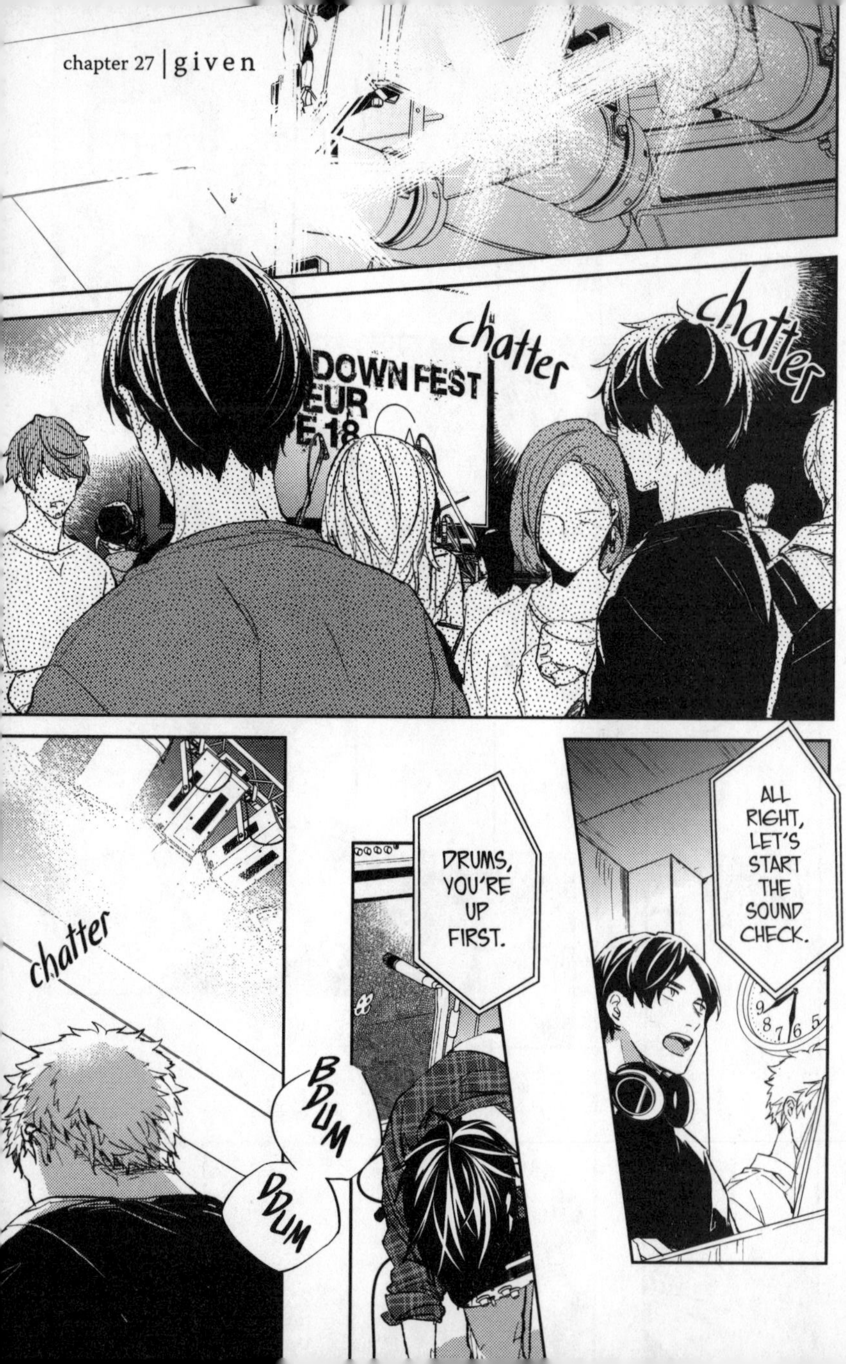
chatter
chatter
DOWN FEST
EUR
E 18
ALL RIGHT, LET'S START THE SOUND CHECK.
DRUMS, YOU'RE UP FIRST.
BDUM
DDUM
chatter

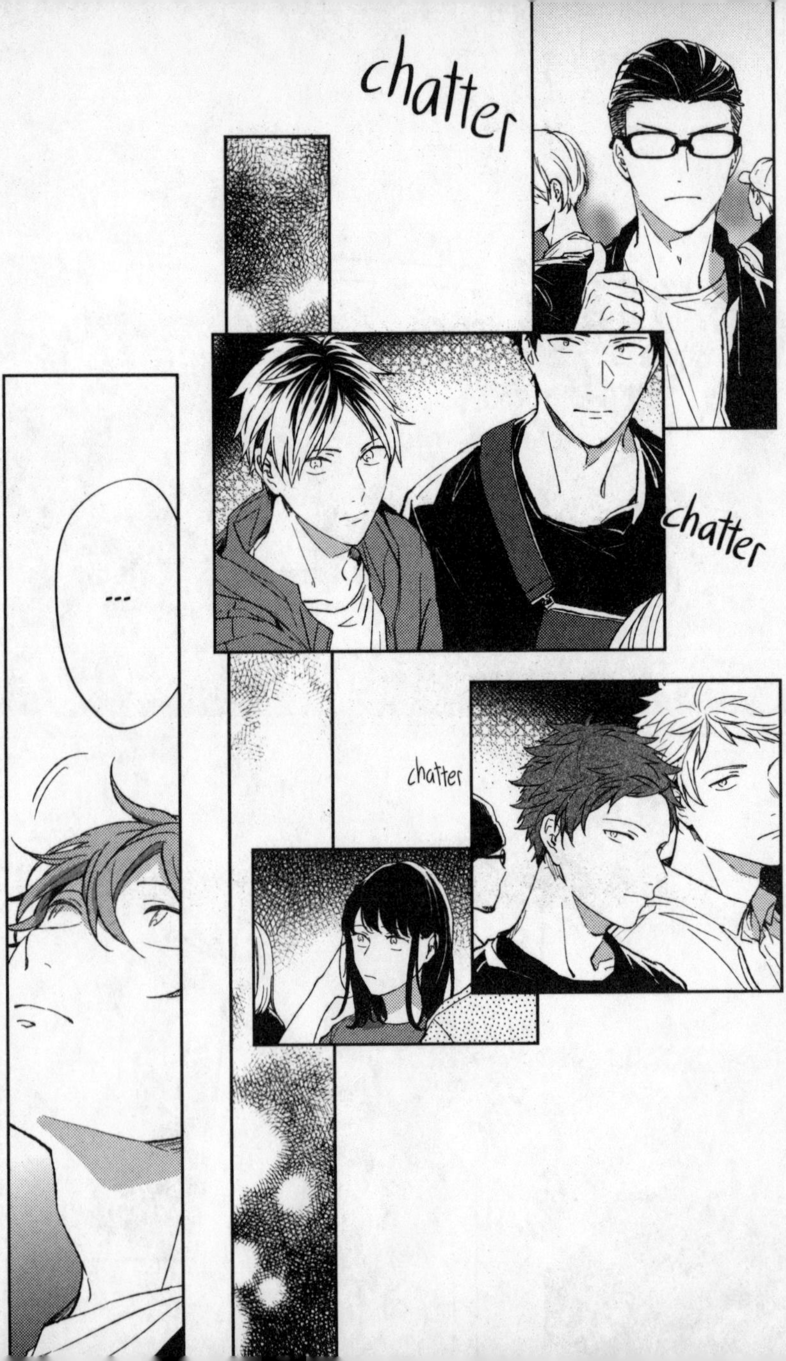
chatter
chatter
chatter
...

chapter 27
given

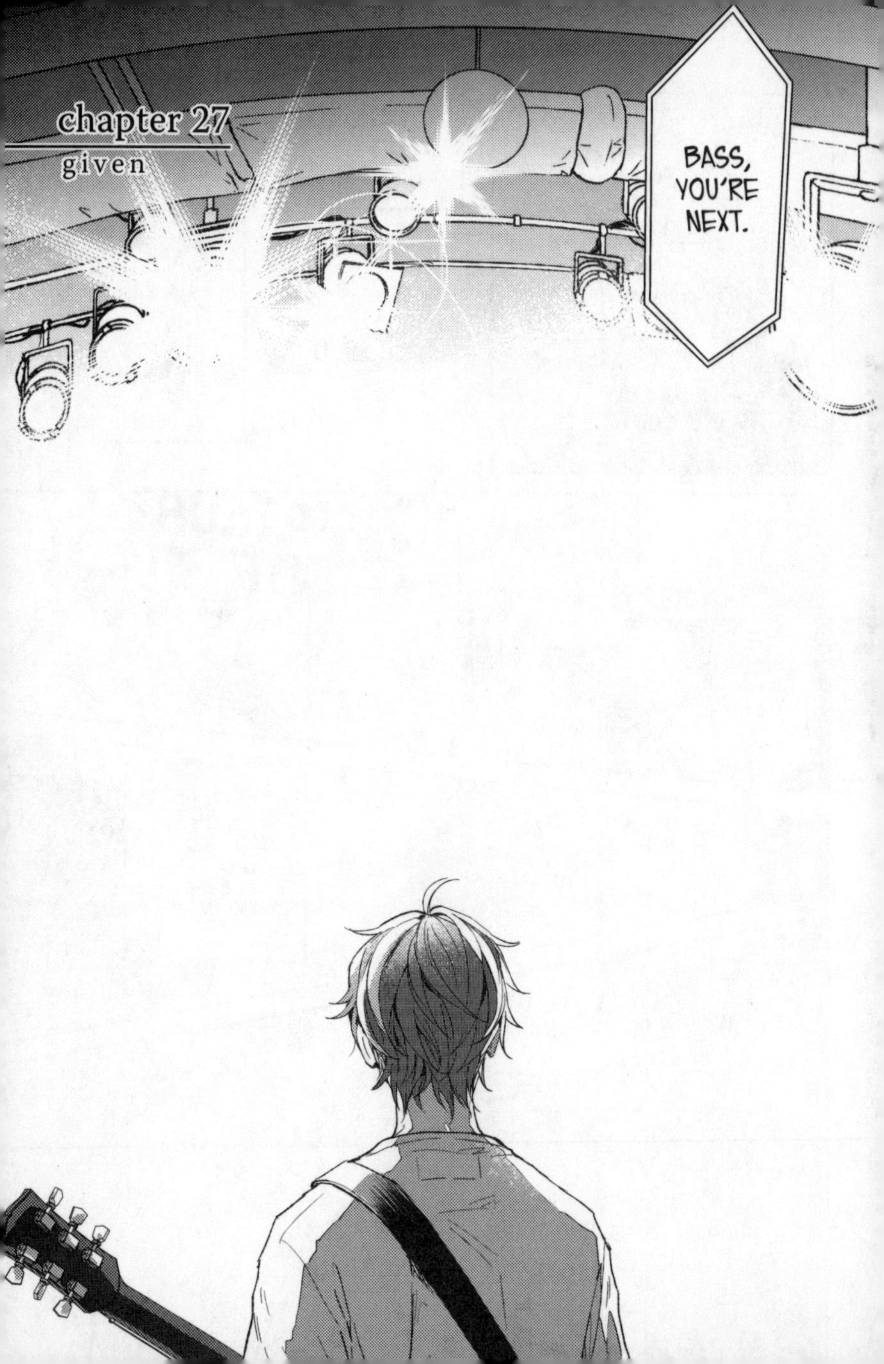
BASS, YOU'RE NEXT.

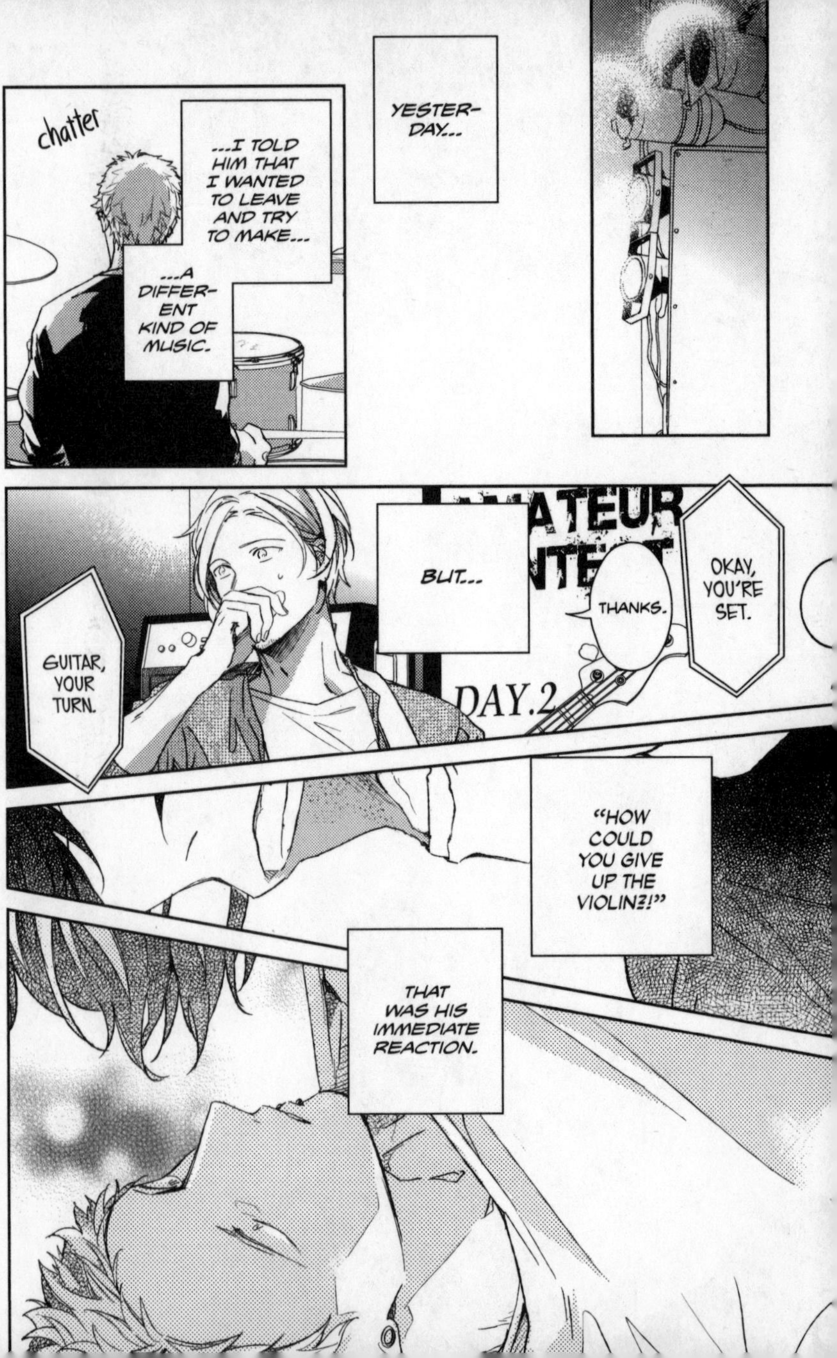
YESTER-DAY...
...I TOLD HIM THAT I WANTED TO LEAVE AND TRY TO MAKE...
...A DIFFERENT KIND OF MUSIC.
chatter
OKAY, YOU'RE SET.
THANKS.
DAY.2
BUT...
GUITAR, YOUR TURN.
"HOW COULD YOU GIVE UP THE VIOLIN?!"
THAT WAS HIS IMMEDIATE REACTION.

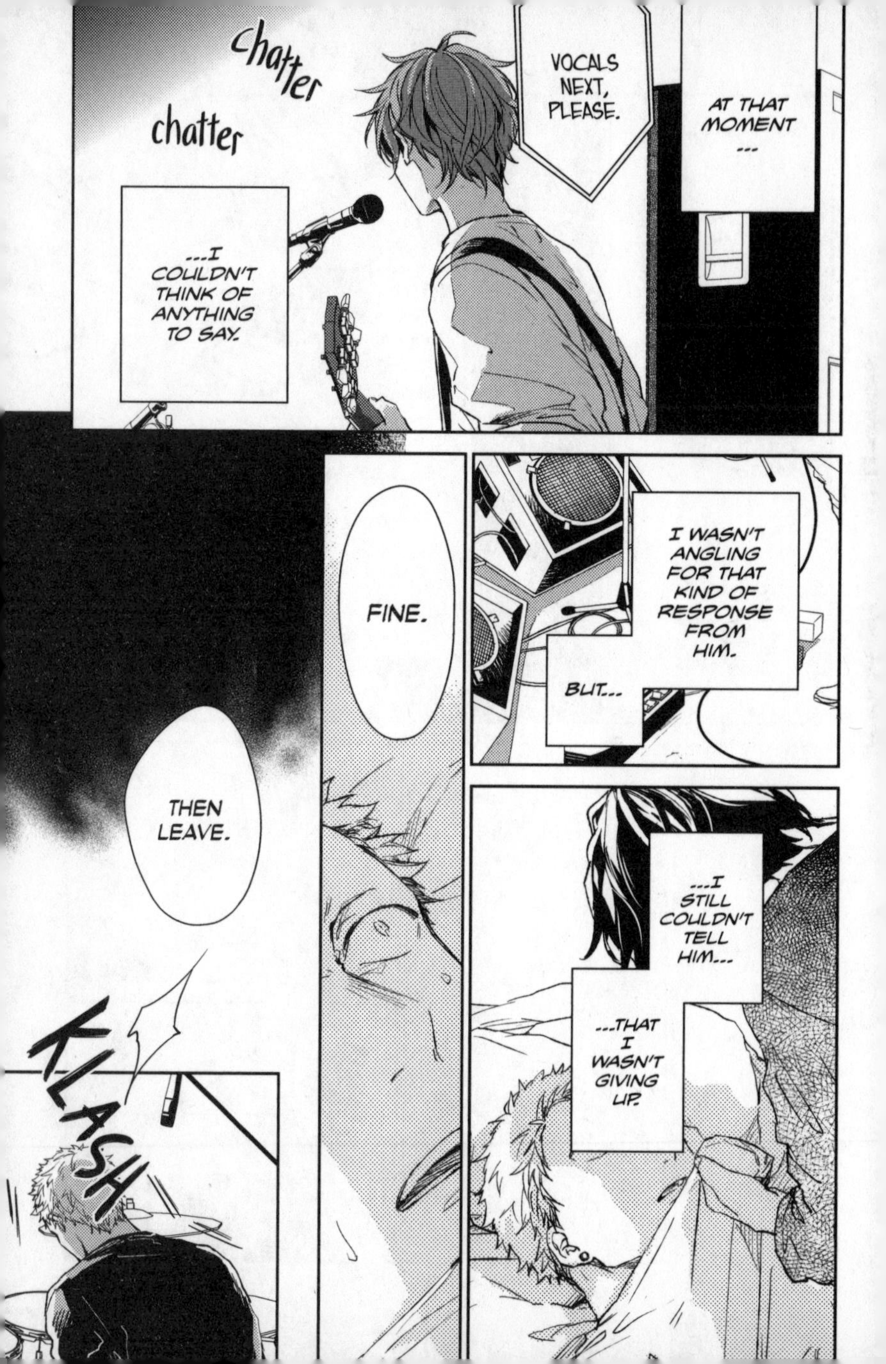
AT THAT MOMENT ---
VOCALS NEXT, PLEASE.
chatter
chatter
---I COULDN'T THINK OF ANYTHING TO SAY.
I WASN'T ANGLING FOR THAT KIND OF RESPONSE FROM HIM.
BUT---
---I STILL COULDN'T TELL HIM---
---THAT I WASN'T GIVING UP.
FINE.
THEN LEAVE.
KLASH

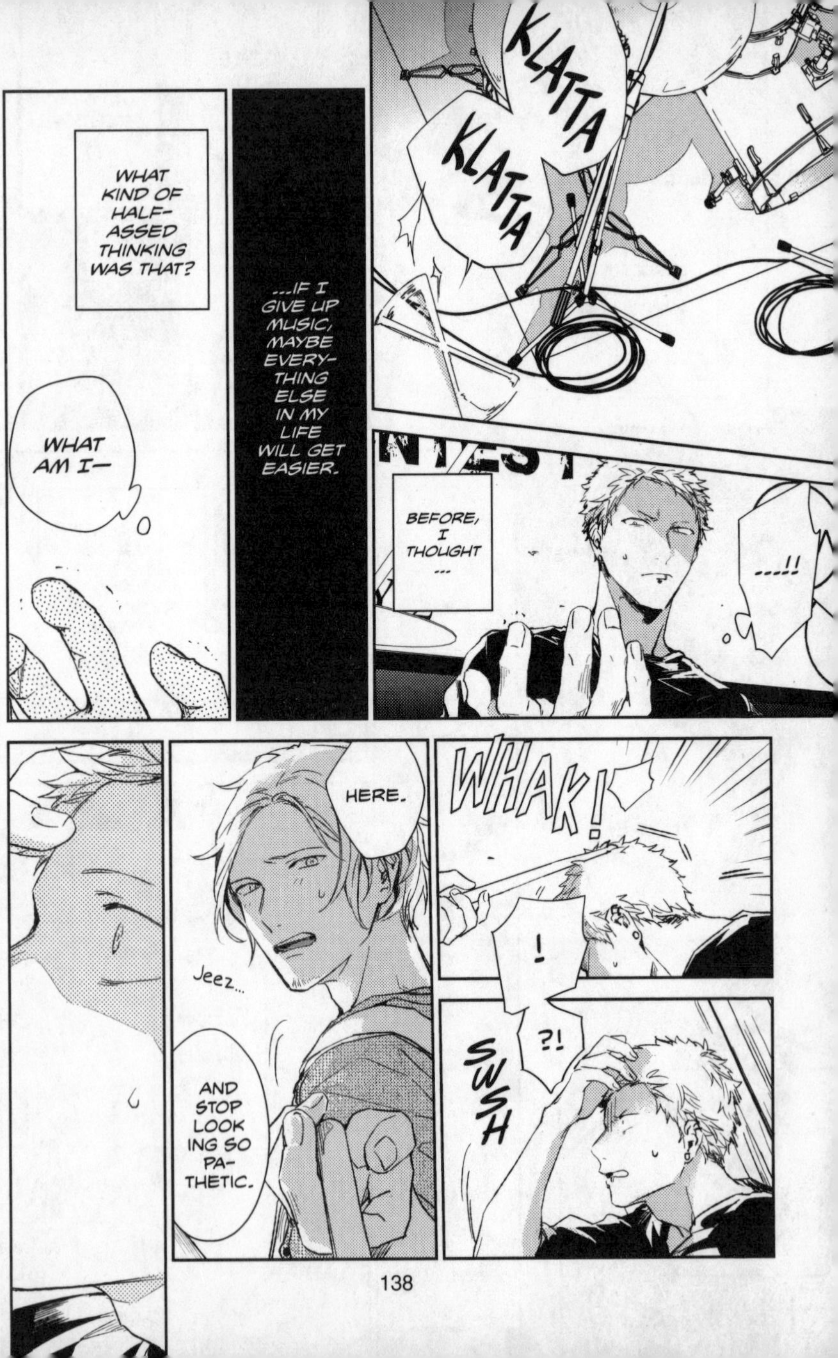
KLATTA
KLATTA
KLATTA
...!!
BEFORE, I THOUGHT...
...IF I GIVE UP MUSIC, MAYBE EVERYTHING ELSE IN MY LIFE WILL GET EASIER.
WHAT KIND OF HALF-ASSED THINKING WAS THAT?
WHAT AM I—
WHAK!
!
?!
SWSH
HERE.
Jeez...
AND STOP LOOKING SO PATHETIC.

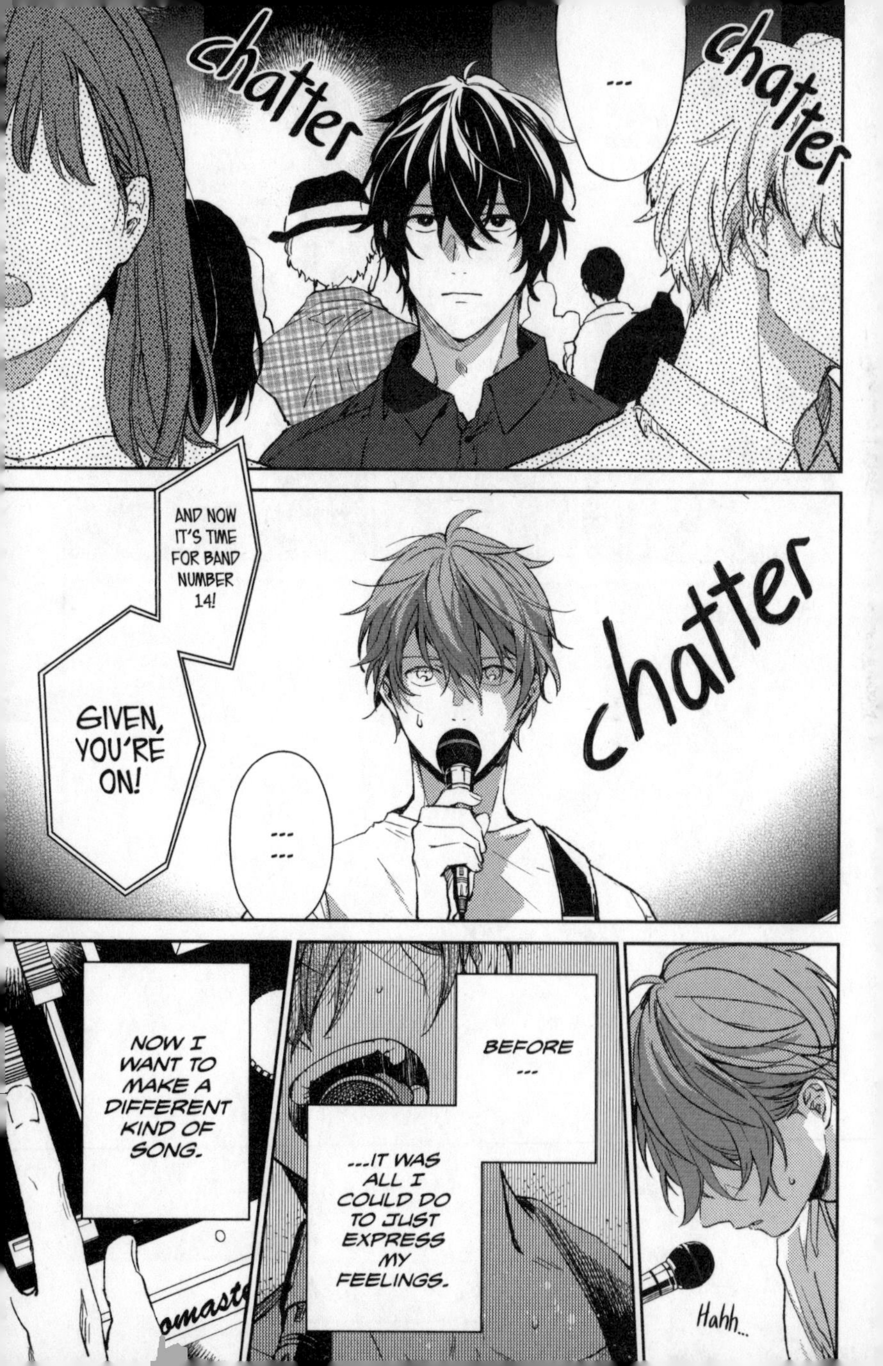
chatter
...
chatter
chatter
AND NOW IT'S TIME FOR BAND NUMBER 14!
GIVEN, YOU'RE ON!
... ...
Hahh...
BEFORE...
...IT WAS ALL I COULD DO TO JUST EXPRESS MY FEELINGS.
NOW I WANT TO MAKE A DIFFERENT KIND OF SONG.

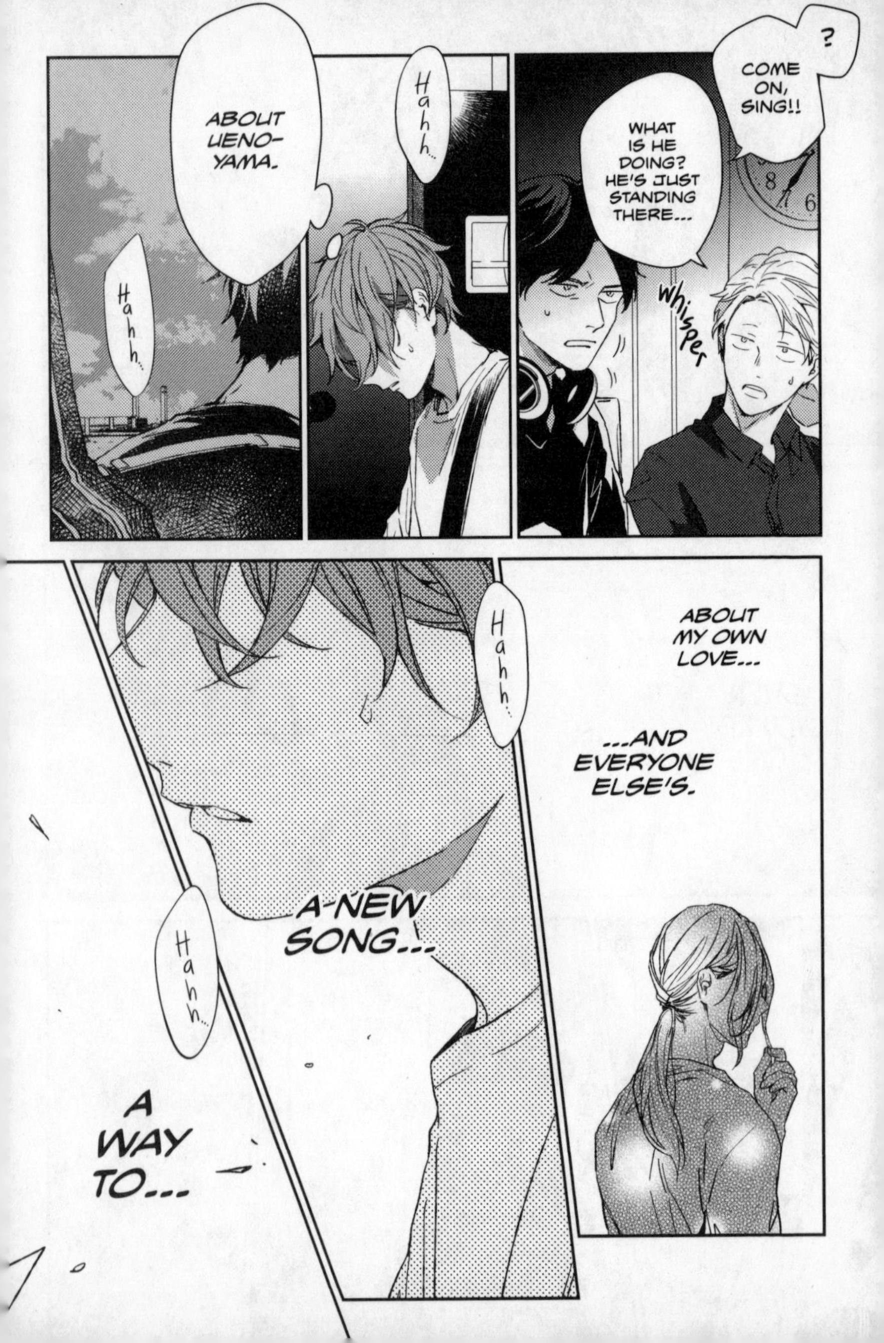
?
COME ON, SING!!
WHAT IS HE DOING? HE'S JUST STANDING THERE...
whisper
Hahh...
ABOUT UENO-YAMA.
Hahh...
ABOUT MY OWN LOVE...
...AND EVERYONE ELSE'S.
Hahh...
A NEW SONG...
Hahh...
A WAY TO...

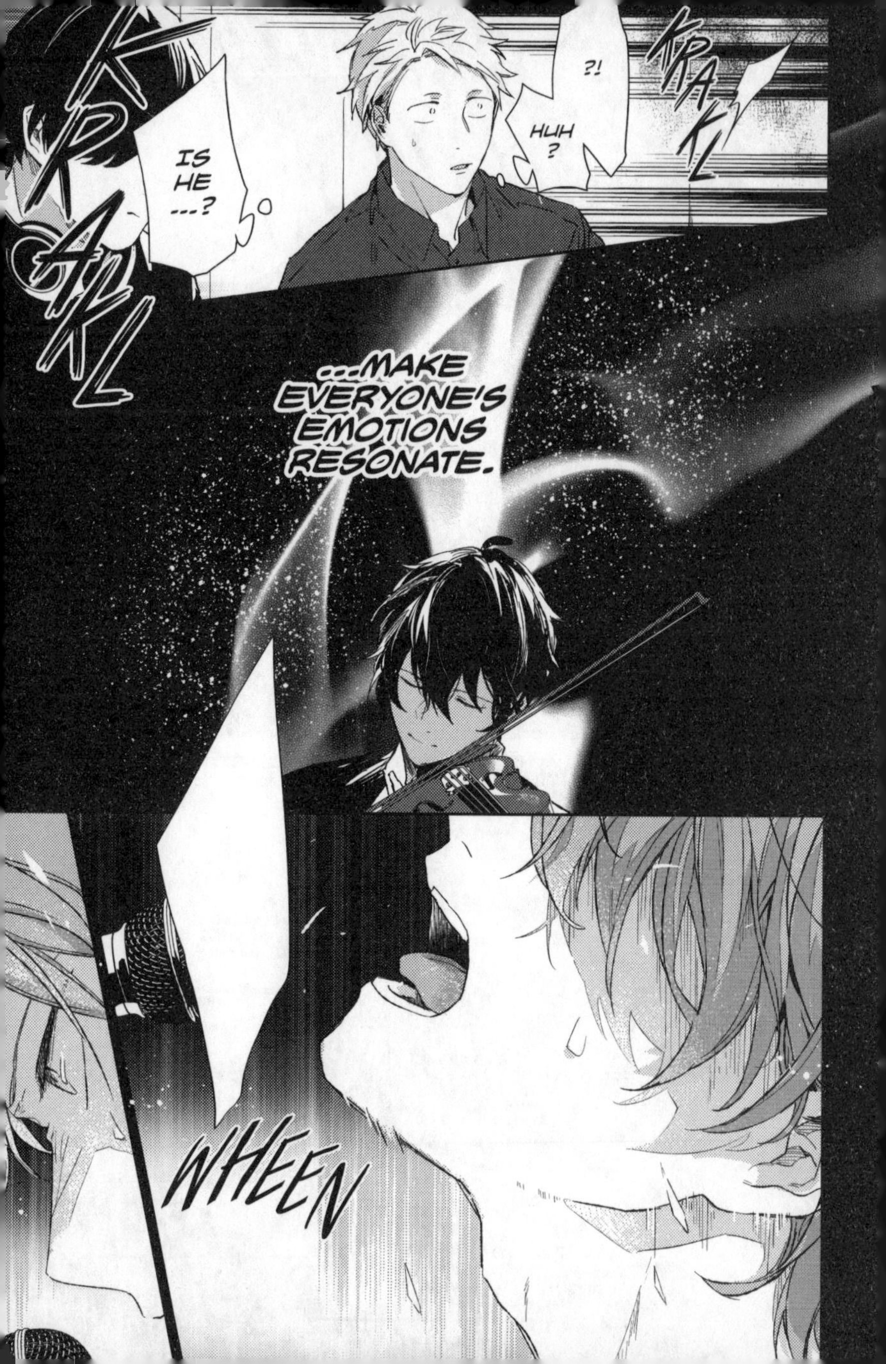
KRAKL
?!
HUH?
IS HE---?
KRAKL
...MAKE EVERYONE'S EMOTIONS RESONATE.
WHEEN

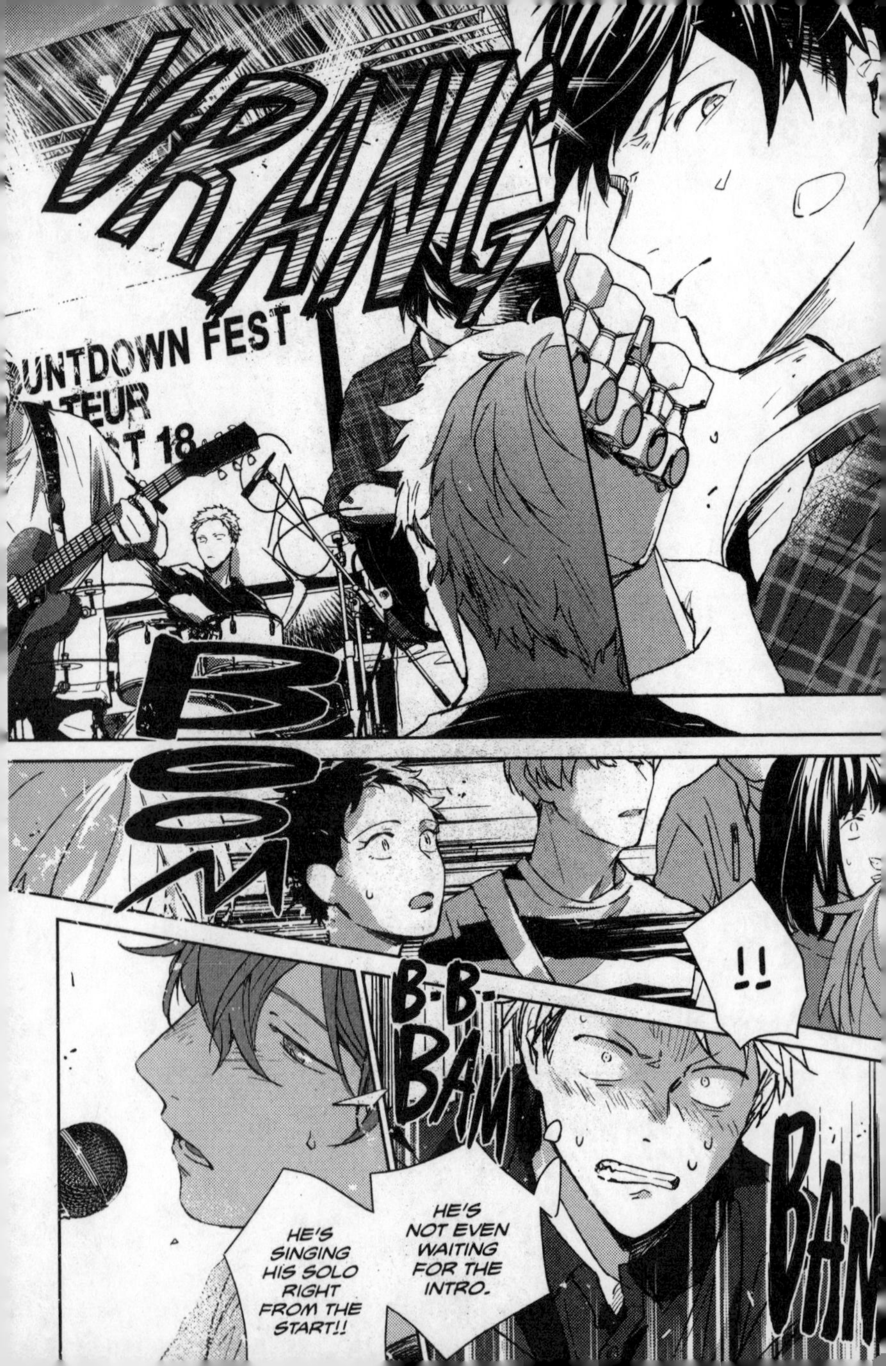
VRANG
UNTDOWN FEST
BOOM
!!
B-B-BAM
BAM
BAM
HE'S NOT EVEN WAITING FOR THE INTRO.
HE'S SINGING HIS SOLO RIGHT FROM THE START!!

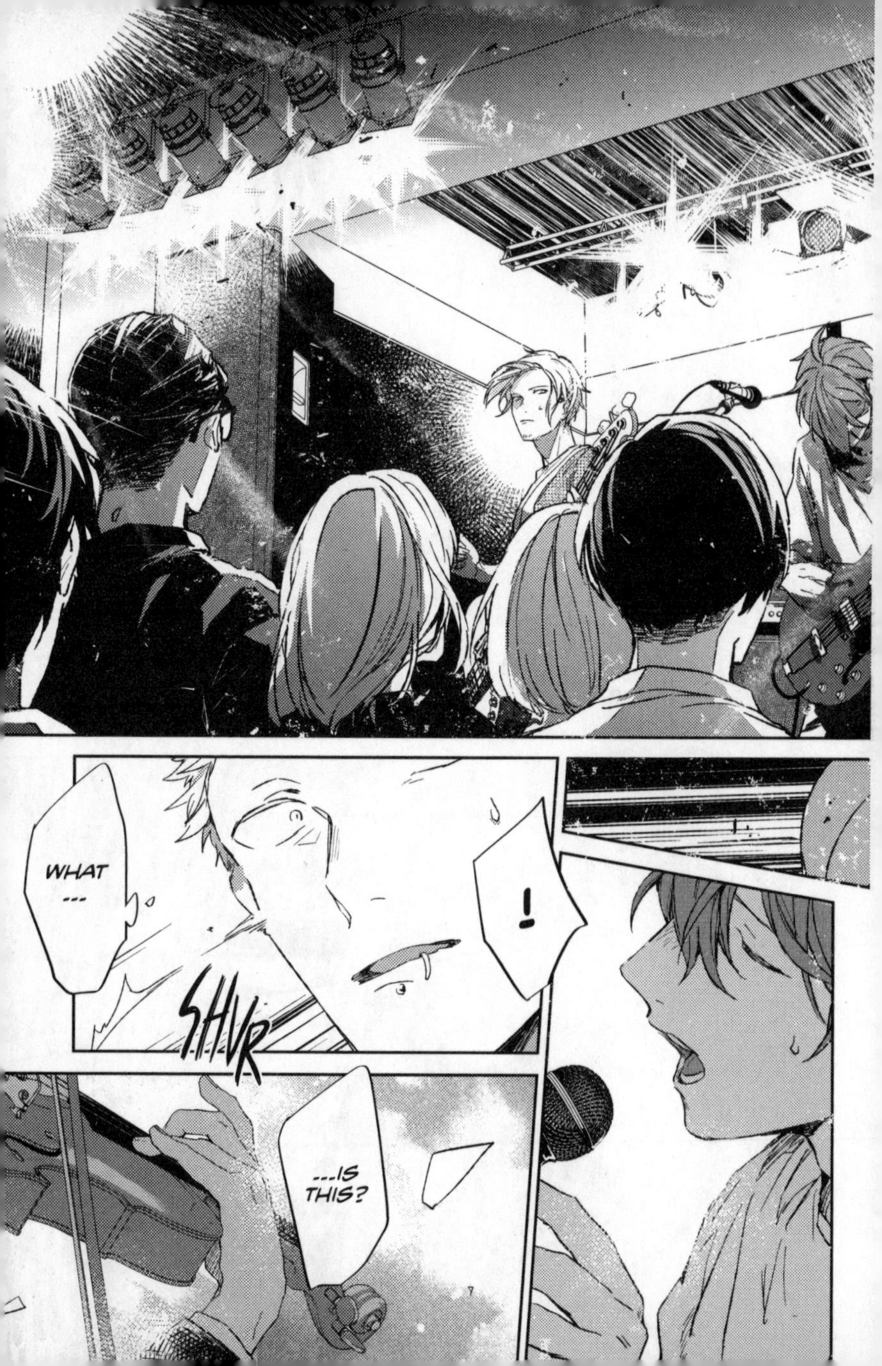
!
WHAT ---
SHVR
---IS THIS?

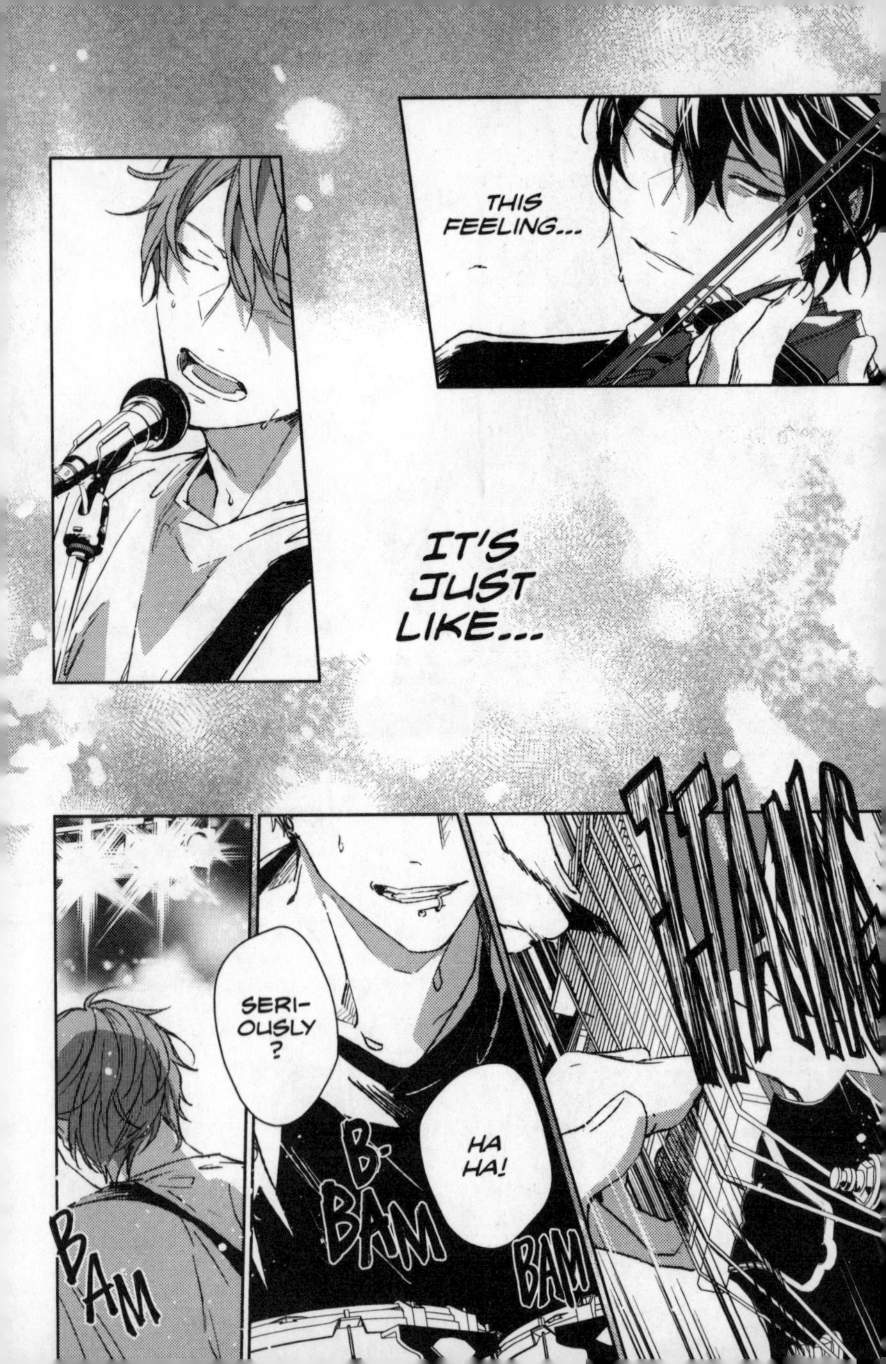
THIS FEELING...
IT'S JUST LIKE...
THANG
HA HA!
BAM
SERI-OUSLY?
B-BAM
BAM

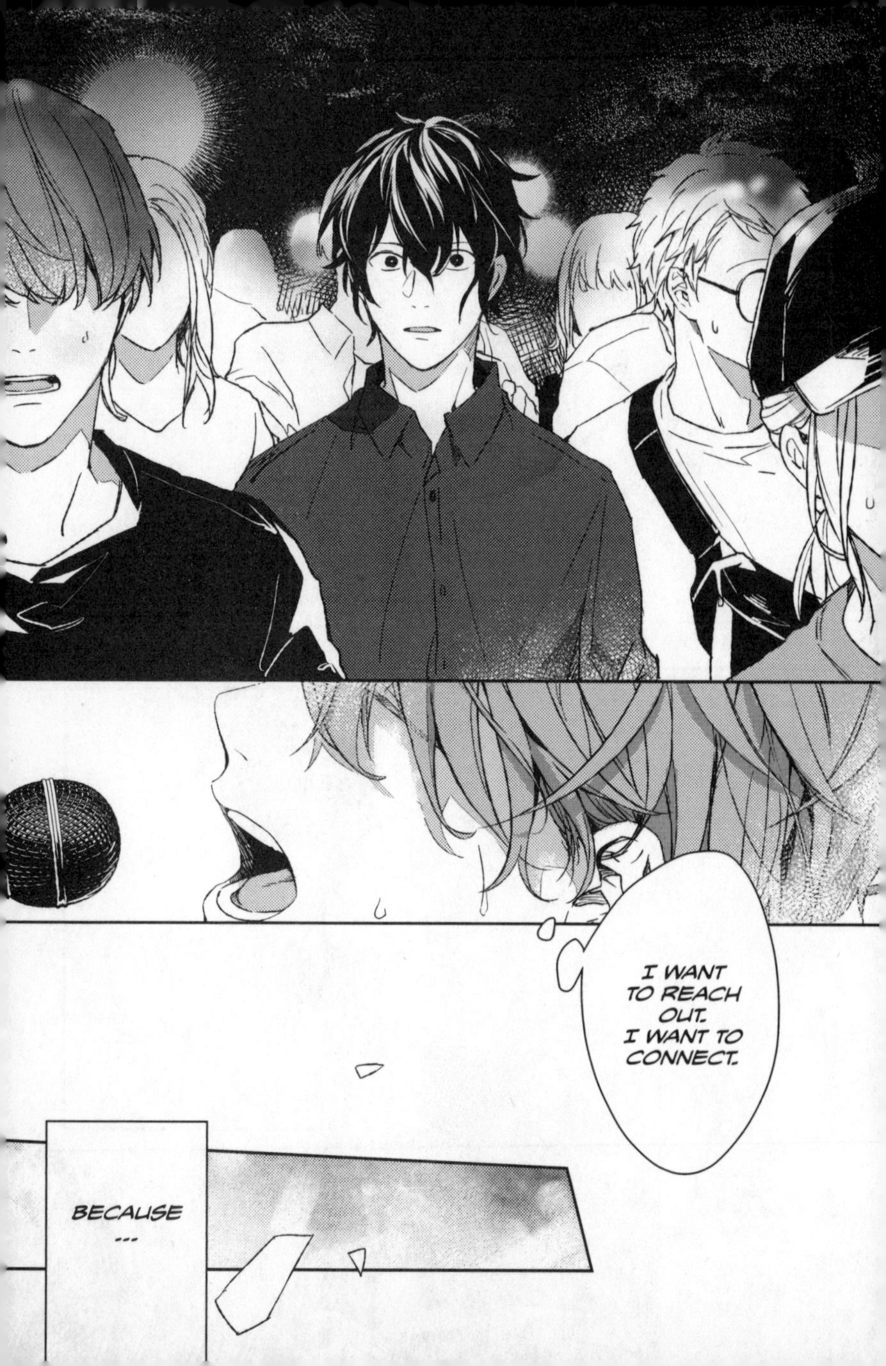
I WANT TO REACH OUT. I WANT TO CONNECT.
BECAUSE ...

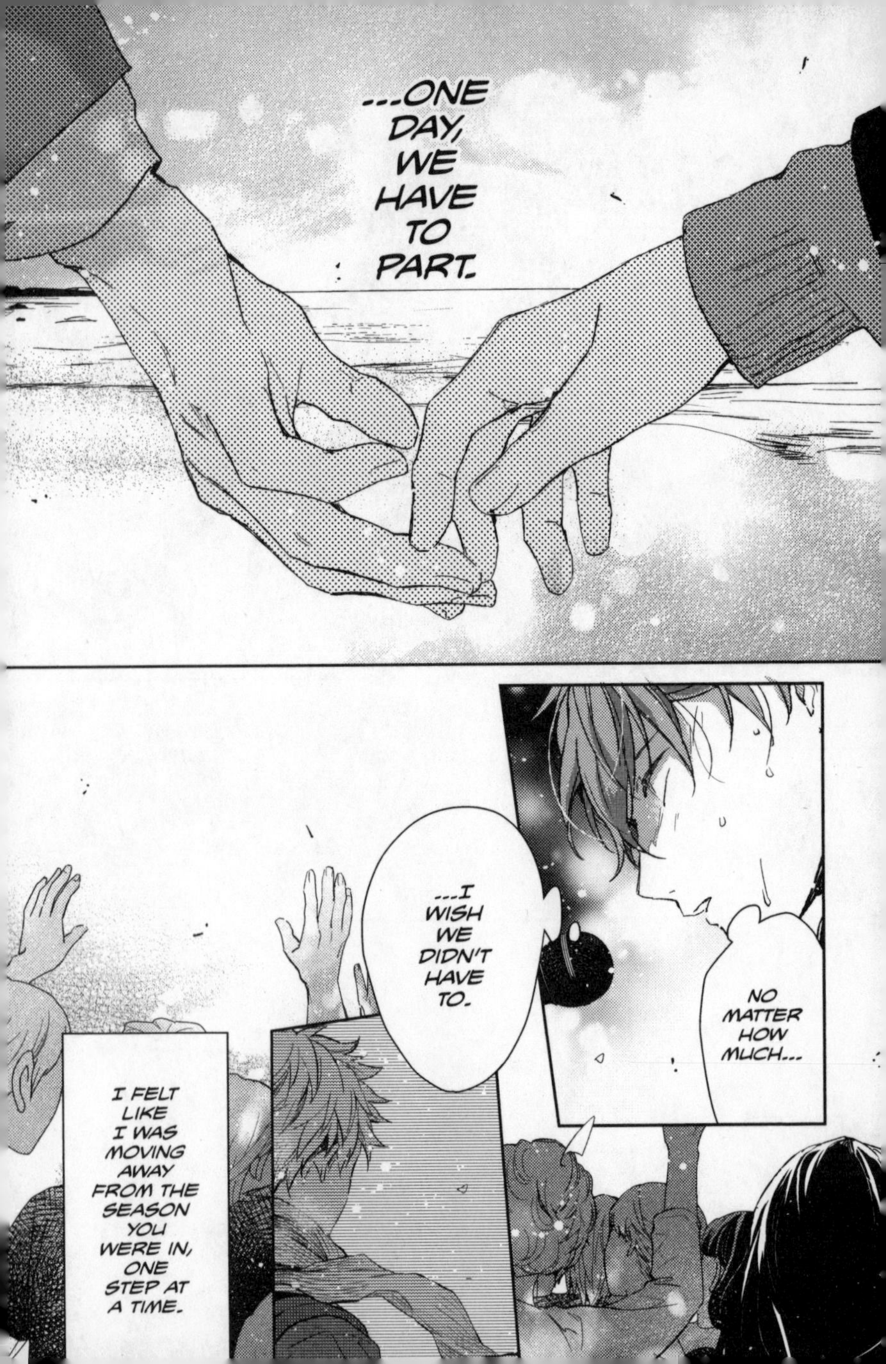
...ONE DAY, WE HAVE TO PART.
...I WISH WE DIDN'T HAVE TO.
NO MATTER HOW MUCH...
I FELT LIKE I WAS MOVING AWAY FROM THE SEASON YOU WERE IN, ONE STEP AT A TIME.

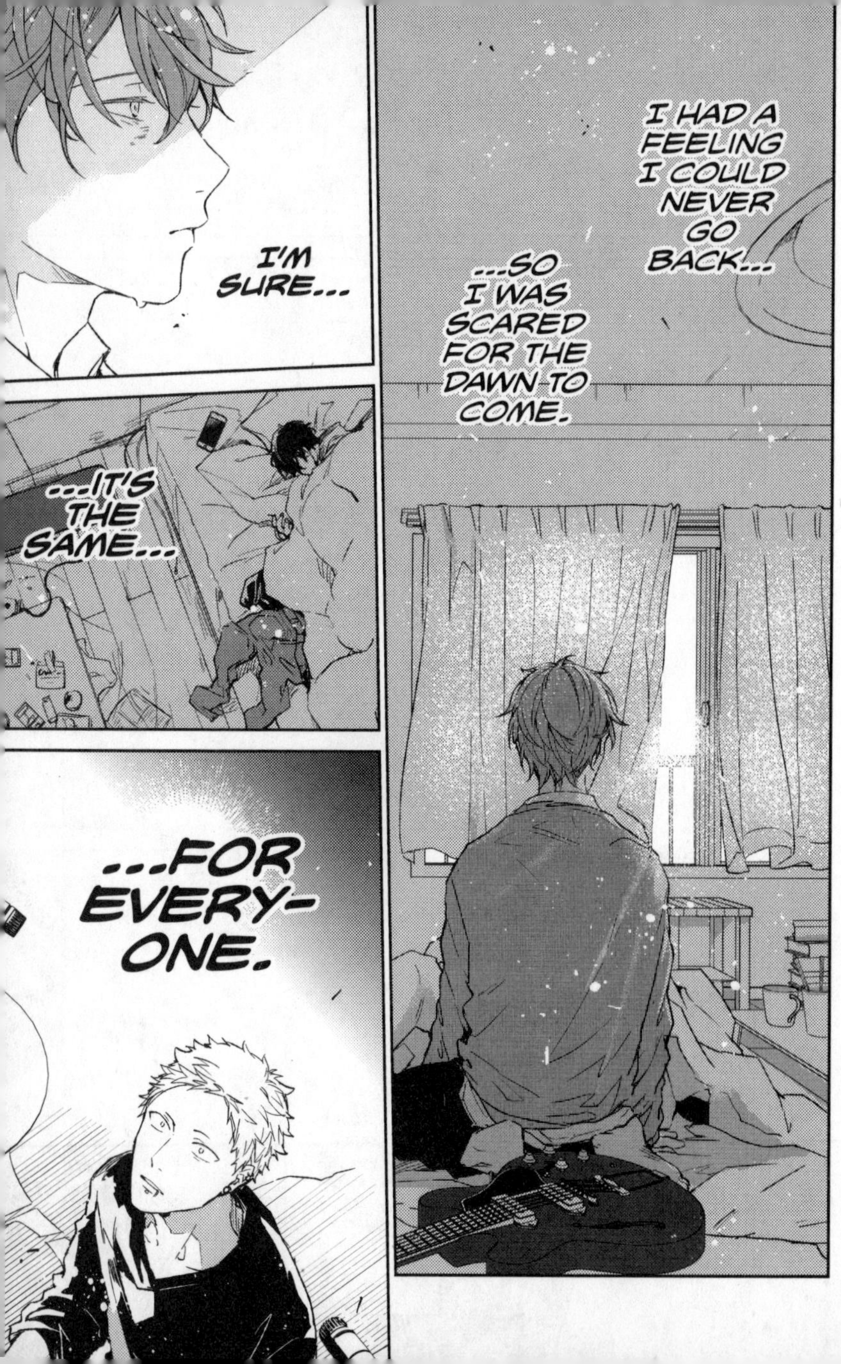
I HAD A FEELING I COULD NEVER GO BACK...
...SO I WAS SCARED FOR THE DAWN TO COME.
I'M SURE...
...IT'S THE SAME...
...FOR EVERY-ONE.

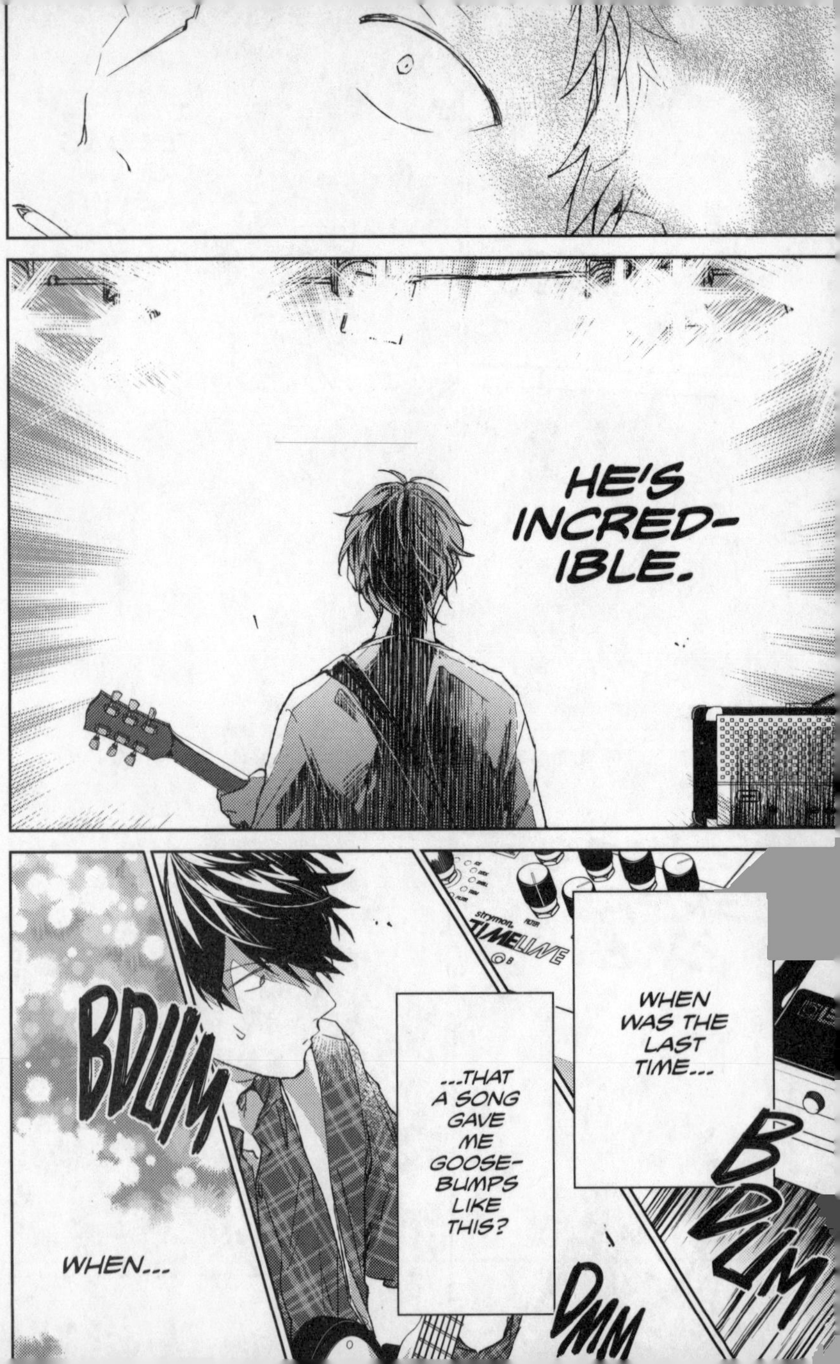
HE'S INCRED-IBLE.
strymon.
TIMELINE
WHEN WAS THE LAST TIME...
...THAT A SONG GAVE ME GOOSE-BUMPS LIKE THIS?
BDUM
DMM
BDUM
WHEN...

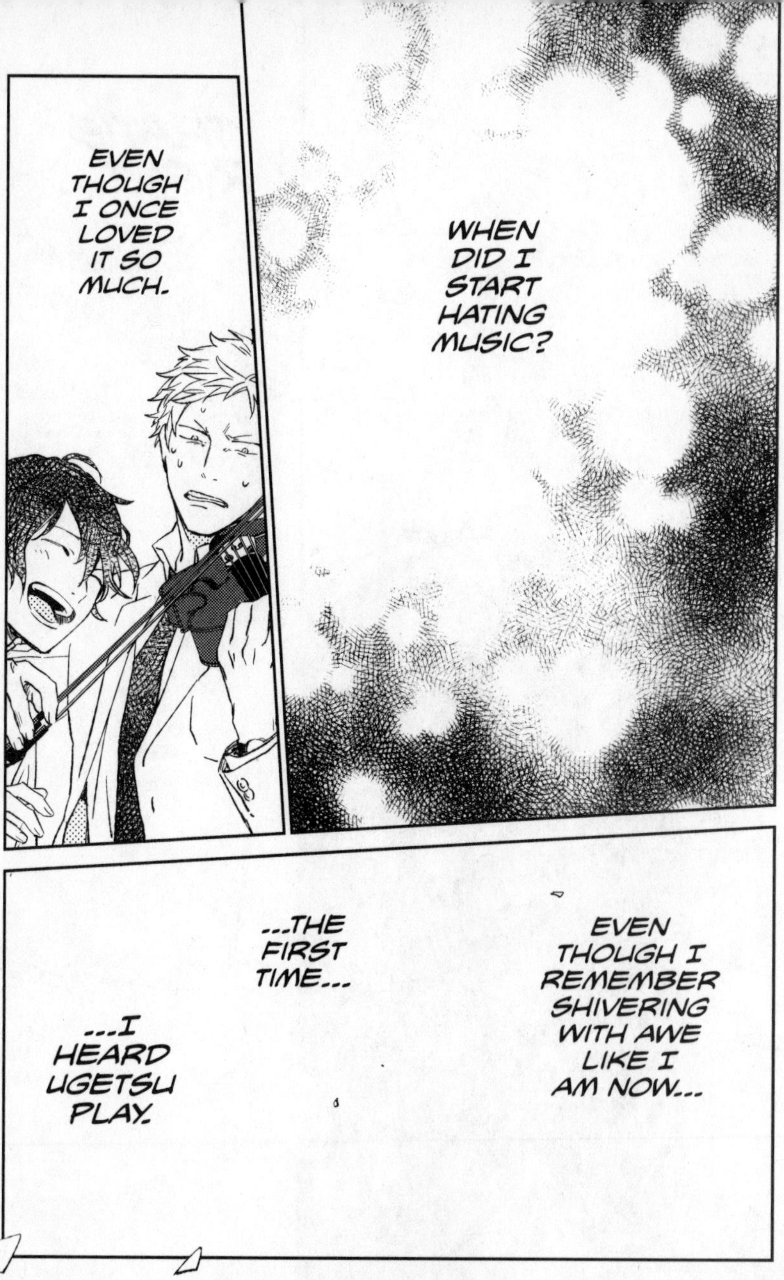
WHEN DID I START HATING MUSIC?
EVEN THOUGH I ONCE LOVED IT SO MUCH.
EVEN THOUGH I REMEMBER SHIVERING WITH AWE LIKE I AM NOW...
...THE FIRST TIME...
...I HEARD UGETSU PLAY.

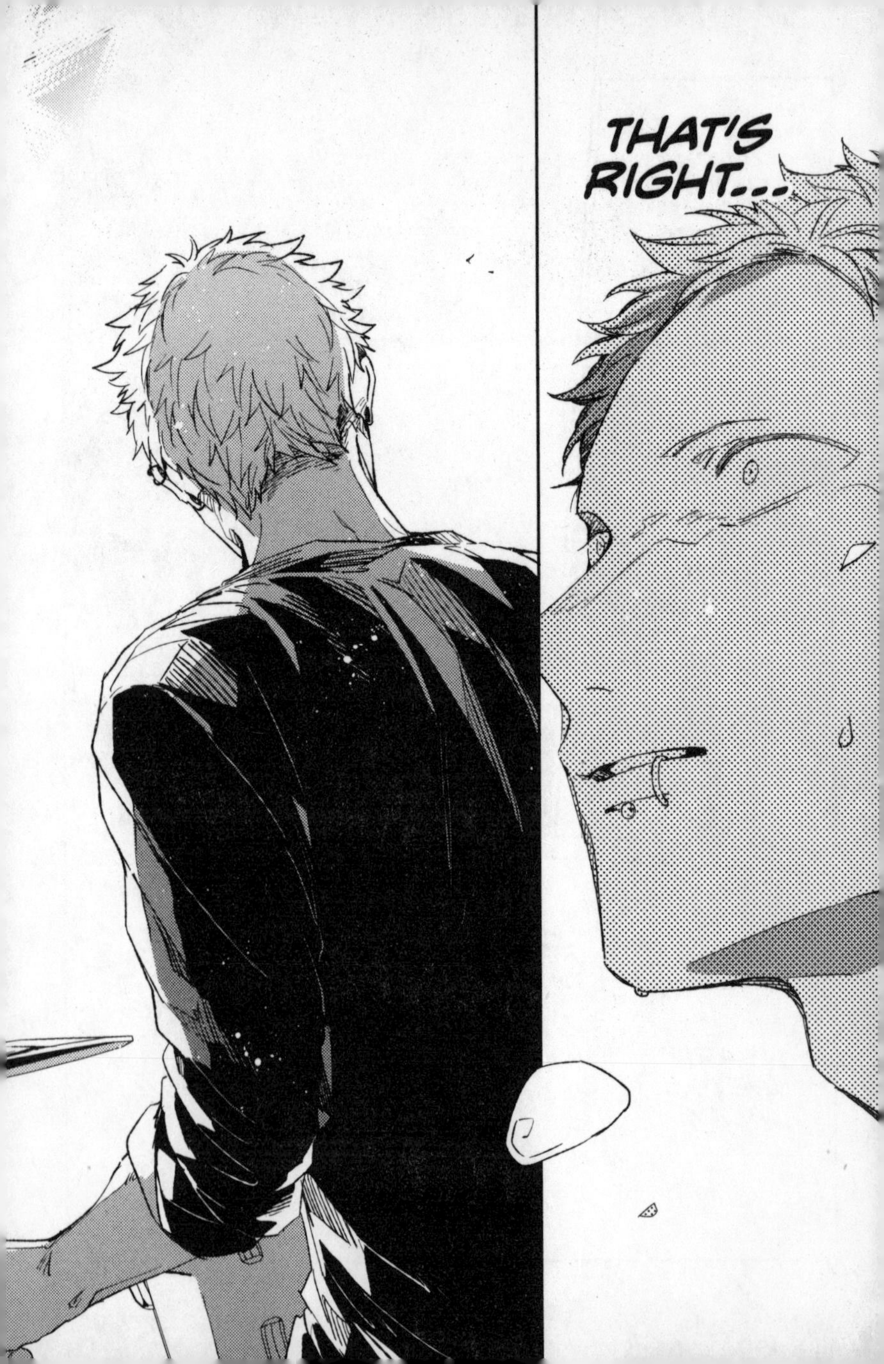
THAT'S RIGHT...

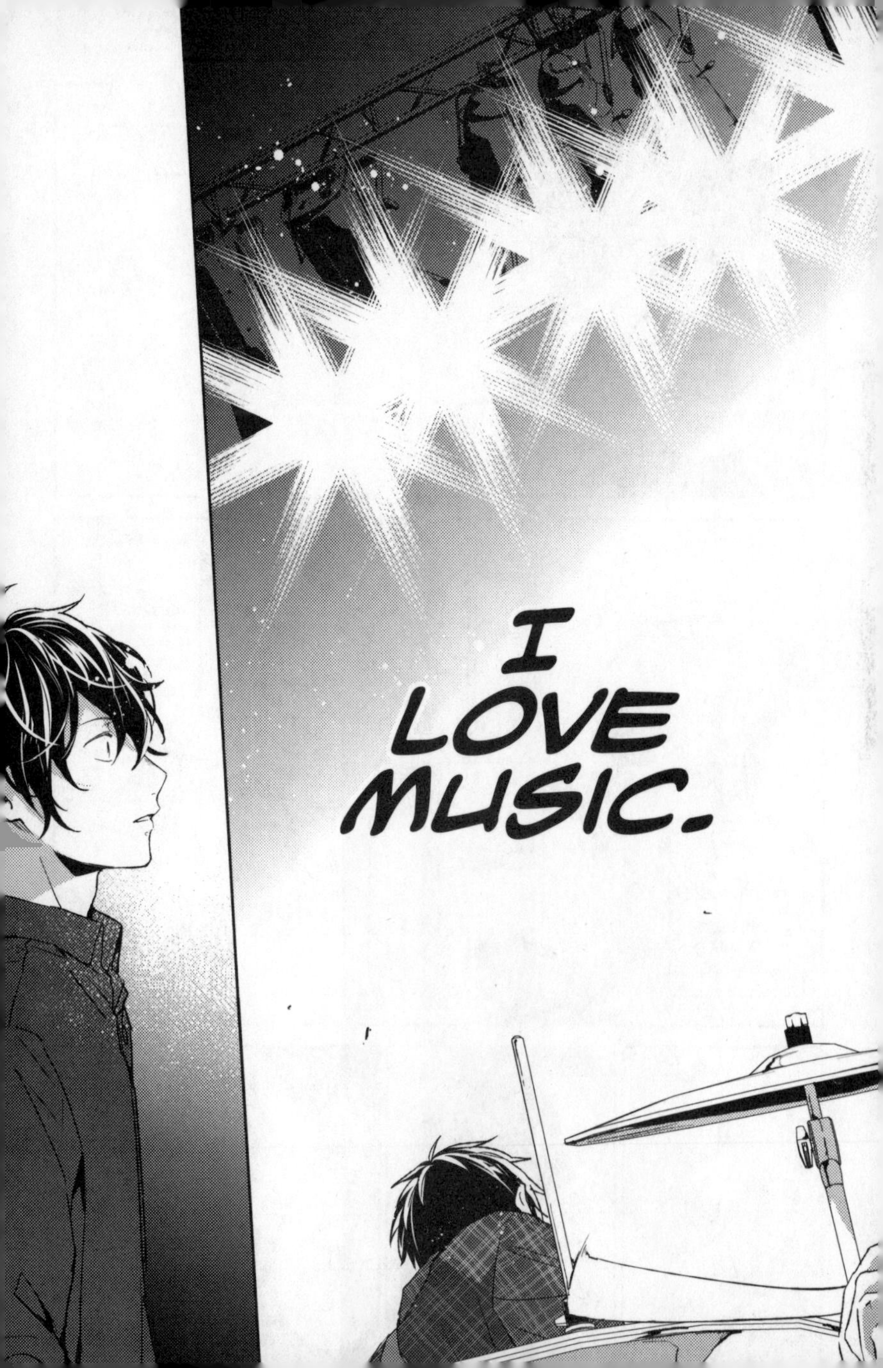
I LOVE MUSIC.

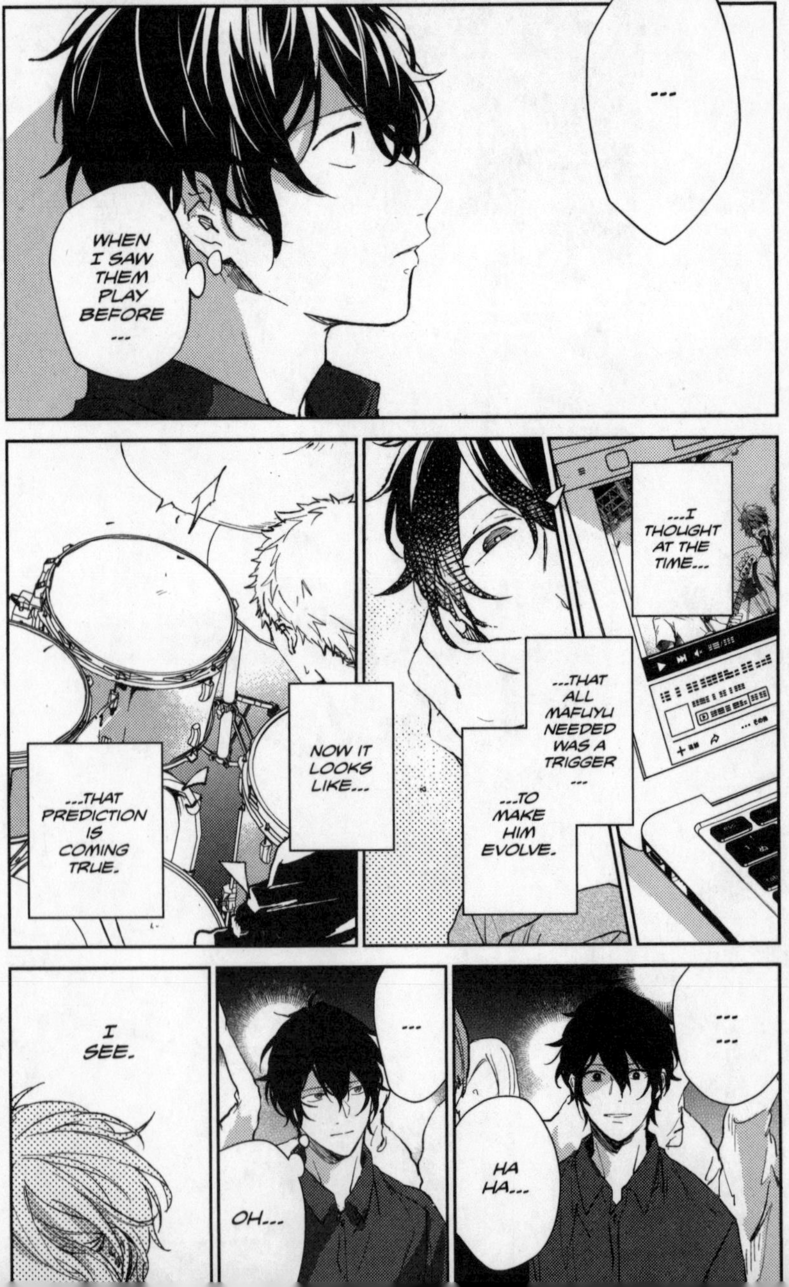
...
WHEN I SAW THEM PLAY BEFORE...
...I THOUGHT AT THE TIME...
...THAT ALL MAFUYU NEEDED WAS A TRIGGER...
...TO MAKE HIM EVOLVE.
NOW IT LOOKS LIKE...
...THAT PREDICTION IS COMING TRUE.
... ...
HA HA...
...
OH...
I SEE.

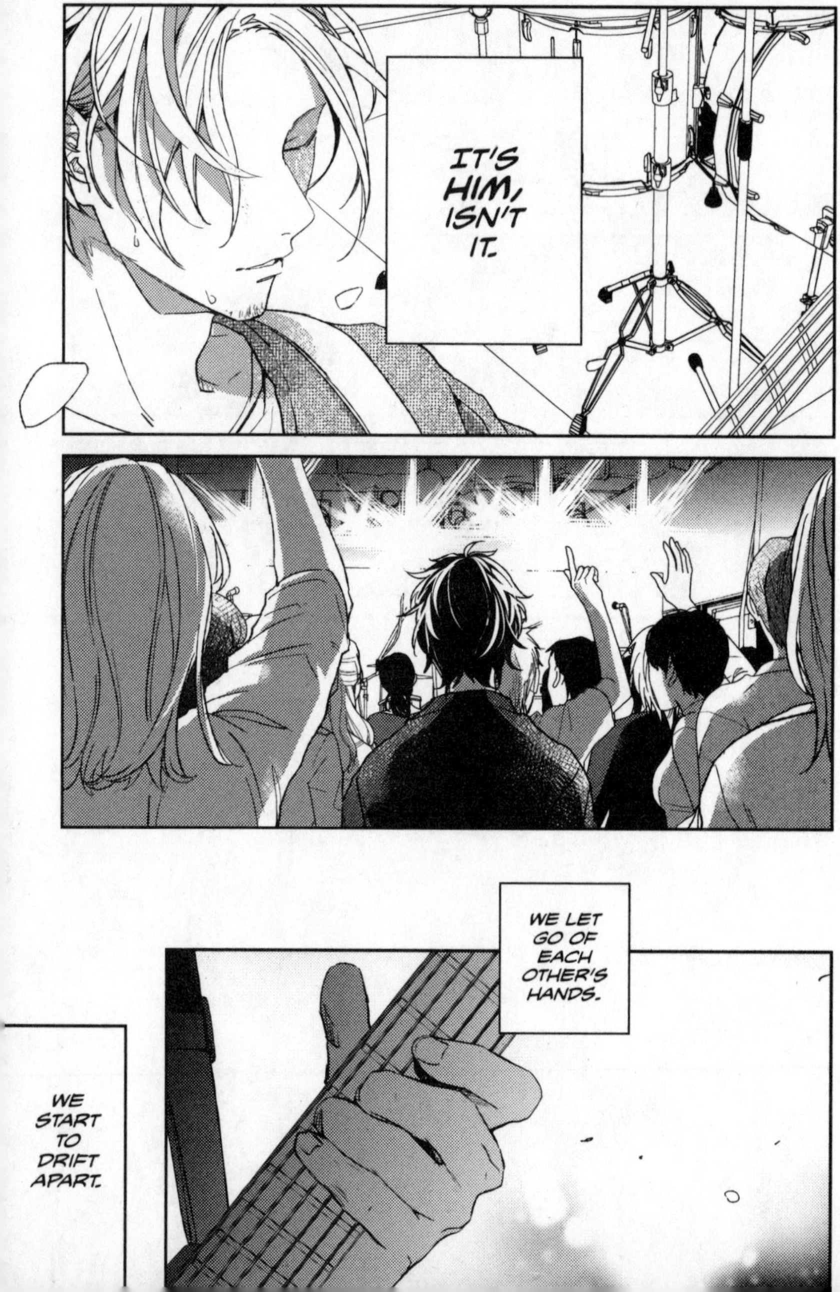
IT'S HIM, ISN'T IT.
WE LET GO OF EACH OTHER'S HANDS.
WE START TO DRIFT APART.

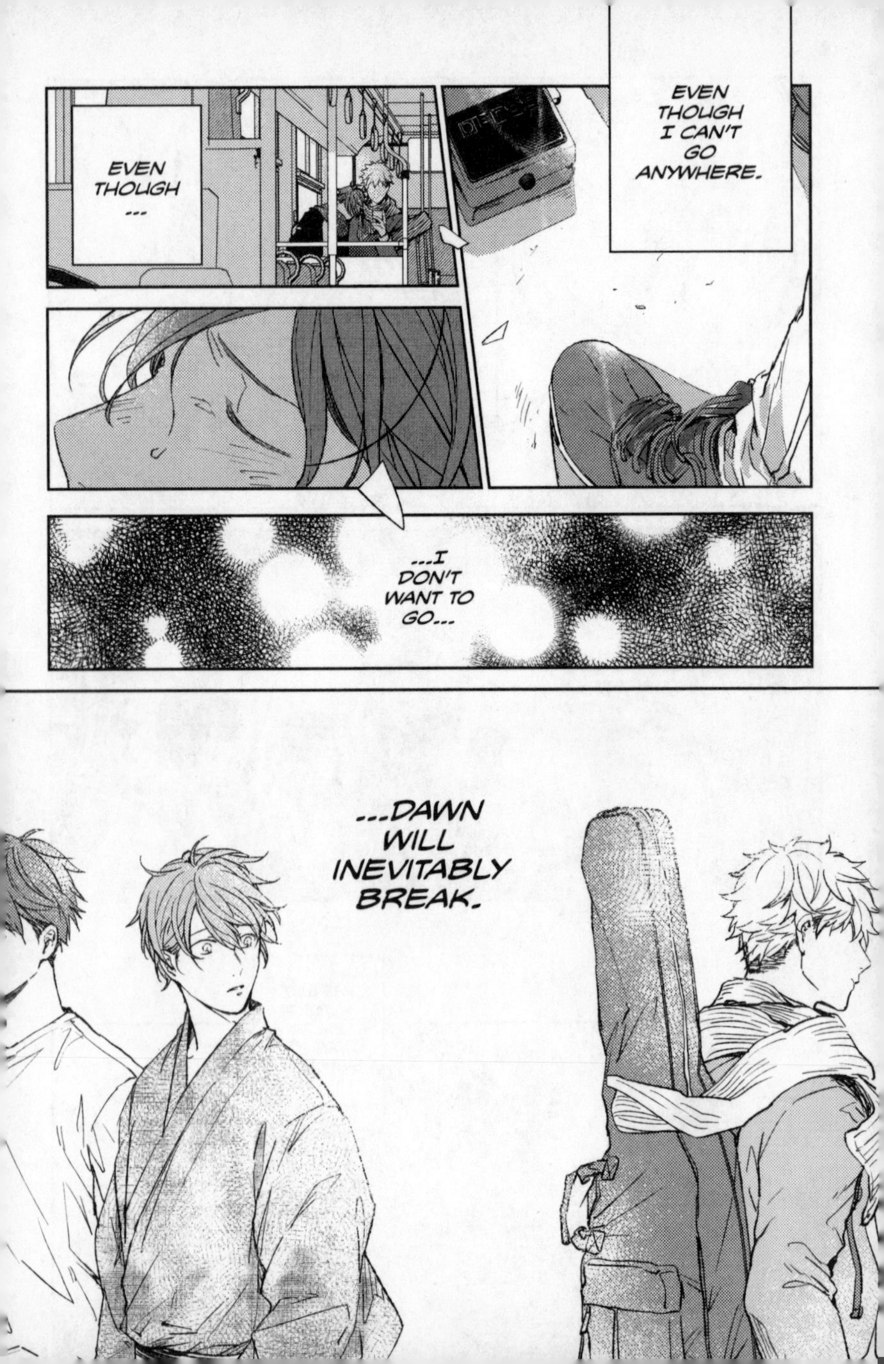
EVEN THOUGH I CAN'T GO ANYWHERE.
EVEN THOUGH ...
...I DON'T WANT TO GO...
...DAWN WILL INEVITABLY BREAK.

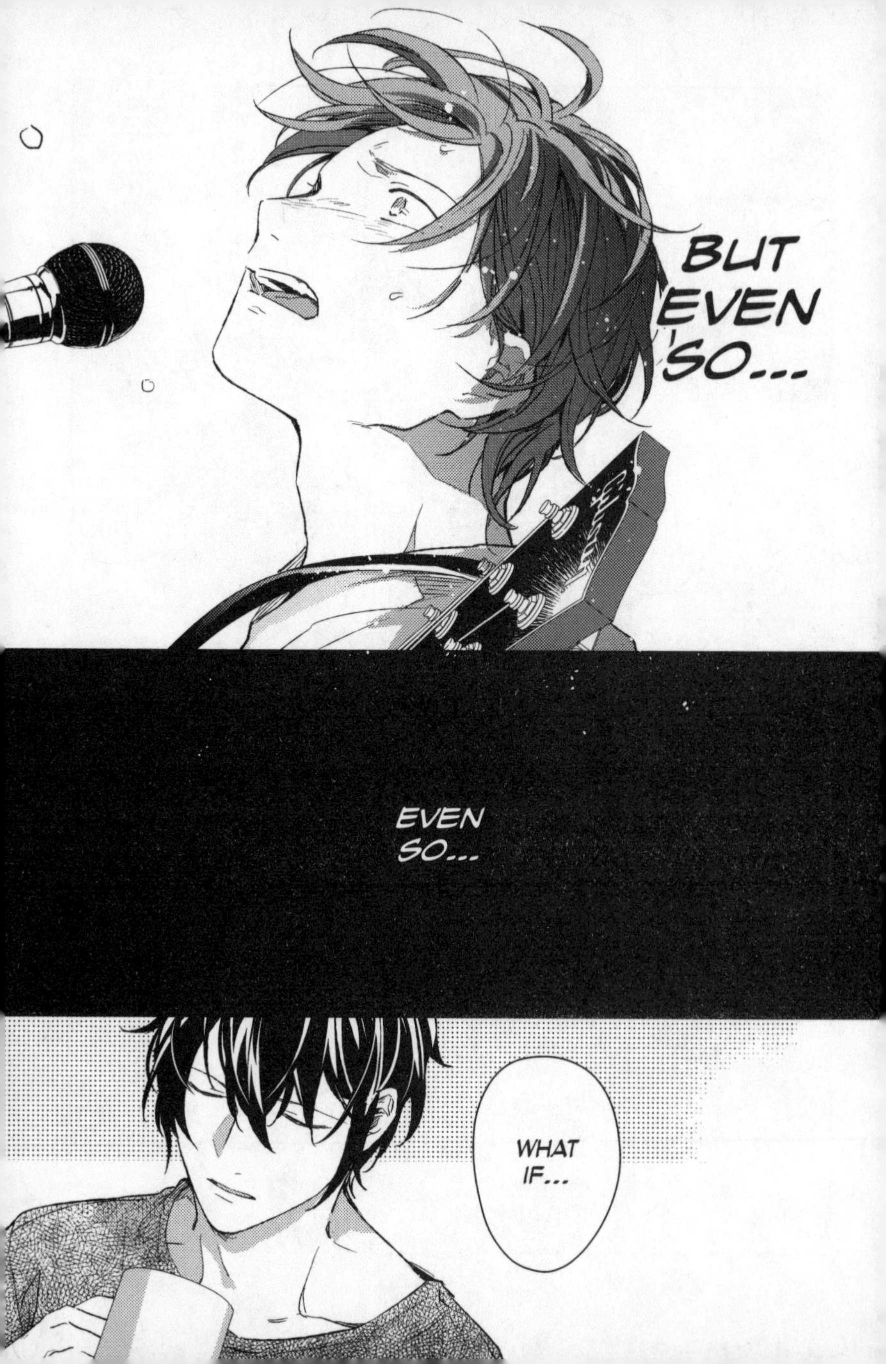
BUT EVEN SO...
EVEN SO...
WHAT IF...

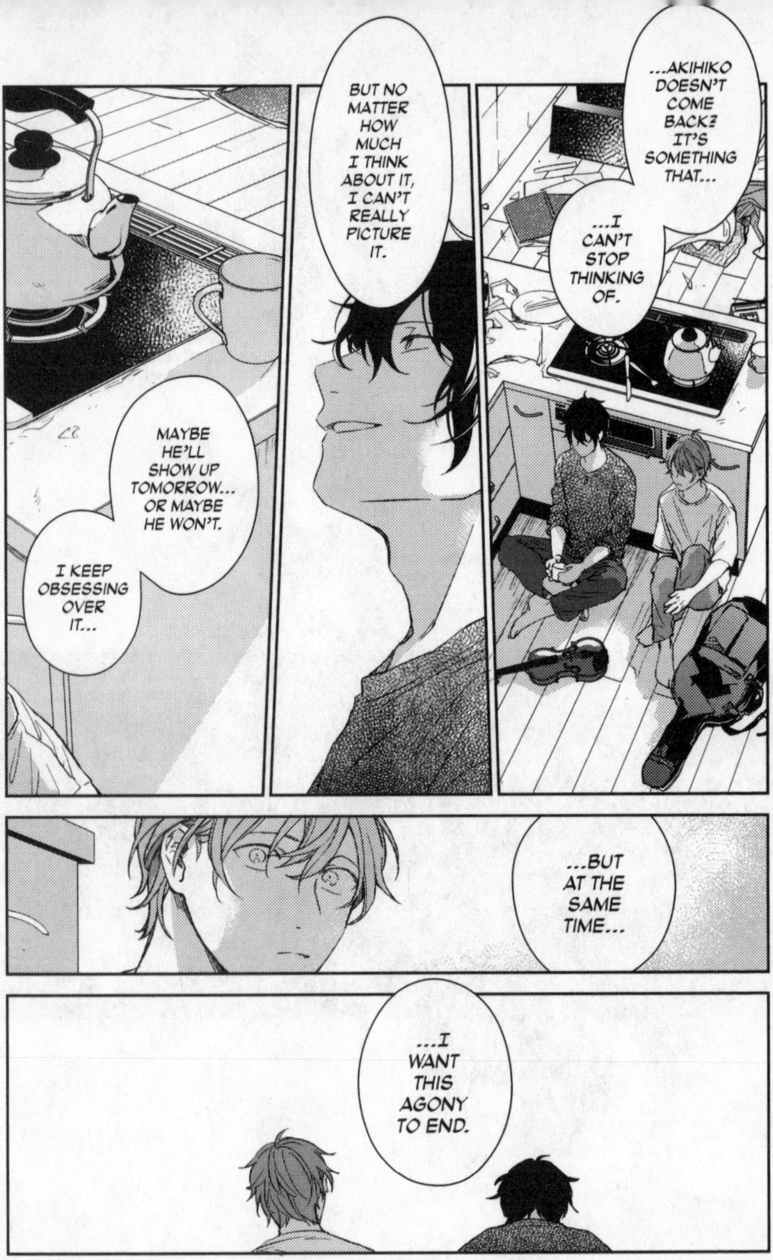
...AKIHIKO DOESN'T COME BACK? IT'S SOMETHING THAT...
...I CAN'T STOP THINKING OF.
BUT NO MATTER HOW MUCH I THINK ABOUT IT, I CAN'T REALLY PICTURE IT.
MAYBE HE'LL SHOW UP TOMORROW... OR MAYBE HE WON'T.
I KEEP OBSESSING OVER IT...
...BUT AT THE SAME TIME...
...I WANT THIS AGONY TO END.

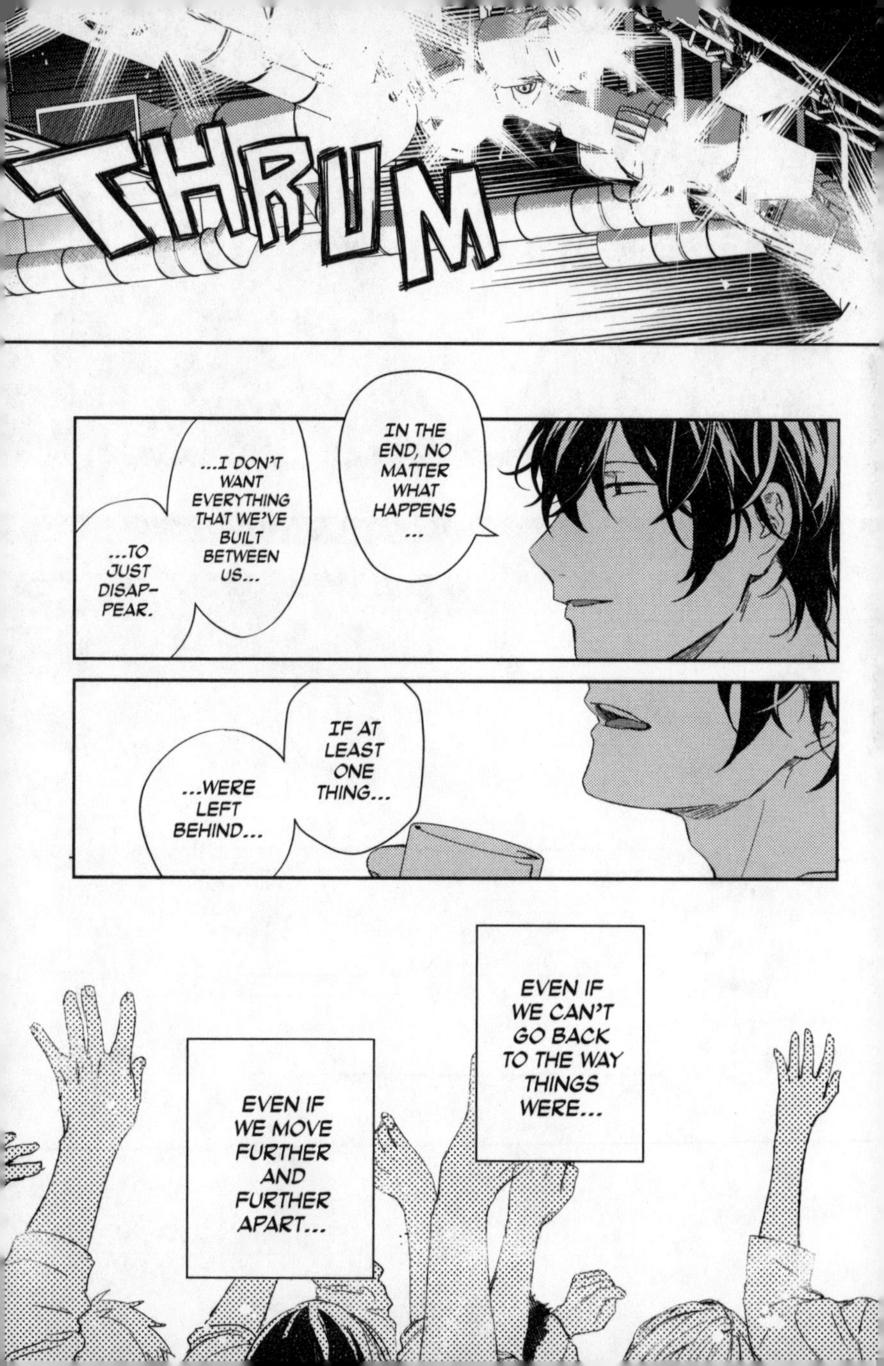
THRUM
IN THE END, NO MATTER WHAT HAPPENS ...
...I DON'T WANT EVERYTHING THAT WE'VE BUILT BETWEEN US...
...TO JUST DISAP-PEAR.
IF AT LEAST ONE THING...
...WERE LEFT BEHIND...
EVEN IF WE CAN'T GO BACK TO THE WAY THINGS WERE...
EVEN IF WE MOVE FURTHER AND FURTHER APART...

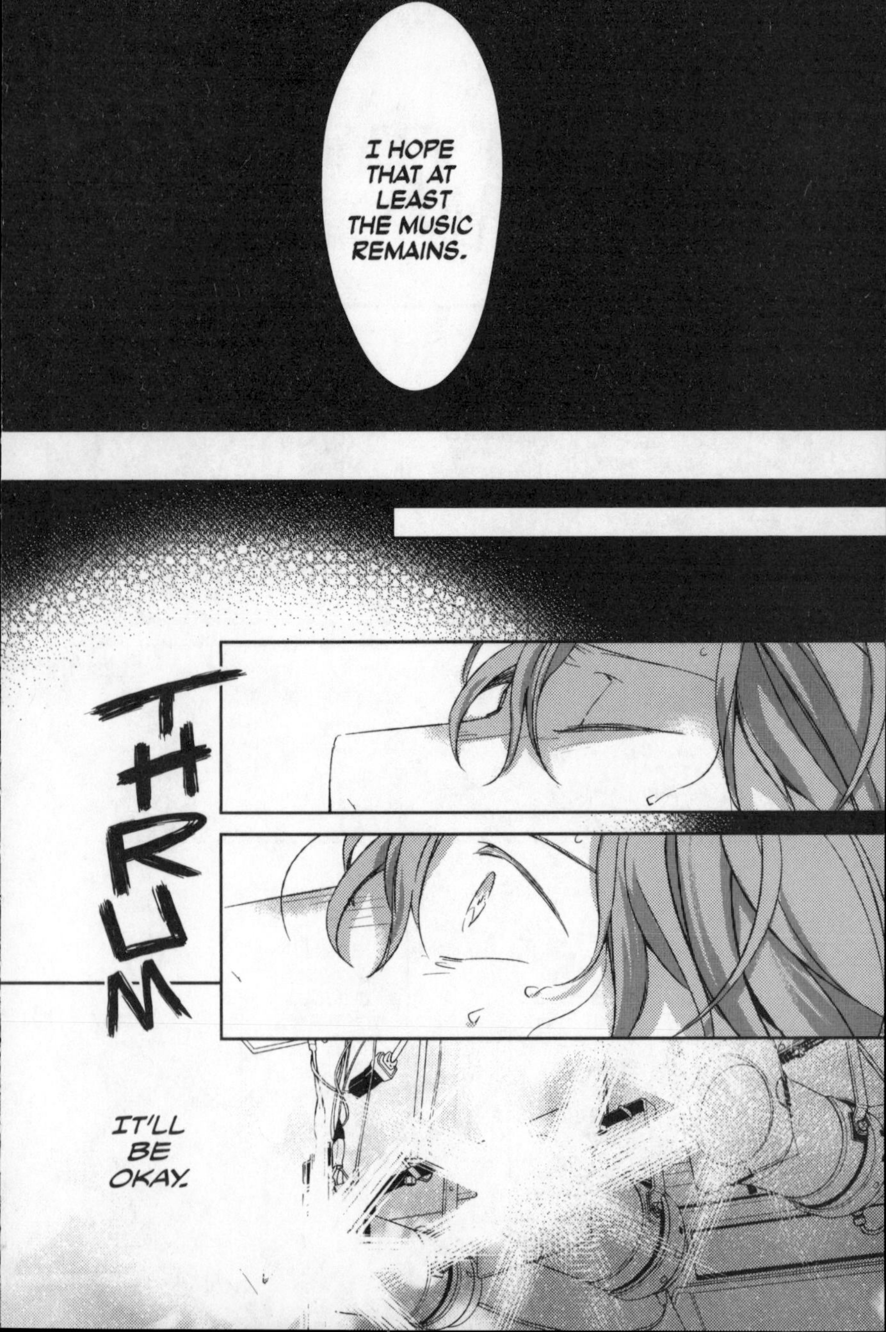
I HOPE THAT AT LEAST THE MUSIC REMAINS.
THRUM
IT'LL BE OKAY.

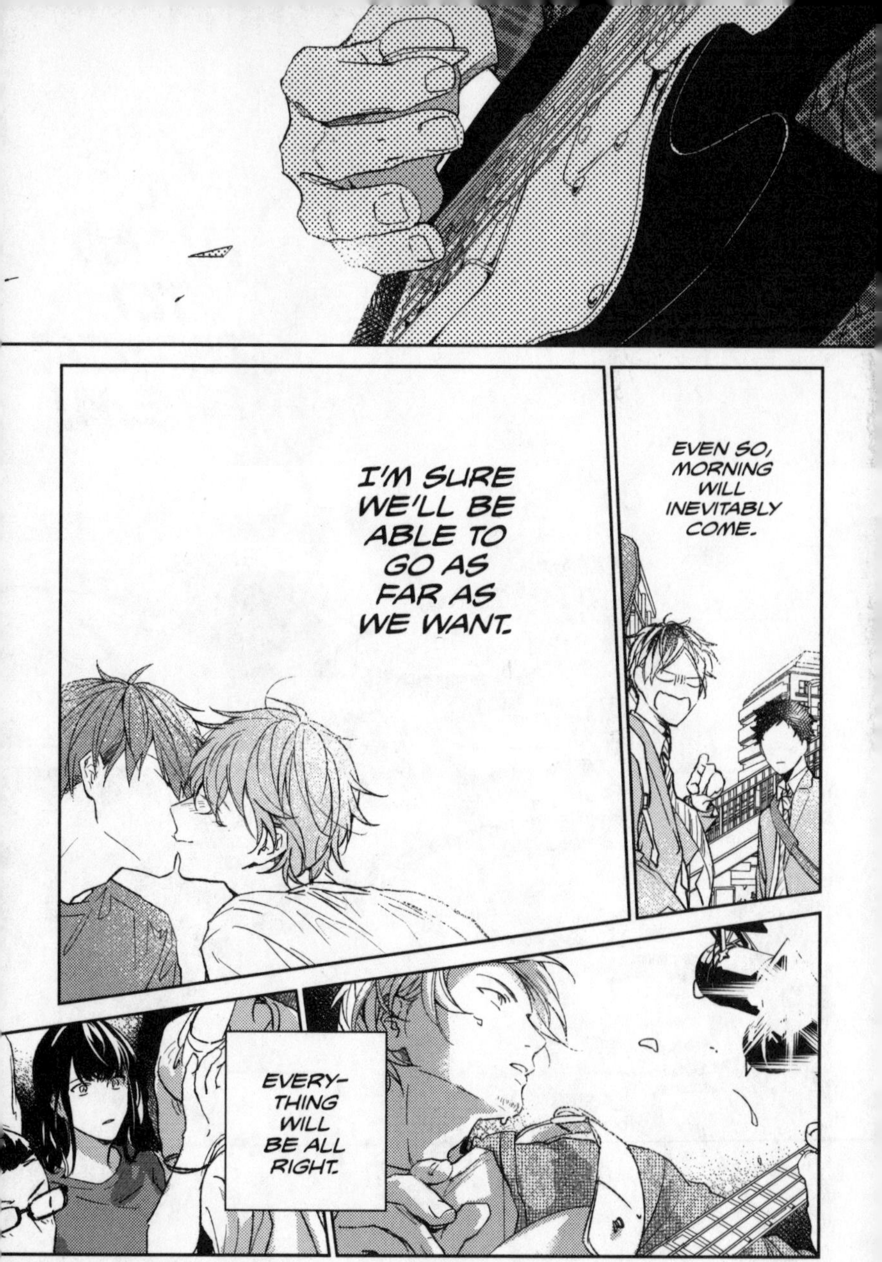
EVEN SO, MORNING WILL INEVITABLY COME.
I'M SURE WE'LL BE ABLE TO GO AS FAR AS WE WANT.
EVERY-THING WILL BE ALL RIGHT.

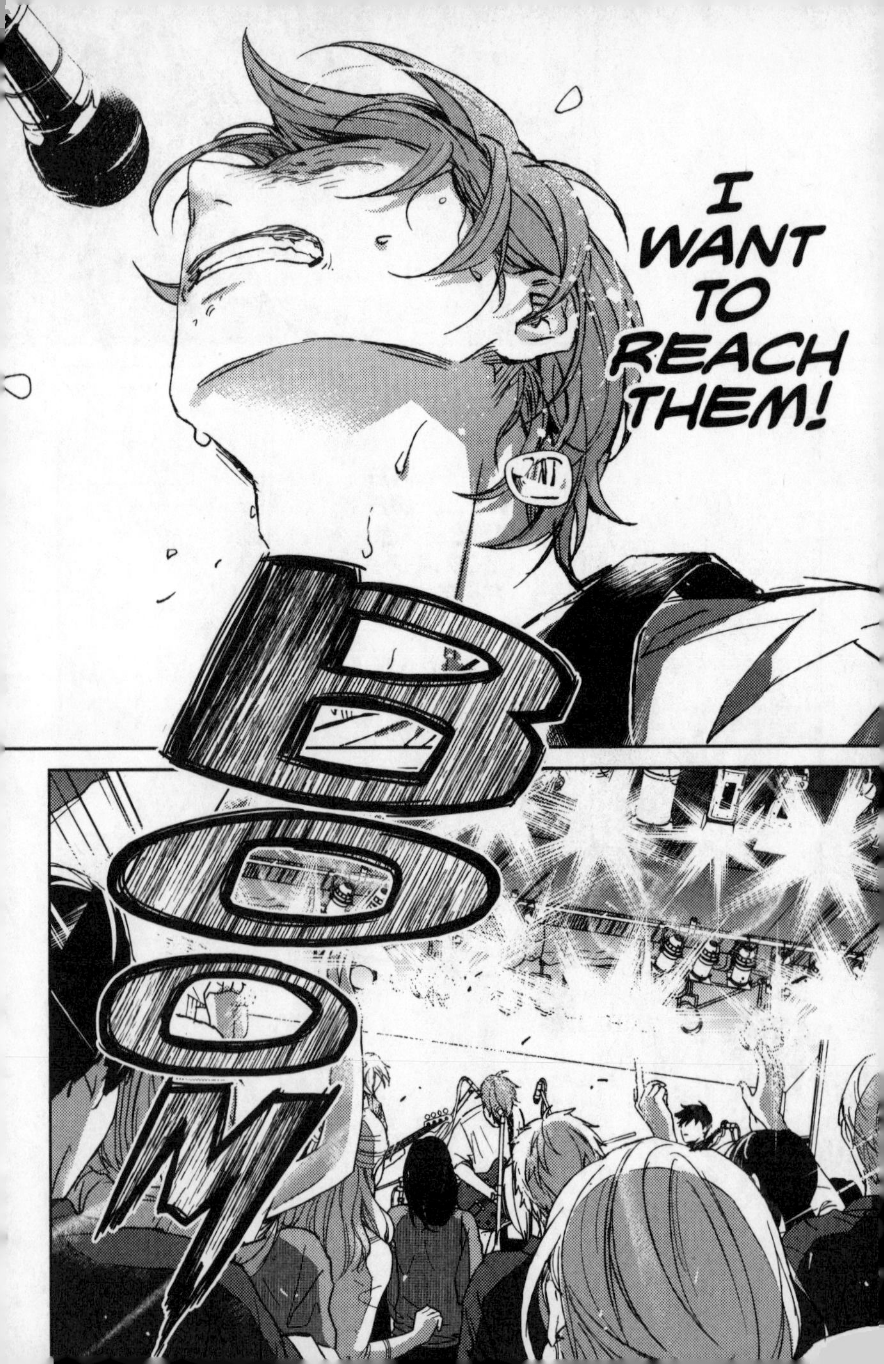
I WANT TO REACH THEM!
BOOM

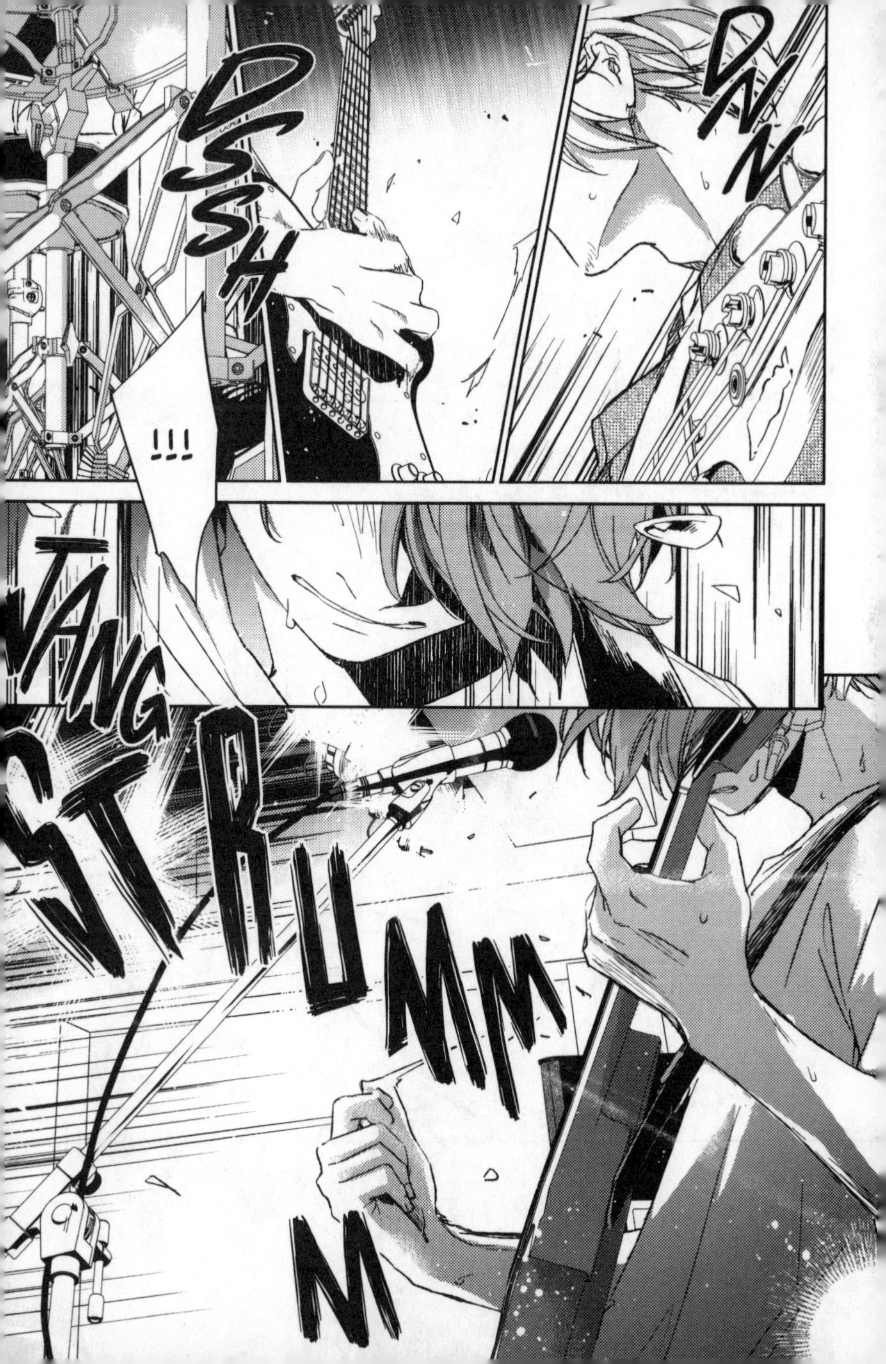
DWN
DSSH
!!!
TWANG
STRUMMM

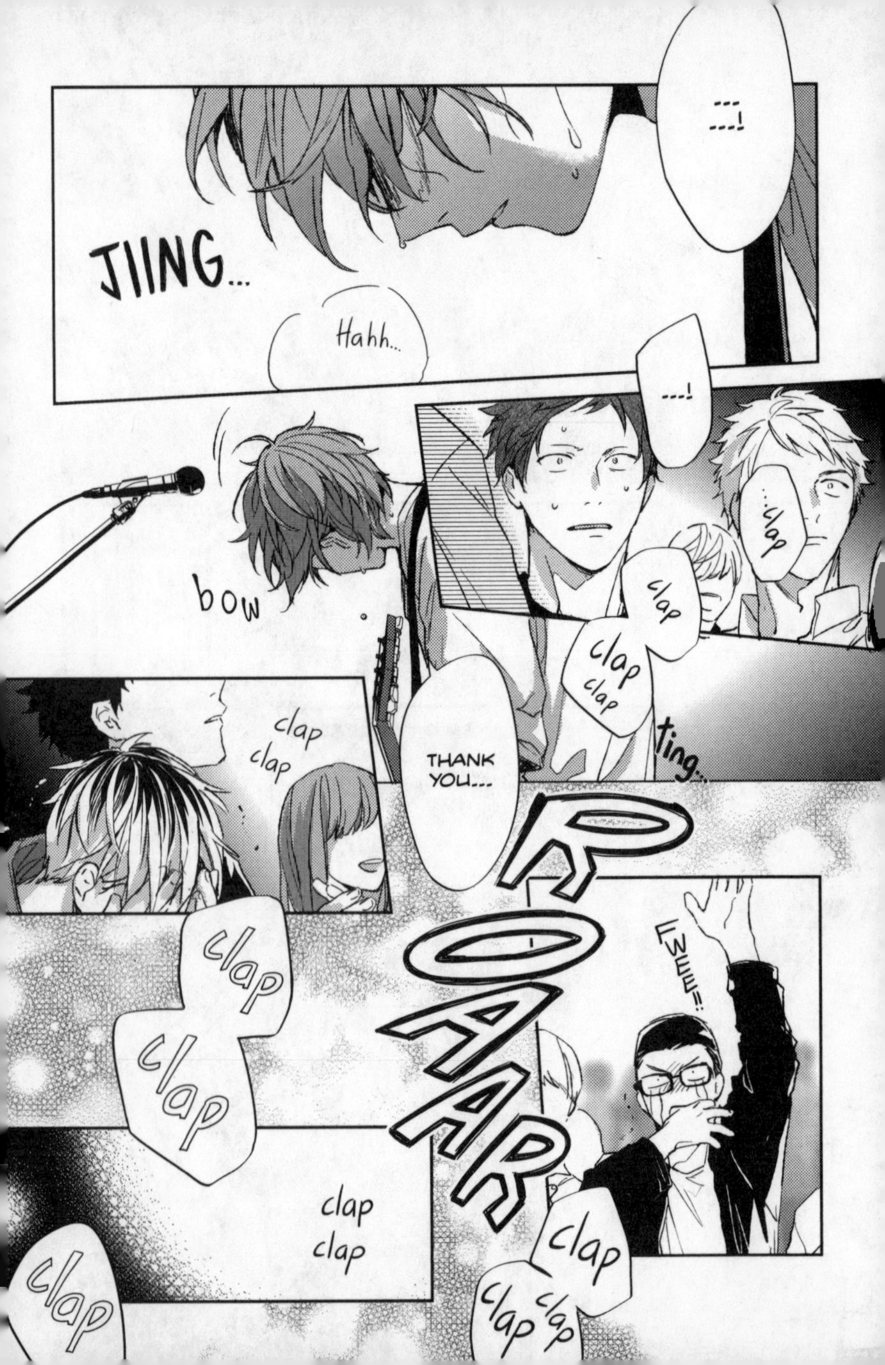

---!
JIING...
Hahh...
---!
...clap
clap
clap
clap
bow
ting...
THANK YOU...
clap
clap
ROAR
FWEE!!
clap
clap
clap
clap
clap
clap
clap
clap

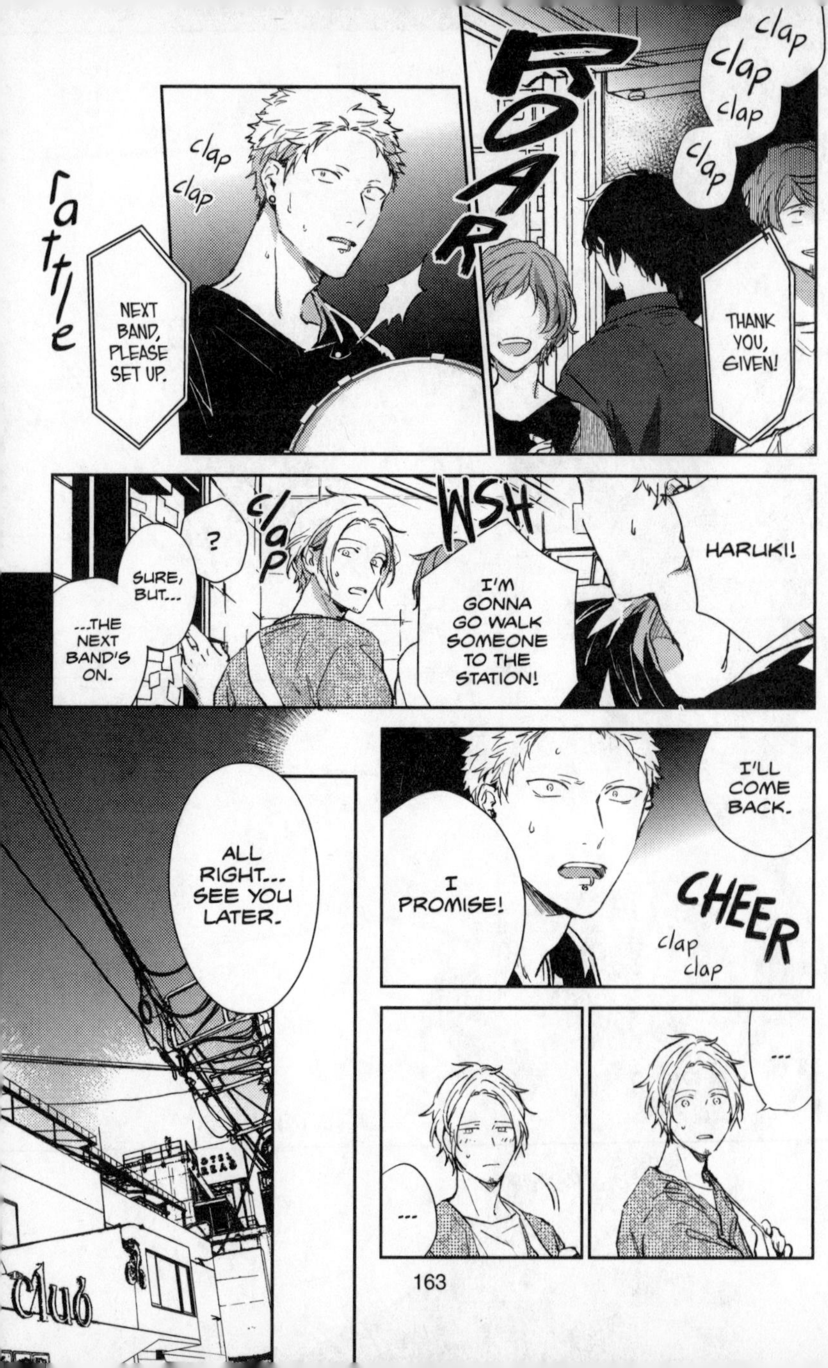
clap
clap
clap
clap
ROAR
THANK YOU, GIVEN!
clap
clap
rattle
NEXT BAND, PLEASE SET UP.
HARUKI!
WSH
I'M GONNA GO WALK SOMEONE TO THE STATION!
clap
?
SURE, BUT...
...THE NEXT BAND'S ON.
I'LL COME BACK.
I PROMISE!
CHEER
clap
clap
...
...
ALL RIGHT... SEE YOU LATER.
Club

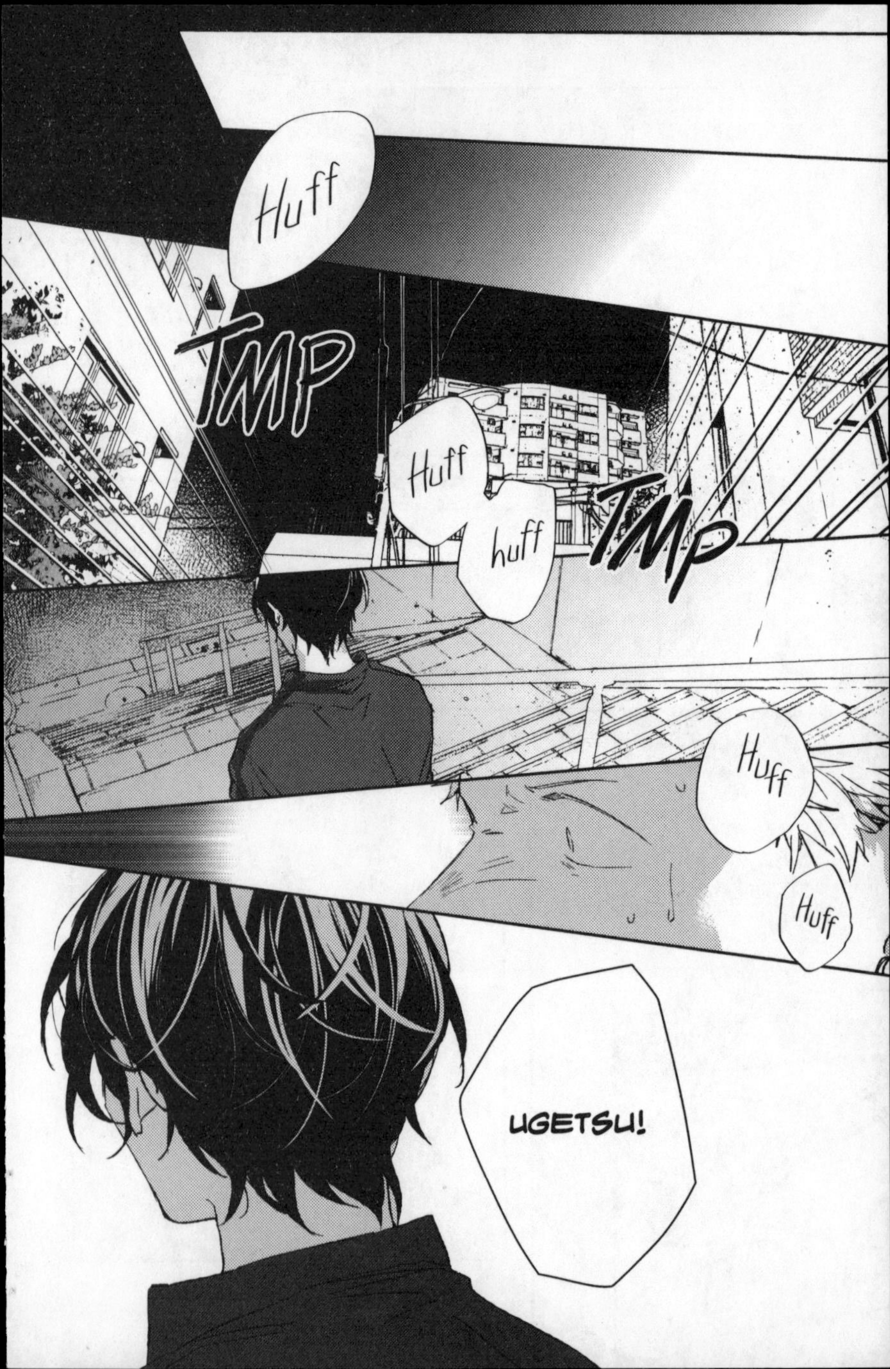
Huff
TMP
Huff
huff
TMP
Huff
Huff
UGETSU!

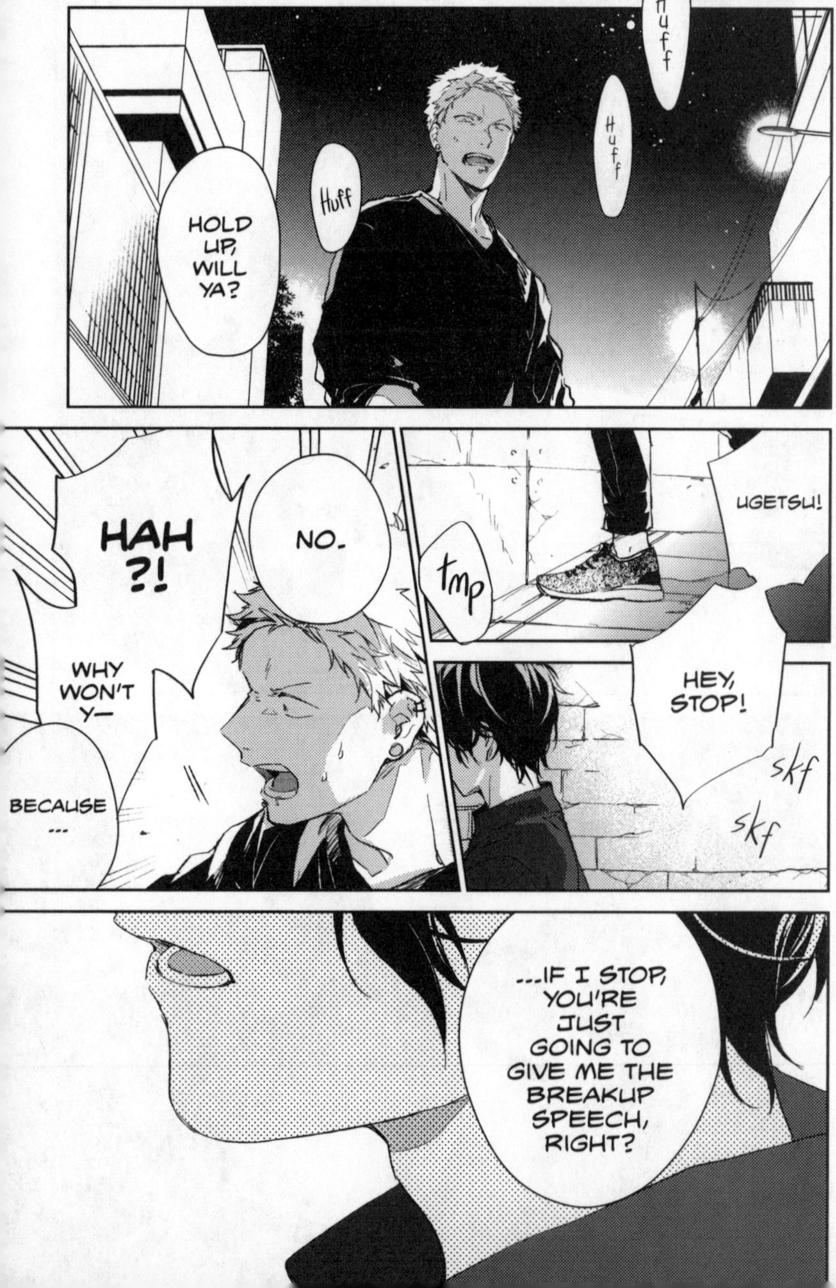
Huff
Huff
Huff
HOLD UP, WILL YA?
UGETSU!
tmp
HEY, STOP!
skf
skf
NO.
HAH?!
WHY WON'T Y—
BECAUSE ---
---IF I STOP, YOU'RE JUST GOING TO GIVE ME THE BREAKUP SPEECH, RIGHT?

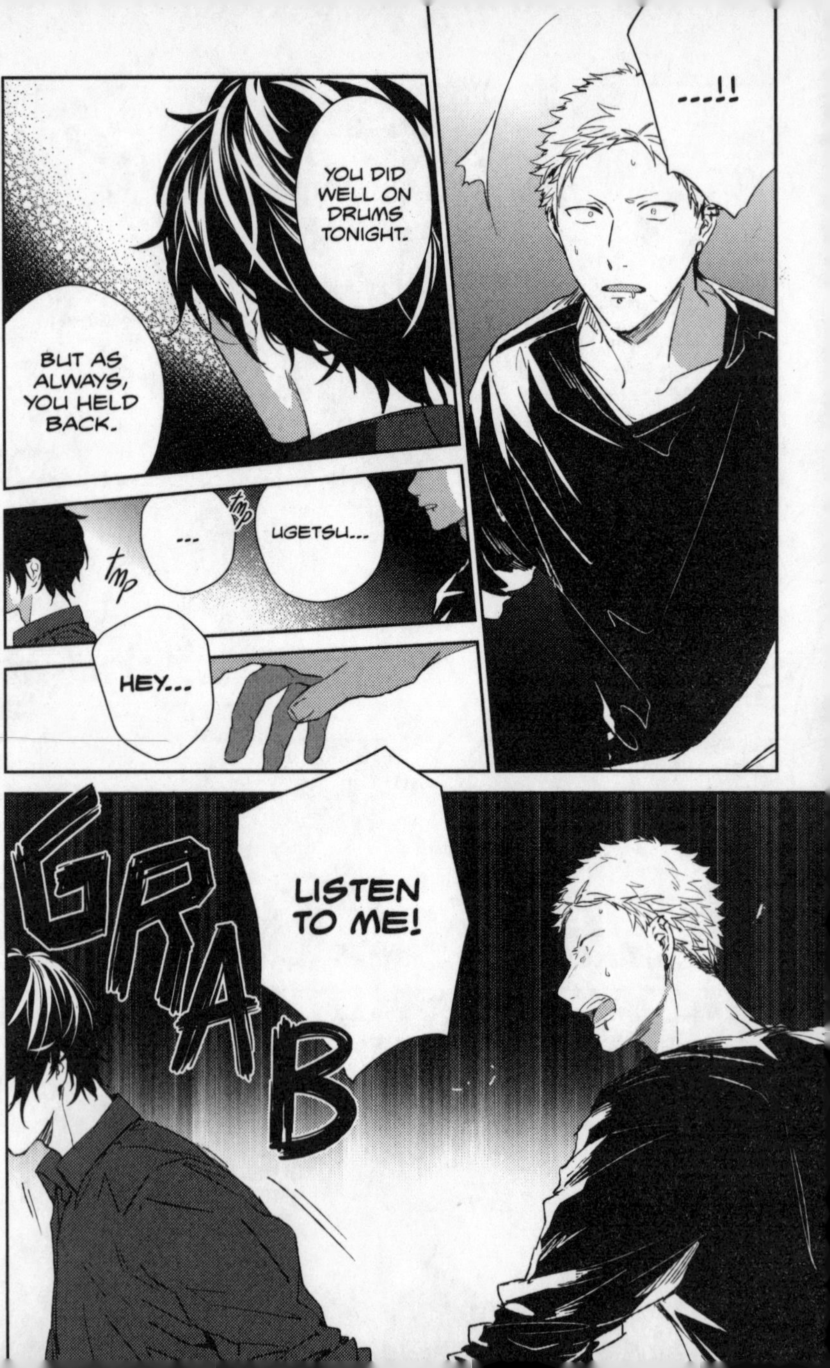
...!!
YOU DID WELL ON DRUMS TONIGHT.
BUT AS ALWAYS, YOU HELD BACK.
UGETSU...
tmp
...
tmp
HEY...
LISTEN TO ME!
GRAB

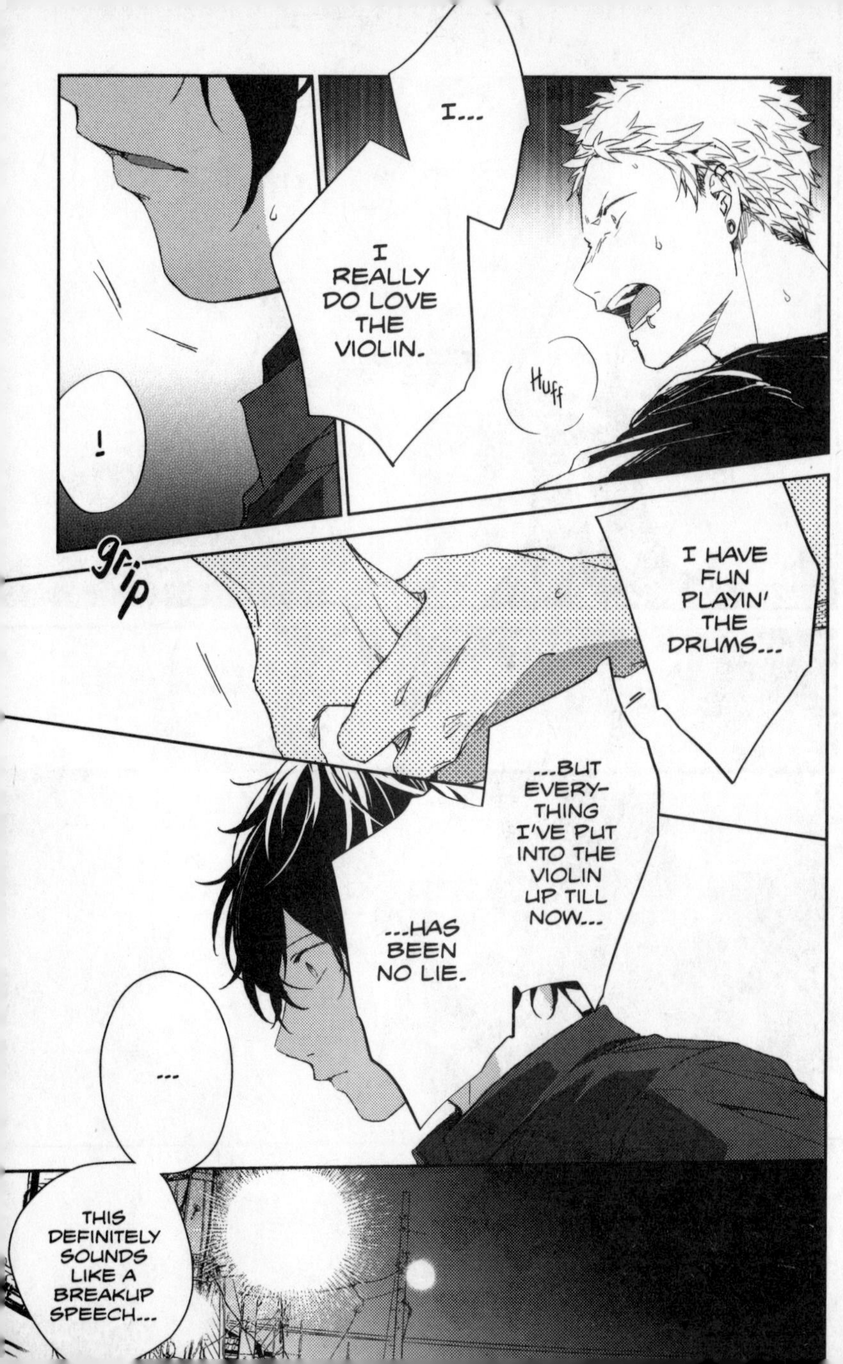
I...
I REALLY DO LOVE THE VIOLIN.
Huff
!
I HAVE FUN PLAYIN' THE DRUMS...
grip
...BUT EVERY-THING I'VE PUT INTO THE VIOLIN UP TILL NOW...
...HAS BEEN NO LIE.
...
THIS DEFINITELY SOUNDS LIKE A BREAKUP SPEECH...

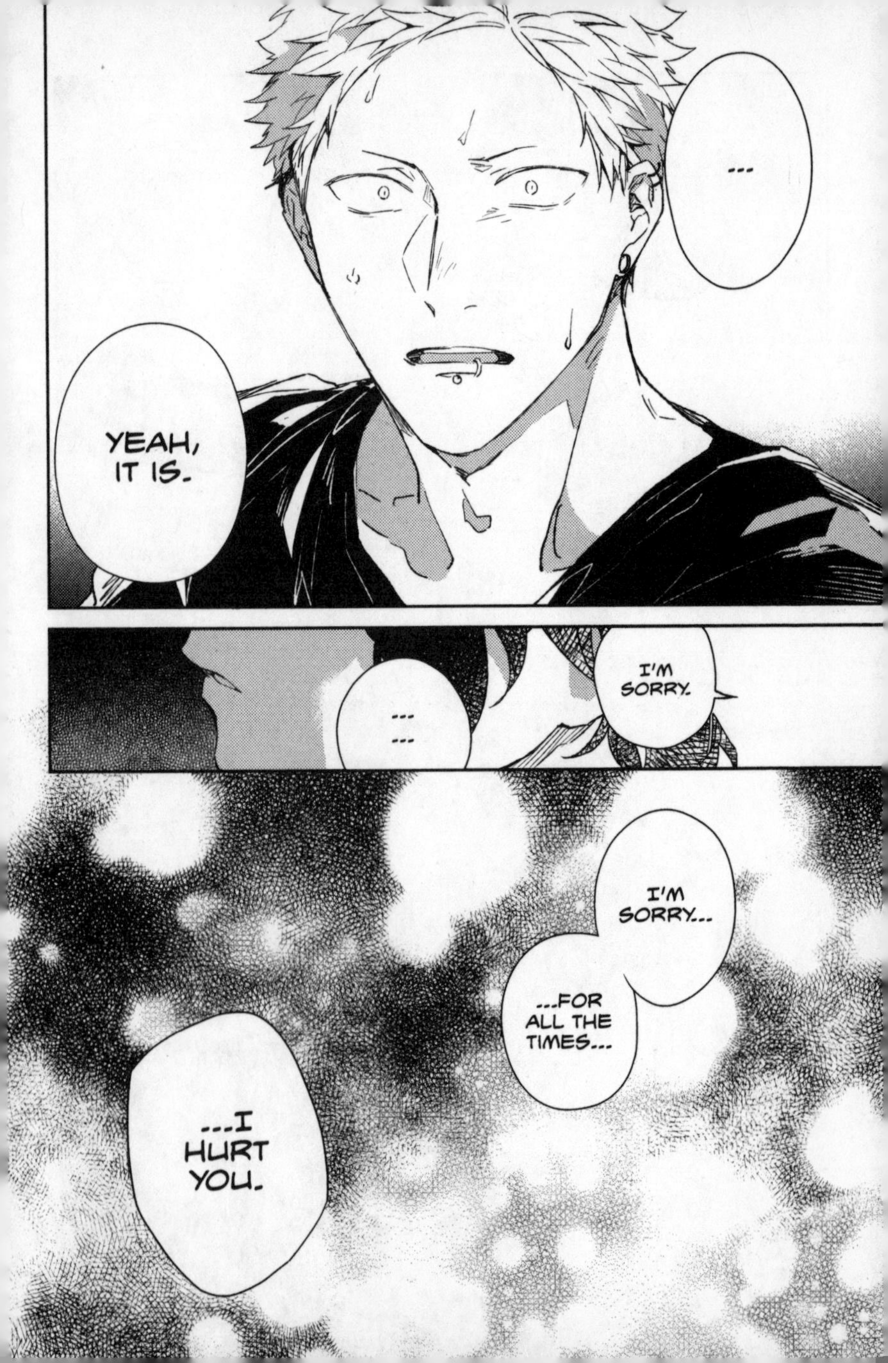
...
YEAH, IT IS.
I'M SORRY.
... ...
I'M SORRY...
...FOR ALL THE TIMES...
...I HURT YOU.

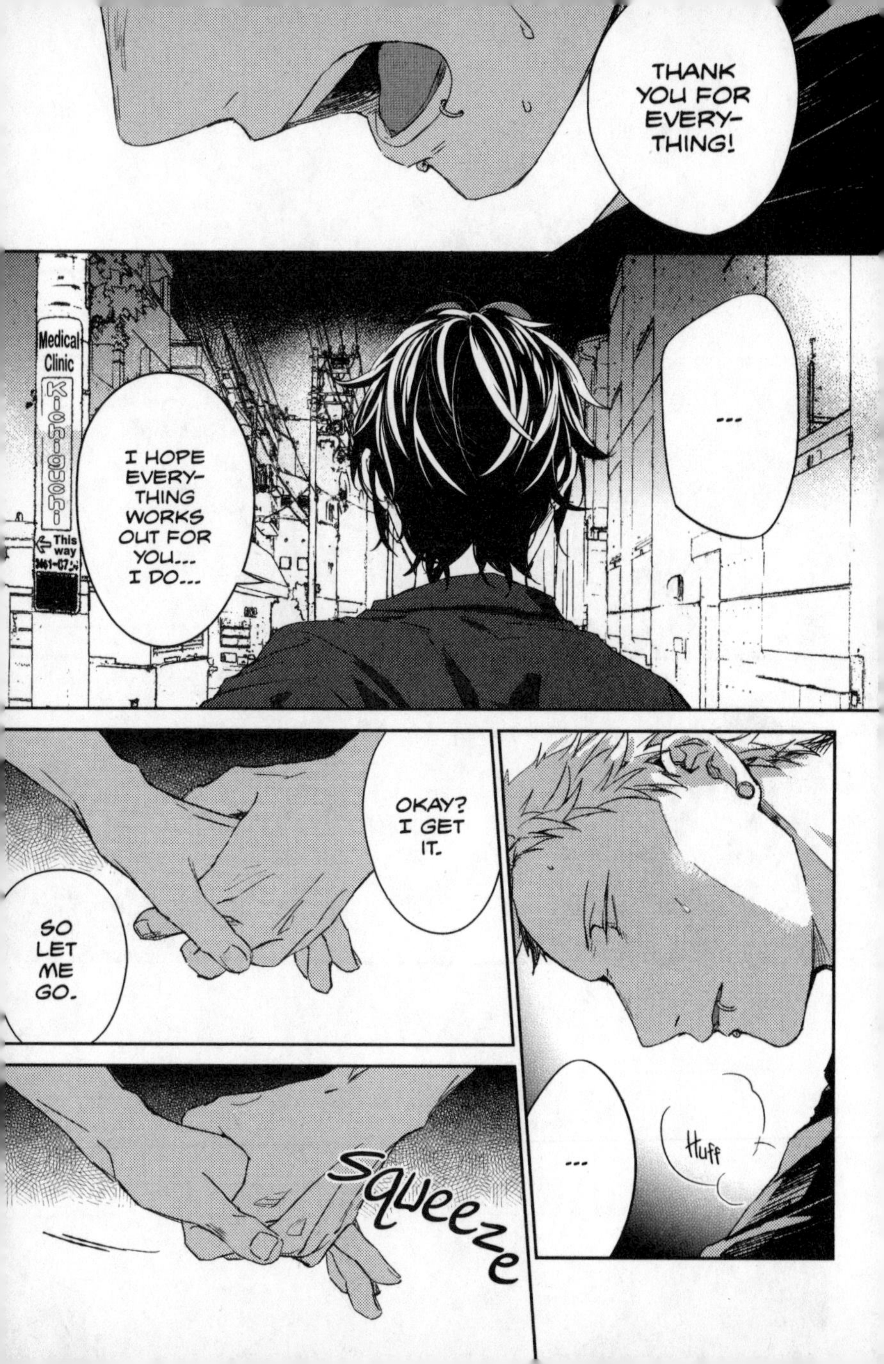
THANK YOU FOR EVERY-THING!
...
Medical Clinic
Kichiguchi
This way
I HOPE EVERY-THING WORKS OUT FOR YOU... I DO...
...
Huff
OKAY? I GET IT.
SO LET ME GO.
Squeeze

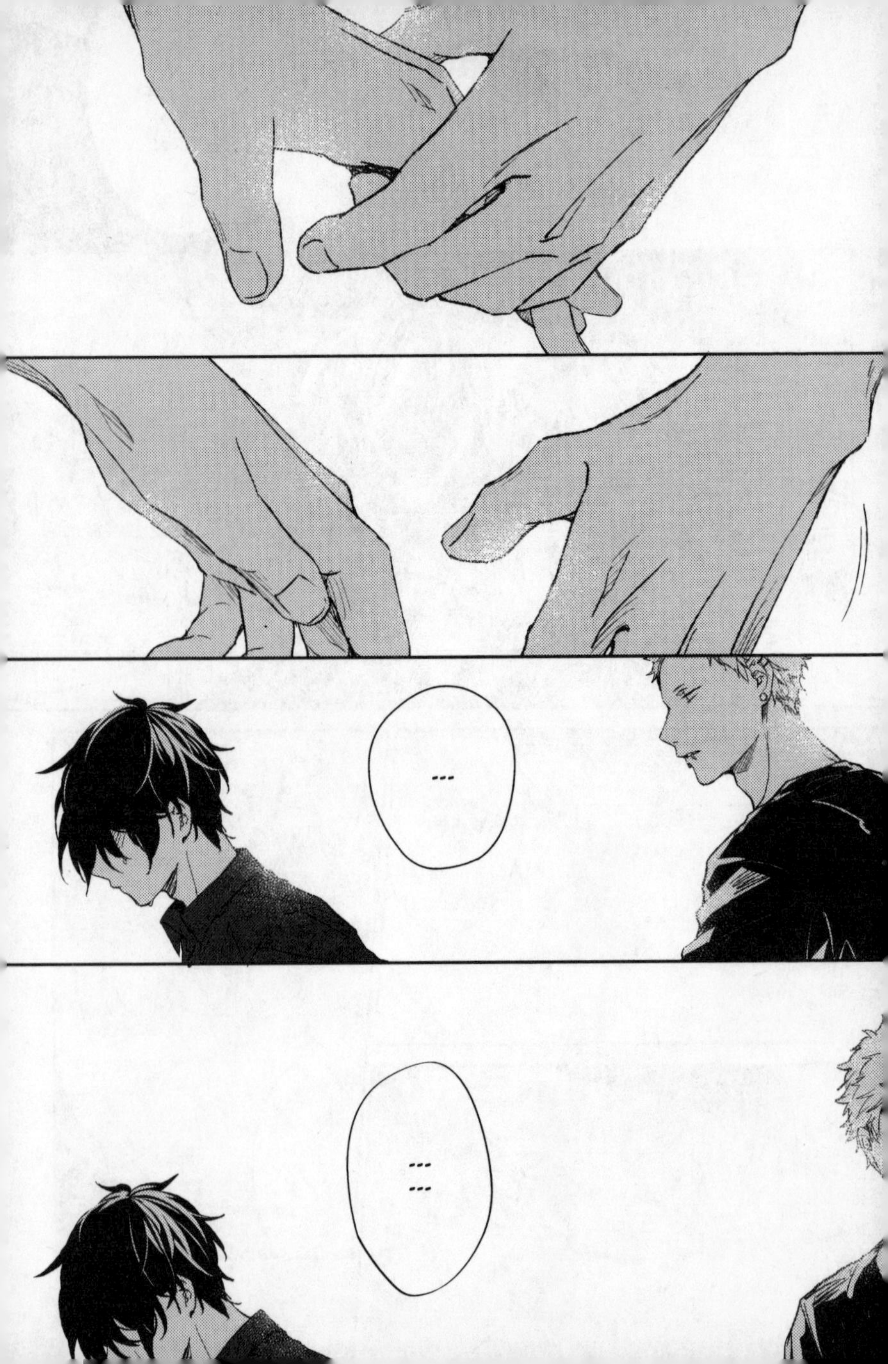
...
...
...

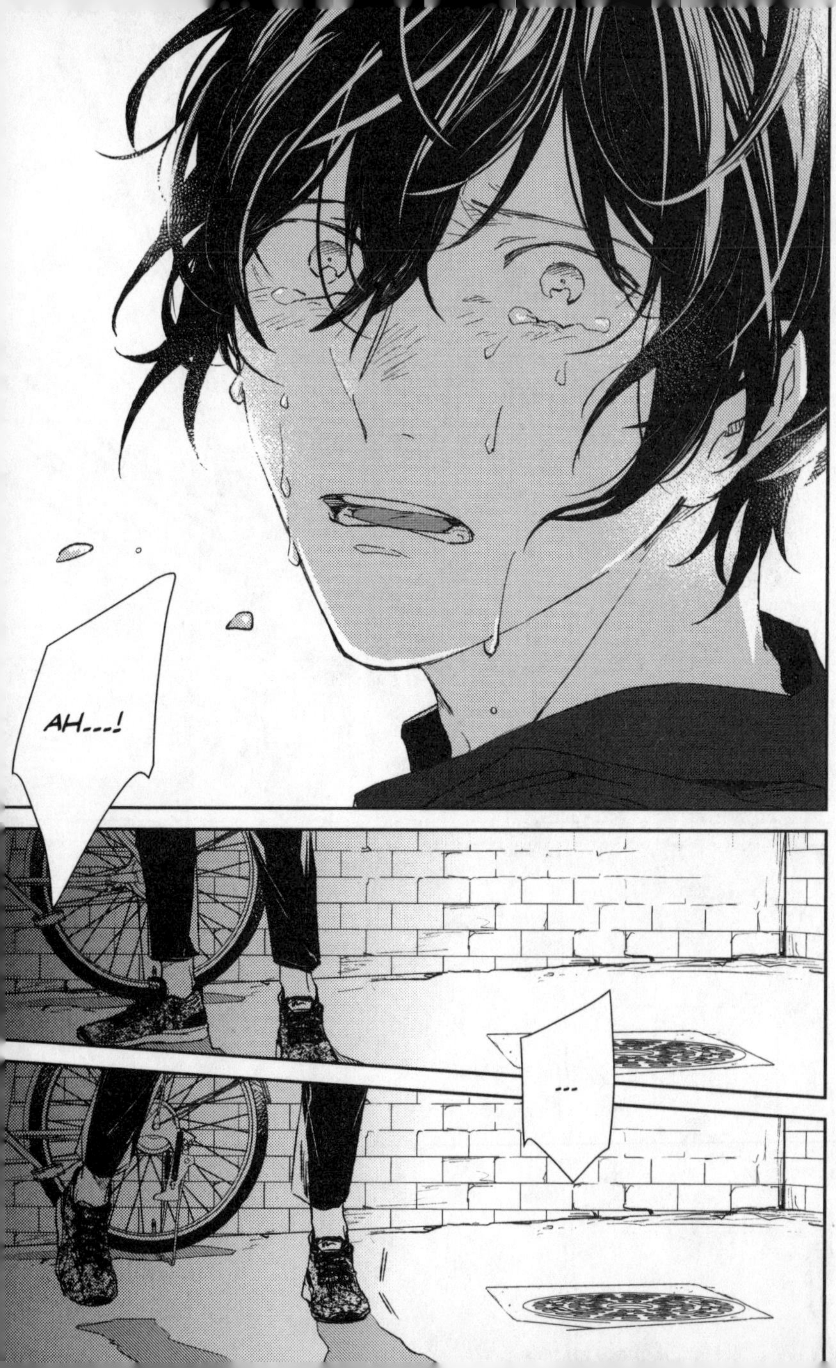
AH...!
...

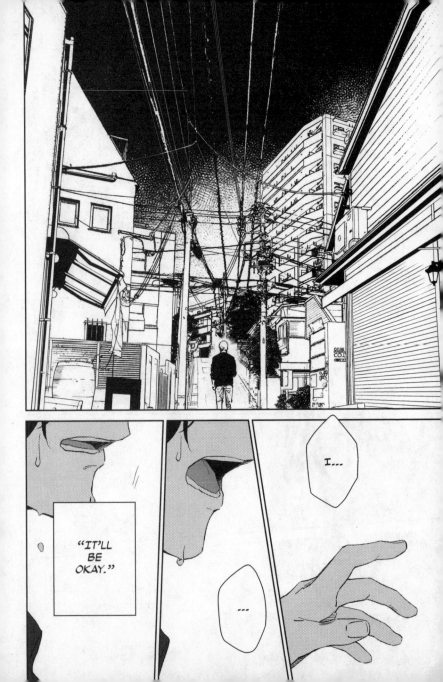

I....

"IT'LL
BE
OKAY."

....

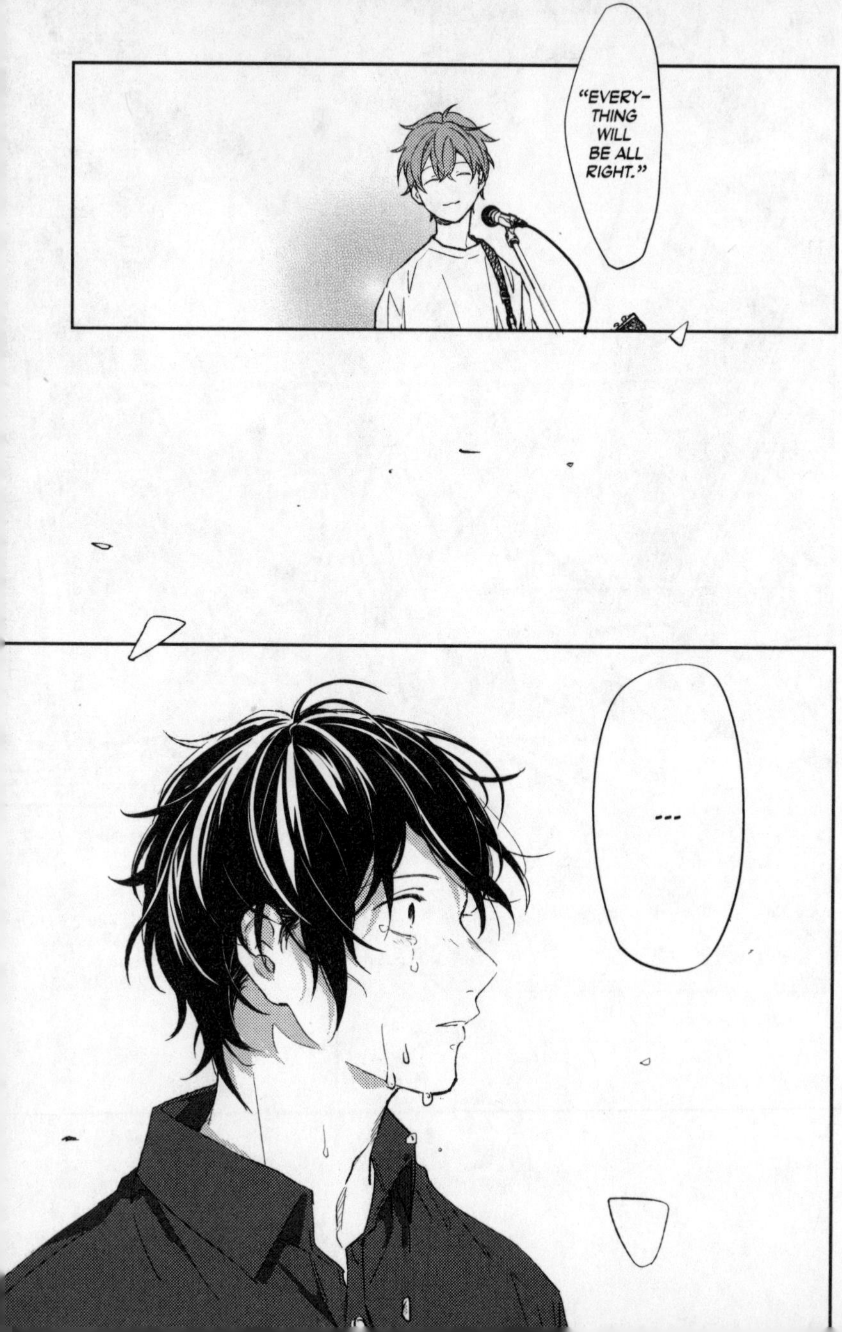
"EVERY-THING WILL BE ALL RIGHT."
...

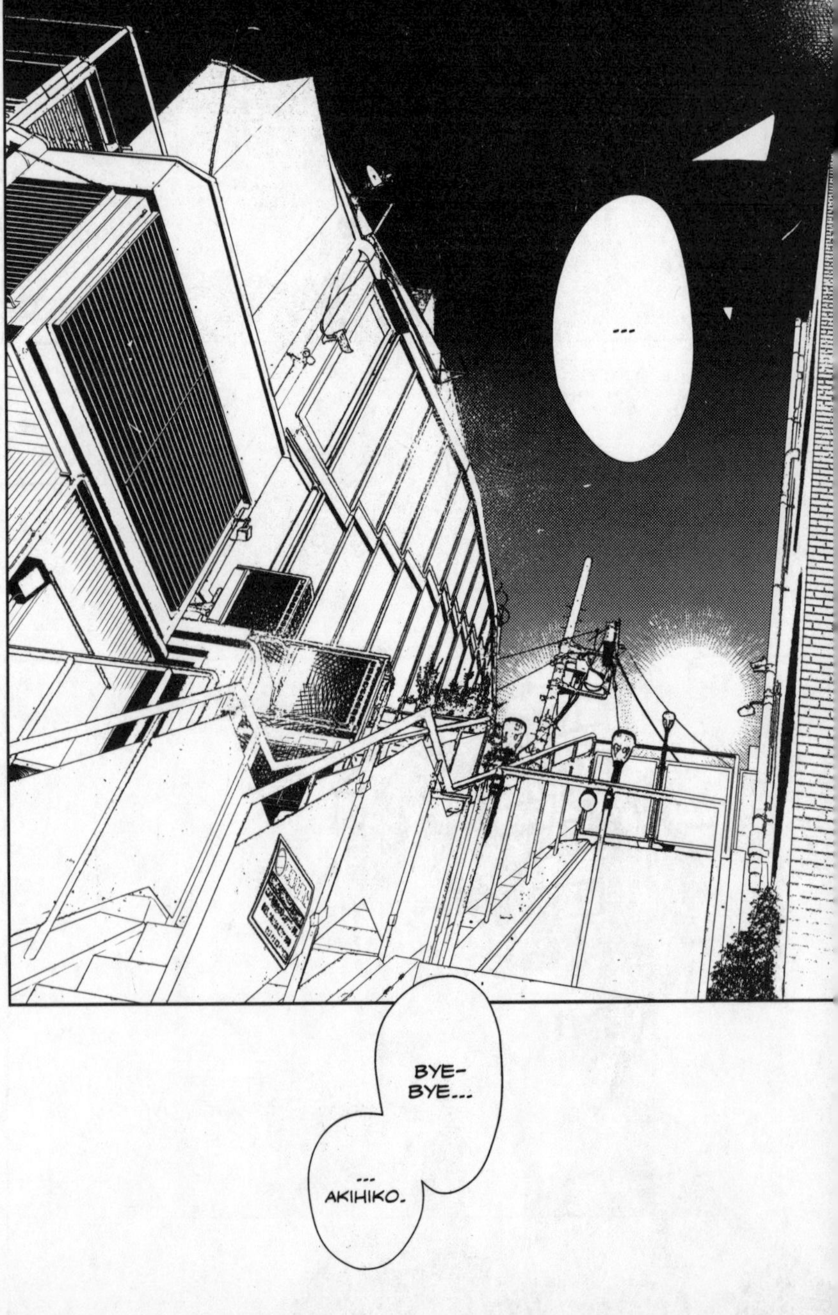
...
BYE-BYE...
...AKIHIKO.

chapter 28

given

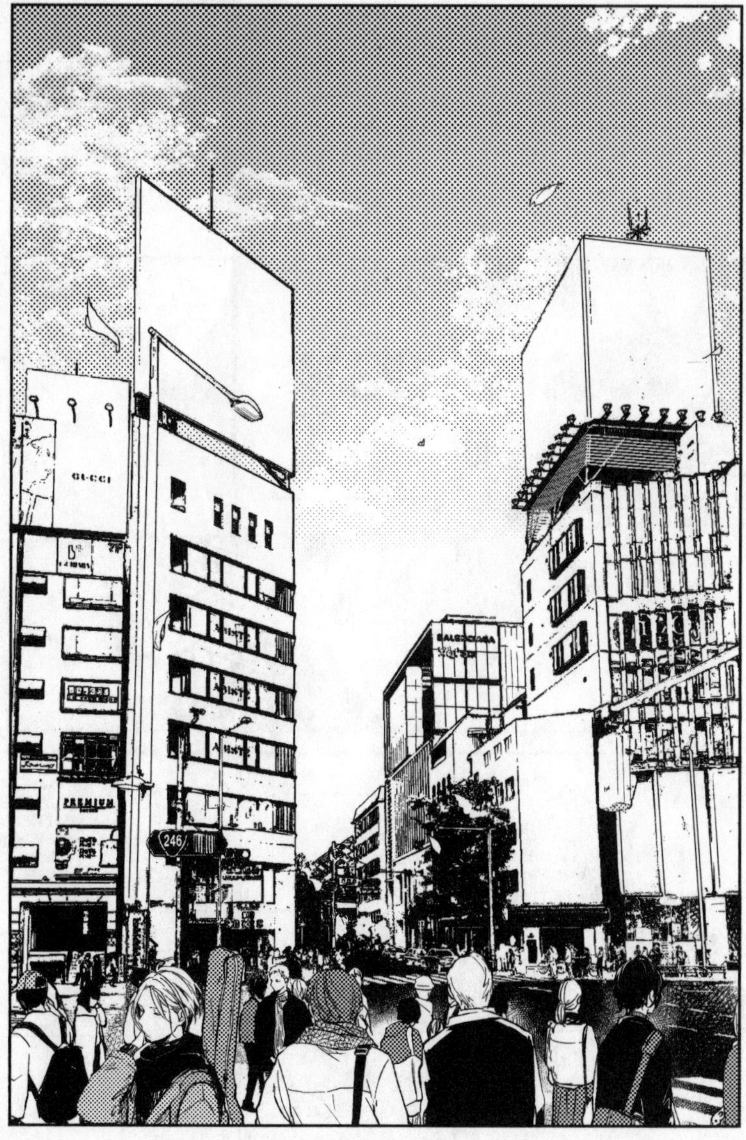

PREMIUM
246

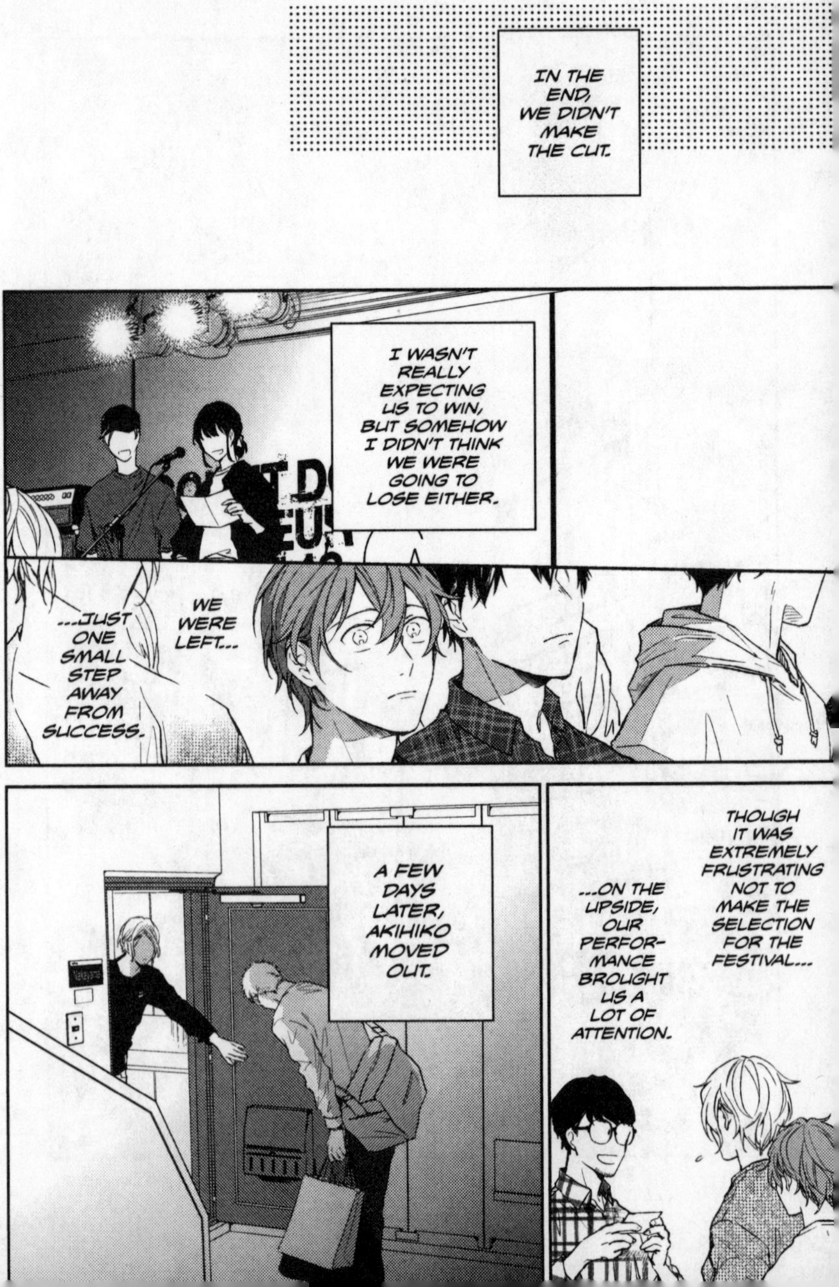
IN THE END, WE DIDN'T MAKE THE CUT.
I WASN'T REALLY EXPECTING US TO WIN, BUT SOMEHOW I DIDN'T THINK WE WERE GOING TO LOSE EITHER.
WE WERE LEFT...
...JUST ONE SMALL STEP AWAY FROM SUCCESS.
THOUGH IT WAS EXTREMELY FRUSTRATING NOT TO MAKE THE SELECTION FOR THE FESTIVAL...
...ON THE UPSIDE, OUR PERFOR-MANCE BROUGHT US A LOT OF ATTENTION.
A FEW DAYS LATER, AKIHIKO MOVED OUT.

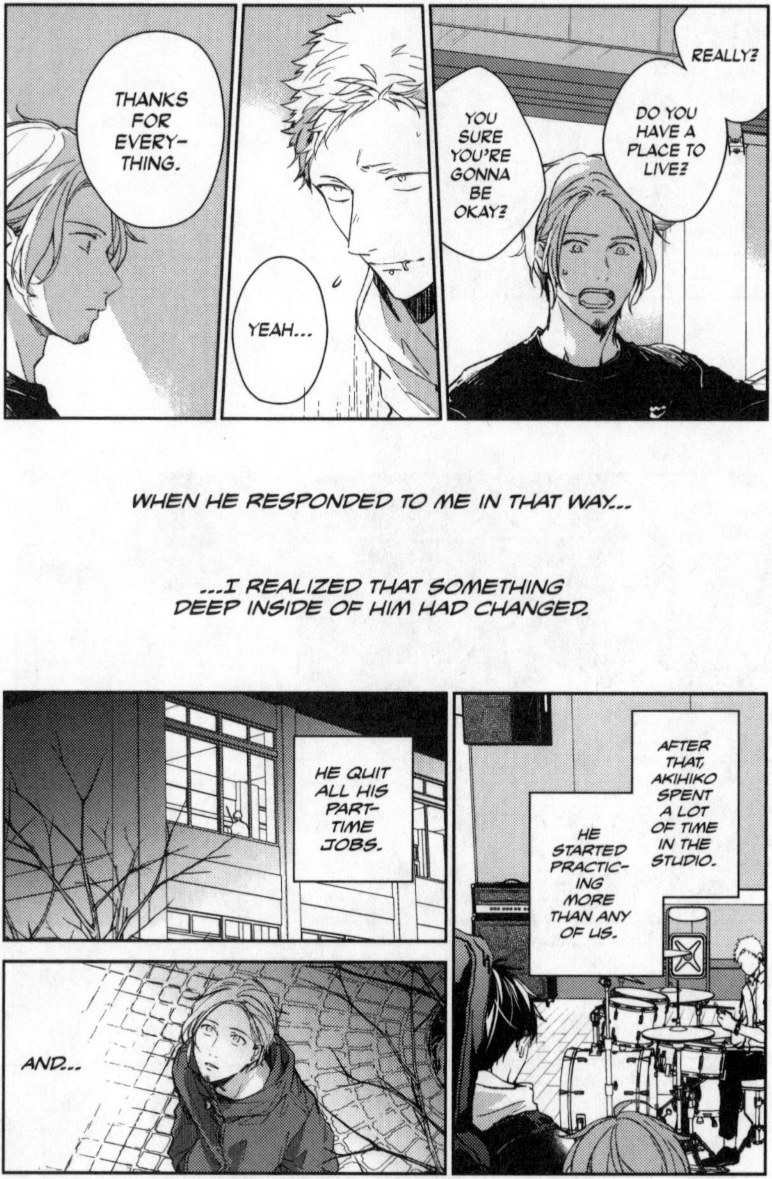
REALLY?
DO YOU HAVE A PLACE TO LIVE?
YOU SURE YOU'RE GONNA BE OKAY?
YEAH...
THANKS FOR EVERYTHING.
WHEN HE RESPONDED TO ME IN THAT WAY...
...I REALIZED THAT SOMETHING DEEP INSIDE OF HIM HAD CHANGED.
AFTER THAT, AKIHIKO SPENT A LOT OF TIME IN THE STUDIO.
HE STARTED PRACTICING MORE THAN ANY OF US.
HE QUIT ALL HIS PART-TIME JOBS.
AND...

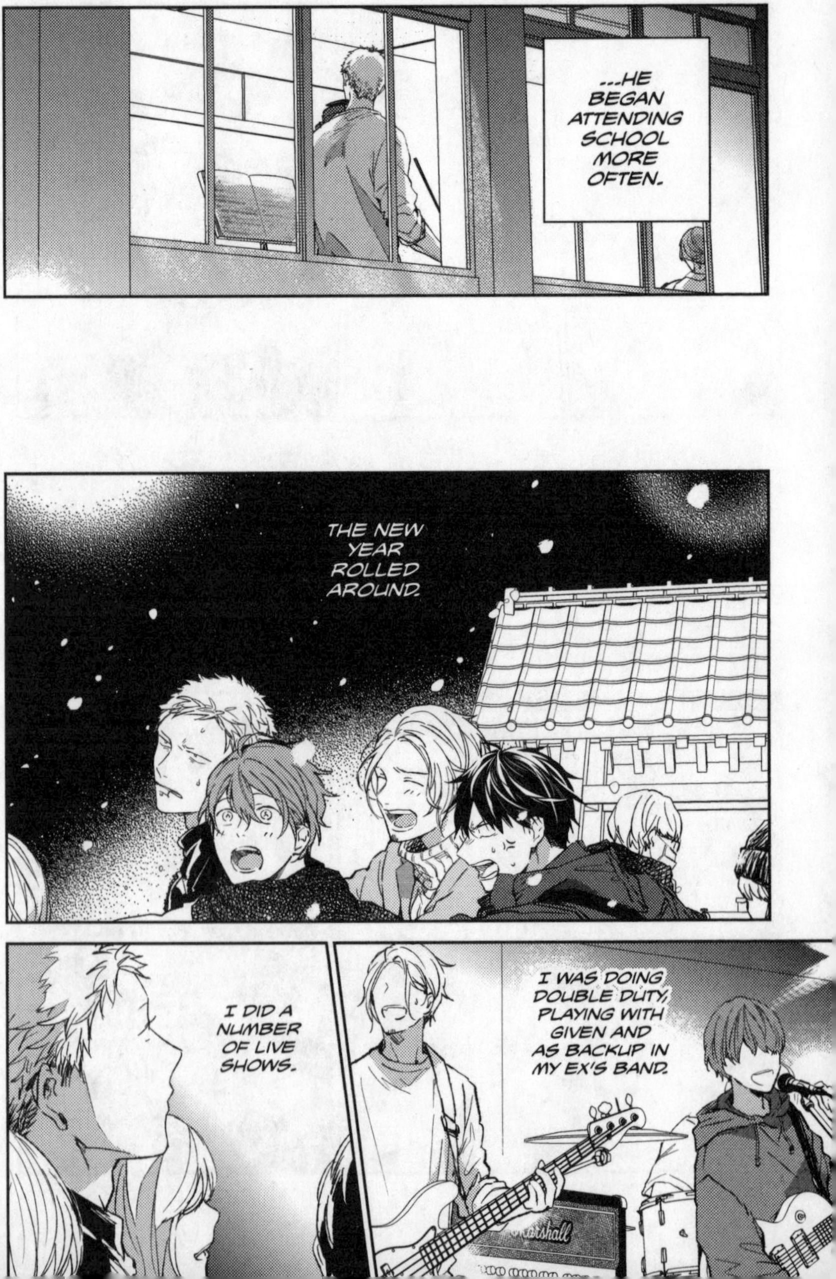
...HE BEGAN ATTENDING SCHOOL MORE OFTEN.
THE NEW YEAR ROLLED AROUND.
I WAS DOING DOUBLE DUTY, PLAYING WITH GIVEN AND AS BACKUP IN MY EX'S BAND.
I DID A NUMBER OF LIVE SHOWS.

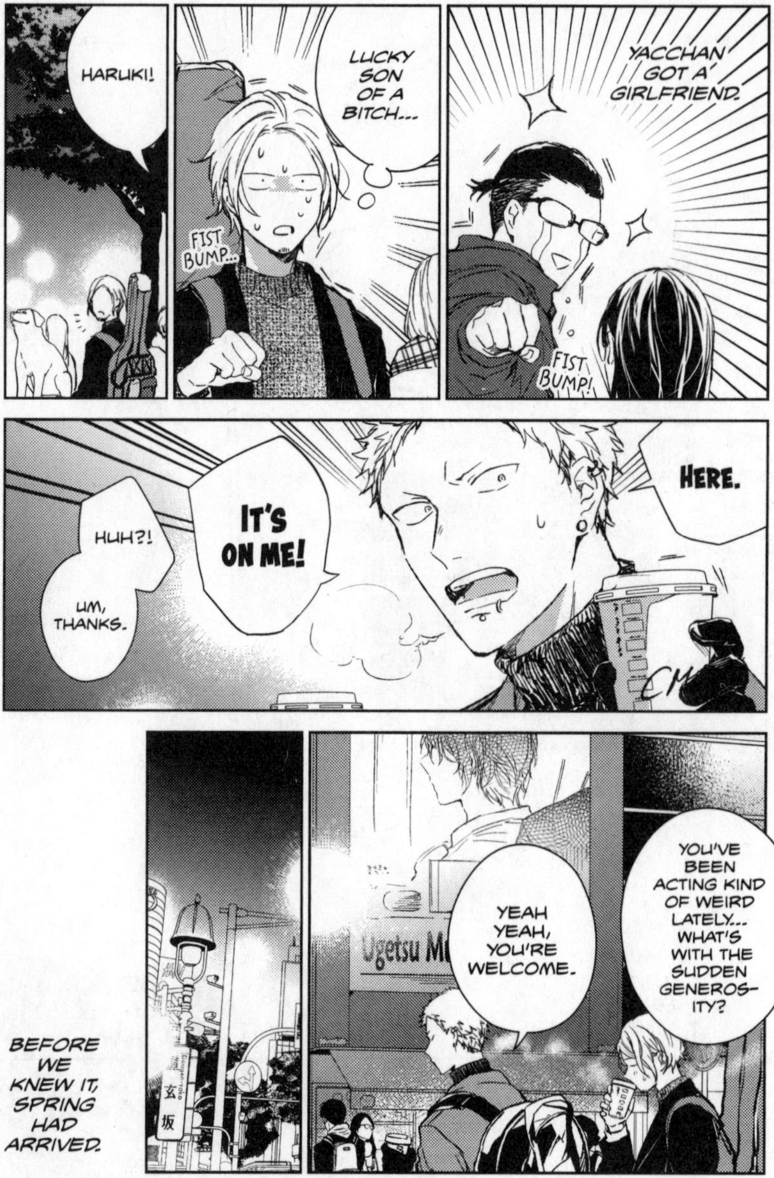
YACCHAN GOT A GIRLFRIEND.
FIST BUMP!
LUCKY SON OF A BITCH...
FIST BUMP...
HARUKI!
HERE.
CM
IT'S ON ME!
HUH?!
UM, THANKS.
YOU'VE BEEN ACTING KIND OF WEIRD LATELY... WHAT'S WITH THE SUDDEN GENEROSITY?
YEAH YEAH, YOU'RE WELCOME.
BEFORE WE KNEW IT, SPRING HAD ARRIVED.

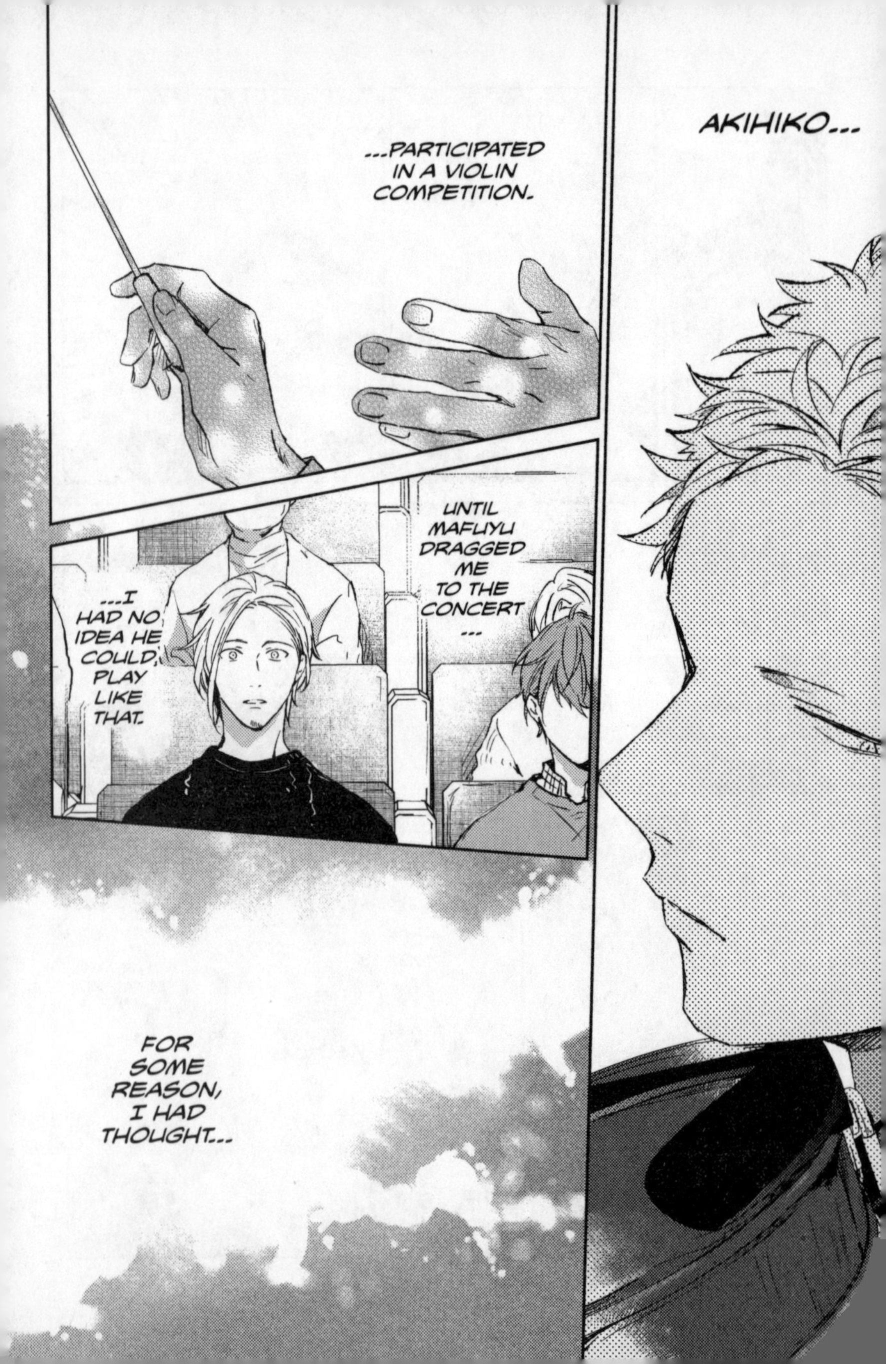
AKIHIKO...
...PARTICIPATED IN A VIOLIN COMPETITION.
UNTIL MAFUYU DRAGGED ME TO THE CONCERT...
...I HAD NO IDEA HE COULD PLAY LIKE THAT.
FOR SOME REASON, I HAD THOUGHT...

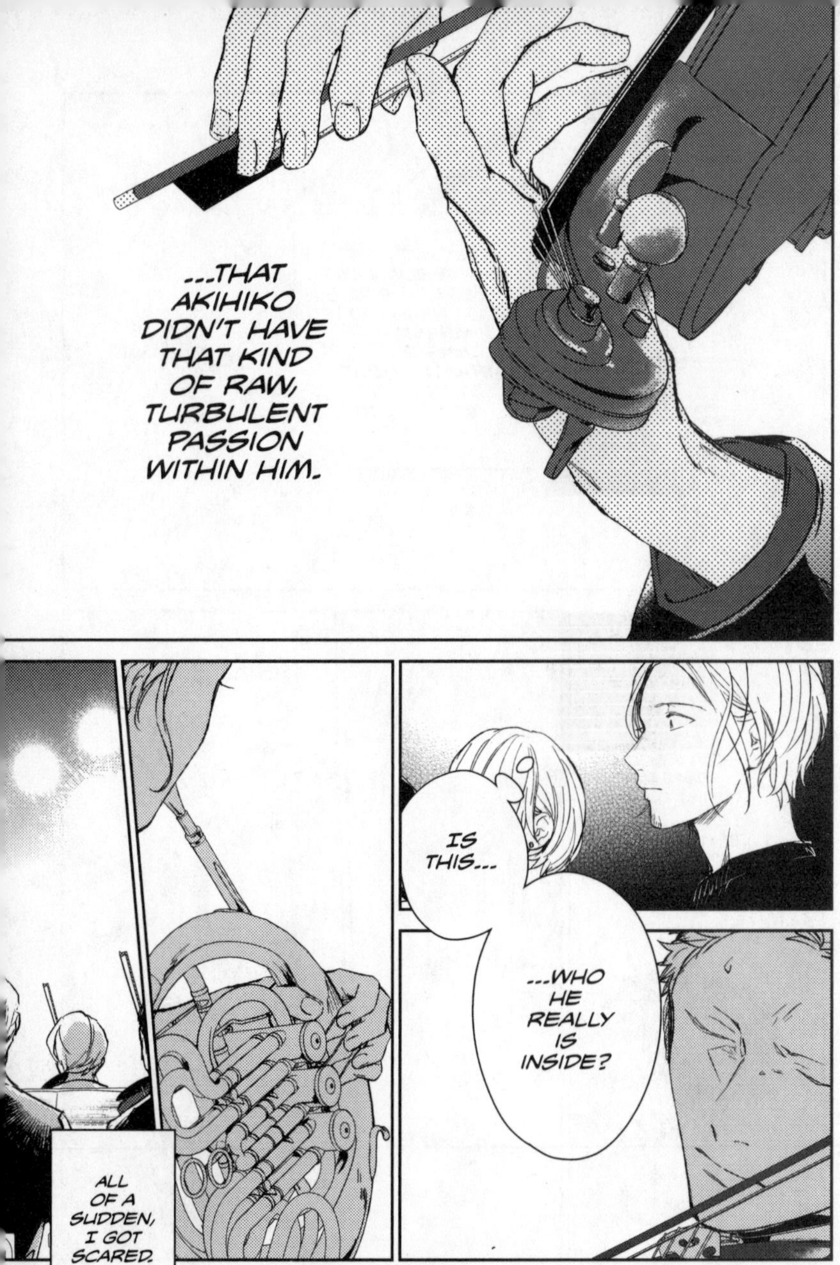
...THAT AKIHIKO DIDN'T HAVE THAT KIND OF RAW, TURBULENT PASSION WITHIN HIM.
IS THIS... ...WHO HE REALLY IS INSIDE?
ALL OF A SUDDEN, I GOT SCARED.

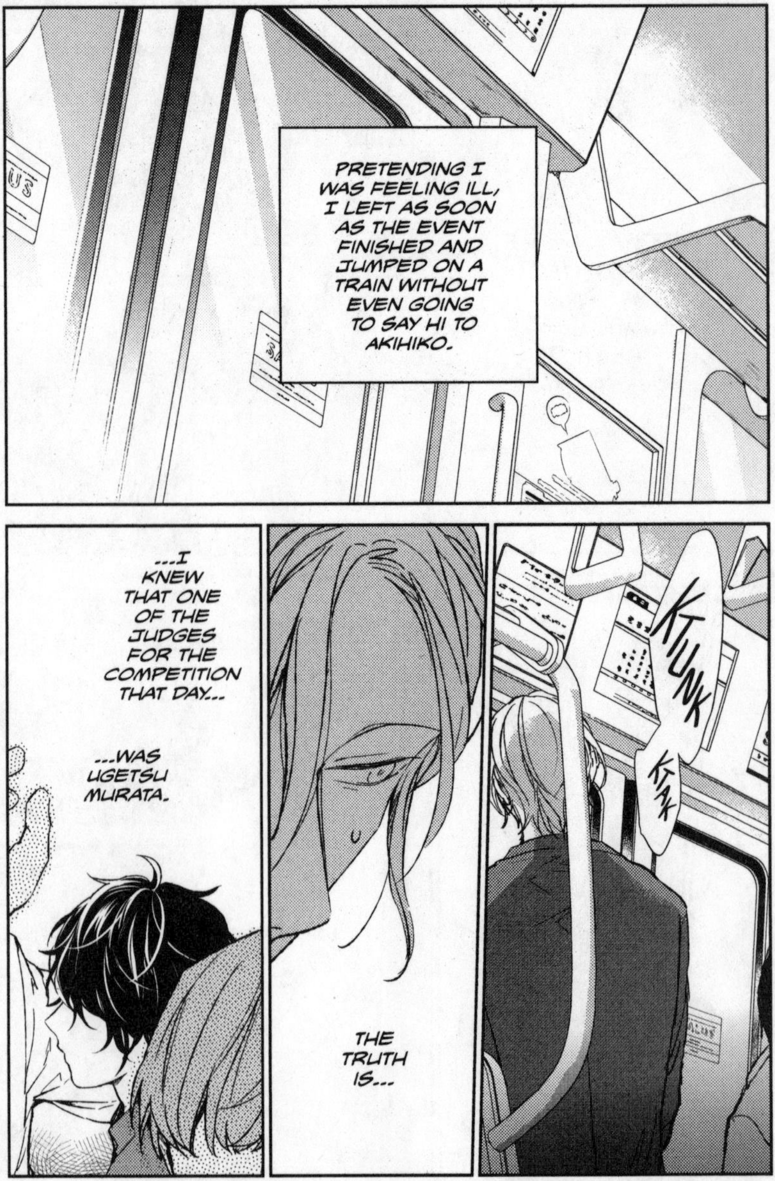
PRETENDING I WAS FEELING ILL, I LEFT AS SOON AS THE EVENT FINISHED AND JUMPED ON A TRAIN WITHOUT EVEN GOING TO SAY HI TO AKIHIKO.
KTUNK
KTAK
THE TRUTH IS...
...I KNEW THAT ONE OF THE JUDGES FOR THE COMPETITION THAT DAY...
...WAS UGETSU MURATA.

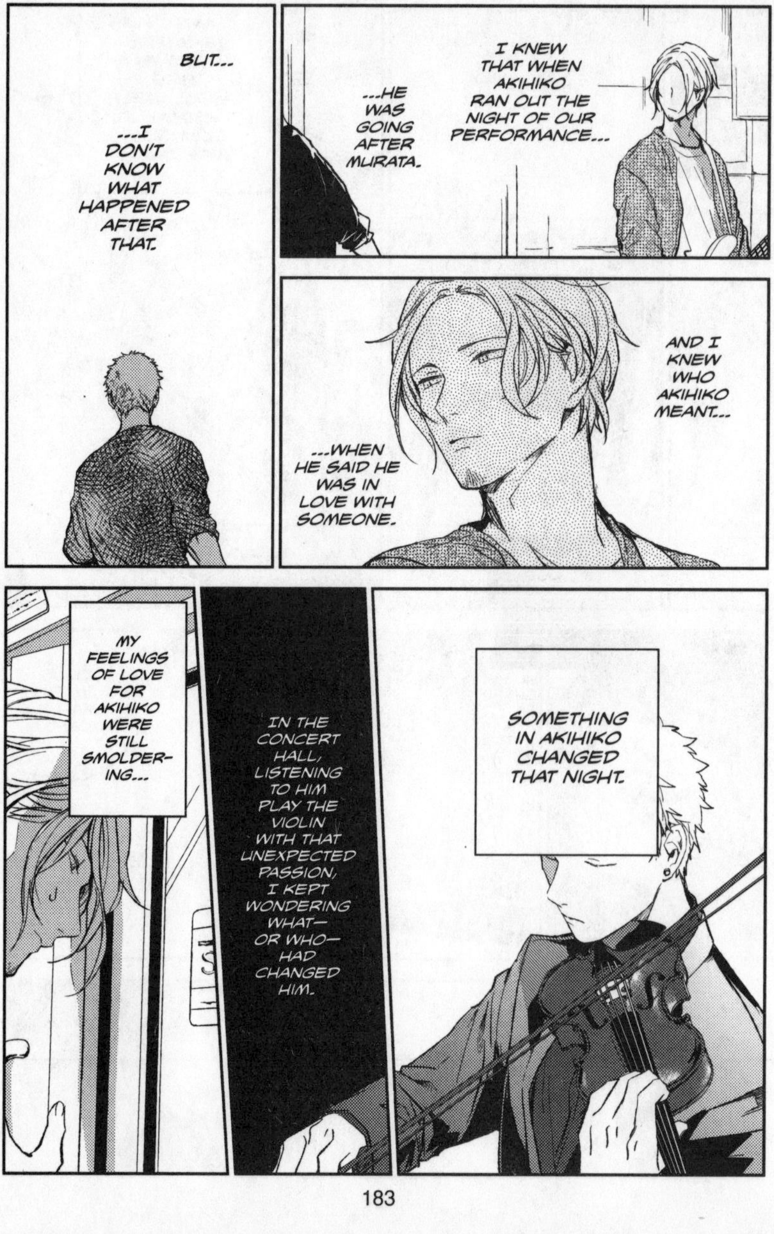
I KNEW THAT WHEN AKIHIKO RAN OUT THE NIGHT OF OUR PERFORMANCE...
...HE WAS GOING AFTER MURATA.
AND I KNEW WHO AKIHIKO MEANT...
...WHEN HE SAID HE WAS IN LOVE WITH SOMEONE.
BUT...
...I DON'T KNOW WHAT HAPPENED AFTER THAT.
SOMETHING IN AKIHIKO CHANGED THAT NIGHT.
IN THE CONCERT HALL, LISTENING TO HIM PLAY THE VIOLIN WITH THAT UNEXPECTED PASSION, I KEPT WONDERING WHAT— OR WHO— HAD CHANGED HIM.
MY FEELINGS OF LOVE FOR AKIHIKO WERE STILL SMOLDER-ING...

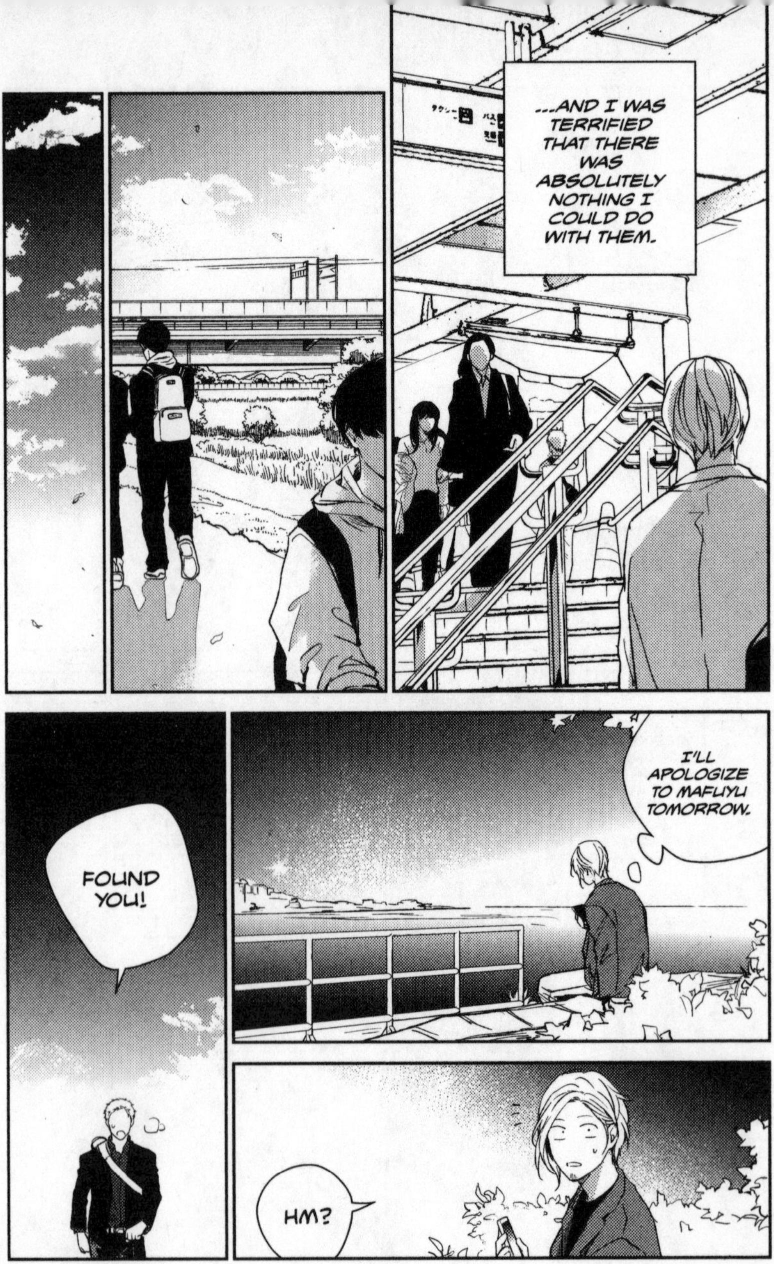
...AND I WAS TERRIFIED THAT THERE WAS ABSOLUTELY NOTHING I COULD DO WITH THEM.
I'LL APOLOGIZE TO MAFUYU TOMORROW.
HM?
FOUND YOU!

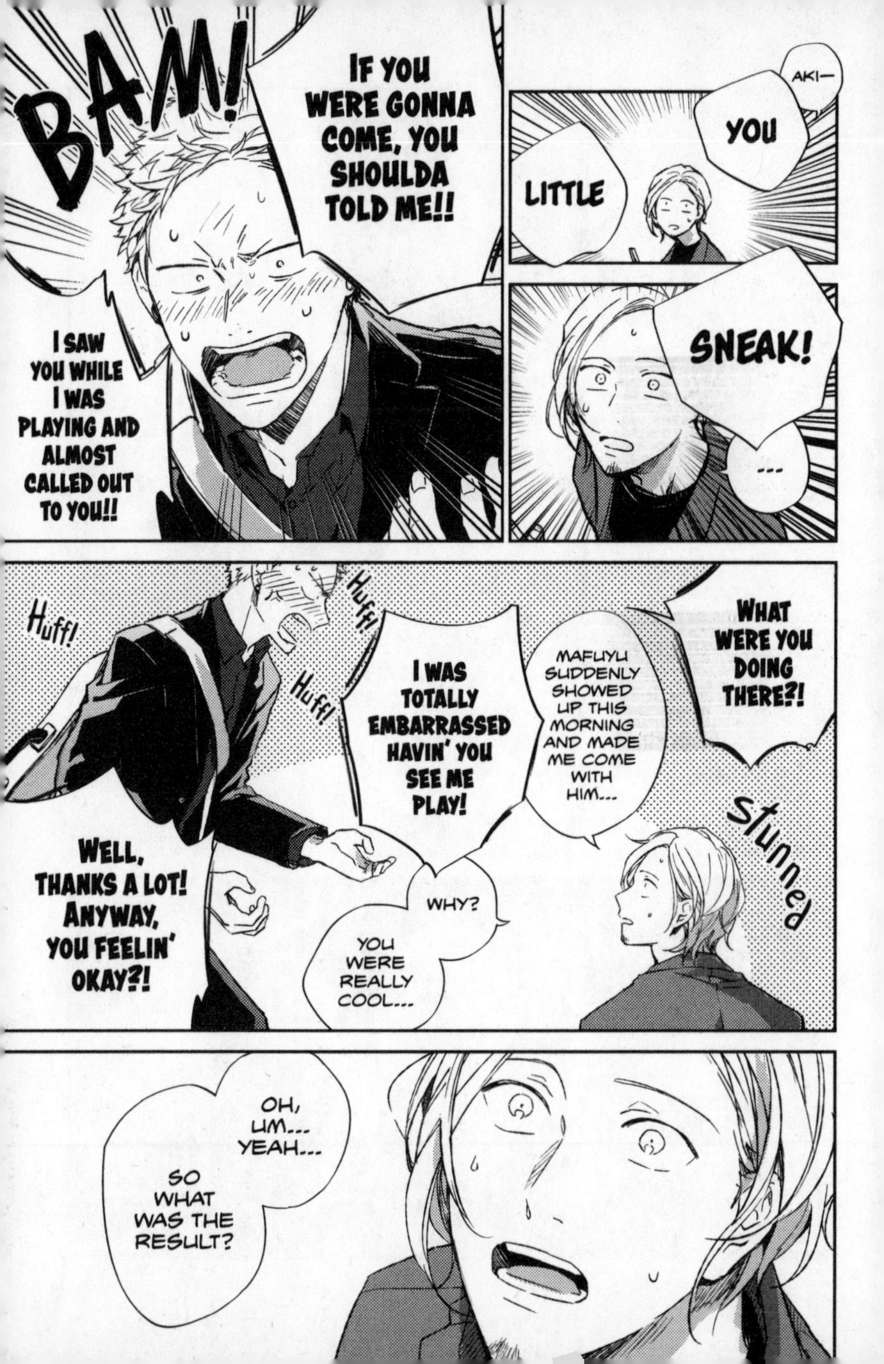
AKI—
YOU
LITTLE
SNEAK!
...
BAM!
IF YOU WERE GONNA COME, YOU SHOULDA TOLD ME!!
I SAW YOU WHILE I WAS PLAYING AND ALMOST CALLED OUT TO YOU!!
WHAT WERE YOU DOING THERE?!
Stunned
MAFUYU SUDDENLY SHOWED UP THIS MORNING AND MADE ME COME WITH HIM...
I WAS TOTALLY EMBARRASSED HAVIN' YOU SEE ME PLAY!
Huff!
Huff!
Huff!
WHY?
YOU WERE REALLY COOL...
WELL, THANKS A LOT! ANYWAY, YOU FEELIN' OKAY?!
OH, UM... YEAH...
SO WHAT WAS THE RESULT?

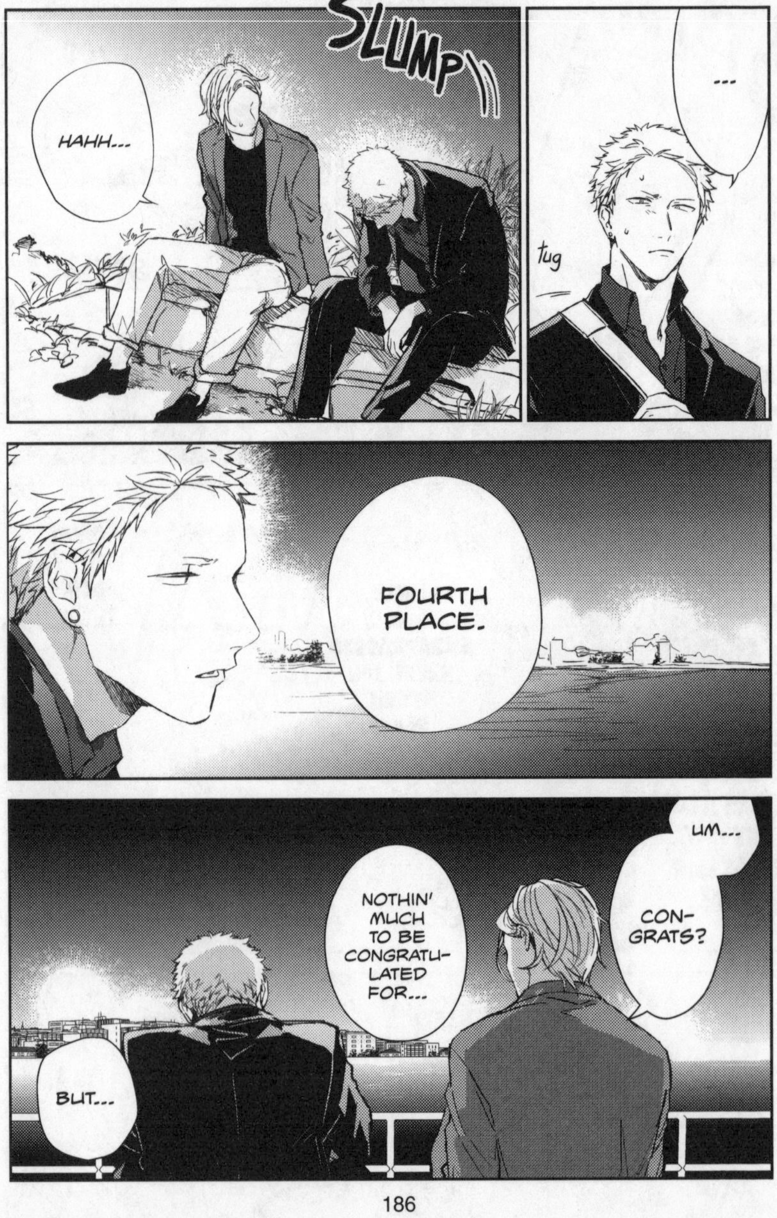
...
tug
SLUMP
HAHH...
FOURTH PLACE.
UM...
CON-GRATS?
NOTHIN' MUCH TO BE CONGRATU-LATED FOR...
BUT...

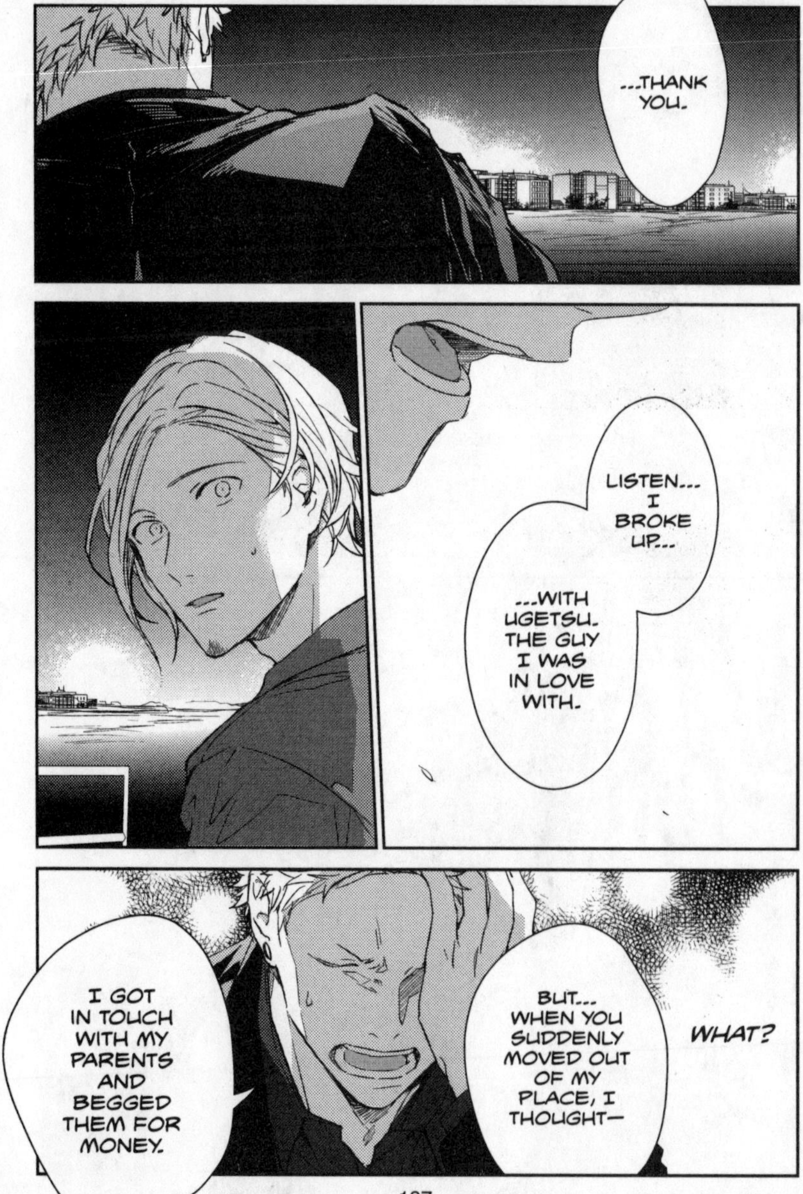
...THANK YOU.
LISTEN... I BROKE UP...
...WITH UGETSU. THE GUY I WAS IN LOVE WITH.
WHAT?
BUT... WHEN YOU SUDDENLY MOVED OUT OF MY PLACE, I THOUGHT—
I GOT IN TOUCH WITH MY PARENTS AND BEGGED THEM FOR MONEY.

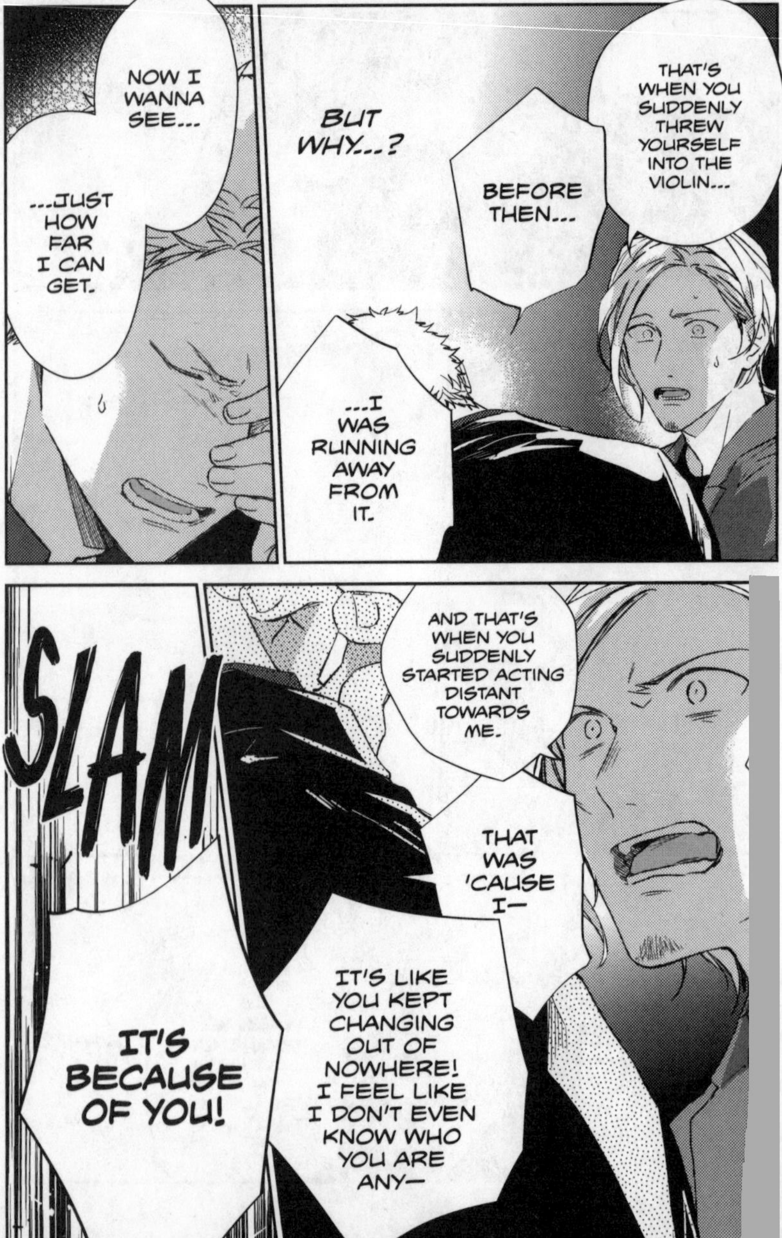
THAT'S WHEN YOU SUDDENLY THREW YOURSELF INTO THE VIOLIN...
BUT WHY...?
BEFORE THEN...
...I WAS RUNNING AWAY FROM IT.
NOW I WANNA SEE...
...JUST HOW FAR I CAN GET.
AND THAT'S WHEN YOU SUDDENLY STARTED ACTING DISTANT TOWARDS ME.
THAT WAS 'CAUSE I—
IT'S LIKE YOU KEPT CHANGING OUT OF NOWHERE! I FEEL LIKE I DON'T EVEN KNOW WHO YOU ARE ANY—
SLAM
IT'S BECAUSE OF YOU!

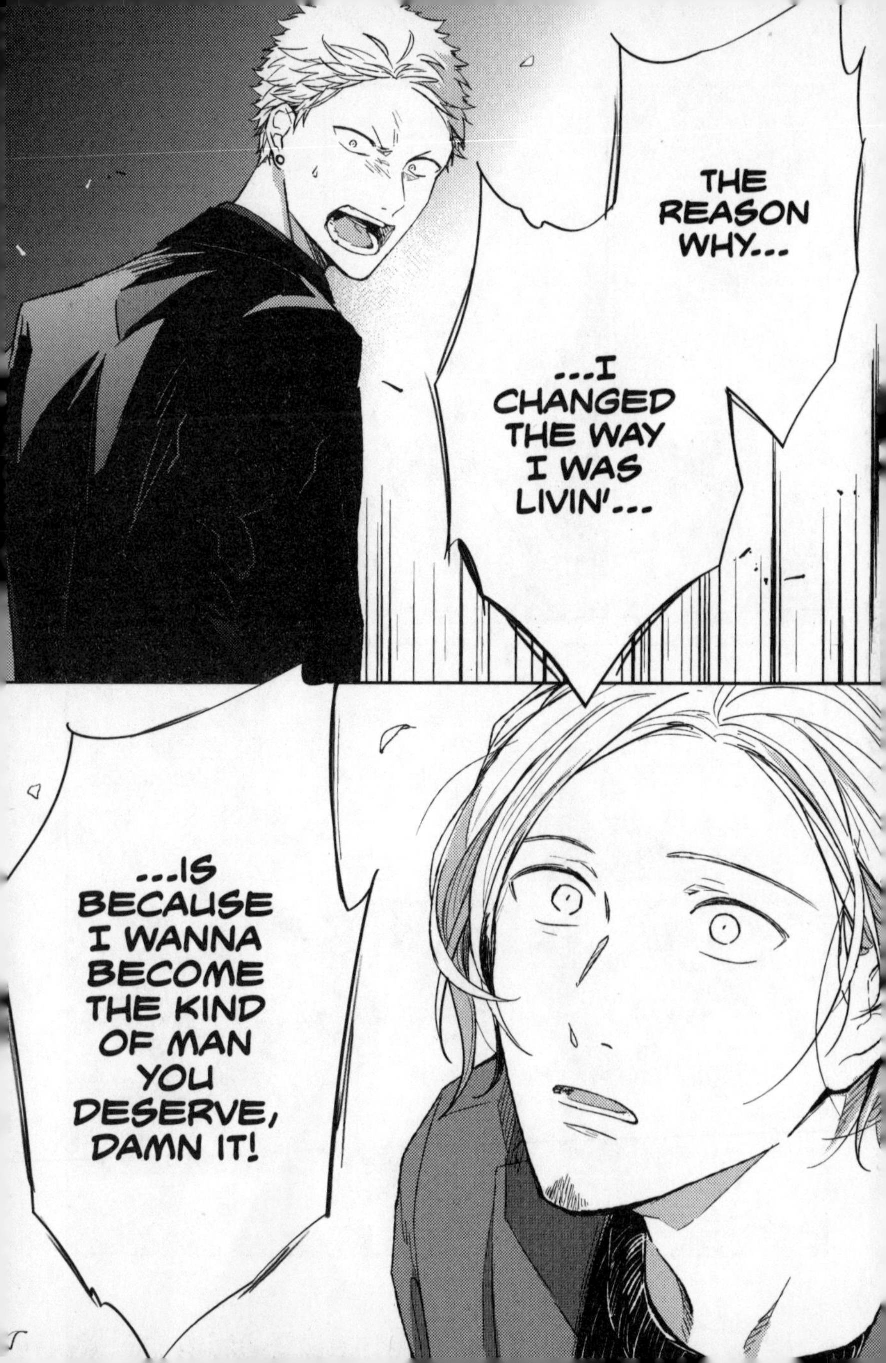
THE REASON WHY...
...I CHANGED THE WAY I WAS LIVIN'...
...IS BECAUSE I WANNA BECOME THE KIND OF MAN YOU DESERVE, DAMN IT!

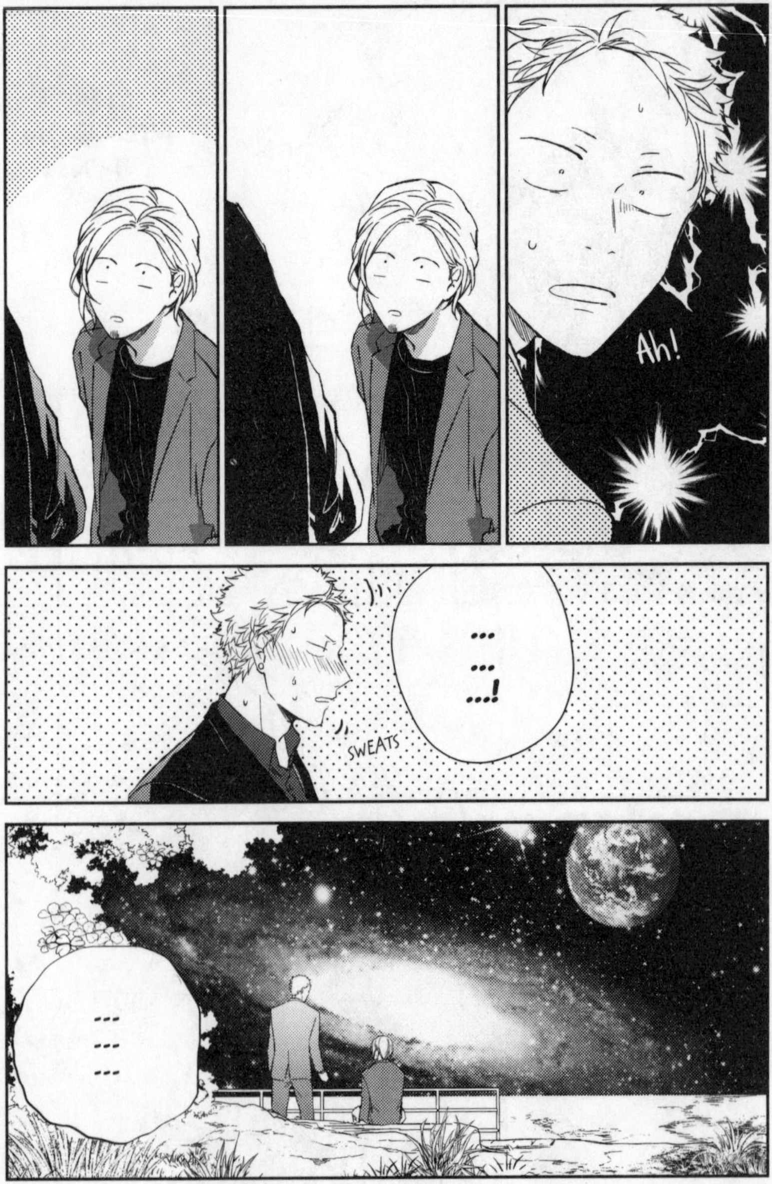
Ah!
...
...
...!
SWEATS
...
...
...

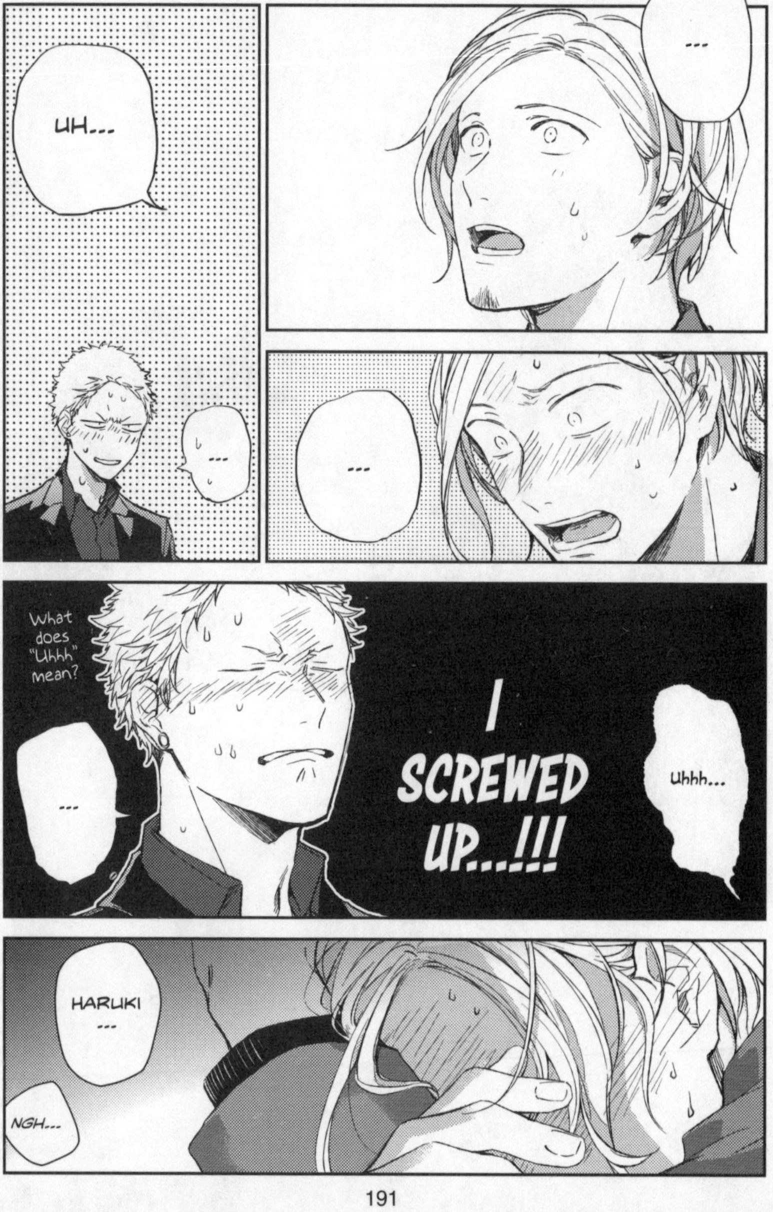
...
...
UH...
...
Uhhh...
I SCREWED UP...!!!
What does "Uhhh" mean?
...
HARUKI ...
NGH...

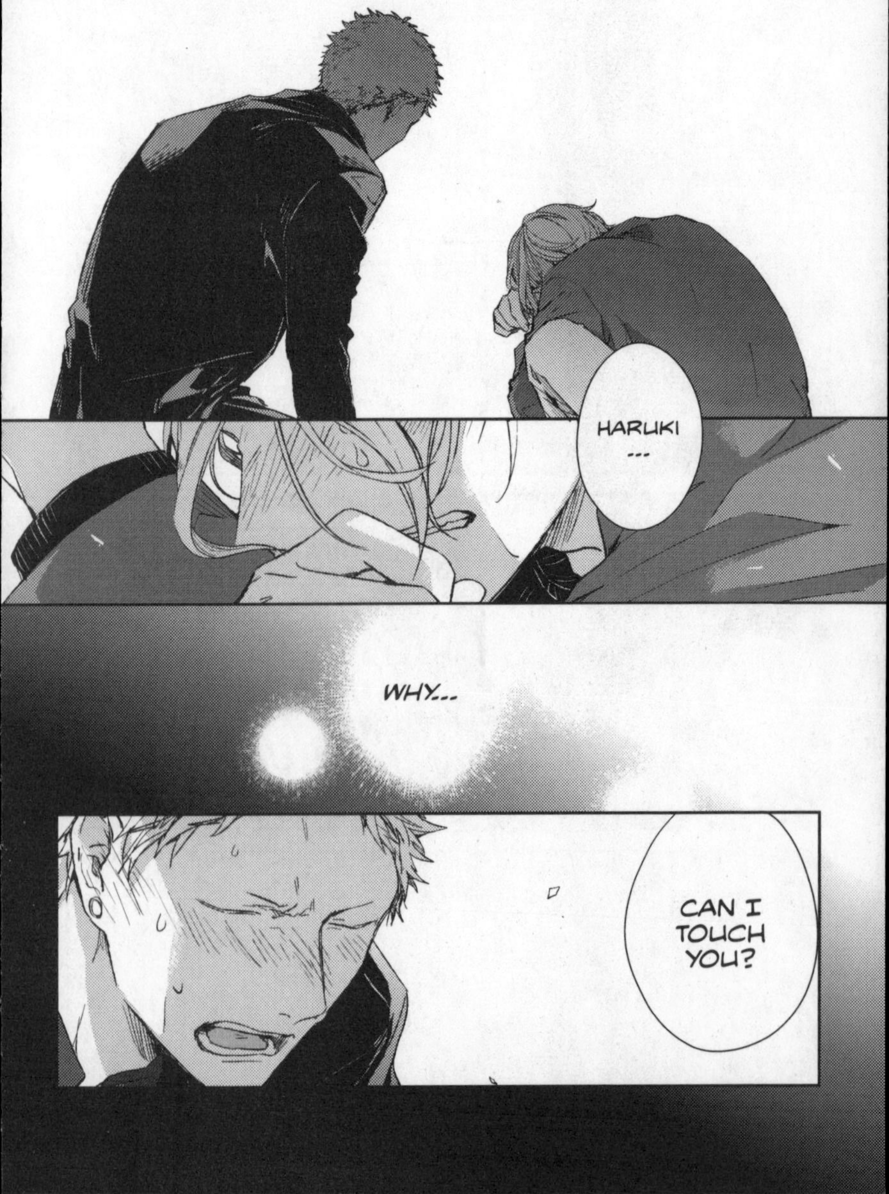
HARUKI
...
WHY...
CAN I TOUCH YOU?

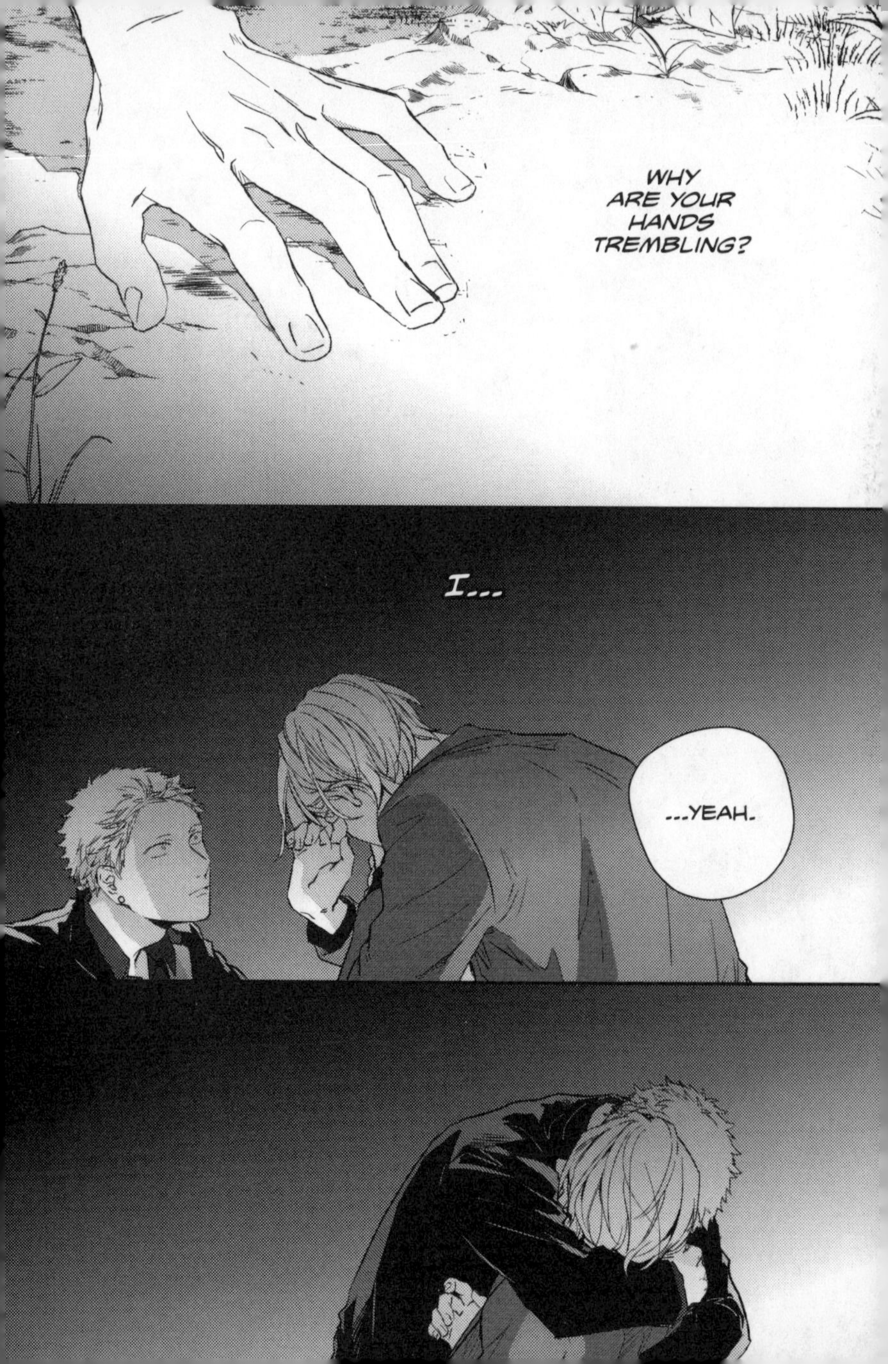
WHY ARE YOUR HANDS TREMBLING?
I...
...YEAH.

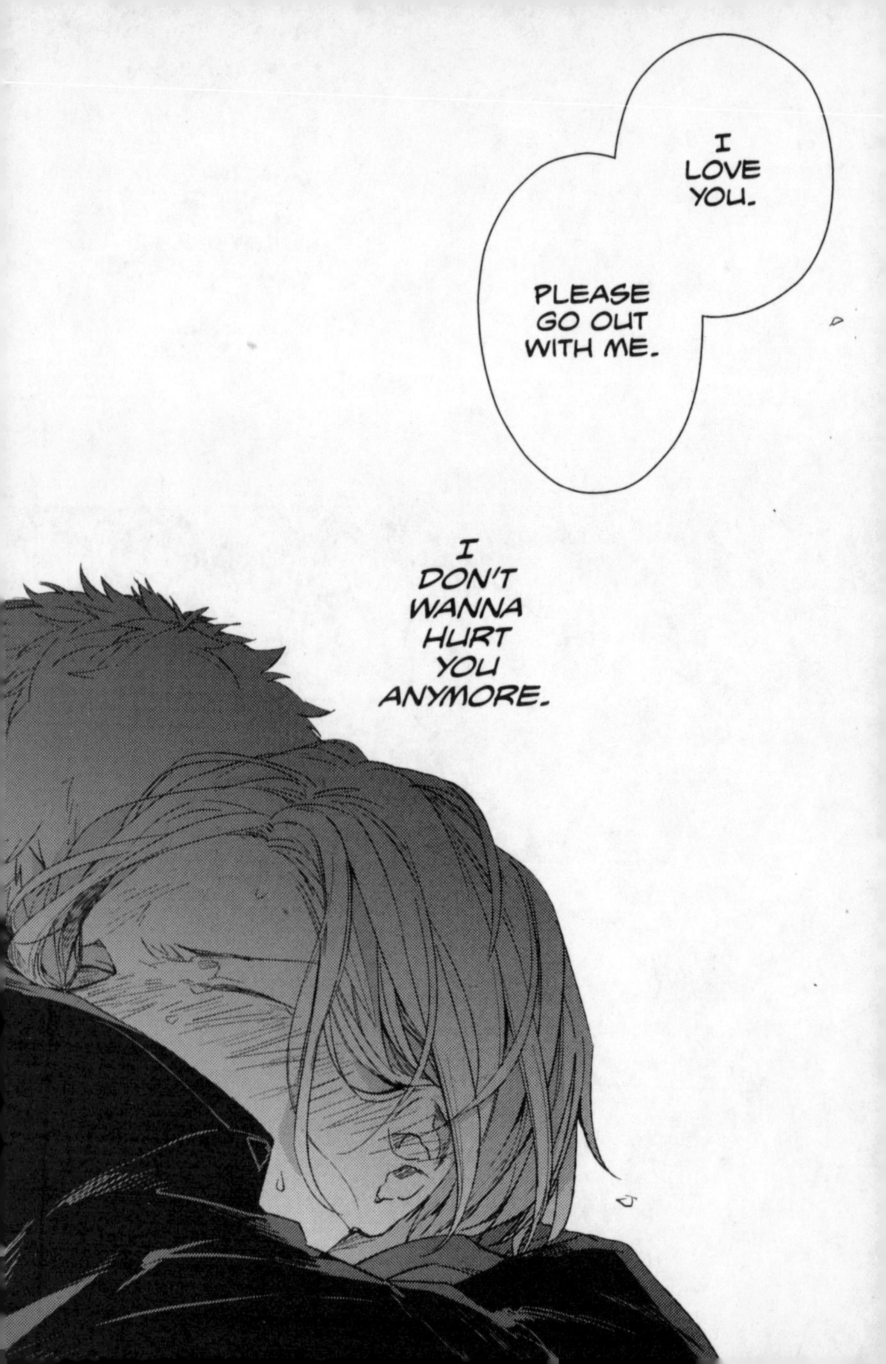
I LOVE YOU.
PLEASE GO OUT WITH ME.
I DON'T WANNA HURT YOU ANYMORE.

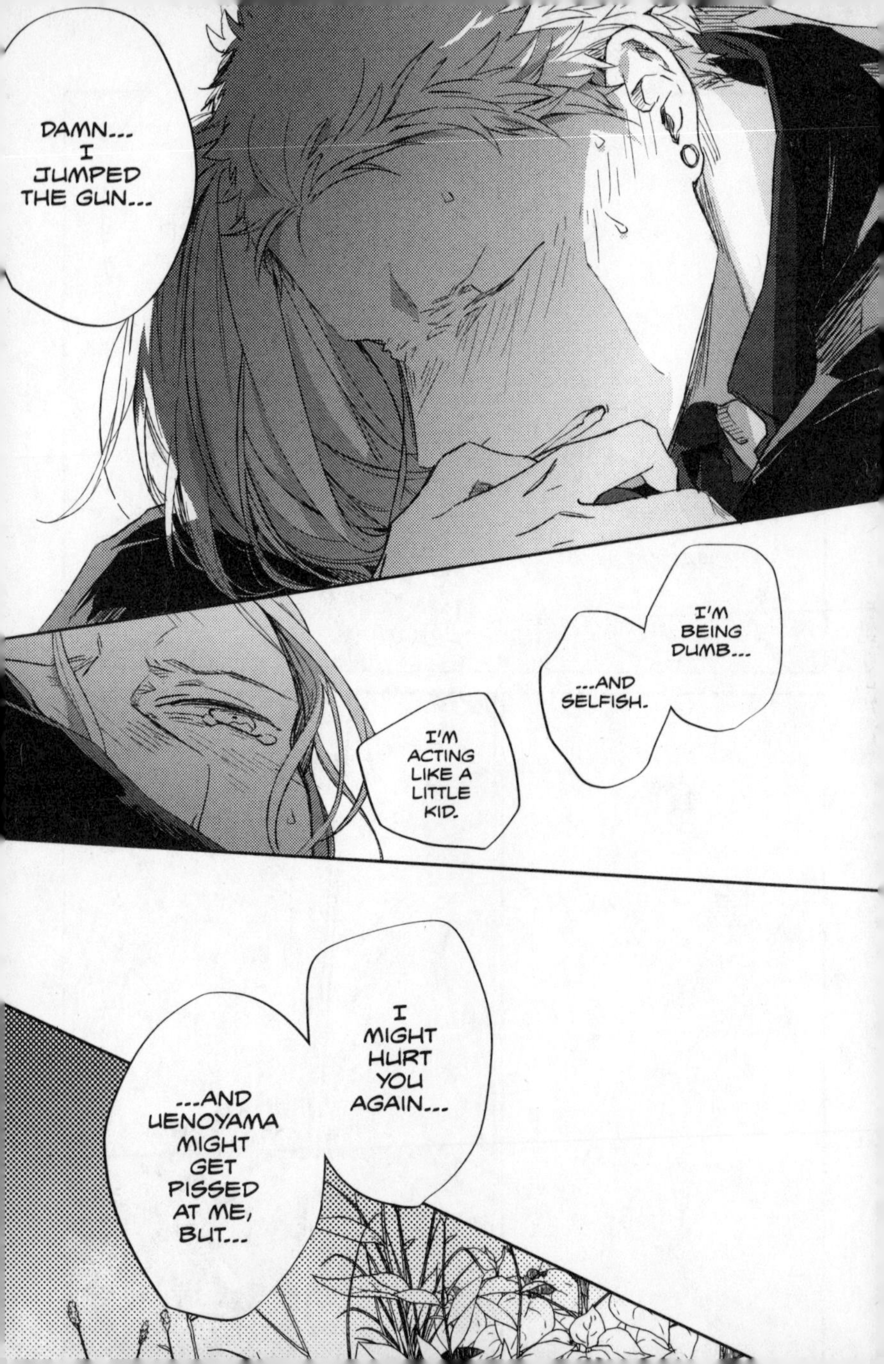
DAMN... I JUMPED THE GUN...
I'M BEING DUMB...
...AND SELFISH.
I'M ACTING LIKE A LITTLE KID.
I MIGHT HURT YOU AGAIN...
...AND UENOYAMA MIGHT GET PISSED AT ME, BUT...

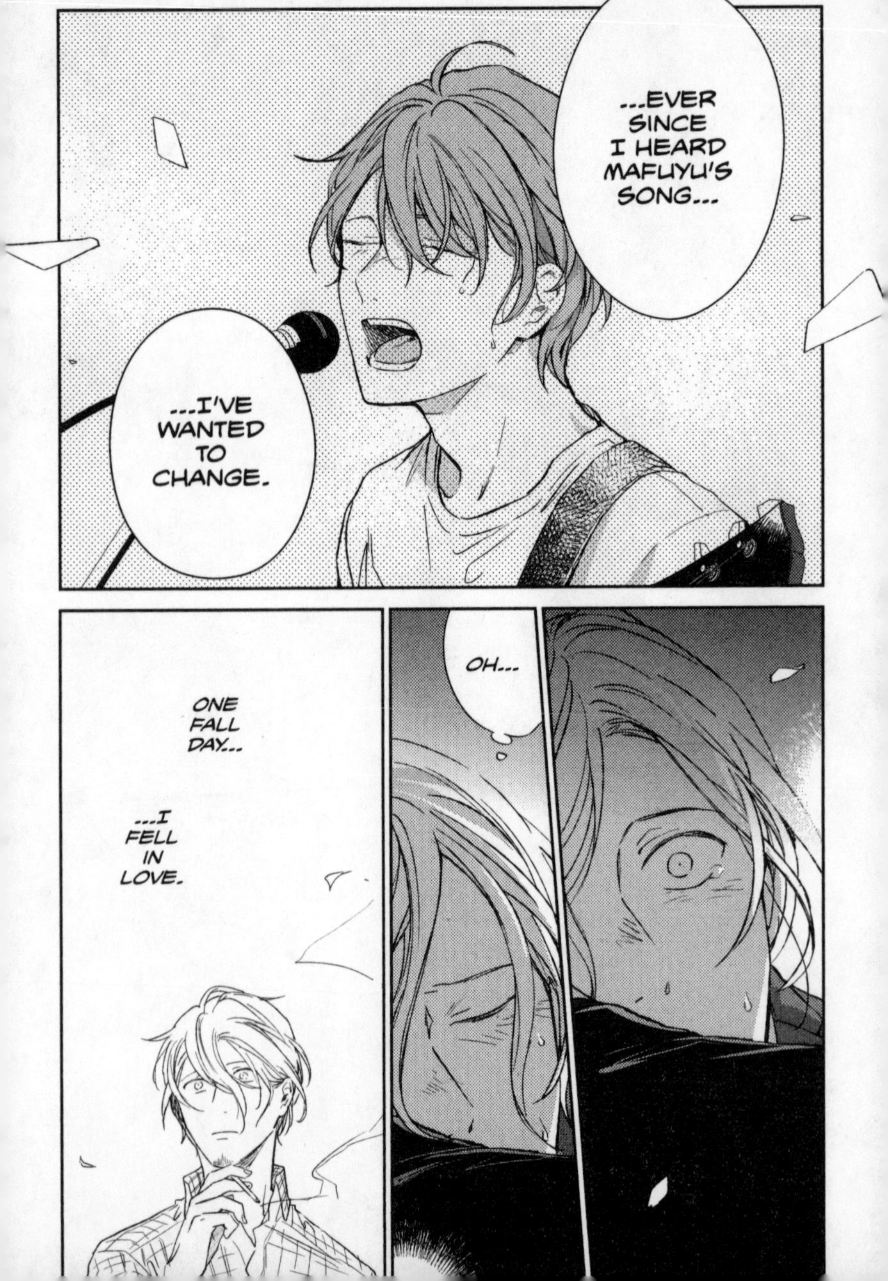
...EVER SINCE I HEARD MAFUYU'S SONG...
...I'VE WANTED TO CHANGE.
OH...
ONE FALL DAY...
...I FELL IN LOVE.

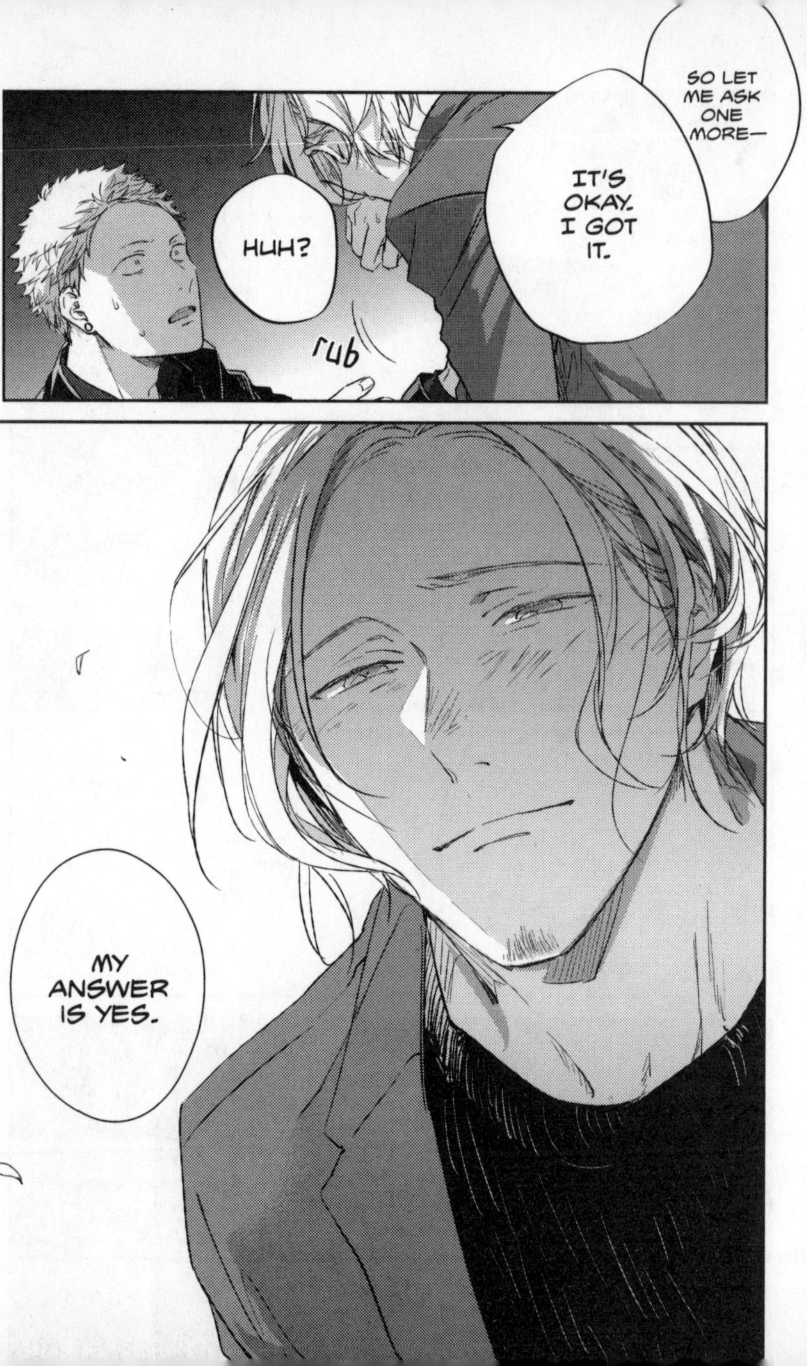
SO LET ME ASK ONE MORE—
IT'S OKAY. I GOT IT.
HUH?
rub
MY ANSWER IS YES.

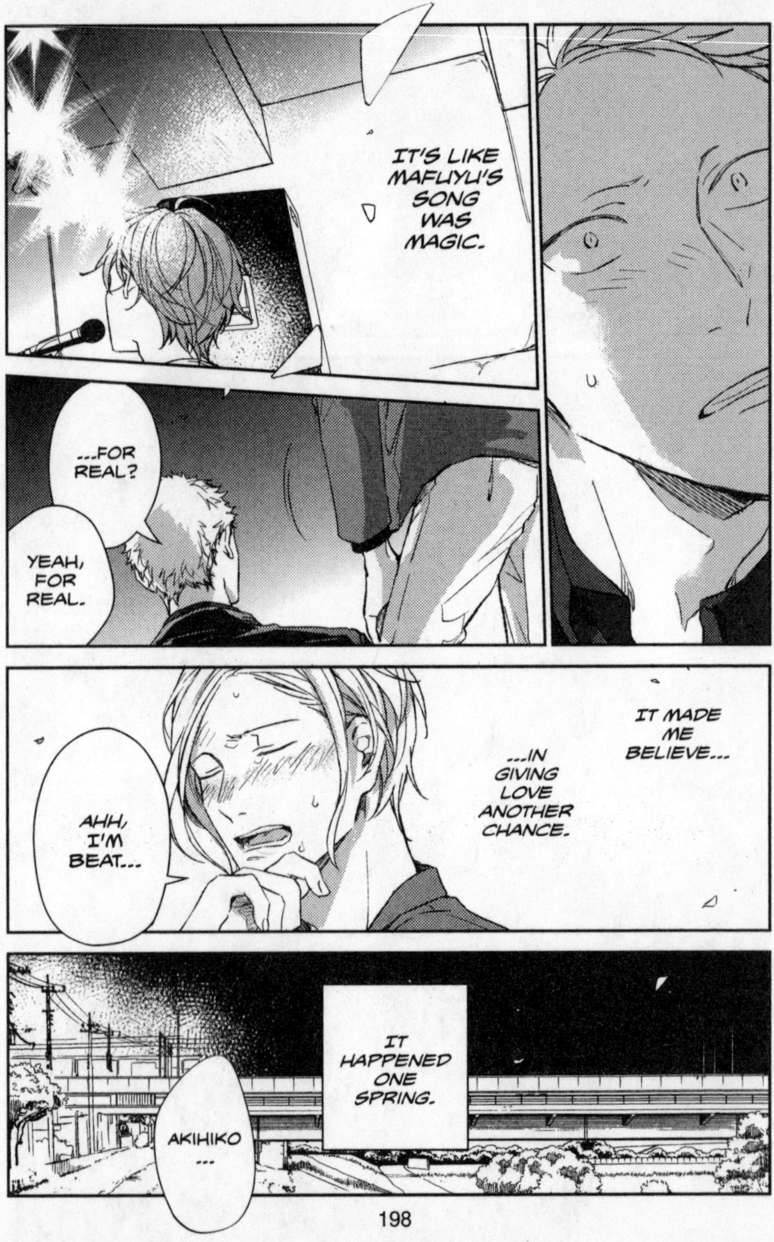
IT'S LIKE MAFUYU'S SONG WAS MAGIC.
...FOR REAL?
YEAH, FOR REAL.
IT MADE ME BELIEVE...
...IN GIVING LOVE ANOTHER CHANCE.
AHH, I'M BEAT...
IT HAPPENED ONE SPRING.
AKIHIKO ...

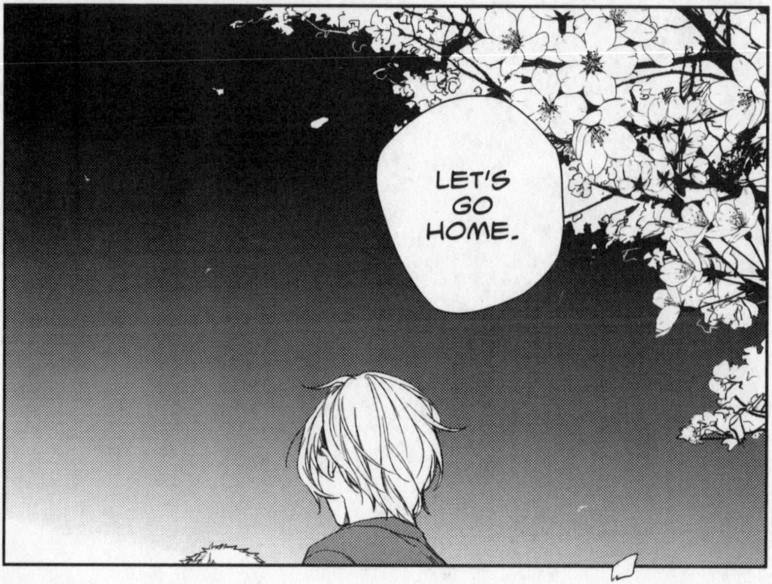
LET'S GO HOME.

A SIMPLE LOVE STORY BEGAN.

To Be Continued...

given

by Natsuki Kizu

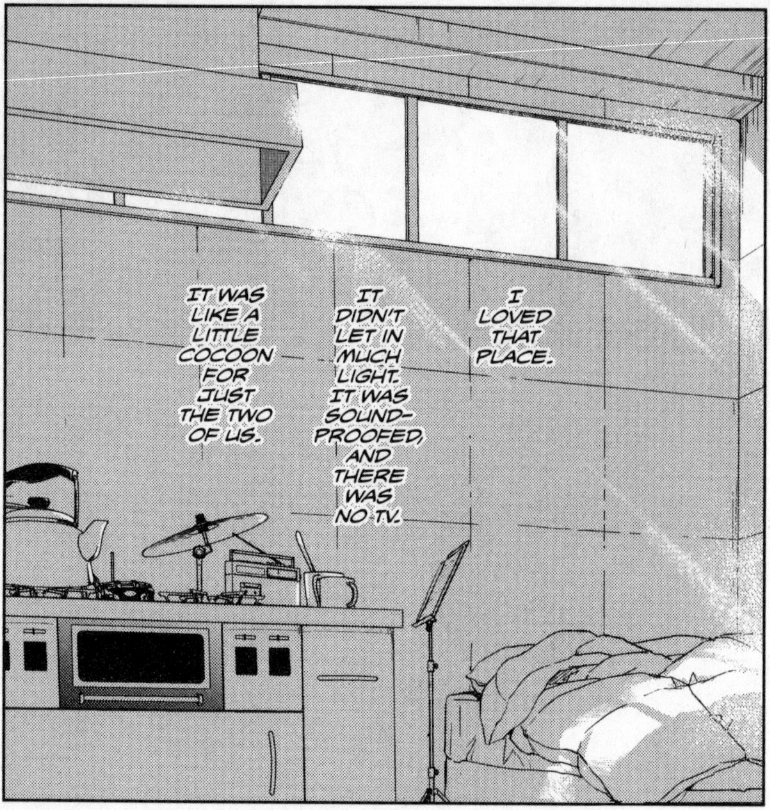
I LOVED THAT PLACE.
IT DIDN'T LET IN MUCH LIGHT. IT WAS SOUND-PROOFED, AND THERE WAS NO TV.
IT WAS LIKE A LITTLE COCOON FOR JUST THE TWO OF US.

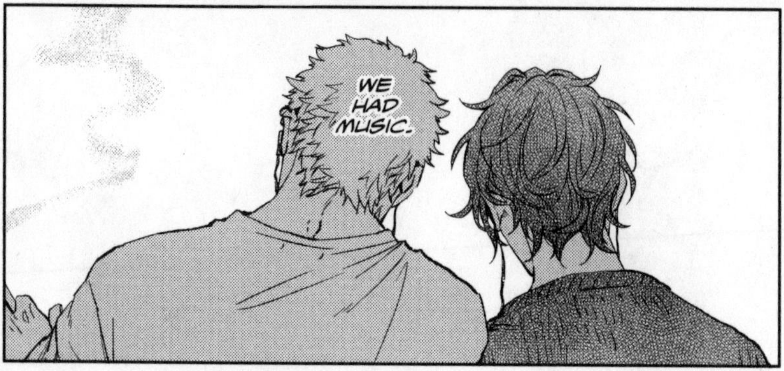
WE HAD MUSIC.

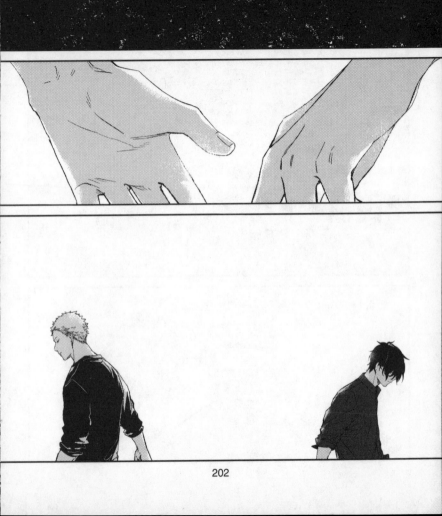

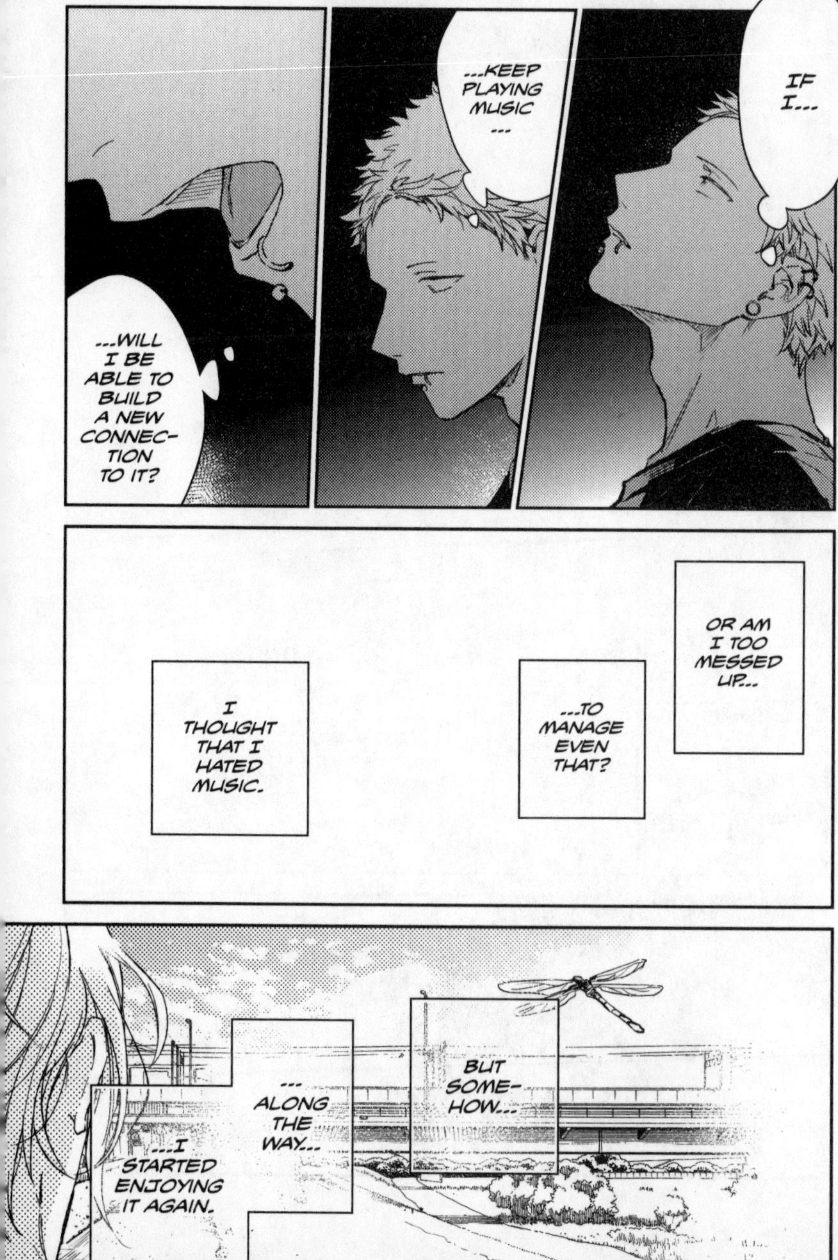
IF I...
...KEEP PLAYING MUSIC ...
...WILL I BE ABLE TO BUILD A NEW CONNECTION TO IT?
OR AM I TOO MESSED UP...
...TO MANAGE EVEN THAT?
I THOUGHT THAT I HATED MUSIC.
BUT SOMEHOW...
... ALONG THE WAY...
...I STARTED ENJOYING IT AGAIN.

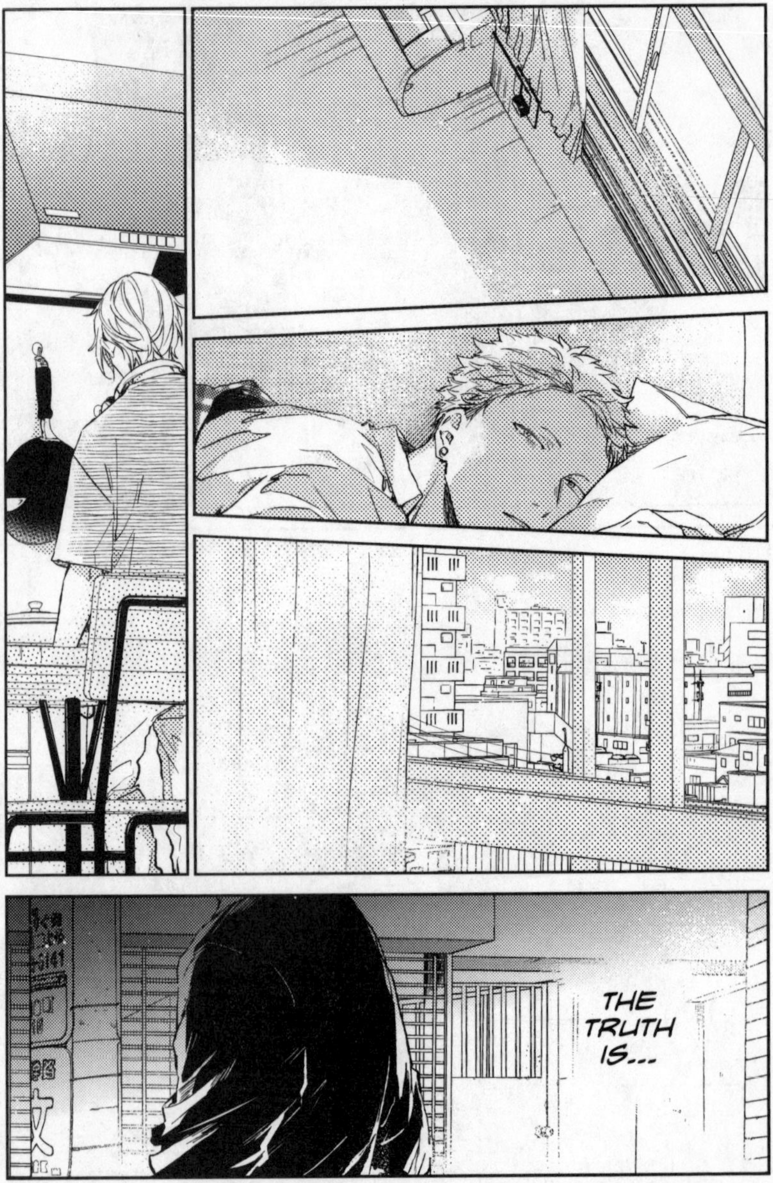
THE TRUTH IS...

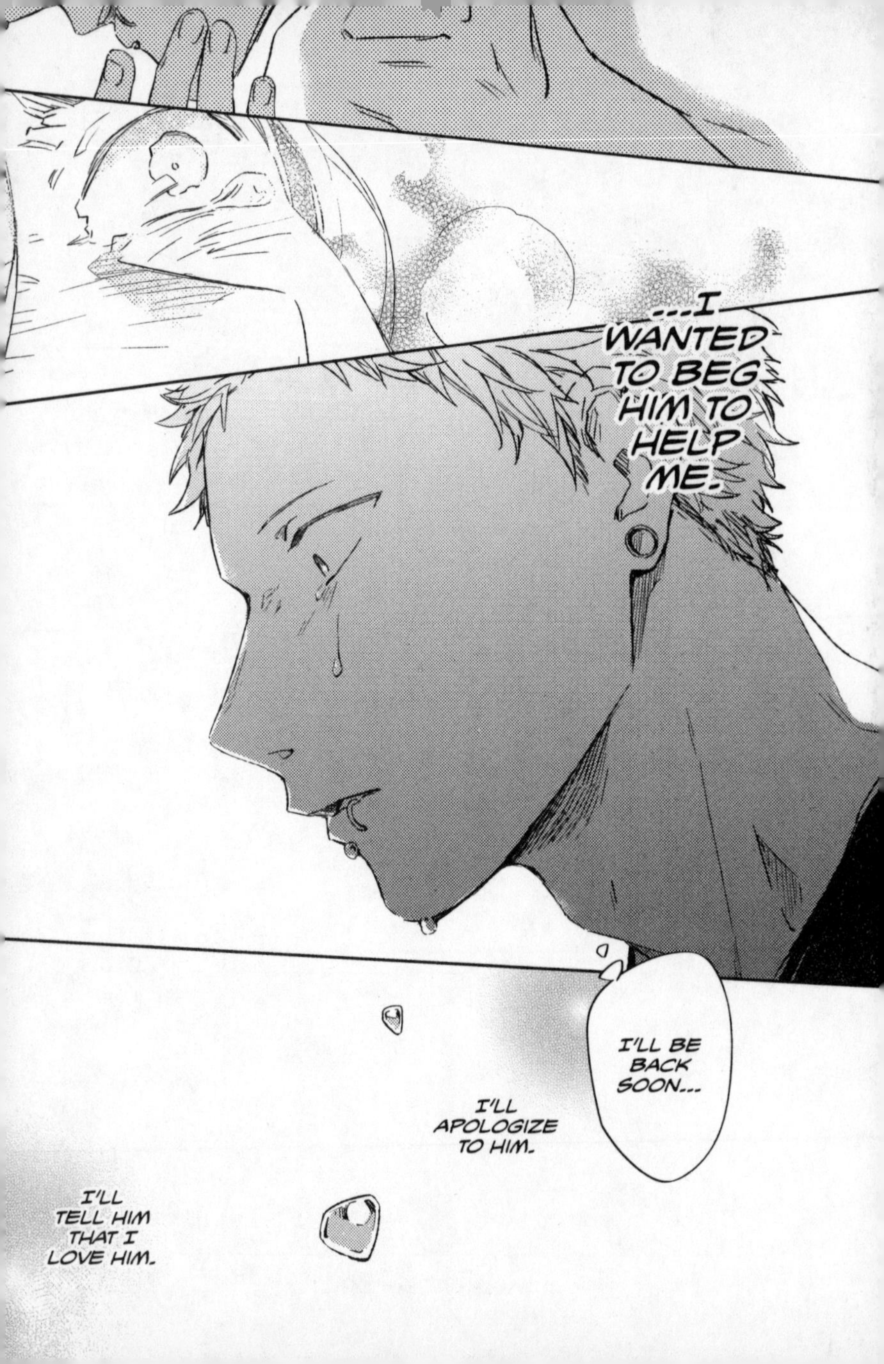
...I WANTED TO BEG HIM TO HELP ME.
I'LL BE BACK SOON...
I'LL APOLOGIZE TO HIM.
I'LL TELL HIM THAT I LOVE HIM.

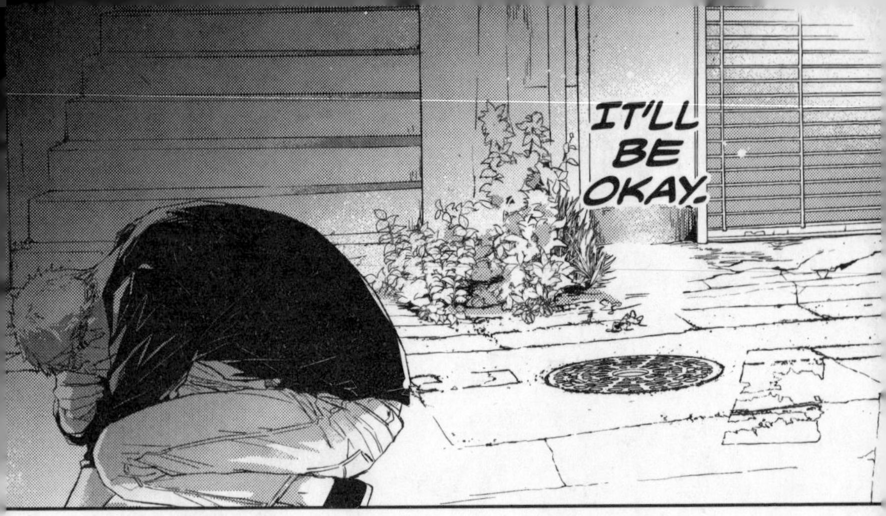
IT'LL BE OKAY.

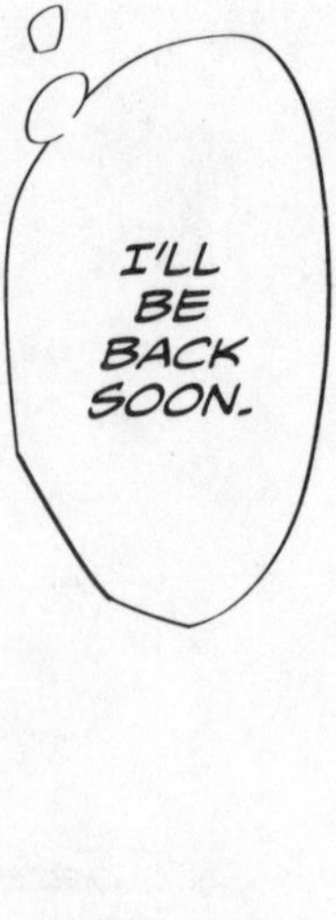
I'LL BE BACK SOON.

Emergence—End

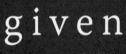

given

by Natsuki Kizu

About violin shoulder rests

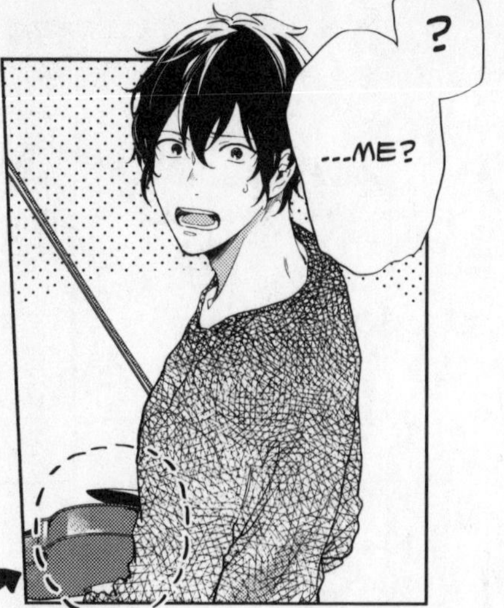

?
---ME?

He usually practices standing up.

Musicians have differing opinions(?) about shoulder rests. Ugetsu doesn't use one. →

This is because he likes to feel the response from the instrument. It has absolutely nothing to do with me taking artistic shortcuts...

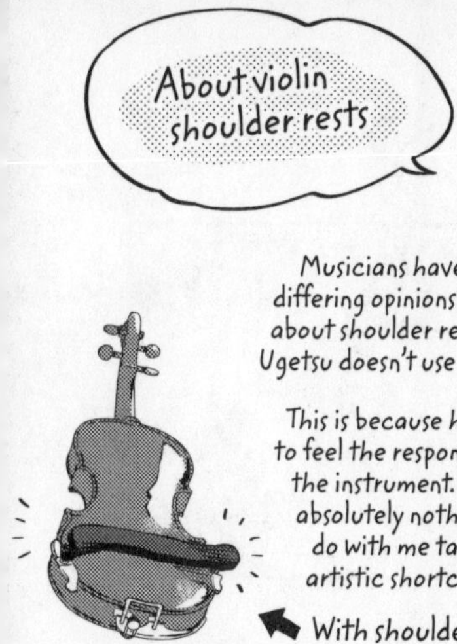

With shoulder rest

Without shoulder rest

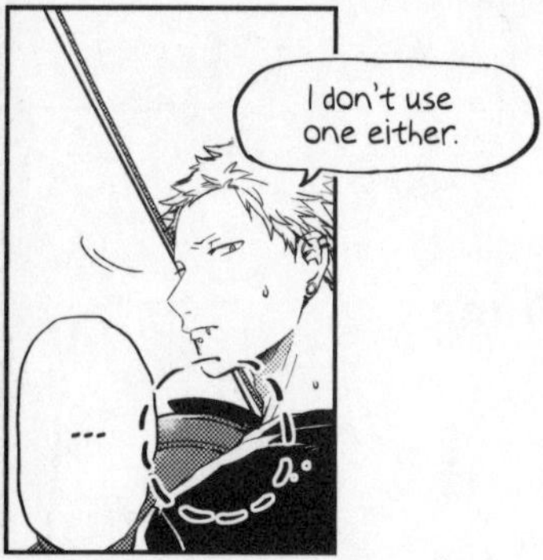

I don't use one either.

(The violin performance on the drama CD was recorded live.)

At the recording, the violinist, Ms. Aoshima, graciously allowed me to observe her for research purposes. She even brought out a bunch of broken bowstrings from the studio!!

S-S-S-So cool!!!

Inspiration for this panel. →

{Apparently you can rehair violin bows.}

Bonus! Concept notes and sketches

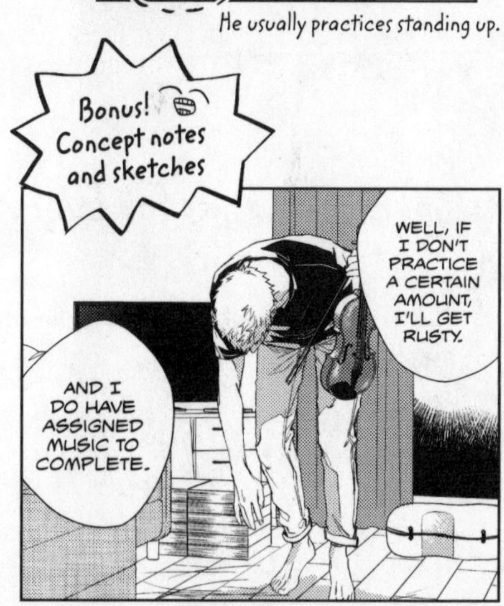

WELL, IF I DON'T PRACTICE A CERTAIN AMOUNT, I'LL GET RUSTY.
AND I DO HAVE ASSIGNED MUSIC TO COMPLETE.

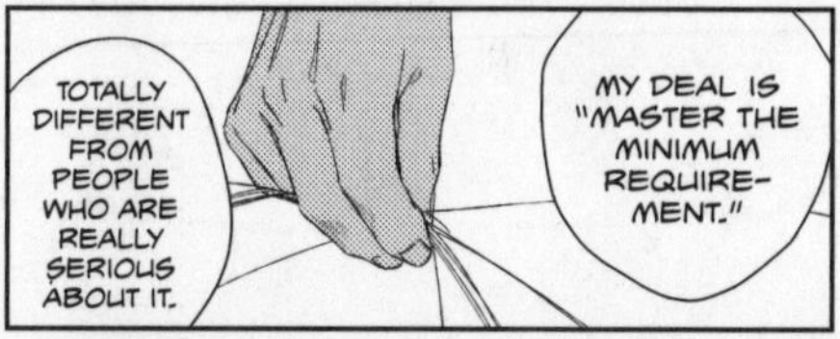

MY DEAL IS "MASTER THE MINIMUM REQUIRE-MENT."
TOTALLY DIFFERENT FROM PEOPLE WHO ARE REALLY SERIOUS ABOUT IT.

I show Kaji picking up broken strings...

About a character profile from volume 1

Correction

Sorry!

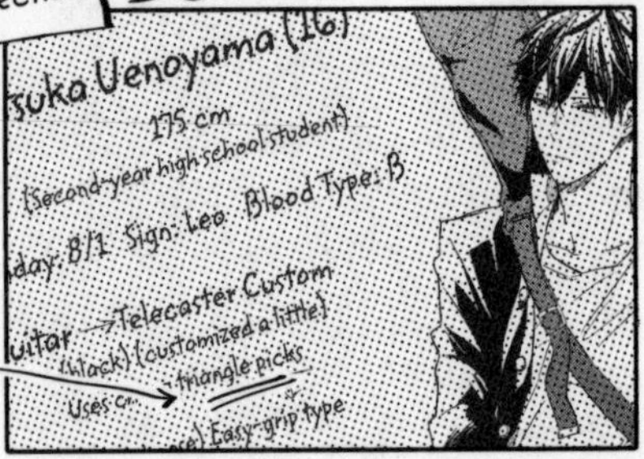
suka Uenoyama (16)
175 cm
(Second-year high school student)
day: 8/1 Sign: Leo Blood Type: B
uitar → Telecaster Custom
(black) (customized a little)
triangle picks
Easy-grip type

In the first version of this page, I called these "teardrop" picks, but later I corrected it to "triangle" picks.

Triangle

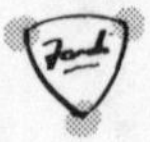

Can use all three edges

Teardrop

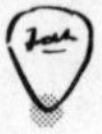

Can use only one edge

Special Thanks for Everything

Editor-in-chief, Ayaka, Matsushita, Tamura

My assistant Eri Hayashi

3D modeling production Rin

For research cooperation Cö Shu Nie, Yama-san (WHITE ASH), Sachiyo Aoshima
@co_shu_nie @sotto_yamasan @Sachiyo_violin

For material cooperation Yoneji, Fujioka, Daisuke, Ko

Live house Machida WEST VOX (former)

My editor Matsumoto

I've never been in a band, so you've all been a great help!

About the Author

Natsuki Kizu made her professional debut in 2013 with *Yukimura Sensei and Kei-kun*, followed by the short story collection *Links* and her breakout series, *Given*, which has been adapted into drama CDs and an animated TV series. To find out more about her works, you can follow her on Twitter at **@kizu_ntk**.

Given

Volume 5

SuBLime Manga Edition

Story and Art by **Natsuki Kizu**

Translation—**Sheldon Drzka**
Touch-Up Art and Lettering—**Sabrina Heep**
Cover and Graphic Design—**Jimmy Presler**
Editor—**Beryl Becker**

Originally published in Japan in 2019 by Shinshokan Co., Ltd.

Printed in the U.S.A.

Published by SuBLime Manga
P.O. Box 77010
San Francisco, CA 94107

10 9 8 7 6 5 4 3 2
First printing, February 2021
Second printing, July 2021

PARENTAL ADVISORY
GIVEN is rated T+ for Older Teen and is recommended for ages 16 and up. This volume contains suggestive themes.

SUBLIME
www.SuBLimeManga.com

For more information

on all our products, along with the most up-to-date news on releases, series announcements, and contests, please visit us at:

SuBLimeManga.com

twitter.com/**SuBLimeManga**

facebook.com/**SuBLimeManga**

instagram.com/**SuBLimeManga**

SuBLimeManga.tumblr.com

SUBLIME
MANGA

The rules were clear: they could date for a week.
But someone forgot to tell love!

SEVEN DAYS

MONDAY → SUNDAY

On a whim, high school third-year Yuzuru Shino asks out first-year Toji Seryo, who is notorious for being a weeklong lover—he'll date the first girl to ask him out Monday morning and then promptly dump her by the following Monday! The boys start dating, and by Tuesday, the first inklings of attraction hit. Can these two put words to their feelings before Monday comes, or are old habits too hard to break?

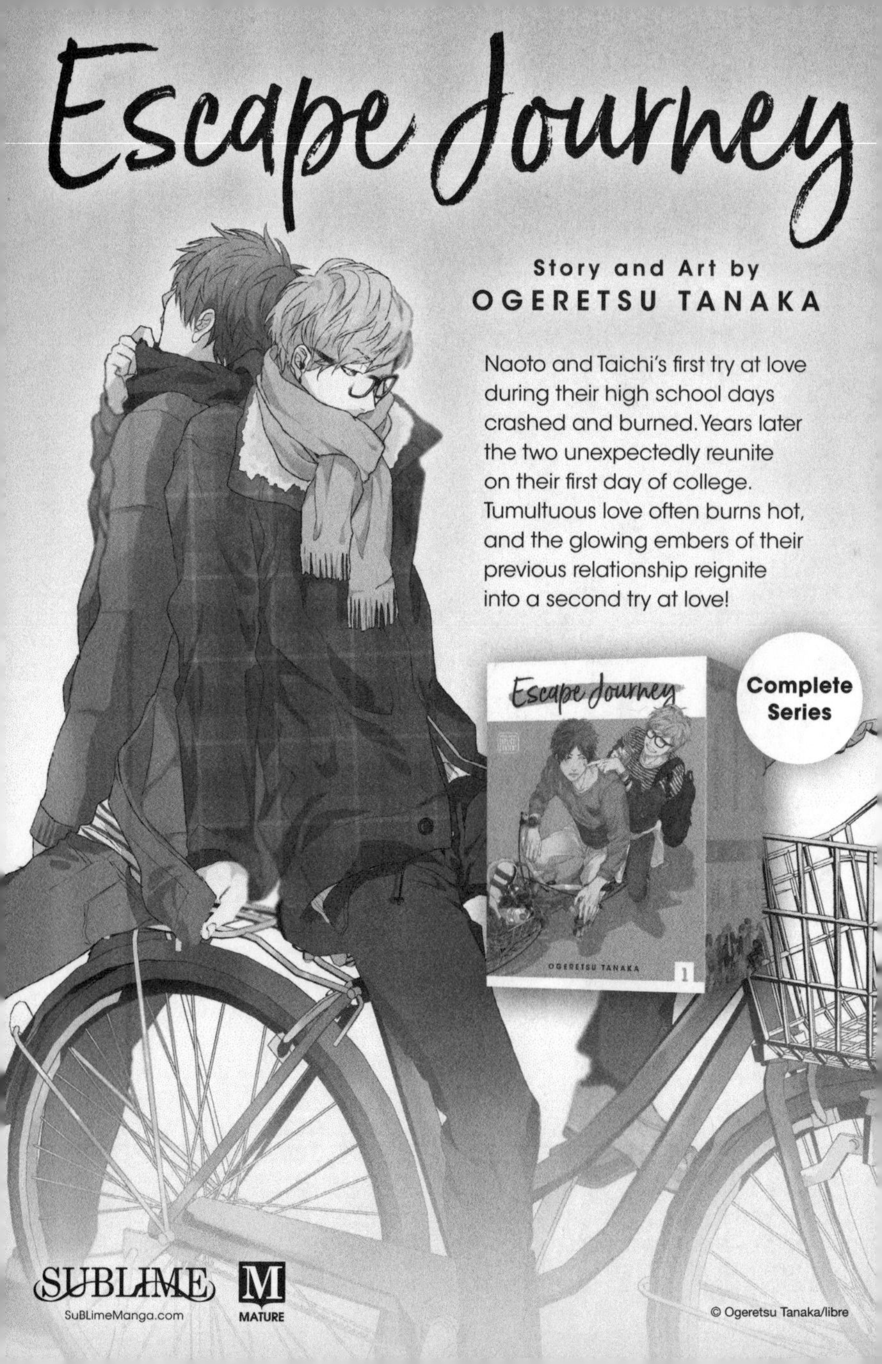
Escape Journey
Story and Art by
OGERETSU TANAKA
Naoto and Taichi's first try at love during their high school days crashed and burned. Years later the two unexpectedly reunite on their first day of college. Tumultuous love often burns hot, and the glowing embers of their previous relationship reignite into a second try at love!
Escape Journey
OGERETSU TANAKA
1
Complete Series
SUBLIME
SuBLimeManga.com
M
MATURE
© Ogeretsu Tanaka/libre

SECRET XXX

MEGURU HINOHARA

SHOHEI'S JUST TRYING TO FIND LOVE IN A PET SHOP, SO WHY ARE ALL THESE BUNNIES MAKING IT SO DIFFICULT?

Shohei *loves* bunnies! He loves them so much he's even taken to volunteering at a local pet shop. Store owner Mito is as sweet and kind as the fuzzy critters he cares for, and it's not long before Shohei finds himself wanting to cuddle with him as much as the bunnies! But Shohei is hiding a dangerous secret, one that makes this dream an unlikely reality.

FOLLOW THE ROMANTIC HIJINKS OF THEIR BROTHERS IN THE SPINOFF SERIES, *THERAPY GAME!*

MATURE   SuBLimeManga.com